A FUNCTIONING
ANARCHY?

A FUNCTIONING ANARCHY?

ESSAYS FOR

RAMACHANDRA GUHA

Edited by SRINATH RAGHAVAN
and NANDINI SUNDAR

PENGUIN
ALLEN
LANE

An imprint of Penguin Random House

ALLEN LANE

USA | Canada | UK | Ireland | Australia
New Zealand | India | South Africa | China

Allen Lane is part of the Penguin Random House group of companies
whose addresses can be found at global.penguinrandomhouse.com

Published by Penguin Random House India Pvt. Ltd
7th Floor, Infinity Tower C, DLF Cyber City,
Gurgaon 122 002, Haryana, India

Penguin
Random House
India

First published in Allen Lane by Penguin Random House India 2021

Uttarakhand was the site of Ramachandra Guha's first work and the Pahar Foundation,
Nainital is close to his heart. All proceeds from this book will go to the Pahar Foundation.

This book is a work of non-fiction. The views and opinions expressed in the essays that
make the book are those of the respective authors only and do not reflect or represent the
views and opinions held by any other person.

These essays are based on a variety of sources including published materials and interviews and interactions conducted by the authors with the persons mentioned in the
manuscript. Each essay reflects the author's own understanding and conception of such
materials and/or can be verified by research.

The objective of this book is not to hurt any sentiments or be biased in favor of or against
any particular person, region, caste, society, gender, creed, nation or religion.

ISBN 9780670093700

Typeset in Adobe Garamond Pro by Manipal Technologies Limited, Manipal
Printed at Thomson Press India Ltd, New Delhi

www.penguin.co.in

CONTENTS

Introduction by Nandini Sundar and Srinath Raghavan   ix

Books by Ramachandra Guha   xxi

Part I: Environment and Equity

1. Empire's Nature in the Garo Hills: A Microhistory of
   India's Environmental Movements
   Arupjyoti Saikia   3

2. The Heart of the Matter: Studying Institutional Structures
   in Historical Perspective
   Shashank Kela   21

3. The Authoritarian Biologist Reloaded and Deep Ecology
   Redux: Conservation Imperialism and the Control of
   Knowledge, Money and Space
   Kartik Shanker and Meera Anna Oommen   37

4. Nation's Body, River's Pulse: Narratives of Anti-dam Politics
   in India
   Amita Baviskar   55

5. Weaving Our Way through Environmental Justice
   Movements in India
   Brototi Roy and Joan Martinez-Alier   71

Part II: The Makers of Indian Democracy

6. Travels within the Self: M. Lakshmi and Her Letters
   from London
   A.R. Venkatachalapathy   91

7. The Singing Satyagrahi: Khurshedben Naoroji and the
   Challenge of Indian Biography
   Dinyar Patel   105

8. 'Grocer, Tailor, Champion Wrestler': The Transnational
   Career of Buttan Singh, c. 1900–1912
   Prashant Kidambi   126

9. Agyeya: Hindi Literature's First Freethinker
   Akshaya Mukul   146

10. Alone at Home, Among Friends Abroad? B.R. Shenoy
    from Austrian School Monetary Economist to Cold-War
    Public Intellectual
    Aditya Balasubramanian   165

Part III: The Making of Indian Democracy

11. The Road to Sevagram
    Venu Madhav Govindu   183

12. Flights of Freedom: German Émigrés, Aeronautics and
    Self-Reliance in India
    Jahnavi Phalkey   200

13. The Supreme Court and Democratic Consolidation
    Madhav Khosla   214

14. From Autonomy to Insurgency: Jammu and Kashmir in
    the Long 1970s
    Srinath Raghavan   228

Part IV: On Ramachandra Guha

15. Ram Guha: A Radical Progressive
    Madhav Gadgil   249

16. The Unquiet Ram
    Rukun Advani   257

17. The Many Rams of Ramachandra Guha
    David Gilmour   266
18. 'What Do They Know of History Who Only
    History Know?'
    Suresh Menon   271

About the Contributors   277
Acknowledgements   281
Notes   283
Index   347

INTRODUCTION

NANDINI SUNDAR AND SRINATH RAGHAVAN

SOME FIFTY YEARS ago, the eminent economist and US envoy John Kenneth Galbraith famously described India as 'a functioning anarchy'. Galbraith's comments captured both the fascination and frustration with which observers around the world, including in India, saw the country's efforts at economic development within the framework of a fully fledged constitutional democracy. Often invoked as sardonic commentary, Galbraith in fact wanted to emphasize the point that 'the success of India did not depend on the government. It depended on the energy, ingenuity . . . of the Indian people'.[1] Galbraith's phrase thus reflected a cautious pessimism about the prospects of the Indian experiment. Ramachandra Guha has often seemed to echo this view, such as in his book *India after Gandhi*, published in 2007 on the sixtieth anniversary of India's Independence, where he calls India a '50-50 democracy'. However, in doing so, Guha is clearly voicing a cautious optimism.

Currently, the robustness of India's democracy seems more precariously poised than ever before, not excepting the infamous years of the Emergency, with authoritarian and even fascist tendencies becoming dominant in society as well as the state. Yet, as the winter of 2019–20 shows us, with its protests against the Citizenship (Amendment) Act (CAA) and National Register of Citizens (NRC), significant numbers of Indians are deeply invested in the secular and egalitarian principles of the

Constitution. Among the memorable images of the protests was one of Ramachandra Guha being dragged away by the police mid-sentence while giving an interview to a television channel against the CAA.

If Ramachandra Guha has been one of the most public and outspoken defenders of Indian democracy, he has also been one of its foremost scholars and chroniclers. In a long and versatile career spanning thirty-five years, Guha has produced a series of remarkable studies that have approached this issue from several vantage points. In each of these, Guha has broken new ground: his pioneering environmental histories of India, both alone and with distinguished scholars like Madhav Gadgil and Joan Martinez-Alier; his social histories of Indian cricket; his monumental history of the Indian republic; his biographies of Verrier Elwin and Gandhi; his anthologies of ecological, social and political thought in India; and his collections of biographical and political essays.

Guha's originality as a scholar has been matched by the accessibility of his writings, both as a historian and columnist. In consequence, he is also one of India's most admired (and at times most reviled) public intellectuals. Insofar as Twitter is any indicator,[2] Guha has over 2 million followers, and is by far the most influential scholar as far as journalists are concerned.[3] In part, this is because of his ability to dig up nuggets of historical information to put every issue in perspective, bringing the archives into conversation with everyday politics. In equal part, however, Guha's fame and notoriety stem from his tendency to pick arguments with a wide range of people and to make ex cathedra pronouncements on a variety of issues. Guha admits to his propensity to 'express moderate views in an extreme fashion'.[4] This formulation is worth comparing with that of another historian fond of periodically winding up his readers, A.J.P. Taylor, who once pleaded that he did not have strong views but extreme ones that were weakly held.[5]

Guha once published an essay titled 'The Last Liberal', yet his own oeuvre shows that while the Indian liberal may be an endangered species, she is hardly extinct. Indeed, when a liberal archetype is needed for a public attack, Guha often serves as the target of choice. To be sure, Guha has given as good as he has got. Among his numerous polemics, the most memorable and notorious one was his put-down of Arundhati Roy as the 'Arun Shourie of the left', for her 'black-and-white' 'moral certificates' in the context of the Sardar Sarovar dam. Roy responded by describing him to an interviewer as a stalker who insistently showed up with his 'angry little cottage industry' of friends and supporters.[6] This 'exchange' has had lasting snide effects, surfacing in differing appraisals of Gandhi, Kashmir, or the Maoists. The irony, of course, is that on many momentous public issues they have also been on the same side.

Another emblematic kerfuffle is an article Guha wrote in the *Indian Express* in 2018, 'Liberals, Sadly', where he argued that 'India's liberals must take on both Hindu and Muslim communalists'.[7] At one point, he compared the wearing of burkas to the wielding of *trishuls* as a sign of backwardness and religious revanchism in the public sphere. This ill-conceived comparison elicited howls of protest. The *Express* carried at least fourteen irate rejoinders to Guha's article, including from a politician whose party is an ally of the Bharatiya Janata Party and the Rashtriya Swayamsevak Sangh (RSS). The *Express* may, of course, have given so much space to this debate merely to milk the dissension for greater readership. Besides, there is the liberal's tendency to argue with her own while treating the larger right-wing challenge as beneath intellectual engagement. And yet, debating with Guha is rewarding, for unlike many others, he engages seriously with criticism and, on occasion, apologizes. If you happen to be a friend, he will be especially contrite. In any case, the opposition to Guha from sections of India's left-leaning reading public is nothing compared to the copious quantities of vitriolic mail he gets from India's non-reading Hindutva public.[8]

In focusing on the trenches of such controversial debates, we risk losing sight of the vast hinterland of scholarship and research that Guha has opened up to a large non-specialist audience. The serious historian as a paperback writer is a rare bird in the Indian landscape. Lucidity and elegance in writing is not always considered a virtue, especially in certain quarters of academia where obscurity and turgidity masquerade as intellectual depth and profundity. Guha took his scholarly bearings, however, from historians like E.P. Thompson and Marc Bloch, who aimed their path-breaking research and writing at the educated, general reader. The defining characteristics of Guha's scholarship have been the desire to consistently break new ground and to reach ever wider circles of readership. No Indian historian has succeeded comparably in taking serious history to the laity. What is more, unlike some celebrity historians in the west, Guha has done so without having to tailor his books to the demands of a television series or of streaming platforms. This is not the place to list his numerous scholarly accomplishments and recognitions, but it is perhaps worth pointing out the intellectual company he keeps. In 2019, the American Historical Association made him an 'Honorary Foreign Member', a recognition accorded to only two other Indian historians so far—Jadunath Sarkar (1952), and Romila Thapar (2009). This recognition also places him in the select league of outstanding non-American historians of earlier generations such as Eric Hobsbawm, Joseph Needham or Fernand Braudel. And it is his scholarship and research that this book celebrates—the broad canvas, the copious footnotes, the analytic insights, and the judicious summing up—rather than his occasionally exasperating but always readable articles in the popular press. The calmness and sobriety of his academic work is, in fact, a remarkable contrast to the passion and verve of his popular writing. Yet, one needs to keep all these qualities in mind to understand the peculiarities of Ramachandra Guha.

CAREER AND CREDO

Born in 1958 in Dehradun where his chemist father, S.R. Guha, worked at the Forest Research Institute, and educated first at Cambrian Hall School where his mother taught geography, Hindi and economics, and then at the elite Doon School and St. Stephen's College, Guha was quintessentially a child of Nehru's India. His parents were first cousins, themselves second- or third-generation professionals, members of an urban cosmopolitan Tamil family, with democratic instincts and a desire to do social work. Some members of the family were also notoriously fractious: for instance, the historian Dharma Kumar and the civil-servant-turned-economist S. Guhan stopped speaking to each other after public disagreements over affirmative action. While this may contextualize Ramachandra Guha's privilege, his liberalism, as well as his argumentative instincts, it does not, however, account for his particular set of varied interests, extraordinary productivity or generosity to younger scholars.

As a child, Guha's interests took him to the cricket field, birding (he wrote on birdwatching for the Doon school magazine), and the Himalayan forest—interests that followed him into his academic career. The greatest regret of his life, Guha has often said, was his failure to become a top-class cricketer—one that he tried to compensate by writing first-class books on the history of cricket (*Wickets in the East*, and *A Corner of a Foreign Field*) and later by agreeing to serve on the board of a Supreme Court-mandated committee of administrators to clean up the Board of Control for Cricket in India (BCCI). As Suresh Menon remarks in his essay in this volume, it is perhaps because cricket or rather the art and craft of cricket has remained Guha's first love, that he is so proficient in the historical craft.

Guha tried all the traditional professions before he settled down as an independent historian. He took a year off after college to study for the civil services exam because 'his friends were doing so'. Fortunately, he failed. Indeed, the succession of jobs that Guha did not join is revealing—he turned down an offer from the *Times of India*, a professorship at the Department of Sociology, Delhi School of Economics (DSE) (because he had decided by then to move to Bengaluru), a professorship at the National Law School of India University in Bengaluru (because it would have meant attending from 9 a.m.–5 p.m.). And then there are the jobs he didn't get—a sociology lectureship at the DSE because his MA was in economics and not in sociology, and a sociology professorship at the Institute of Social and Economic Change, Bengaluru, for the same reason. More recently, in 2018, he did not join Ahmedabad University as professor and director of the Gandhi Winter School because the Akhil Bharatiya Vidyarthi Parishad (ABVP), the student wing of the RSS, threatened to agitate, claiming that if exposed to Guha, 'the youth power of the country will have no feeling for the country or our world-best culture and will become directionless and reckless by the courses created under the direction of such a directionless person'.[9] Guha's various arguments and his passionate involvements in projects may betray a certain recklessness, but to charge him with the ability to undermine the morals of the country's 'youth-power' or ruin its 'world-best culture' is perhaps an overestimation of his reach.

Guha admits that he was directionless—missing class in college, playing bridge and cricket—till he met his wife, the talented designer Sujata Keshavan, in 1979, when she was studying at the National Institute of Design.

With an indifferent BA and MA in economics, and a girlfriend who refused to let him join the Institute of Rural Management Anand (because she could not practise design while living in a village), Guha applied to the Indian Institute of Management (IIM) Calcutta, to do a PhD in sociology. His early environmental interests were strengthened by a summer study trip in college to Koraput where he researched adivasi productivity in Hindustan Aeronautics Limited. A local veterinarian, Dr Das, suggested he read Verrier Elwin, which began a lifelong romance with his work.

Other early influences were E.P. Thompson, Lewis Mumford, and C.L.R. James. Never one to neglect his intellectual debts—on the contrary, he is extravagant with his acknowledgements—Ram has ascribed much of his early acquaintance with social history and sociology to the sociologist Anjan Ghosh: 'I wouldn't have become a scholar without him; I wouldn't have written a single book had I not studied with him'.[10]

While Ghosh was no doubt a remarkable mentor, whether he can be burdened with (or blamed for) Guha's subsequent productivity is doubtful. As his first editor, Rukun Advani, recalls here, 'Ram Guha was from the word go rather like an unstoppable force, a volcano spilling over with more ideas for books that he wanted to write than his brain was able to contain'. This energy and this passionate interest in ideas and issues as well as the people around him is evident to anyone who knows Guha. Less easily observed is his incredible discipline and work ethic. In a real sense, he embodies the injunction of Max Weber, whom Guha once called the greatest of sociologists, that 'in the field of science only he who is devoted *solely* to the work at hand has "personality" . . . we know of no great artist who has ever done anything but serve his work and only his work'.[11] Illness, injury or a death in the family—none of these seem to keep Guha from writing, any more than a singer can stop singing or an artist painting. This single-minded pursuit of scholarship has been made possible by Sujata Keshavan, whose calm management of the family and its finances has ensured for him the time and space to write.

Soon after his PhD, Guha spent a year teaching at the School of Forestry and Environmental Studies at Yale, followed by a stint at the Indian Institute of Science in Bengaluru where he collaborated with the ecologist Madhav Gadgil. He then moved to Delhi and was employed at the Institute of Economic Growth, the Wissenschaftskolleg zu Berlin, and the Nehru Memorial Museum and Library—three research positions which he used to full advantage, before moving to Bengaluru in 1994 as an independent writer.

While Guha has since held several other visiting positions abroad—for instance, as Philippe Roman chair of International Affairs and History at the London School of Economics (2011–12)—his heart, as he has noted in his interview to John Harriss, remains in India, 'invested in the lives of his fellow Indians'.[12] The poem by Nissim Ezekiel with which he concludes that interview well summarizes his choice of place and of commitment:

I have made my commitments now.
This is one: to stay where I am,
As others choose to give themselves
In some remote and backward place.
My backward place is where I am.

If energy is one term that characterizes Guha, another might well be his modesty. Despite his considerable public standing and numerous awards,[13] he continues to engage with a variety of people, each encounter—whether in person or print—marked by an essential humanism. As David Gilmour writes in his essay, Guha is 'someone who takes friendship seriously'. This book is a small attempt by several people he has mentored, inspired or befriended to reciprocate his multiple acts of friendship and generosity. It is also a tribute to his groundbreaking scholarship that cleared the tracks for subsequent research in three distinct areas: environmental history and sociology, historical biography and contemporary history.

ENVIRONMENT AND EQUITY

The 1980s, when Ramachandra Guha began his scholarly career, was a period marked by attention to subaltern voices in history writing, as well as a time when environmental issues entered scholarship in a serious way. The first two reports of the Centre for Science and Environment involved massive documentation on India's contemporary ecological problems, ranging from water to urban air pollution to forests. The Chipko movement had caught the popular imagination and the Forest Act was being debated. Guha's first article—written for the *Economic and Political Weekly* (EPW) whose cause he has championed ever since—was on the history of the 1878 Forest Act, showing the contesting ideologies at work. Intellectual history has remained an abiding interest, as shown by his co-authored work with Joan Martinez-Alier.

The Unquiet Woods, his first monograph, based on his thesis at IIM Calcutta, located the Chipko movement within a longer history of peasant movements against the disruption of existing moral economies. This was followed by two wide-ranging, synthesizing works on India's environment, co-authored with Madhav Gadgil, *This Fissured Land* and *Ecology and Equity*, which yet again espoused the concerns as well as conservation strategies of ordinary people as against colonially entrenched bureaucracies. In the mid-1990s, the field of Indian environmental history came to be dominated by the Grove-Guha debate on whether colonialism was the watershed for Indian forests, and whether scientific forestry was dictated by imperial interests (Ramachandra Guha) or by the desiccationist concerns of East India Company surgeons perturbed by the links between deforestation and drought (Richard Grove). It is not coincidental that *The Unquiet Woods* was followed by a number of monographs on forests and adivasis in different parts of the country, making that the dominant stream in Indian environmental history and sociology as against, say, the study of rivers, winds or the commons.

The essays in this volume bear testimony to Guha's deep influence in this field, with scholars continuing to debate and discuss his ideas even as they have extended the field. Arupjyoti Saikia's essay on Garo resistance to forest restrictions is in keeping with Guha's close historical exploration of environmental struggles, while Shashank Kela looks at the functioning of the forest bureaucracy in shaping environmental history, moving away from the dominant focus on policy or law. Amita Baviskar and Joan Martinez-Alier and Brototi Roy present two—perhaps contrasting—essays on the trajectory and current shape of Indian environmental movements today, with Baviskar pointing to the decline of boots on the ground in the struggle against large dams and a greater emphasis on technological critiques and legal challenges, while Martinez-Alier and Roy point to the resilience of movements and their reach in different arenas.

Ever a coiner of provocative yet descriptively apt terms, Guha has characterized environmental politics as underpinned by three major intellectual strands—Crusading Gandhian, Ecological Marxist and Appropriate Technologist—all of whom combined, one might argue, go towards characterizing Guha himself. In their essay, 'The Authoritarian Biologist Reloaded', Kartik Shanker and Meera Anna Oommen take Guha's critique of American-style wilderness conservation further to explore its current manifestations on the conservation circuit.

BIOGRAPHY AND THE MAKERS OF INDIAN DEMOCRACY

Guha's own trajectory took him from environmental historian to romantic biographer with his unputdownable biography of Verrier Elwin, the missionary-turned-anthropologist whose enchanting accounts of adivasi life in central and North-east India had long fascinated him. Indeed, so romantic was Guha about his subject that he visited Bastar in 2005 at the height of the Salwa Judum, a state-sponsored counter-insurgency campaign involving huge loss of civilian lives and property, to see where Elwin lived, and went on to help defend the adivasis that Elwin wrote about before the Supreme Court in a case on Salwa Judum.

As a field, biography has been considerably underdeveloped in India, for the reasons that Dinyar Patel outlines in his essay in this volume, such as the lack of private papers and archival indifference. But Indian lives may also be understood differently by their subjects, as David Arnold and Stuart Blackburn argue: 'Indians present individual lives within a network of other lives and that they define themselves in relation to larger frames of reference, especially those of family, kin, caste, religion, and gender'.[14]

Guha's major biographies are of people who maintained copious records of their lives, and he follows a fairly standard chronological account in the tradition of Western biography. Yet it is a mark of his originality that even on a subject as much written about as Gandhi, Guha presents a life that seems rather less familiar yet even more arresting. How does he pull this off? For starters, unlike many recent works on Gandhi, Guha's two-volume biography ranges far beyond his subject's published writings. Over years of archival work spanning four continents, he accessed private papers and archival materials, newspapers and magazines that no previous biographer had tapped. This immense pool of materials was crucial to Guha's methodological approach to life-writing, which emphasized the centrality of his subject's family and friends, detractors and foes, in the fashioning of Gandhi. Indeed, a striking feature of his biography is the extent to which we learn about Gandhi through the worlds and words of those around him. Guha credits this approach to the great Goethe scholar Nicholas Boyle,[15] but we may also see it as an attempt to turn the tables on Gandhi, who carefully and self-consciously moulded his own public self.

Equally important is Guha's attempt at portraying Gandhi against a wider historical backdrop. Not only is Gandhi's life deftly situated in the imperial and global contexts of the late nineteenth and twentieth centuries, but the books also trace a worldwide web of interest in and influence of Gandhi. The fidelity to such detailed historical reconstruction is also important for Guha's attempt to trace the evolution of Gandhi's ideas on a host of critical issues such as empire and race, caste and gender among others. The Gandhi that emerges from this biography is a man who stubbornly clung to some ideas and principles while modifying and discarding others. Finally, the biography is written deliberately in a spare and unadorned style that simultaneously makes it highly accessible and captures something of Gandhi's own notion of the relationship between writing and living.

His own works apart, Guha has been an evangelist for biography in India. In particular, he has underscored the importance of writing lives beyond those of the elites or subalterns on whom historians typically tend to work. Exemplary are Guha's own brief and coruscating yet moving and perceptive accounts of persons he has known—the editor of EPW, Krishna Raj, the Naxalite-turned-civil-liberties activist C.V. Subbarao, the economist Dharma Kumar, or the writer U.R. Ananthamurthy, among others.

It is in this tradition that the range of biographies that populate this volume have been written—about several fascinating if lesser-known characters in history, who each made a significant mark in their fields—from the wrestler Buttan Singh who made his name in Australia in the early twentieth century, to the college teacher Lakshmi Ammal, whose travelogue was perhaps the first Tamil autobiography by a woman, and the Hindi writer Agyeya, whose writings and politics excited significant controversy in his day. Dinyar Patel takes us through the life of Khurshedben Naoroji who was trained as a professional singer but chose to become a satyagrahi instead, while Aditya Balasubramanian describes the career of B.R. Shenoy, a right-wing Cold-War intellectual.

Contemporary History and The Making of Indian Democracy

Along with Balasubramanian's account of Shenoy, Venu Govindu's essay on the context for Gandhi's decision to relocate to Sevagram in the mid-1930s takes us from biography to the contemporary history of India. Guha's *India after Gandhi* (2007) was a pioneering and monumental account of the world's largest democracy. In retrospect, Guha's decision to embark on this book seems audacious. To be sure, he had dealt with India's post-independence history obliquely in *A Corner of a Foreign Field*, his history of Indian cricket. Yet, there was hardly any historiography on independent India. As Guha has noted, it seemed as though 1947 had become a boundary between historians and political scientists—the former stuck to the period before while the latter focused on the years after. The only significant work by any historian was Sarvepalli Gopal's biography of Jawaharlal Nehru, the second and third volumes of which dealt with the years between 1947 and 1964. If the absence of historiography was one deterrent, then the lack of official archival material should have been another. At the time Guha had published his book, neither the National Archives of India nor any of the state archives had begun systematically acquiring declassified government files and materials. In such a situation most professional historians would have quailed at the thought of writing a history of India from 1947 to the present. Luckily, for historians as well as lay readers, Guha was up to the challenge.

Guha creatively dealt with both the problems. To compensate for the absence of laid-down markers of historiography, he engaged closely and widely with work in the social sciences on Indian politics, democracy and development. The conceptual scaffolding of the book as well as its analytical focus were provided by ideas drawn from this massive body of writing: the primacy of the political and the five axes of conflict—caste, language, religion, class and gender. Yet the historical sociologist in Guha knew how to deploy these to craft an analytic narrative of the arc of Indian democracy. The historical materials themselves were equally eclectic. Guha undertook extraordinary research in the private papers, newspapers and periodicals housed in the Nehru Memorial Museum and Library, and elsewhere. Prior to his efforts, it seemed inconceivable that a history of Indian politics and democracy could be written without access to the official archive. Yet Guha's book showcased and analysed a dazzling array of public debates and deliberations carried out in English-language publications—an account that suggested that India's improbable democracy was also a many-voiced chorus.

The result was a rare work of history to which the often-misused epithet, 'magisterial' actually applied. At just under 900 pages, the book is a remarkable instance of the historian's craft: an unflagging narrative is nicely balanced with crisp analytical sections and sure judgements. The liberal historian's sympathies with the project of Indian democracy are evident, but he is never blind to its deformities and brutalities. One could argue with his political judgements and sympathies, but that had no bearing on what one could learn from this humane work of history. In the thirteen years since the book's publication, Indian democracy has undergone many vicissitudes, but no remotely comparable historical account has yet emerged. It remains a towering landmark in the historiography of contemporary India.

Guha's work has helped establish contemporary history as a serious area of inquiry within the study of Indian history. Apart from the contributions by Mukul, Balasubramanian and Govindu, three other essays deal with aspects of the contemporary history of India. Madhav Khosla examines the relationship between the government and the judiciary during the formative decade of the 1950s. Srinath Raghavan analyses the tangled history of Kashmir's autonomy in the 1960s and '70s. Jahnavi Phalkey considers the history of big science in independent India through the quest for developing a military aircraft.

Although he has worked outside formal academia for large parts of his career, Guha has encouraged and mentored hundreds of younger scholars, quite apart from opening up new fields of research. Alongside his own research culminating in *India after Gandhi*, Guha, along with Nandan Nilekani, set up the New India Foundation (NIF), which has supported and enabled a significant new body of work on independent India. Guha was at once mentor and reader, editor and publishing agent for authors who held a NIF fellowship.

It is fitting that this collection of essays to honour one of India's foremost and fiercely independent scholars should have brought together an assortment of academics, researchers and writers who might never otherwise find themselves under a single roof or between the covers of a single volume. This book is a testimony to the range, depth and vitality of Guha's scholarship, which has in turn sparked new directions that draw on his work but also go beyond it in interesting and important ways.

BOOKS BY RAMACHANDRA GUHA

ENVIRONMENT

Guha, R. (1989) *The Unquiet Woods: Ecological Change and Peasant Resistance in the Himalaya*. New Delhi: Oxford University Press.

Gadgil, M. and R. Guha (1992) *This Fissured Land: An Ecological History of India*. New Delhi: Oxford University Press.

Gadgil, M. and R. Guha (1995) *Ecology and Equity: The Use and Abuse of Nature in Contemporary India*. London and New York: Routledge.

Guha, R. and J. Martinez-Alier (1997) *Varieties of Environmentalism: Essays North and South*. London and New York: Routledge.

Guha, R. (2000) *Environmentalism: A Global History*. New York: Longman.

Guha, R. (2006) *How Much Should a Person Consume? Environmentalism in India and the United States*. Berkeley, CA: University of California Press.

BIOGRAPHIES

Guha, R. (1999) *Savaging the Civilized: Verrier Elwin, His Tribals and India*. Chicago, IL, and London: University of Chicago Press.

Guha, R. (2014) *Gandhi Before India*. New York: Alfred A. Knopf.

Guha, R. (2018) *Gandhi: The Years that Changed the World*, 1914-1948. New York: Alfred A. Knopf.

Essay Collections

Guha, R. (2001) *An Anthropologist Amongst the Marxists and Other Essays*. New Delhi: Permanent Black.
Guha, R. (2003) *The Last Liberal and Other Essays*. New Delhi: Permanent Black.
Guha, R. (2012) *Patriots and Partisans*. New Delhi: Penguin Books.
Guha, R. (2016) *Democrats and Dissenters*. New Delhi: Penguin Books.

Cricket

Guha, R. (1992) *Wickets in the East: An Anecdotal History*. New Delhi: Oxford University Press.
Guha, R. (1994) *Spin and Other Turns: Indian Cricket's Coming of Age*. New Delhi: Penguin Books.
Guha, R. (2002) *A Corner of a Foreign Field: The Indian History of a British Sport*. London: Picador.
Guha, R. (2020) *The Commonwealth of Cricket*. New Delhi: HarperCollins.

History

Guha, R. (2007) *India after Gandhi: The History of the World's Largest Democracy*. New York: Ecco.

Edited Volumes

Guha, R, and T.G. Vaidyanathan (eds) (1994) *An Indian Cricket Omnibus*. New Delhi: Oxford University Press.
Guha, R., ed. (1999) *Social Ecology*. New Delhi: Oxford University Press.
Guha, R. and D. Arnold (eds) (1995) *Nature, Culture, Imperialism*. New Delhi: Oxford University Press.
Guha, R. and J. Parry (eds) (1999) *Institutions and Inequalities: Essays in Honour of Andre Beteille*. New Delhi: Oxford University Press.
Guha, R. ed. (2000) *The Picador Book of Cricket*. London: Picador.
Guha, R. ed. (2000) *Nature's Spokesman: M. Krishnan and Indian Wildlife*. New Delhi: Oxford University Press.
Guha, R. ed. (2012) *Makers of Modern India*. New Delhi: Penguin Books.
Guha, R. ed. (2016) *The Makers of Modern Asia*. Harvard University Press.

Research Papers and Journal Articles

Ramachandra Guha has also published some twenty research papers in journals such as *Contributions to Indian Sociology, Development and Change, Economic and Political Weekly, Environmental Ethics, Indian Economic and Social History Review, Journal of the Royal Anthropological Institute,* and *Past and Present.*

PART I

ENVIRONMENT AND EQUITY

1

EMPIRE'S NATURE IN THE GARO HILLS: A MICROHISTORY OF INDIA'S ENVIRONMENTAL MOVEMENTS

ARUPJYOTI SAIKIA

EARLY IN THE twentieth century, massive political turbulence swept across the Garo Hills in what is now Meghalaya, but was formerly a district in the British Indian province of Assam. The unnerved colonial state was forced to institute an enquiry commission in 1906. It was not, however, as if the colonial state was entirely unprepared for this turn of events since the Garo predicament had begun to unfold by the late eighteenth century itself, followed by strong resistance towards the British East India Company (EIC) government throughout the nineteenth century. Given their centrality in pre-modern trade networks, the Garo Hills had long attracted EIC traders, who bought elephants, coal, limestone and timbers from the locals. Rudyard Kipling's Kala Nag, the elephant from the Indian kheddah department who 'served the Indian Government in every way that an elephant could serve it for forty-seven years' was from the wilds of the Garo Hills.[1]

By the turn of the nineteenth century, vast tracts of the Garo Hills became part of the empire's forestry programme.[2] The Garos detested the idea that their *jhum* lands used for shifting cultivation were converted into *sarkari* (government-owned) forests. The British government also enforced compulsory labour service on their Garo subjects—known as *begaar*—to overcome the shortfall in manpower. The Garos had already been fighting a long-drawn battle against the zamindars of Goalpara on the begaar issue. Garo anger against begaar and restrictions on jhum was eventually drawn into the larger orbit of anti-colonial resistance by Garo leader Sonaram Sangma, who galvanized the Garo struggles into a movement from 1899 to 1910 on the basis of legality, rights and justice. This extraordinary act of defiance of 'Empire's nature',[3] was perhaps the most significant precursor to those later environmental struggles brilliantly described in Guha's *The Unquiet Woods*.

THE DEFIANT GAROS

Despite the powerful presence of Mughal and Afghan chiefs in their proximity,[4] with forts in places like Mymensingh or Sherpur designed to coerce the Garos into supplying their regimes with wild elephants and other services,[5] the Garos could still retain their political control over their territories till well towards the end of the eighteenth century.[6] When this Garo sovereignty began to lapse, the zamindars of Bengal intensified their raids on the Garo Hills. They partially succeeded in pushing the Garos into the interior of the Garo Hills, and taxed those living in the plains of Goalpara. Accounts of the Garos' fierce retention of their resources and territories became legend—and part of the empire's graphic account of India's rude wild tribes. In 1919, William Carey, an American missionary, described the Garos not only as of 'fiercer fame' but 'as the most uncouth and barbarous of all the border tribes'.[7] Similar ideas percolated deeply into the sensibilities of the Assamese literary elites of the nineteenth century. Ratneswar Mahanta, writing in the Assamese literary journal, *Assam Bandhu*, reserved the harshest words to describe the stubbornness and 'primitive lifestyle' of the Garos.[8]

British commercial interests in the Garo Hills began in the late eighteenth century,[9] requiring subjugation of these areas by the EIC government. However, company officials realized these areas could not be governed at par with the Bengal Presidency, leading the governor general in council to pass an unusual law—Regulation X of 1822—for the Garo Hills. The regulation exempted 'the Garrow mountaineers, and other rude Tribes on the North-Eastern Frontier of Rungpore' from the scope of acts of Bengal.[10] This gave EIC officials a free hand in Garo territory.

Yet, subduing the Garos remained a tough job, despite the colonial imposition of fines and tributes. David Scott, the first commissioner of Assam, sought permission from the Bengal government to 'march into a village and give notice that if the Chief did not surrender himself in two days and pay tribute, the village would be burnt and cultivation laid waste'.[11] Scott collected Rs 8000 in fines between 1817 and 1832.[12] Francis Jenkins, Assam commissioner (1836–61) had to repeatedly re-enact these low-intensity expeditions to the Garo Hills for their 'outrages and contumacy'.[13] When the Garo villagers refused to pay fines, as a measure of further punishment, they were not allowed to come to the border markets.[14] The Garos retaliated by raiding the plains.[15] Some of the villagers challenged their clan chiefs who asked them to pay tribute.

Punitive expeditions were resurrected at regular intervals to subdue the Garos until 1862. In the official narrative, by 1867–70, the Garos had come firmly under the control of the colonial government: 'only a comparatively small group of villages in the center of the hills remains independent and unvisited'.[16] The empire used various technologies of governance including topographical surveys to affirm its full control over the hills. An *English, Bengali, and Garrow Vocabulary* was published in 1867, as proof of mastery over the Garos by Bengali and English officials.[17]

Yet the Garos remained reluctant to part with the fruits of their labour easily, and the intensity of their raids into British territory only increased. British officials attributed this resistance to their nature as 'wild and barbarous tribes', and repeatedly reiterated their own resolve to 'reclaim [the Garos] to the habits of civilized life'.[18]

ZAMINDARS, COTTON AND THE GAROS HILLS

Barring the eastern side, the Garo Hills were ringed by the thickly forested estates of the zamindars of Bengal and Goalpara, who tried to maintain control over the foothills. During the Mughal times, the zamindars 'held all the low country under the Garo Hills on the Assam side, and it was their principal duty to repress the incursions of the savage tribes of the uplands'.[19] In turn, the Mughal government imposed only light taxation on these zamindars, in the form of cotton collected from the Garo Hills. In the late eighteenth century, the EIC government confirmed three zamindari estates as *istimary* mahals—to be lightly taxed—in return for their role as bulwark against the Garos.

The lands occupied by the zamindars had actually been captured from the Garos. Early in the nineteenth century, Francis Buchanan, the East India Company surgeon, botanist and surveyor, described the Garos cultivating with the plough 'with fully as much care as any of the neighbouring Bengalese'. He noted that 'the best villages and longest portion of that district are recent and violent usurpations' from the Garos.[20]

In addition to taking over their land, the zamindars asserted their superiority over the Garos by occasionally extracting rent from them, mostly in cotton, but also as cash. The zamindars had also established *haats*, or weekly markets, in all the passes of the foothills, which ensured they regulated the lucrative trade with the Garo Hills. The Garos who refused to accept the authority of the zamindars were eventually pushed to the hills by them. This perpetual violence between the zamindars and the Garos occupied the centre stage of political life in the Garo Hills throughout the nineteenth century.

In this long history of Garo resistance, at least one episode metamorphosed into a charismatic and millennial character: the rebellion of the Pagal Panthis (madmen) which traumatized the zamindars as well as the company government. The Pagal Panthi sect, mostly populating the present-day Mymensingh district of Bangladesh, came into existence in the later decades of the eighteenth century.[21] Born out of syncretic Sufi and local political–cultural traditions, the Pagal Panthis were a close-knit group who violently resisted the oppression of the Bengali zamindars. The Garo peasants from the southern Garo foothills teamed up with these rebellious tenants to challenge zamindari oppression, and between 1824 and 1833, the two together regularly outnumbered the zamindars.

Why were these hills so prized? The answer would be found in cotton, the most valuable article of export from this area. Trade in cotton had already flourished during the Mughals; these exports reached Bengal through a nexus of merchants and zamindars. Prospects of lucrative trade attracted both Bengali and Assamese merchants including Bhabananda, the sixteenth-century Assamese merchant, into the Garo Hills.[22] Eighteenth-century India's vibrant textile trade was propelled by a vastly spread out network of cotton production in which the Garos were no small player. Considered one of the best varieties found in Bengal, cloth made from Garo cotton was highly prized by Bengal's rich.[23] The fame of the Garo Hills' cotton, whose fibre was considered 'to be harsh and to twist badly' and was 'better adapted for mixing with wool than for any other purpose' came from its use as a good mix with wool to make carpets.[24] At one point, the Bengal government even thought that the Garo Hills could fulfil the needs of the Manchester mills.[25] The Garo Hills produced the largest share of the cotton output of Assam; of the total area of 38,815 acres, the Garo Hills alone cultivated 22,933 acres.[26] Broadly categorized as *bor kopah* (large cotton) and *saru kopah* (small cotton), and cultivated as part of their jhum crop, George Watt identified the Garo Hill cotton as 'very remarkable' and of 'very rare form'.[27] William Carey, the famed missionary from the Garo Hills, reminded his readers that 'who read this may be resting their feet . . . on cotton grown in a Garo jhum'.[28]

The zamindars effectively controlled the cotton trade, and till 1788, paid their revenue to the EIC in cotton.[29] Unless authorized by these zamindars, no trader from Bengal could access the cotton produced in the Garo Hills. The Garos also depended exclusively on the Bengal markets for their vibrant cotton trade, despite 'fraud, falsehood, and extortion'.[30] 'When the Garrow arrives at the market the zemindar commences by taking part of the cotton as his share, the remainder is exchanged for nothing literally'.[31] Zamindars collected astronomical tax from the cotton sold in the markets, often amounting to one extra load of cotton against every load brought to the market.[32] Zamindari extortion at the foothill markets led to violent retaliatory raids by the Garos.

The zamindars of Goalpara also regularly extorted taxes from their Garo tenants but this rent was not shared with the company government. In 1824, zamindars paid only one thousand part of such collection to the company government.[33]

By the mid-nineteenth century, the zamindars' access to the Garo Hills was curtailed by the EIC. As they were deprived of their lucrative commercial ventures, the zamindars pushed the southern boundaries of their estates, subjected the Garo peasants there to rent and made them buffers against the Garos of the uplands. This led to increasing territorial disputes between the two. During 1849–51, the company government decided to draw boundaries between the Garos and zamindars. The indomitable Garos retaliated; an official estimate claims that in 1852 there were seven raids by the Garos. When early in the 1870s those boundaries were resurveyed by the British official W.O. Beckett, he restored some of those lands to the Garos from the estate of Bijni, one of the five zamindars of Goalpara. The zamindars sought legal remedies but this gave them insignificant reprieve, and they continued to push the southern limits of their estates.[34] The zamindars' attempt to realign their territory signalled the unfolding of a larger political crisis.

EMPIRE'S FORESTRY IN THE GARO HILLS

The Garo Hills were, wrote the EIC officials, '. . . undisturbed by agriculture, the mountains are covered with a noble forest, containing an infinite variety of curious and ornamental plants'.[35] By 1872 the empire's men realized how lucrative the Garo timber trade would be: 'Government may expect a fair return . . . wild elephants are said to be very numerous, and probably khedda operations would prove profitable'.[36] Logs from the Garo Hills found ready customers; the rich from Bengal bought them to build house posts and boats.

Crude lac, extensively used as a textile dye, in varnishing and oil paintings, was another promising product. An estimated 4 per cent of Assam's export earnings came from trade in lac in 1793.[37] A winter crop, the Garo villagers reared the lac insect on 'plant arhar dal [*Cajanus cajan*]' primarily on the northern face of the hills. Once harvested, these villagers, many of them recent converts to Christianity, brought this crop to the haats in the foothills. The forest department exercised full control over the lac market by issuing licences to shopkeepers to buy the lac and collecting duty from them.[38] In the 1900s, the annual duty was on an average Rs 10,000, while the value of lac was Rs 50 per maund. These petty shopkeepers were 'agents of the Marwari traders' who operated from Goalpara.[39]

The other prized forest product was a superior-quality sal (*Shorea robusta*), covering an estimated 8 per cent of the Garo Hills.[40] Speculative timber markets in Bengal and Assam had increased the value of other timber trees too since the 1860s, with nearly 'all the timber sold being brought down to sand churs at the mouths of the affluents of the Brahmaputra, at the end of the rainy season'.[41] The timber trade was regulated through a nexus of Bengali or Marwari timber merchants, contractors (known as *duffadars*) and timber cutters. The duffadars, mostly Bengalis, provided credit in advance and paid all royalty and taxes on the timber. The timber cutting was done by several non-Garo tribes including the Rabhas and Meches of Goalpara. The Garos refrained from timber cutting in part because of their comradeship with nature, and in part because of their hostile relationship with the timber merchants. Swidden agriculture (colloquially called *jhum kheti* or *aba-oa*), which also involved cutting trees, was regulated through elaborate rituals, making it inherent to the Garo living world.[42]

The first official survey of the Garo Hills forests was conducted during 1868–76. In the 1870s, Assam's forest department brought a large portion under its control as Reserved Forests (RF). Between 1883 and 1888 the department declared eighteen RFs in the Garo Hills, including a few patches of Unclassed State Forests. The declaration of the RFs extinguished the rights of the Garos to jhum. Despite warnings by the deputy commissioner of the Garo Hills that formation of the RFs would entail hardship for the Garos and they should not be alienated from their lands,[43] the department went ahead on the principle that 'all land is absolutely at the disposal of Government unfettered by any rights' of the Garos.[44]

The demarcation of RFs was arbitrary with no consideration of Garo claims: 'If the Deputy Commissioner was satisfied on a casual inspection that certain villages had sufficient land outside the proposed reserves, the reservation was effected without more ado than notice to quit and the tender of Rs. 15 for each house required to shift'.[45] Compensation was rarely paid for the acquisition of village lands or for extinguishing rights of shifting cultivation. Such restrictions often spilled beyond the RF.[46] An age of restrictions engulfed the Garo Hills.

Yet, at the same time, the department did not want to dislodge the extensive forest trade centred on the Garo Hills. The forest department kept alive this trade network through a permit system and a series of checkpoints on the rivers. The Garos, and others too, were allowed to buy permits—known as *gurkati*—for 1 rupee. This gave 'the holder a right to sell bamboos, canes, grass, fuel, and unreserved poles under 6 inches in girth to outsiders'.[47] But it was essentially those who lived outside the Garo Hills who bought these passes for Rs 3 annually [known as foreign pass]. Of the average revenue of Rs 26,000 in the first decade of the twentieth century, only one-sixth came from the Garos.[48] A few Garo villagers were permitted to graze their cattle in the borders of the RF, but on condition that they worked for the department in clearing fire lines and boundaries.

By the early twentieth century, the forestry programme in the Garo Hills became an economic success. The Indian Railways, the largest customer of the forest department, regularly procured narrow gauge sleepers from the sal forests.[49] A cheerful forest department wanted to add more areas as RFs, proposing to incorporate approximately 25,000 acres more in 1900. The extinction of their jhum rights invited the wrath of the Garos. The department could finally reserve only 8000 acres.[50] But senior foresters repeatedly complained against vast tracts of forests still remaining as waste in the Garo Hills, and the destruction of valuable sal. In 1896, H.C. Hill, inspector general of forests, complained how the '[o]pen area is far in excess of that required for the shifting cultivation of so scanty a population'.[51]

The ideologically competing views of nature and agricultural method crystallized on the topic of jhum cultivation. For the empire, it was a wastage of land while for the Garos it was a continuation of traditional choices regarding their relationship with nature. An early critique of jhum warned that '[Due to] jhooming . . . the whole forest area is . . . subjected to gradual deterioration which is all the more dangerous'.[52] The angry forest department noted that the Garos, despite being under British rule, 'still look on the forest par excellence as their natural and legitimate means for increasing the yield from their fields by burning . . .'[53]

The Assam government began regulating shifting cultivation on the southern boundaries of the Garo Hills, passing the Sylhet Jhum Regulation of 1891.[54] But efforts to encourage permanent cultivation faced resistance, leading the inspector general of forests, S. Eardley-Wilmot, to propose that within RFs some areas should be demarcated as jhuming areas which should be endowed with 'liberal grant of rights' for all possible domestic and agricultural needs.[55]

The colonial practice of begaar, begun earlier by the Bengali zamindars and resisted by the Pagal Panthis,[56] further dismantled Garo lives. By the turn of the century, there were at least three distinct labour services which formed part of the begaar: work on bridle paths, bamboo bridges and inspection bungalows; porterage for touring officers; and labour for the forest department, such as the removal of sleepers from inside the RFs.[57] All these were crucial for strengthening government presence as well as integration of the interior trade of the Garo Hills with the wider markets.

Begaar survived through the network of contractors, many of whom had experience of supplying workers to the Assam tea gardens. To ensure a continuous supply of labour, the government regularly served warrants—legal notices demanding free labour—to the nokmas, Garo headmen. The tone and tenor of these notices were intimidating. Petty government officials regularly demanded that begaar be provided for their personal work.[58] Garo village headmen were threatened. 'If you cannot send begaars you shall have to do the job of a begaar with your own hands', Playfair, the deputy commissioner warned one of the Nokmas.[59] The colonial state blamed the rise of the Garo's political radicalism and refusal to carry out begaar on their brush with Christianity and new-found prosperity from trade in lac.[60]

THE TURBULENT GARO HILLS

Early in the twentieth century, Garo rage against the forest department and zamindars of Goalpara acquired an organized form. The turning point arrived in 1900, when the Bijni estate laid claims on Garo lands and more RFs were proposed in the Garo Hills. In December 1902, hundreds of Garos assembled at Dolgoma, a steamer port on the Brahmaputra. The rebellious Garos, memories of their days with the Pagal Panthis still fresh in their collective memory, sought to reclaim the Garo Raj and also prohibit their fellow Garo tenants from paying rent to the zamindar.[61] Officially termed the 'Dalgoma Disturbances', this insurgency greatly worried the colonial state. The chief commissioner of Assam imprisoned several Garo leaders including Sonaram Sangma. Months before the Dalgoma Disturbances too, several of the Garos, including Sonaram, were prosecuted for organizing a panchayat and collecting subscriptions.[62] Sonaram collected the subscriptions through an elaborate network of hereditary nokmas. He was imprisoned till April 1904 and again in 1905. The Garos were not demoralized by their leader's imprisonment. Rather, Commissioner J.C. Arbuthnott admitted, from 1902–03, the Garo agitation had 'assumed dangerous proportions',[63] with the Garos entirely declining to pay rent to the zamindars.

Sonaram Sangma's rise as a messianic leader of the Garos culminating in the Dalgoma Disturbances was of very recent origin. Only years before the disturbances, he was dismissed from the payroll of the Public Works Department (PWD) where he had worked for ten years as a clerk.[64] He came from a reasonably well-off family but his schooling remained inconclusive. After his dismissal as a PWD worker, Sonaram secured re-employment as a small-pox vaccinator in the Garo Hills which was suffering from an outbreak of this epidemic.[65]

Personally, it was a difficult time for Sonaram's family, with the British taking over the forests and the Bijni zamindar's possession of their lands leading to a decline in their income.[66] However, much of Sonaram's authority came from his position within the Garo social structure, in particular from his wife's family. By virtue of being the grandson-in-law of a powerful Garo headman (*malik*), he ensured a superior position within the Garo society. Calling himself *skhutong* (head nokma), Sonaram also claimed to be the political heir to Dhansing, his grand-father-in-law and a chief headman; he even produced before Arbuthnott a seal belonging to Dhansing to carry the latter's authority. Sonaram's wife, Thokje, still received rent from nokmas. Sonaram told his prosecutors that all the 'Nokmas of all these villages have paid my wife . . . They pay this in recognition of her rights'.[67]

Both situations—Sonaram's acquaintance with Assam's Congress leaders and his dismissal from service—empowered him to oppose the empire.[68] Sonaram claimed that his first major outreach to seek legal recourse began when he visited Calcutta towards the end of 1901 or early 1902.[69] Sonaram knew Bengali 'but not thoroughly', and he could write his name in English. He used all the force that he could assert to challenge the might of the zamindars and forest department. Sonaram's ultimate weapon was a book published by him. Priced at Rs 50, a reasonably high charge, 600 copies of Sonaram's book were printed; he himself sold about fifty to sixty copies. This tiny work contained old official records, survey papers, *parwana*s (notices), etc., proving the cruelty inflicted by the zamindars and the colonial state on the Garos. The book served three purposes: it contained evidence of British and zamindari cruelty to the Garos; it was a Garo proof of loyalty to fight against these cruelties; and finally, a part of the profit from sales could meet Sonaram's costly legal battles.

If Sonaram's book became a symbol of subscribing to the idea of resistance, it also became evidence for the colonial state to penalize Sonaram. Most witnesses who deposed before Arbuthnott admitted that they had acquired a copy of this book. The book also represented Sonaram's case against the empire. Jacob, a lawyer for Sonaram, and who was well known for his sympathetic defence of the Mundas during their trial by the turn of the nineteenth century, pleaded before Arbuthnott that Sonaram may not be considered as a witness in the RFs and begaar question as the evidence supplied in this book in the form of parwanas 'speak for themselves'.[70]

Two aspects of this political mobilization—collection of subscriptions and collective meetings, panchayats, as they were called—worried the

British officials. Sonaram became a force who could mobilize thousands of poor Garos and take on the might of both the zamindars and forest department. To underscore the question of mass support, Sonaram's memorials never forgot to mention the signatures of 1,00,000 Garos. His fellow companions were 'well-educated men having received their education in America and in other parts of the world'.[71] Not a novice, Sonaram devised an intelligent mechanism of monetary subscription as a way to mobilize his fellow countrymen. Sonaram maintained a basic office system—with five clerks—to organize and maintain this legal war. He engaged more than five leading lawyers who were either British or Bengali. The British lawyers, by virtue of their social proximity to the officials posted in the Garo Hills and Goalpara, allowed Sonaram to have access to information, legal papers and other support.

Sonaram's legal battle was preceded by several decades of intense territorial disputes between the Garos and the zamindar of Bijni, when the colonial state often sided with the latter.[72] The Garo agitation was shaped by three distinct issues: alienation of the Garos due to the new regime of forest governance, territorial disputes with the Goalpara zamindars, and their subjection to the malicious system of begaar. This had also united the Garos living in the plains and in the hills.

Apart from filing lawsuits against the zamindars' wilful practices, Sonaram submitted well-written, argumentative and lengthy memoranda to the viceroy. His memorials were authoritative, legally precise, informed by details and evidence, and further armoured by maps to show the encroachments made by the zamindars of Goalpara. One of the last petitions, prepared by Calcutta-based barrister Surendra Nath Ghosal, was shot off to Lord Minto, the viceroy, in 1906. Sonaram's memorials reprimanded the forest department for enclosing the forests with great haste and within a short period.[73] Sonaram reminded Minto that 'compensation, however, has never been paid for the acquisition of village lands or for extinguishing rights of shifting cultivation'.[74] Sonaram's petition demanded that the government either give compensation or return some of the lands to the Garos. That the Garos be given access to forests, right to use and sell forest produce besides rights of 'cultivation and rights of pasturage'. His memorial insisted that the government 'should give the villagers concerned a fair sum in compensation, representing roughly the approximate value of the land so lost. This should be offered as a sovereign act of grace and not as a matter for bargaining'. The amount of compensation should be carefully estimated and 'paid as a gift' to families and villagers 'who would now be entitled under Garo custom to cultivate the lands we shall now retain'. Sonaram also spelled out a territorial limit for jhum, restricting it to the hills.[75] Sonaram demanded that 'no system of forced labour' should be allowed to exist 'under the British government', noting that 'coolies are either not paid at all, or that they were remunerated most inadequately'.[76]

The Garo agitation was strengthened by the forest department softening its hostility to shifting cultivation. In 1905, for instance, S. Eardley-Wilmot advised that shifting cultivation might be allowed within the RFs. Assam's conservator of forests was quick to qualify that this was meant only for future RFs, not the existing ones.[77] The anti-forest-department mobilization was strongest on the northern side of the Garo Hills though southerners too joined them, largely because this was where the trade in forest products and imperial forestry flourished. Extortion and aggression of the powerful zamindars of Goalpara and the memories of resistance to them also helped in the escalation of defiance.[78]

The British officials spared no opportunity to censure Sonaram's political activities, calling him 'notorious' and 'criminal'. He was repeatedly restrained from entering the Garo Hills.[79] Declared persona non grata in the headquarters of the Garo Hills, Sonaram was repeatedly asked by the colonial state to 'give security for good behaviour'. From 1900 onwards, the administration regularly persecuted Sonaram and looked for evidence to sanction harsher punishments. However, Sonaram continued to collect subscriptions, organize small meetings, travel to Calcutta to plan memorandums to the governor general, travel around the interiors of the Garo Hills to secure more support and convince his fellow Garo peasants that they would get back their lands, and collect old records from the courts as evidence against the zamindars.

An Inquisition of the Garos

As widespread insurgency gripped the Garo Hills in the early 1900s, a worried government first asked Joseph Bampfylde Fuller, lieutenant governor of Eastern Bengal and Assam, to conduct an enquiry. Unpersuaded by his dismissal of Garo complaints, the government then asked John Campbell Arbuthnott, commissioner of the Surma Valley, to make a fresh enquiry. Arbuthnott, a Scot, was educated in Edinburgh and joined the

Indian Civil Service in 1877 and was subsequently posted in Bengal and Assam.[80] From December 1906 till February 1907, he made several visits into the Garo Hills, and summoned large numbers of villagers and their headmen to answer his aggressive questions. Assisted by officials from the revenue, survey and forest departments, his enquiry was welcomed by the Garos who effortlessly answered his queries. Most of his time was spent in enquiring about the complex world of tenancy, rent and territorial limits of the zamindars of Goalpara and their relations with their Garo subjects. His investigation revealed the collective will of the Garos to outmanoeuvre the might of the colonial state and zamindars.

Arbuthnott interrogated his witnesses on the questions of forestry and begaar. Each one of them told Arbuthnott, in Garo, of the 'existence of irksome forest rules and fines and penalties imposed on them for fishing, hunting, collecting honey and wax, camping out in reserves, and for the spread of accidental fires due to burning jhums in the vicinity of reserves'.[81] Many questioned the forest department's wisdom of 'selfishly' retaining the RFs as a 'sacrosanct area'.[82] They did not shy away from telling their interrogator: 'We want to get back our village lands which have been taken from us and formed into the Forest Reserve. If we get it back and can cultivate within the Reserve the other land will get a rest, the jungle will grow up and be again fit for jhuming. We also want to "be exempt from impressed labour".'[83] Some others complained about how there was 'no forest lands left for cultivation, only ekra and bamboo jungles. The land [they have] . . . been fallow for three or four years and is no use.'[84] Others were more forthright. 'I am not troubled under the Forest Rules nor have my people been fined. We simply want our land back in order to be able to jhum and cultivate', retorted one.[85] Others complained how they 'got no compensation for the land. It was taken from us by Government by force [zabardusti]'.[86]

The forest department had a long list of crimes committed by the Garos. It punished those who set on fire their lands for jhum as this fire would spread to the RFs.[87] 'I was fined for burning my jhum.'[88] Others were fined for hunting, some were fined for entering RFs to collect honey,[89] some were fined for cutting even unreserved trees, some for sleeping inside the RFs (while on their way to work as begaar) and for fishing near RFs. Singiram's village which was 'ordered to supply coolies to make road near Dambu to get sal sleepers out of the reserve' was fined 'Rs. 120 for camping in the reserve, and lighting fires'. The villagers claimed that they camped on the edge of a stream with permission and cooked their food. The men were fined Rs 5 each.[90] Fire could spread fast during the dry and winter months, even if the reserves were located at a far distance, and punishment for this was obviously and strongly detested by the Garos. For some, the RFs had fragmented their jhums: 'My cultivation lies between two reserves Rajasimla and Ildek and it is difficult for my people to cultivate'.[91] Temporarily abandoned hamlets, part of the Garos' agrarian landscape and cycle, were considered forests without customary rights. It is not clear when this process began to take place, but by the turn of the century, intense dispersal of the Garo villages was noticeable. Such disintegration and consequent thinning out of the original villages did not, however, empty the original villages of their cultural memories completely. The original villages which owned sacrificial stones (shong-kosi) were rarely abandoned. Mistaken by the emptiness of such habitation, in 1903, the forest department included at least one such village within a RF much to the bitterness of the Garos.[92]

Begaar interfered with the Garos' busy agrarian life. 'We do not like clearing the roads in the rains as we can't leave our crops which have to be watched on account of wild elephants and pigs. We do not like working in the cold weather either', angrily retorted one lac and cotton cultivator to Arbuthnott.[93] Singiram Nokma and his ryots were 'afraid of being impressed in future as coolies . . . We want a clear order that we shall not be impressed'.[94] Some 'paid money' so that they would 'not be impressed as coolies'. 'They do not want [to] carry loads . . . [even] willingly if the rate was raised to 8 annas'.[95]

While he lent a sympathetic ear to the Garos' plight and was critical of the forest department, Arbuthnott also remained firmly apprehensive of Sonaram, whose replies to his interrogation were alert, and full of wit and conviction, while his legal papers had the powers to challenge the might of the forest department and zamindars. Sonaram not only responded to Arbuthnott with facts and figures, but also gave the larger picture of Garo rights. Some of his statements are worth quoting at length.[96]

Court: Was it not because you issued a proclamation to the Garos not to pay rent to Bijni or the Government?

Sonaram: I did issue a proclamation, because Bijni first issued one.

. . . .

Court: What do the Hill Garos expect to get out of this case?

Sonaram: They expect the reserved forests to be thrown open and impressed labour to be abolished. They want to cut trees and bamboos wherever they like without taking passes and also to jhum where they please, inside the reserves. They think that their own lands have been taken from them by Government and turned into forest reserves. I have not made the hillmen any promises about reserves being thrown open or about the abolition of beg[a]ar.

. . . .

Court: Were you described in the judgments of Mr Cuming as a professional agitator, and a man of dangerous character?

Sonaram: I cannot say.

In the eyes of the colonial state, Sonaram had not confined his agitation to the Garo Hills alone but had spread it to other areas too. Sonaram unequivocally denied this but not before admitting that he 'jointly' worked with the Garos from other areas. Sonaram also used his knowledge of the Garo Hills' tumultuous past to outwit the colonial state, citing Garo relationships with the Mughals. He was ever-ready with evidence and proofs: 'I can call 200 or 300 witnesses to prove that we did nothing at Dalgoma'.

The colonial state considered the collection of monetary subscription by Sonaram as a crime against the empire. But Sonaram told Arbuthnott that the 'subscriptions were paid voluntarily'. As in previous proceedings conducted against Sonaram by Captain Playfair,[97] where every witness stated that they had voluntarily given the money to Sonaram,[98] this time around too, his followers were explicit. Nacheng Nokma told Arbuthnott that he collected monetary contribution from his ryots as they 'object to do begaar'. 'If we subscribed we would get off and be exempt from all calls for labour and that we would be able to cultivate our lands at our leisure . . . we would get back our lands which are included in the reserves and that we would be able to take and sell forest produce when we go to the bazars in the plains'.[99] 'Money is required for the Vakils and Barrister who will plead our case for us', said another headman.[100] In the popular understanding, Sonaram had to collect money to get official papers needed 'for proper boundaries of the Garo lands'.[101] 'I hear that Habarghat pergana really belongs to the Garos and I subscribe because the lands are claimed by our people . . . we want the reserves back in order to cultivate'.[102] Thomal said, 'Now your case is to be heard, those who want to be exempt from begar must bring money'.[103] 'We have subscribed to the fund because we have no good land left outside the reserve for our cultivation . . . If we get it back and can cultivate within the Reserve the other land will get a rest, the jungle will grow up and be again fit for jhuming',[104] 'We have given larger sums of late because we hear that we are to be exempt from begaar and that we shall get back our village lands'.

Arbuthnott noted that while the movement had widespread support, it was the rich Garo villagers who grew lac and cotton who contributed most towards Sonaram's legal costs. These crops brought good profit from the extensive markets which sprang up all along the Goalpara borders. The combined participation of Garos in the plains and hills also reinforced Sonaram's agitation. The former's anger was against the Goalpara zamindars while the latter had accumulated grievances against the forest department. Others like Kachari and Rabha tribes—who were tenants of the zamindars—were also with the Garos in their struggle. The intensity of the movement was most powerful in those places where RFs were created by carving out village lands, and in such cases, 'whole villages have subscribed . . . according to the ability of the individual'.[105]

ONE STEP FORWARD AND TWO STEPS BACK

In May 1907, Arbuthnott submitted his lengthy report which included some unusual proposals.[106] Arbuthnott, who had little doubt about 'the unanimous testimony of the hillmen',[107] agreed that 'the manner in which forest reservation has been carried out is largely responsible for the present unsatisfactory attitude of the Garos'.[108] Arbuthnott, who realized that creation of RFs had led to a decline in the agricultural land, admitted that the process of demarcation was arbitrary, that compensation was never paid for 'acquisition of village lands or for extinguishing rights of shifting cultivation',[109] and that when compensation was given, it was peanuts. That this serious crisis did not lead to any massive resistance against the forest department, Arbuthnott thought, was because of the memories of the Garo expedition (1872–73) which led to the subjugation of the tribe by the empire. Others did not complain either because a legal recourse was considered time-consuming or could attract further trouble.[110]

Arbuthnott also realized that several RFs were created without any economic logic. Bereft of their utilitarian goal, these forests should 'be made over, within certain limits, to the villages from which the lands were taken' which would bring down the Garo agitation.[111] While total de-reservation would be 'a retrograde step', exclusion of 'worthless' areas of the RFs was still possible.[112] Those unworkable areas needed to be reconstituted as protected forests. But what about the expenses incurred by the forest department 'in opening out a wretched tract of country'?[113] This could be derived, Arbuthnott proposed, from levying more taxes on the marketed lac.

What would happen to the world of jhum? Notwithstanding his suggestion to the forest department to abdicate their rights on forests, and despite being aware of the fact that 'jhuming is the only kind of cultivation possible from the nature of the country',[114] Arbuthnott stressed the need to curb jhum, and encourage Garos to adopt permanent cultivation. Arbuthnott also toyed with the idea of *taungya*, where jhum within RFs would be allowed. But the issue was not entirely about jhuming, but of sovereignty and customary rights over land, which were considered superior to colonial law. As Sonaram proudly asked Arbuthnott—why should the government offer him ownership over land when he already possessed this?

What about begaar? Arbuthnott, who disliked the practice, agreed that it had already begun to decline. Gone were the days when one could expect to deploy military police 'to compel villagers to turn out to work'.[115] The system was bound to end, as recent economic prosperity amongst the Garos stood against the idea of begaar. Only transition to a contract labour system, like that of the Assam tea plantation, could save the empire's authority in the Garo Hills, Arbuthnott concluded. However, he also justified the conditional continuance of begaar: 'But it is not unreasonable that the Garos should be expected to carry the baggage of the few district officials . . .'[116]

Months later, Eastern Bengal and Assam's financial secretary and conservator of forests sat down to examine Arbuthnott's report. The proposals, however, did not go down well within the forest department. 'If it is absolutely necessary on political and administrative grounds', M. Hill, the conservator grudgingly agreed to resurvey the RFs so that 'worthless' areas could be excluded and compensation for the remaining reserved areas considered.[117] Hill opined that conversation of RFs to the category of protected forests would be a regressive step as this would only partially empower the forest department and still allow various human activities though 'Garos have more or less acquiesced in their reservation'. Hill angrily dismissed Arbuthnott's suggestion to abandon all future proposals to create RFs. Rather, he insisted that the Garos should be discouraged from jhuming and encouraged to take up permanent cultivation.

William James Reid, the finance secretary, did not agree with the conservator: rather he thought that the Garo Hills' 'upper slopes are never jhumed, as the prevailing mists are believed to make cultivation there a failure'. Reid also concluded that 'no form of cultivation can entirely take the place of jhuming' in the hills of Assam. 'The nature of soil, the conformation of the ground and the crops raised are all against such complete substitution', Reid argued. He also agreed that compensation should be given for which 'the basic of calculation should be not only the supposed value of any land reserved, but the extent to which individual villages were deprived of their culturable lands and the amount of land fit to be jhumed which was left to them'.[118] Weeks later, despite the forest department's opposition, the Assam government agreed with Arbuthnott's proposals that the RFs, 'areas which it is not found worthwhile to retain should be surrendered to the villagers'.[119] The Indian government recommended awarding compensation.[120] Withdrawal of the governmental authority from the RFs—in the form of giving back these areas back to the Garos—was an undesirable idea, but for political reasons and 'in favour of liberality' such an unusual practice could be thought about. Similarly, begaar should also be slowly discontinued.

Those were the big promises; but in the end, the imperial government could not jeopardize its economic foundations and took only minor corrective steps to redress the Garo grievances except the demands of de-reservation and compensation.[121]

Sonaram died in 1917. A nationalist hero for the Garos, Sonaram's statue proudly stands in the heart of a Garo township. However, the causes for which he fought still remain. The total area of the RFs in the Garo Hills today remains almost similar to what was there in the 1900s. Shifting cultivation is still practised, and the old ideological wars about the merits and demerits of jhum refuse to die down.[122] The forests continue to be contested.

Acknowledgements: I am specially grateful to Bengt G. Karlsson, Dwijen Sharma and Sanat K. Chakraborty for helping locate select archival materials on Sonaram Sangma.

2

THE HEART OF THE MATTER: STUDYING INSTITUTIONAL STRUCTURES IN HISTORICAL PERSPECTIVE

SHASHANK KELA

IN THE LATE 1980s, forest management in India made a sharp break with the past—this, at least, is the generally accepted view. During this period, official pronouncements (exemplified in the new forest policy of 1988) shifted from a predominantly extractive orientation to one more nuanced and conciliatory, stressing environmental considerations and popular participation. Joint forest management (JFM) was introduced in the 1990s. Judicial intervention in environmental questions is another bellwether: in 1996, the Supreme Court's Godavarman judgment redefined forests, restricted the scope of permissible activity in them and established the Central Empowered Committee as a regulatory body.[1]

Two books by Ramachandra Guha serve as inflection points in the debate over forest management that gained momentum during this period.[2] *The Unquiet Woods* traced contemporary conflicts between local communities and the state in the western Himalayas back to colonial forest policies. *This Fissured Land*, written with Madhav Gadgil, put forward a broader argument about people and natural resources in South Asia. It argued that the precolonial past had been marked by a rough equilibrium between resource use and resource preservation, mediated through the caste system. Colonialism disrupted this relationship by commodifying forests

21

and taking them into state ownership, outlawing traditional practices of use and management. The effect was to break down pre-existing patterns of stewardship and promote unsustainable extraction.

Its publication provoked a sharp debate. Three years later, a major study by Richard Grove traced the beginnings of modern environmentalism to colonial fears over desiccation and deforestation, and examined their influence on forest conservancy in South Asia.[3] Other scholars challenged the assumption of ecological harmony in the past by citing conflicts over resource use before the advent of colonialism.[4] More recently, Kathleen Morrison has argued that environmental change was a constant feature of South Asia's history from prehistoric times.[5]

Quite clearly, the arguments advanced in *This Fissured Land* must be re-evaluated in the light of subsequent scholarship. By now, we possess a substantial body of evidence pointing to major episodes of environmental change in the past—but much less discussion of their precise effects. It has been argued, for example, that the dry forests of peninsular India gradually became adapted to periodic fires of low intensity over thousands of years, once humans colonized the interior of the Deccan. These fires were set by local communities to create optimum conditions for foraging, hunting and grazing.[6] The result was a savanna-like landscape of open forests and grasslands.

In a transformation of this kind, one interlocking suite of plants and animals is replaced by another. By contrast, the conversion of forests to fields subtracts many species (but also adds some). The ecological effects of agrarian expansion are determined by human density and farming techniques: secondary forests growing over zones of shifting cultivation shelter fewer bird species than natural forests but more than plantations.[7] Industrial farming, on the other hand, empties landscapes of much of their flora and fauna. The effects of deforestation are variable and complex: they can only be uncovered through detailed regional studies.

A comparative perspective is built into Guha's writings—the colonial period serves as a vantage point to look before and after. An early paper examines continuities in the realm of forestry during the decades after Independence.[8] Considerable stress is laid upon the commercial considerations informing colonial forest policy; these remained unchanged after 1947, engendering growing conflict with local communities with very different patterns of resource use.

This viewpoint finds broad acceptance in much of the subsequent literature on forest management. This essay is concerned with some of the issues raised by it. The debate is an intricate one with many strands. Most of its participants take policy prescriptions or legislation as their point of departure. The introduction of JFM led to the first studies of forestry in terms of rule-making.[9] The campaign around the Forest Rights Act (FRA) and its passage in 2006 marked a noticeable shift to problems of governance. In the words of two scholars,

> [t]he questions have shifted from 'how to conserve forests' or 'how to afforest wasteland' to 'who are the stakeholders relevant to the forest question', 'who should have the primary say', 'what are the rights of non-local stakeholders', and 'what should be the process of converting to non-forest land'. Questions of forest rights, responsibilities, regulatory structures, transparency, and accountability have increasingly become central to the discourse . . .[10]

Some ecologists approach analogous problems from the vantage of biodiversity conservation: Ghazala Shahabuddin provides a comprehensive critique of the official paradigm and explores its alternatives.[11] This viewpoint accepts the need for 'inviolate' spaces, kept free of human activity, but argues for democratizing forest management and extending legal rights to forest dwelling communities.[12] Another criticism, emerging in recent years, takes bureaucratic opaqueness and hostility to science as its theme.[13]

From forest (and park) management, we have advanced to a very different set of questions to do with effectiveness, accountability, legal rights, democracy, justice, even organizational theory. Yet the sophistication of this debate (and the policy prescriptions generated by it) conceal a striking paradox—the actual behaviour of the state has not changed very much despite a series of legislative and policy reforms beginning with the Forest (Conservation) Act (FCA) of 1980.

An illuminating study by Kanchi Kohli and Manju Menon dissects the procedural infirmities with which the FCA is riddled, allowing the state to divert forest land at discretion.[14] This is not uncommon; the Indian state has always shown a marked preference for ambiguity in legal wording, reserving a range of discretionary powers for itself.[15] Even without this, it would be difficult to make legislation watertight, for implementation depends, in the final analysis, upon the good faith of state agencies. JFM lacked legal backing, and its actual purposes were utilitarian and instrumental: Sharachchandra Lele argues that its failure shows that forest officials 'are opposed to any serious devolution of powers, and even to a pragmatic de-concentration of functions'.[16] The FRA, by contrast, had the force of law. It was supported by the tribal welfare ministry and passed in the teeth of objections from the ministry of environment and forests and a powerful conservation lobby. Some states, in some regions at least, tried to make it work despite obstruction from the forest department.[17] Its uneven record is ascribed to this hostility and a number of legal loopholes (the scope of the gram sabha's authority, conflict with the FCA and so on).[18]

New laws, policy enactments and procedural rules continue to be suggested to reform practices that have proved resistant to similar proposals since the 1980s. This is not to deny some progress, but few scholars would suggest that we are anywhere near a satisfactory resolution of intractable problems of conservation, land rights and participatory management. Since 1988, and especially after 1996, the state has laid increasing stress on the environmental aspects of its stewardship—climate change bulks large in its recent pronouncements and proposals—but its actual record is worse than mediocre.

Here, I suggest that this failure cannot be understood on its own terms, from within the discursive grid of policy and legislation. Instead, it may be more fruitful to examine it in terms of the *institutional* history of forest management from the late nineteenth century on. Colonial forestry has received considerable attention in the environmental history of South Asia.[19] Since land management policies were informed by silvicultural (and occasionally environmental) considerations, they have been examined largely from this perspective. This leaves significant gaps: many themes, including the history of botanical research and the evolution of bureaucratic structures, remain virtually unexplored. Here, I outline an argument for their significance in shedding new light upon contemporary problems.

Most scholars ignore the actual structures of the forest department. Organizational studies exist, mostly in specialized journals, but their scope is restricted to institutional *behaviour*. Sushil Kumar and Sashi Kant map variable attitudes to JFM within the department—its hierarchical structure, marked by asymmetric flows of information, is viewed as a problem of organizational culture.[20] Forrest Fleishmann examines individual behaviour in terms of the mechanisms that underpin this culture; his stated subject is 'the conceptual space in which individuals make decisions and take action'.[21] I would suggest, on the contrary, that organizational culture is the outcome of a historical *process* embodied, above all, in the evolution of bureaucratic structures and the institutional attitudes reflected and perpetuated in them.

The basic structures of forest management took shape during the late nineteenth century in order to carry out a specific set of tasks. Their limits were determined by the nature of colonial rule—here, I take the Madras Presidency as an example. They were carried over with only a few changes after 1947: this structural continuity is quite distinct from that in the domain of policy, which monopolizes scholarly discussions. From the 1970s, the responsibilities of the forest department grew steadily to encompass wildlife conservation, park management and environmental protection, but without any commensurate effort to change its structures and augment its capacities to tackle these challenges.

A succession of new laws, procedural frameworks and rules were put in place, but the agency responsible for implementing them remained substantially unchanged. Its structures and institutional habits are mired in a very different past. Because of this, the chronic failures of an earlier period were carried over into new settings, becoming more acute from the turn of the century as economic growth took off and resource use intensified.

COLONIAL FOREST MANAGEMENT IN THE MADRAS PRESIDENCY: BROAD TRENDS AND POLICIES

The Madras government created a separate agency to manage forests in the 1850s. Its stated goal was to extract timber profitably, efficiently and sustainably. This was coupled with a quasi-environmental ethic whose acceptance, both within and outside the department, was never total and waxed and waned in subsequent decades. Emerging from the desiccationist discourse identified by Richard Grove as a springboard for environmental thought in the nineteenth century, this coupled tree cover with precipitation and surface flows. Its adherents argued that forests played an essential role in trapping rainfall, regulating run-off and preserving streams and rivers on which agriculture depended.[22] As time went on, the economic aspects of this argument—what would now be called ecosystem services—received increasing emphasis.

The second feature of colonial forest management was a near-total indifference to the natural composition of forests. Since the overriding goal was to extract commercially valuable species, the desirability of introducing them where they did not exist (or not in large enough quantities) seemed obvious. Ambitious schemes to plant native or exotic species were proposed. In 1876, forests in the Western Ghats were put forward as an ideal site for the introduction of *Castilla elastica* (a rubber tree).[23] In 1882, Dietrich Brandis, praising the Australian blue gum (*Eucalyptus globulus*) as 'a most remarkable and valuable forest tree', suggested planting it in scrub and the remains of old *sholas* in the Nilgiris.[24]

The principal reason why so few of these plans came to fruition was the conservatism of the Madras government, its reluctance to spend more than the absolute minimum on forest management and its insistence on holding the department to a rigid system of cost accounting. Forest officials saw teak (*Tectona grandis*) and wattle plantations as pilot projects: as such, they received attention quite disproportionate to their scale. Planting operations inflicted substantial damage in some regions—the destruction of grasslands in the Palni Hills being a prime example—but in many other places their effects were mitigated by the lack of sustained support and funding.

At the core of forest management was the prevention of fire. In the beginning, foresters regarded fire as a calamity everywhere, but this opinion was eventually modified. In Bengal, after many decades of failed experimentation, it was admitted that mosaicized landscapes dominated by sal (*Shorea robusta*) had been created through regular burning by local communities over many decades.[25] The ideal was forests where timber trees grew straight and tall, preferably in pure stands. Where fire appeared to aid their growth—notably sal and teak, but also anjan (*Hardwickia binata*)—officers were prepared to reconsider its prohibition, if only under strictly controlled conditions.

The relationship between fire and forestry is a complex one. In Madras the formative period of railway expansion in the 1860s and '70s had a dual effect on the thorn and dry deciduous forests of the southern Deccan. After being logged for sleepers, they became a favoured source of fuelwood supply for railway companies (whose locomotives continued to burn wood until the early years of the twentieth century).[26] The regular removal of large trees may have magnified the intensity of forest fires though varied ecological mechanisms including the proliferation of the exotic weed

Lantana camara: this was identified as a threat to sandalwood (*Santalum album*), a characteristic tree of the southern Deccan, by the early 1900s.[27]

ADMINISTRATIVE STRUCTURES AND KNOWLEDGE PRODUCTION

The administrative structures of the Madras forest department remained largely ad hoc and amateur for several decades. Professional expertise or training were rare: its first head, Hugh Cleghorn, was a doctor, and although there were a few plant collectors (Cleghorn himself) and botanists (Richard Henry Beddome described a number of species new to science), most conservators concentrated on the task of timber extraction. In time, recruitment became formalized. Candidates for the forestry service were chosen in Britain, where they were given a course of training, followed by field trips to Europe (France or Germany) to observe the principles of managed forests at first-hand.

From the turn of the century, the Imperial Forestry Service gradually became professionalized. The Forest Research Institute (FRI) in Dehradun was set up in 1906. In the interwar period it produced a small body of 'pure' research, mainly on taxonomy and vegetation analysis. Some of this stemmed from practical questions of revenue: the spike disease in sandalwood, the most profitable forest 'crop' in the Deccan, became the subject of official concern for several decades. It eventually led to a close study of its parasitic mechanism (the sandal tree is a root parasite) and a wide-ranging survey of insect fauna associated with it, including the identification of several species new to science with the help of experts in Britain, France, Germany and the United States.

This research was produced in the teeth of significant institutional limitations. Some specialists were recruited, but a good deal of scientific data was collected by men working in their spare time, in addition to their normal administrative duties. The forest department's research budget was minuscule, the bulk of it being devoted to forestry. The FRI examined problems of extraction and yield, industrial processes, and methods of exploiting forest 'products', old and new. The stress on keeping costs low and turning a profit meant that the Imperial Forestry Service remained chronically undermanned and underfunded, its members swamped with logistical tasks. In 1935, H.G. Champion described some of the difficulties involved in compiling his pioneering classification of forests by vegetation type while serving as silvicultural expert at the FRI. His survey was partly based on vegetation lists 'with very varying amount of detail' compiled by provincial silviculturists. To these, he added his own observations and field notes:

> Although I have been fortunate enough to have been able to see, even if in some cases only from the railway carriage window, nearly all the types described in the following pages, it has often been impossible for me to make detailed studies, and I have made use of what seemed to me the most suitable accounts and lists for the purpose in hand, irrespective of their source.[28]

The fact that a small proportion of forest officers continued to pursue research problems despite these obstacles can be attributed to their social background. Administrators sent to India had always been recruited from the middle and upper classes. Candidates for the Imperial Forestry Service were no exception, and the requirement of a university degree merely amplified this tendency. They belonged to a powerful landed gentry whose political ascendancy dated back to the seventeenth century. As imperial expansion opened the world to its gaze, many of its members acquired a strong interest in natural history. This was a pan-European process—specimens of every kind began pouring into herbariums and museums from the sixteenth century. These collections were to lay the groundwork for startling advances in the natural sciences.[29]

One of the key texts in the development of the Linnaean system of classification is the *Hortus Malabaricus*, compiled by the Dutch administrator Hendrik van Rheede from a mass of information provided by local physicians in Malabar and published (in Latin) from 1678. 'In the first edition of *Species Plantarum* Linnaeus (1753) included 254 of van Rheede's names in the protologues of his species. Linnaeus also adopted some of van Rheede's Malayalam names for genera e.g., *Pavetta* and *Basella*. Eleven Linnaean species names . . . were solely based on van Rheede's illustrations.'[30] By the nineteenth century, a stream of specimens collected by professional and amateur botanists in the company's employ was making its way to botanic gardens in the UK, notably Kew and Edinburgh.[31]

Thus some members of the Imperial Forestry Service brought an abiding interest in the physical aspects of the countryside—soils, trees, wild flowers, butterflies, birds—with them to India. The bureaucratic nature of colonial administration and its class cohesion—virtually all its senior representatives from district collectors to members of the viceroy's council shared the same social background—encouraged the pursuit of knowledge for its own sake. Individual forest officers not only had the social incentive to do unpaid research but a long tradition of scientific investigation to draw upon. Research projects undertaken in support of silvicultural operations included Champion's survey and studies of individual species like *Hardwickia binata*.[32]

Administratively, the Madras forest department was a hierarchical organization marked by two sharp divisions. One separated conservators from field staff. The latter were Indian, and no qualifications apart from literacy were demanded of them. They were trained after recruitment, principally in logistical tasks like policing, surveying (marking fire lines, measuring trees for felling, etc.) and keeping accounts. Any data collection performed by them remained at a basic level: gathering specimens, counting trees and so on.

The other line separated white and Indian administrators: Indians were trained at the FRI and allotted junior positions in the cadre. The devolution of power to provincial governments in the 1930s led to a restructuring of the service. By then, much of the routine scientific–technical work of the FRI was being performed by Indian experts, and Indian conservators were being promoted to independent charge, albeit in forests regarded as relatively insignificant from the silvicultural point of view.

The Decades after Independence

The period from 1947 to the early 1970s is marked by the absence of any kind of environmental *discourse*. The category of protection forests vanishes without a trace and, with it, the ecological argument for preserving them. Vasant K. Saberwal lays stress on the unscientific nature of this argument and its instrumental use by forest officers seeking to curtail grazing in the Punjab hills.[33] The Himachal Pradesh forest department occasionally cited the ecological value of forests to justify stricter rules after 1947: this did nothing to prevent the steady loosening of grazing regulations under political pressure, or the enormous extraction of timber by the department itself.[34]

It can be demonstrated that deforestation by itself has no effect on water flows, but this would not be regarded as a sound argument for cutting forests where they do exist. In practical terms, protection forests were largely symbolic; there is no evidence to show that the colonial state allowed them to interfere with its economic objectives. But once the classification was jettisoned, there remained no grounds, even in theory, for mitigating the more extreme consequences of 'development'.

After the First World War, forestry came to be based on surveys and working plans. Foresters aimed to balance timber extraction with natural regeneration and replanting to replicate the management of European woodlands. This model was a loose one: during the 1940s, working plans were set aside and timber cut indiscriminately to supply an imperial economy mobilized for war. After 1947, the forest department was to pay no more than lip service to sustainability in timber operations even as it abandoned its tenuous commitment to research.

Forestry generated revenues and provided raw material for industry as part of the effort to build a modern economy. Arguably, this promoted more reckless extraction—national interest being a more compelling justification than profit—but wider developments should also be borne in mind. The post-war economic boom in western Europe and the United States, the rapid growth of east Asia, and ambitious projects of modernization in the Third World converged to generate a spiralling demand for raw materials and consumer goods. It was an era marked by unprecedented growth and consumption, and reckless environmental destruction. To this, India was no exception.

There is some evidence to show that efforts to alter the natural composition of forests became more sustained and effective. The private (zamindari) forests of Midnapore in West Bengal were taken over by the forest department: by the 1970s, these sal-predominant, intensively coppiced woodlands had acquired a large proportion of eucalyptus and acacia species in addition to teak.[35] As late as 1976, the National Commission on Agriculture was advocating clear-felling natural forests in order to plant timber trees.[36]

One of the most noteworthy aspects of forest management during this period is the abrupt collapse of knowledge production. By the 1970s, the forest department had ceased to produce research of any quality. The reasons for this collapse are twofold. One stemmed from a mode of recruitment largely unchanged from the colonial period: forest officers continued to be generalists with a basic degree rather than specialists with advanced training. But where the colonial state had recruited from a landed class with a long-standing interest in natural history (fostered by generations of leisure, social privilege and university training) and embedded in a vast imperial apparatus, the new nation recruited its candidates from a very different urban (and upper-caste) milieu.

Education in the natural sciences was regarded as redundant for the task of timber extraction. No other tasks were set before the forest department, and its recruits lacked the inclination to pursue research on their own initiative as their predecessors had done. The FRI's umbilical cord to the department was never cut: its administrators remained serving forest officers rather than specialists. This ensured its decay: the focus on utilitarian problems was the symptom, not the cause, of a wider malaise. Ecological research took root only in the 1980s, *outside* the department— with the Wildlife Institute of India in Dehradun (set up in 1982; granted autonomy in 1986), the Centre for Ecological Sciences at the Indian Institute of Science in Bangalore (1983) and the National Centre for Biological Sciences in Bangalore (1991).

The political pressure exerted on officers to approve industrial projects, mines, dams and defence establishments is another side of the story. Here, my focus is on the *institutional* structures that played a key part in subverting the state's professed objectives. By refusing to recruit specialists and set aside funding for basic research, it allowed the tenuous achievements of the interwar period to lapse.

Yet another reason for the decline in research capacity was the retention of the divide between administrators and field staff. In a colonial context, the hierarchical division between (largely) white administrators and Indian subordinates mirrored the racial division of labour, the normative distinction between rulers and ruled. In a democratic context, it makes very little sense. In most developed (and some developing) countries, the park ranger or forester is a professional, trained to collect and interpret data.[37]

By contrast, the recruitment and training of rangers and forest guards in India embodies an institutional failure that has never been recognized, leave alone acknowledged. They occupy the base of a rigid hierarchy reliant upon giving and receiving orders rather than collecting data and sharing information. A number of alternative mechanisms could be envisaged: a separate wing for protected areas, distinct personnel for policing as opposed to observation and data collection, and so on. All of them depend

on blurring the entrenched division between blue-collar 'workers' and
white-collar 'administrators' inherited from the colonial state and never
subjected to scrutiny.

THE 1970S TO THE 1990S: REFORM OR STASIS?

From the 1970s, wildlife conservation became a key objective of forest
management.[38] This new emphasis coexisted comfortably with older
patterns of extraction. Its principal achievement—an expanding network
of protected areas—was counterbalanced by the absence of experts needed
to manage them. The state actively discouraged overseas researchers:
Kailash Sankhala, the first director of Project Tiger, rejected a proposal by
the Smithsonian to set up field stations in India at a time when indigenous
ecological expertise was conspicuous by its absence.[39]

The nineties saw the first attempt to formulate a new paradigm of
management, ostensibly in cooperation with local communities. JFM
emerged, for the most part, out of external conditions: the empirical failure
of policing and the desire to reduce costs of protection combined with
pressure from international aid agencies. The victory of the Communist
Party of India (Marxist) in Bengal formed the political context in which
the first experiments were incubated. Where an autonomous tradition of
forest protection already existed (as in Orissa), the department preferred to
bypass its structures or bring them under its own control.[40]

One of the defining features of JFM from 1990 to 2000 was the
provision that only degraded forest land (with less than 40 per cent
crown cover) qualified for co-management. Essentially, the department
sought to outsource protection of the least rewarding patches to local
communities. Particularly striking was the overriding emphasis on
forestry. Natural regeneration has been identified as a sensible method of
renewing some forests—it is estimated that approximately 63 per cent
of India's forest lands, or 40 million hectares, fall in this category (out
of which 30 million hectares are degraded to a significant degree).[41] Yet
land under JFM was afforested rather than being allowed to regenerate,
species for planting were chosen by the department, benefits were
couched in terms of timber sharing and revenue from 'harvesting'
timber, and forest produce and grass were systematically subordinated
to timber value. The department kept firm control of every aspect of the
process, from drawing up working plans to determining wage rates and

the final division of profits. Its field staff controlled JFM committees, operated bank accounts and disbursed funds.[42]

The first organizational studies of the forest department appear during this period. Bhaskar Vira sees a paradox in its rigid hierarchy, marked by lack of flexibility and aversion to innovation, coupled with its reliance upon individuals to come up with new ideas. An outcome of ineffective monitoring, this is seen as a positive feature, promoting flexibility through the back door as it were.[43] I would argue, on the contrary, that these ideas were intrinsically fragile; the large-scale adoption of JFM rapidly led to its dilution as the institutional structures of the department reasserted control.

Forest governance in India operates within a dual legal framework. One element comprises central laws and policies (the Forest [Conservation] Act of 1980, the National Forest Policy Resolution of 1988, the JFM circular of 1990), but actual jurisdiction is exercised by state governments, and laws passed by state legislatures also apply. The Bengal Private Forests Act of 1948 transferred zamindari forests to state ownership; Tamil Nadu's Janmam Abolition Act of 1969 did the same (to be followed by a flurry of legal suits that took more than thirty years to resolve).[44] The fact that Tamil Nadu took significantly longer than Bengal to abolish private forests indicates the degree of latitude exercised by state governments before the centralizing effects of the Godavarman judgment took hold.

This dual jurisdiction generates ambiguity, especially with respect to forest rights. The Panchayati Raj Extension to Scheduled Areas (PESA) Act of 1996 was supposed to give adivasi panchayats wide-ranging powers over natural resources. In Madhya Pradesh, a legislative enactment of 1997 modified it by adding a provision that community rights to non-timber forest produce could only be exercised 'with due regard to the spirit of other laws from the time being in force'. From this, the department argued the Forest Act took precedence over PESA in reserve forests.[45] The FRA makes diversion of forest land conditional upon recognizing and settling the rights of forest dwelling groups—but the centre can and has circumvented this obligation by accepting the contention of state governments that no such rights exist.[46]

There are significant variations in forest management across states. In the south, where the political influence of farming castes is deep-rooted, it becomes difficult to maintain a wholly adversarial relationship with them. The forest department is forced to be more pragmatic and less authoritarian, if only in comparison with adivasi regions.[47] The existence of forest panchayats in Uttarakhand can be attributed, partly at least, to the preponderance of upper-caste peasants—in contrast to Madhya Pradesh and Chhattisgarh, where adivasi peasants enjoyed no formal rights before the passage of the FRA. In the North-east, the department's authority is circumscribed by the fact that a significant proportion of land falls under community control.[48]

A uniform set of structures, attitudes and institutional habits underlie these variations in time and space: the collapse of knowledge production, a rigid hierarchy, lack of specialized training, reluctance to allow communities any share in decision-making and so on. A few officials work with wildlife biologists to improve park management, but the inherent instability of this relationship is laid bare in a recent account. In 1996, Raghu Chundawat set up a pioneering study of tigers in Panna National Park with the encouragement of its field director. Five years later, the director was transferred. His successor decided to promote tourism by using the project—which was tracking tigers fitted with radio collars—to locate them for viewing. When the researchers objected, their permissions were curtailed and their movements restricted. Poachers moved in as soon as research monitoring ceased. When Chundawat went over the director's head to warn of falling tiger numbers, the forest department closed ranks. The project was stopped and its members evicted from the park. Over the next four years, Chundawat's career was all but destroyed.[49]

A common response to these failures is the advocacy of community control, but *community*, like *bureaucracy*, tends to be posed in abstract terms, a category whose content is taken for granted. Most communities are hierarchical, riven by lines of conflict, with benefits and costs unequally shared. The assertion that forest dwelling groups are capable of sustainable resource use is debatable: the experience of colonialism and modernity has eroded traditional patterns of resource management, and created new aspirations.[50] It is less a case of reviving old structures than reinventing them in an entirely new context.

An obvious solution is to democratize governance within the framework of state ownership: most scholarly discussions adhere to this approach. They flag bureaucratic resistance as a sticking point, but the problem of institutional reform is ignored. The tendency is to bypass state institutions (through devolution), laying stress upon popular mobilization, political commitment and bureaucratic re-education.[51] The limited results of legislative enactments since 1990 testify to the failure of this strategy.

CONCLUSION

Since 1947, debates about forest management and conservation have been restricted, for the most part, to bureaucrats without specialized knowledge and experts who supply this deficiency. All the participants in these discussions take the bureaucratic structures of the forest department, its coercive capacity and inherent limits, for granted. In actual fact, this configuration was contingent and historically determined. It took shape around the late nineteenth and early twentieth century, and was governed by three principles—controlling costs, maximizing revenues and setting out a clear hierarchy of command. Expenses of administration were held down by keeping manpower to a minimum. Forest management was designed to yield a profit; research centred on commercial outcomes rather than basic knowledge. Once all rights not expressly recognized by the state were made illegal, coercion became the only method of protecting forests. The department assumed extensive penal powers, underpinned by a strict division of functions.

These structures remained largely unchanged after 1947. There was some regression: timber felling became more indiscriminate and research output collapsed. The department maintained its adversarial relationship with local communities, ameliorated in practice by political considerations. The goals of forest management began to change in the 1970s; during the 1980s and 1990s, an entirely new framework of environmental regulation was put in place. Yet the utility of structures inherited from the colonial period and their capacity to achieve these objectives has never been called into question.

Any regulatory framework relies upon specialized mechanisms to put legislation into practice. In response to public concern over pollution, Richard Nixon's Republican administration released a 'message on the environment' in 1970, asking Congress for funds to upgrade federal facilities, abate pollution and carry out research. It proposed air quality standards, guidelines to reduce emissions, and taxes and safeguards for oil transport and processing. Before the end of the year, the Environmental Protection Agency (EPA) had been established: this consolidated the environmental responsibilities of the federal government under a single department to 'permit response to environmental problems in a manner beyond the previous capability of government pollution control programs'. The EPA was entrusted with monitoring the environment and setting (and enforcing) standards for water and air quality in concert with state governments.[52]

India chose the opposite path. From the 1970s, the state has grafted an expanding set of environmental objectives on to the forest department with little or no effort to augment its capacities. The central ministry for environment and forests (with climate change now added to its remit), originally created in 1985, sits atop the department and works through it. The chronic failures of environmental regulation become much less puzzling when we compare this rickety framework with agencies of economic management, defence production and space exploration: the recruitment procedures and operational structures of the Planning Commission, the Reserve Bank of India, the Defence Research and Development Organisation and the Indian Space Research Organisation were professionalized from the very beginning.

The gradual shift from extractive forestry to conservation and environmental planning has yielded some real achievements. Yet much of this progress remains confined to paper—regulation is ineffective, popular hostility persists, failures of park management are routine, fauna (and the conservation of large mammals in particular) continues to take precedence over flora. The probable effects of climate change have barely been examined. A small but growing body of work by sociologists, anthropologists, environmental economists and ecologists examines the limits of this shift and its shortcomings.

This chapter looks at the problem from the perspective of the historian—it shows that it is all but impossible to change the orientation of a complex institution without changing its structures. Policy reform is unlikely to succeed without addressing this fundamental obstacle. There are two distinct questions here: one involves the state's willingness to act; the other, its *capacity* to act effectively. The two are usually conflated—it is assumed that the state is capable of taking action once the right policies have been adopted—but must in fact be considered separately. Or the question of capacity is treated as a technological problem (requiring better tools), or one of incentives (in order to reform bureaucratic behaviour). In actual fact, it cannot be solved without rethinking institutional structures in the light of history.

3

THE AUTHORITARIAN BIOLOGIST RELOADED AND DEEP ECOLOGY REDUX: CONSERVATION IMPERIALISM AND THE CONTROL OF KNOWLEDGE, MONEY AND SPACE

KARTIK SHANKER AND MEERA ANNA OOMMEN

IN 1989 AND 1997 respectively, nearly ten years apart, Ramachandra Guha published two critiques of prevailing and emerging paradigms in environmentalism, which were of immense significance to India and the Third World.[1] Both essays warned against the pitfalls of adopting a universal ethic, especially an anti-human one that ignored the diverse social and cultural foundations of the developing world. In this essay, we query what (if anything) has changed in the decades since.

Throughout human history, human–environment interactions have taken many forms that have resulted in a range of outcomes from over-exploitation to sustainable use to 'conservation'. The sequestration of resources by the wealthy and the powerful has also been a feature of human societies in recent history, beginning with agrarian and pastoral societies that restricted access to land and resources from competing groups. In India and elsewhere, strategies of enclosure were implemented by local rulers and were further formalized and scaled up during the

37

colonial period.[2] In fact, the recent trajectory of 'conservation' is deeply interlinked with that of European colonialism. Conservation, as it is currently defined and operationalized, owes its origins to settler excesses in these regions as well as responses to the scarcity induced by commodity extraction and the legacies of the Industrial Revolution. The European tradition of exclusionary hunting preserves and exclusive rights in favour of the elites also aligned closely with practices in other parts of the world, including Asia.

In North America, the early 1900s witnessed the birth of the notion of pristine wildernesses, as conceived and romanticized by those such as John Muir and Henry David Thoreau.[3] This was not only a radical shift from the utilitarian approach of American forestry (and its proponents like Gifford Pinchot), but also different from anthropocentric approaches adopted by the British and princely kingdoms in places like India. While some American conservationists such as Aldo Leopold promoted a balance with agrarian systems, and recognized that the value of natural areas also lay in services such as hunting and fishing, a strong movement for exclusionary conservation developed from their ideas, representing a biocentric view of 'nature for its own sake'. Ironically enough, the areas that they considered as untouched by human hand, such as the vast landscapes of California and Yellowstone, turned out to be consequences of centuries of 'manipulation' by native American peoples.[4] In many locations, low population densities of indigenous communities as a consequence of prior contact with Europeans and disease produced seemingly pristine landscapes that masked prior human influence.[5] In places such as Yellowstone and Yosemite, the removal of indigenous communities paved the way for the first national parks. Elimination, eviction and dispossession of native communities, and the 'idealisation of uninhabited landscapes'[6] have been the hallmarks of the American conservation movement.

However, the problematic history of the origins of conservation has largely been neglected in the contemporary conservation arena. On the whole, global conservation continues to be dominated not only by a limited understanding of history, but also by Western paradigms of protection that adhere to narrow frameworks of knowledge and ethics. Following the establishment of the crisis discipline of 'Conservation Biology' in the 1970s, conservationists of all hues have portrayed themselves as saviours of the planet, and have assumed sanctimonious postures about their role in society. In particular, ecologists and biologists have assumed the mantle of leadership in conservation decisions based on the (often misguided) premise that good science axiomatically translates to good management. In an attempt to be apolitical, these groups also tend to project conservation as a wholly righteous exercise without its attendant politics and continuing dispossession. Further, despite the fact that sustainable use is one of the three main tenets of the Convention on Biological Diversity (CBD), protectionist paradigms find widespread support in this community which continues to disproportionately campaign for human-free spaces, exclusionary conservation, and a call to end many forms of use that were once commonplace and continue to be crucial to human existence.

In the first ('Radical American Environmentalism and Wilderness Preservation'[7]) of the two landmark papers, Ramachandra Guha critiqued the emerging, yet powerful American deep ecology movement, which he warned, was 'a radical trend within the wilderness preservation movement' that aimed to shame the anthropocentric stance of traditional conservation discourses into a biocentric one. He questioned its applicability and argued against its adoption in countries such as India. The second ('The Authoritarian Biologist and the Arrogance of Anti-humanism'[8]) critiqued the self-proclaimed role of biologists as the flagbearers of science and the arbitrators of wildlife conservation. He called out various luminaries such as David Ehrenfeld and Dan Janzen who had been at the forefront of the conservation movement and who accorded a central place to biologists in environmental decision-making. Guha also called into question the policies of many large conservation NGOs and their impact on people.

A few years later, Dan Brockington's critique of fortress conservation became a rallying call for conservation social scientists to tear down the walls that biologists had built.[9] In 2003, Mac Chapin addressed an article to 'Big International Non-Government Organizations' (BINGOs), titled 'A Challenge to Conservationists' where he called on them to devise strategies that could simultaneously address conservation issues without sidelining marginal communities and their livelihoods.[10] And in 2005, Mark Dowie labelled conservation as one of the biggest causes of human rights violations (after war) that had resulted in an extraordinary number of conservation refugees.[11]

In general, the role of large Northern NGOs in setting conservation agendas, particularly for the Global South, came under fire.[12] Conservation social scientists also critiqued neoliberal conservation, an emerging conservation paradigm incorporating free market ideologies and privatization, and forging links between unlikely ideological partners, particularly NGOs and private corporations.[13] These led to the emergence of the field of political ecology in conservation.[14] Building on the prior analyses of political ecologists who critiqued the nexus between knowledge and power in Third World environmental research,[15] many of these essays called into question both the ideology of the conservation movement as violating human rights, as well as the movement's ability to be effective, creating as it did a wide swathe of 'victims' who were opposed to the idea of conservation itself. Social scientists pointed out the problematic consequences of 'war by conservation'[16] and described these as proactive, interventionist militarized responses, whereby conservation agencies engaged in violence and use of force against people who were identified as poachers with links to terror networks in areas that were of geostrategic interest to the US-led war on terror.[17]

The parallel and intertwined histories of the engagement of large conservation organizations and conservation biologists in the latter half of the twentieth century has its roots in certain ideologies, which while originating in the West, found a happy resonance in urban elite conservationists across the world (the local whites). This imperialism has manifested itself in three forms—knowledge, money and space. We examine each of these in the course of this essay. Given the changing paradigms of conservation over the years, we ask what has changed in the decades since Guha's seminal papers. Has the politics of conservation evolved? What do the offshoots of the deep ecology movement look like? Have biologists become any less 'authoritarian'? And what does it mean for developing countries like India?

INCURABLE TYRANTS AND OVERGROWN INFANTS

The idea that knowledge is power dates at least to Plato's *Republic*,[18] and is generally attributed to Francis Bacon and Thomas Hobbes in the sixteenth–seventeenth centuries (though it also appeared in sixth-century Islamic literature[19]). A modern scientific interest in the natural world was then already over 200 years old, and developed into the fields of biogeography and evolutionary biology. This interest further broadened into studies of animal behaviour and ecology. However, despite directly addressing questions relating to natural landscapes, flora and fauna, ecology as a discipline remained somewhat separate from movements related to nature preservation till the 1970s.

Modern conservation has its origins in the evolution of the environmental protection movement in the US. Here, environmental measures adopted to counter the Dust Bowl and ecological impacts linked to the Great Depression—followed eventually by concerns surrounding industrial pollution (pioneered by Rachel Carson's 'Silent Spring'[20])—drove the emergence of conservation, and consternation, at a national scale. As the cause gained traction globally via the establishment of several NGOs such as World Wide Fund for Nature (WWF), The Nature Conservancy (TNC) and International Union for the Conservation of Nature (IUCN), there was a rapid development of a priestly class within this enterprise. Further, since the conservation discourse was dominated by Western biologists and ecologists, this 'crisis discipline' began to spread the self-serving rhetoric that these two areas of research were central to conservation.[21] With this machete in hand, biologists from developed countries (US and European mainly) invaded the rest of the world, in pursuit of a particular kind of knowledge (biology or science), not of course for any personal gain, but to benefit the greater common good, namely conservation.

What followed the ordainment of biologists as the high priests of conservation was something akin to a gold rush. The first was disciplinary: from population biology to community ecology to genetics, the case was made for their contribution to conservation. Several journals were started—*Biological Conservation* in 1968, *Environmental Conservation* in 1974, *Conservation Biology* in 1977—and many textbooks were written during this period, establishing conservation biology as a new discipline.[22] In particular, Michael Soulé (the 'father of conservation biology') championed the development of this new field and the idea that good conservation was based on biology.

For example, there were heated debates surrounding the use of island biogeography, a theory proposed by Robert MacArthur and E.O. Wilson (1967),[23] to explain species richness on islands, to create conservation rules. One such rule, based on the idea that smaller islands would have fewer species, was called the SLOSS dilemma,[24] i.e. should conservation reserves consist of Single Large or Several Small patches? This idea became so dominant that it is considered almost axiomatic today that larger areas are better for conservation. However, not everyone supported these ideas;

not only was there considerable disagreement about what ecological theory suggested in this regard, but also about whether some of these rules were based on that theory at all.[25] Needless to say, there was, and is, a need for informed decision-making, but for decades, this was largely centred on a single discipline, namely biology.

Parachute science

At the same time, there was a geographical consequence of the spread of conservation biology. Biologists were already keen to pursue their trade in different parts of the world, a tradition long part of the field, even before the voyages of Darwin and Wallace. For Northern/Western scientists, the allure of the tropics with their vast diversity and countless endemics continued. Increasingly though, it was being frowned upon as 'parachute science'[26] where biologists or ecologists could drop into other parts of the world, collect data or samples, and disappear, sometimes leaving not even footprints or memories. However, conservation now legitimized the presence of these parachute scientists: much as the incursions of large political powers into other parts of the world have been justified as being in response to terror, so has conservation biology found its way there through the narrative of crisis.

This domination over knowledge and science has been facilitated through bilateral state arrangements, support from philanthropic donor agencies and state funding for Western universities, as well as by the presence of large multinational NGOs in many countries. Recent changes in policy leading to greater regulation of such research by developing countries such as India and Indonesia point to increasing concern about this practice.[27] As in economics and health, conservation solutions too are being sourced from Western institutions leading to a mismatch in knowledge as well as context.[28] There are of course exceptions to this, and in many instances, Western researchers are unaware of such asymmetries in power and in most cases are not deliberately exploitative.

When the CBD was ratified in 1993, it sought to bring about a more democratic ownership of intellectual property along with an equitable sharing of benefits. Many nations enacted laws within the framework of the CBD which aimed to restrict biopiracy and increase access to benefits for local communities. An unfortunate side effect of these laws in many countries (including India) is that the free exchange of biological material between scientists (in particular for taxonomic or genetic analysis) has been greatly restricted. The scientific community has felt so inconvenienced by these laws that they have repeatedly endorsed their repealing.[29] While it is certainly true that these laws do pose constraints for legitimate collaborative research, the role of the 'outpost scientist' who serves as a source or conduit for research samples to First World entities is equally worth examining.[30] Moreover, the notion that laws aimed at greater benefit sharing should be changed or dispensed with to serve 'science', disregarding traditional societies who may benefit from Intellectual Property Rights (IPR), only serves to demonstrate the arrogance of the scientific community, and the very anti-humanism that Guha spoke of.

THE AUTHORITARIAN BIOLOGIST RELOADED

In the last couple of decades, the social sciences have breached the bastion of biologists, creating an alternate rhetoric that calls for an explicit recognition of rights, especially of marginalized communities, in conservation. Deriving from the academic disciplines of anthropology, sociology, economics and environmental history, this has had such an impact that the body of knowledge is now largely referred to as 'Conservation Science'. The catalyst for this relabelling came from two respected academics in the conservation field, Peter Kareiva and Michelle Marvier, who in a compelling article (titled 'What Is Conservation Science?') called for a global broadening of the discipline to include other disciplinary inputs (especially from the social sciences) as well as the critical importance of balancing biodiversity conservation and human well-being.[31] This was met with an unprecedented series of vitriolic, and often personal attacks on these authors, their humanistic viewpoints, and their questionable moral standing. Stalwarts of conservation biology promptly denounced their anthropocentrism. Michael Soulé himself launched a scathing attack on the 'chimeric' mistake that was 'new conservation', providing counterarguments with examples from the US as if nowhere else mattered.[32] Richard Primack, then editor of *Biological Conservation*, wrote a similar response along with Philip Cafaro;[33] they were joined by a chorus of conservation scientists.[34] Most of the participants in this debate were from Northern institutions and chided Kareiva and Marvier for losing sight of their morals.

What were the responses from the Global South? For the most part there was silence, because, unless you paid a subscription (to the publishing giant Elsevier),[35] *Biological Conservation* was not accessible to the less fortunate academics, non-academics and others who simply did not care as there were more pressing priorities. To many of us embedded within research and conservation in the developing world, Western conservation biologists opposing the need to address human well-being tend to come across as ignorant relics unmindful of the folly of brushing aside the coupled social-ecological systems that now dominate the planet. They also came across as sympathizers of colonial fortress conservation approaches that have led to large-scale exclusion, translocation and marginalization of local communities. In an earlier era, those opposed to people's participation or more inclusive approaches could dismiss the entire movement as uninformed or unscientific. However, from the 1990s, a large number of social scientists, ranging from environmental historians to political ecologists and anthropologists, had been pointing to the problematic aspects of exclusionary conservation via the protected area approach.[36] Thus, in contemporary conservation milieus, biologists were no longer arguing with so-called 'placard carrying activists' or 'unwashed social workers', but with respected academics sitting in universities.

In the conservation biology camp, the political ecological critique of conservation spawned a range of new movements that purported to be based on rigorous science. One of these was initiated by the eminent ecologist, E.O. Wilson, who argued that half of the earth needed to be set aside for nature.[37] This has generated support largely from biologists and those of biocentric orientation, with the proponents claiming evidence from ecological studies that this is the only preventive to large-scale extinction.[38] The response from the conservation social science community argues that this approach, first, ignores the sources of resource extraction, consumption and environmental impact, which would continue to operate unchecked; second, would have a significant social impact, affecting mostly economically weak and politically marginalized communities; third, does not provide clarity about who would control this biodiversity half; fourth, fails to recognize the value of human–environment relationships; and fifth, offers no path forward for biodiversity in the human half.[39]

While these critiques are based on social, political and economic realities, there are also alternate ecological frameworks, such as reconciliation ecology[40] that have not received sufficient attention from the proponents of pristine spaces. Based on ecological research on the relationship between the number of species and area (the species–area curve), Michael Rosenzweig suggested that the way forward would be to increase the ecological suitability of human-dominated landscapes, i.e. reconciliation between human needs and nature.[41] Such reconciliation landscapes would enhance biodiversity through providing more habitat for species, and through connectivity across habitats for others.[42] Moreover, while they may not protect all biodiversity, the ecological integrity and functionality of such landscapes would obviously be greater than heavily degraded spaces.

For many conservationists however, Half-Earth seems to be a straightforward win with a potential to sequester more land for conservation than they had previously dared to express. Displaying an appalling lack of awareness or acknowledgement about the problematic history of conservation including, most significantly, its repugnant links to colonialism, many biologists have been quick to sign on, questioning neither the science behind this arbitrary figure, nor its practicality. For instance, how would Half-Earth be operationalized by developing countries struggling to even minimally increase land under protection? Would this not entail the forced removal of people? Reflecting an even narrower ethic, a select group of conservationists demands that 'intraspecies justice'—justice for people—should not come at the expense of 'interspecies justice'.[43] How would interspecies justice translate on the ground for a country like India? Referencing a classic philosophical scenario, does this mean that they would pick the last tiger over a human baby?

The difference between these approaches is not, as conservation biologists would have you believe, that one (Half-Earth) is based on science while others are not. In fact, the difference seems largely normative.[44] Do we want to promote policies that are likely to cause social injustice or those that integrate humans with their environments? Do we believe that being connected to nature is an integral part of human culture and should be extended equally to all, which might create better support for conservation? It is richly ironic that biologists believe that science should (or does) provide all the answers when different camps within biology itself advocate (almost) diametrically opposite approaches. This would be amusing if it did not have such dire consequences.

THE DEEP ECOLOGY REDUX

In their effort to argue for the preservation of their favourite species and ecosystems, Northern conservationists have been quick to form a mutually reinforcing nexus with ideologues of the animal rights and liberation fronts, claiming ecocentrism as the ethics of choice. This unholy alliance has spawned new movements such as 'compassionate conservation'[45] and 'just preservation'.[46] Borrowing heavily from the political theory of animal rights,[47] just preservation aims to give voice to non-humans, youth and futurity (future generations of both human and non-human beings) through courts and other legitimate arenas of adjudication.

Compassionate conservation, one of the most prominent of these movements in recent years, is defined by the idea that individuals (of species) matter and amounts to the outcome that animals must never be harmed or killed. Critiquing this framework, Meera A. Oommen et al. have argued against the application of a single universal moral code for conservation.[48] They also point out that the approach could have fatal consequences for people affected by conflict with large dangerous animals such as elephants and crocodiles. There are further concerns about compassionate conservation with regard to its science and rationality. First, its proponents ignore insights from a range of disciplines especially the social sciences, thus using knowledge in a selective fashion.[49] Second, despite the rash of inconsistencies with conservation strategies that various authors have pointed out, they insist that it is not a version of animal rights. But, compassionate conservation cannot accept hunting as a strategy for conservation, even when it has been shown to have social and economic benefits in many contexts.[50] Thus, compassionate conservation may have its place as a value (based on the rights of individual animals) but cannot be argued to be based on conservation science.

Ethical overreach in the guise of science is a widespread feature of Western conservation interventions in places such as Africa. For example, Amy Dickman et al. caution fellow conservationists against the pitfalls of moral relativism and 'misguided respect' for local cultures and traditions in less developed countries, and instead urge the adoption of science-based universal principles to guide conservation.[51] In their words, 'What sympathy should we grant for tradition, whether for cutting down trees in a UK woodland, or for the killing of threatened species for cultural reasons? A lion may represent one man's trophy, another's photo opportunity, another's threat or nuisance, and the ghost of another's enemy . . . the last view in this list represents a traditional yet baseless belief . . .'[52] While no doubt well intentioned, the idea of biologists and conservationists assuming the role of adjudicators of local cultural practices and social contexts outside their own remains problematic.

To be fair, animal-oriented politics in academia is not confined to biologists but affects a larger body of academics, mostly derived from the Global North. A host of sub-disciplines variously known as critical animal studies, more-than-human geographies, etc. have come into vogue in the last few years, with its proponents reinforcing each other. Another feature is their selective dependence on information from the developing world and spiritual traditions elsewhere. For instance, by pointing out the existence of equivalent terms for compassion ('ahimsa' in the Indian context) in multiple languages, Arian D. Wallach et al.[53] advance it as a core ethic that automatically translates into a universal value. However, their attribution of India's (questionable) conservation success to inherent compassion and 'progressive' animal protection laws is not only naive but amounts to tacit support for the country's fundamentalist political factions that promote violence against communities that deviate from mainstream consumption norms. Guha's caution about the misrepresentation of eastern traditions in support of a particular ethical position is still very much valid.[54]

GRAB THAT CASH WITH BOTH HANDS

Viewed as another global socio-economic enterprise, conservation is affected by the same forces as the rest of society. Just as large multinationals sequester markets and funds, so have large NGOs (BINGOs) such as Conservation International (CI), TNC, WWF, IUCN, Greenpeace and Wildlife Conservation Society (WCS) cornered a lion's share of conservation funds.[55] With budgets larger than some small countries, one can legitimately ask whether their primary goal is environmental conservation or self-preservation? With offices in dozens of countries, including real estate in Geneva, Washington DC and New York, these organizations are not cheap to support. Further, overhead costs and bloated executive salaries add to costs.[56] Fundraising for survival is in fact one of the key challenges for NGOs worldwide, both large and small. However, many large organizations have pursued and received funds from large corporate donors with dubious environmental credentials. In 2013, the partnership between IUCN and Shell came in for much criticism and was described as 'greenwashing'.[57] In fact, many instances of funding support for environmental projects by corporations have been described as blood money (payments made to victims, here the environment), conscience money or as explicit greenwashing (paying to improve their image).

The money game interlinked with that of increasing corporate partnerships is also evident in the sudden emergence of conservation strategies that are linked to business solutions. In recent years, philanthropic donors, especially those tied to large, powerful corporations have been at the forefront of a more entrepreneurial 'philanthrocapitalism'[58] that seeks to involve features such as venture philanthropy and certain tech-based solutions in social projects related to conservation. Despite being somewhat untested in this sphere, there is a sudden surge in philanthropic interest in supporting these and a concomitant disinterest in conventional interventions.[59] In these contexts, funding support is decided not by experts in the field of conservation, but by prominent business and investment professionals who are confident that successful models in the business sector can be replicated in the environmental field. Problematic interventions that include hidden persuaders or behaviourally engineered compliance strategies such as 'nudge'[60] are sometimes actively pursued.

Apart from creating a nexus between corporations and NGOs, fundraising imposes other constraints. Large-scale funding often needs greater visibility which makes it necessary for organizations to practise one-upmanship in the public sphere. This then begins to define, first, the kind of work that organizations do, and second, how they portray themselves in the media. As funding for charismatic species is easier to obtain, the efforts of a large number of organizations are geared towards this. Thus, approaches to on-ground work which need to be discretionary, low-profile and to share credit with local partners are not pursued as they contribute little to the public profile of organizations and restrict their ability to raise funds.

In both Africa and Asia, a disproportionate amount of funds are received for large, charismatic vertebrates such as elephants, rhinos, tigers and lions, and these are often preceded by creative media campaigns that embellish facts or can be characterized as less-than-candid portrayals of one's work and impacts. For instance, John Mbaria and Mordecai Ogada ask the interesting question of who makes the most money out of elephants in Africa—the government, the poachers, investors in tourism, or conservationists?[61] According to them, '[T]he NGOs' hunt for donor cash starts after a selection of catchy, attractive, and widely used buzzwords that resonates well in a world that stands accused and—to some extent—feels guilty for being unable to live and let other residents of the planet live.'[62]

THE TEMPLES OF 'PRISTIANITY'

Last but not the least, in their zeal for the preservation of wild nature, many biologists and NGOs have colluded with the state in the protectionist paradigm for the creation of exclusionary protected areas, a pursuit of pristine spaces that could be called 'Pristianity' for the religious fervour with which it has been pursued. Given the severity of war and pestilence, it is no mean achievement that conservation has become one of the largest causes of displacement worldwide.[63] Large NGOs have been accused of human rights violations in many of the places where they work. In Africa and other parts of the world, they have been accused of colluding with national governments that have a record of abusing human rights and/or turning a blind eye to rights violations. In many instances, it is alleged they have provided funds, support and even arms to the government.[64]

The land grab can occur in two ways. One is direct ownership. The Nature Conservancy in fact started with the idea of purchasing land for conservation. While this continues in many parts of the world, the economics of landownership has somewhat derailed this strategy. The second type of 'colonization' occurs by control, typically with the state owning the land, and biologists and conservationists determining what should and should not happen on them. There are innumerable examples of collusion between white conservationists from the Global North and the state in creating these new 'colonies'. Perhaps most symbolic is the role of Richard Leakey in the creation of Kenya's national parks.[65] More recently, 'Space for Giants' and similar initiatives in Africa aim to acquire land for species such as elephants using top-down strategies with strong policing of such spaces.[66]

Pristianity has been kept alive by two new movements, Half-Earth[67] and Nature Needs Half,[68] which have argued for a radical increase in protected areas around the world. While there is no doubt that development needs to be curbed, the argument of these movements is flawed on multiple grounds as previously detailed. In terms of geography, it is clear that the creation of such areas will affect the developing world significantly more (the Global South, the tropics, etc.). In those parts of the world, it will affect indigenous and marginalized communities significantly more than the wealthy. There is no talk of rewilding London, New York or even Mumbai.

It has been shown that there are long-term social, cultural and psychological impacts of displacement on individuals and communities.[69] Moreover, disconnecting people from nature seems to be the exact opposite of all that is done in the name of environmental education. Ironically, while many conservationists run programmes where they sensitize urban children to nature by taking them out of the city, the same groups attempt gentrification projects in the name of education that propose to take communities that are far more connected to nature away from their roots, and cut those ties.

(Not an) Indian Summer

The effectiveness of the wilderness ideal which guides environmental research in many parts of the world has been questioned as a paradigm for conservation in the developing world in general as well as for India in particular.[70] In India, conservationists' preoccupation with fortress conservation and the preservation of species has been well-documented.[71] The domination by this narrow group is particularly problematic in a country with a diverse array of human–wildlife relationships. Although the subcontinent has a rich tradition of traditional management (many of them regulating common property and resources), exclusionary strategies have been the mainstay of conservation.[72] Additionally, conservationists have been reluctant to examine alternate strategies that are holistic in their treatment of coupled social-ecological systems.

Modern India's conservation history is steeped in its colonial legacy. Precolonial utilization of forests already had significant elements of exclusion (e.g. hunting preserves), but colonial forestry brought about enclosures on an unprecedented scale. Legal support for this was secured under the Indian Forest Act (1927) which empowered the government to declare any area a reserve forest, regardless of the history of occupation. Post-Independence conservation further strengthened this framework via the Indian Wildlife (Protection) Act, 1972, which enabled the creation of protected areas. The conservation fraternity, largely drawn from the upper classes, reinforced these demands, resulting in more protected areas as well as the exclusion of people.[73] Following long-running human rights and social justice campaigns, the Forest Rights Act (FRA)—the Scheduled Tribes and Other Traditional Forest Dwellers (Recognition of Forest Rights) Act—was passed in 2006 aiming to correct historical injustices towards communities who were expelled from forests in the past. However, before and after the Act was passed, there was and continues to be a cacophony of breast-beating from conservationists and wildlife-focused NGOs, claiming that this would spell doom for Indian forests and wildlife.

As in other parts of the world, the field of conservation in India has been influenced by home-grown conservationists as well as by influences from conservation biology and deep ecology.[74] To this day, both conservation practice and biology in India remain a largely elitist preserve. If one were to construct a profile of its proponents, these conservationists would largely be college-educated, well-to-do individuals from urban, non-agricultural, most likely upper-caste, affluent backgrounds, some with regional affiliations, or caste and class histories (e.g. the liberal sprinkling of conservation professionals from feudal backgrounds). Similar trajectories of the evolution of environmental consciousness and environmentalism attributable to city dwelling, urban lifestyles, leisure, class, etc. have been discussed.[75]

The contrast between 'agrarianism' and 'wilderness thinking' as pointed out by Guha[76] is critical if we want to understand contemporary conservation perspectives relating to the following questions: Why do certain philosophies of conservation find favour while others (often more widespread ones that are tied to utilization) are considered anathema to conservation? Why, despite a long history of utilization and existence of extensive commons, has the preservationist paradigm taken hold? Could these trends be linked to the fact that representation from the vast majority of rural, lower and middle classes—including tribal and Dalit groups, i.e. those with extended ties to the land, forests and land-based occupations and different environmental philosophies—is wholly or partially missing?

We argue that the anti-hunting, animal-rights-based philosophies of Northern deep ecologists have struck a chord with upper-caste/class, urban groups which are religiously and/or culturally embedded in non-exploitative backgrounds (in relation to animal consumption). There have also been romanticized claims of environmentalism originating in Hinduism, Buddhism, Jainism and other eastern religions. Indian environmentalism in general has undergone shifts towards Sanskritization, Brahminization and Saffronization as is evident from the politics of Anna Hazare, Sunderlal Bahuguna and numerous others.[77] This trend of the primacy of conservative Hindu ideologies and a more or less complete failure to address Dalit values and environmentalism is reflective of a larger trend.

The lack of attention to the rights of marginalized groups is paralleled by a pushback not only against the use of species by local communities, but also in the treatment of problem species such as large carnivores, crocodiles, elephants and pigs. As protection regimes are successful, the spillover of wildlife into human-dominated landscapes and resultant conflict has been an emerging issue in India. However, the elimination of problem individuals (e.g. Avni, the tigress) or that of species causing large-scale agricultural disruptions (e.g. wild pigs) has been met with a great deal of opposition from a section of the conservation lobby rooted in animal rights philosophies.[78] Along with a call for stringent protection of animals, many of these groups often make a demand for disproportionate punishment to people who trespass into protected areas (e.g. shoot-at-sight orders in Kaziranga).

Both conservation practitioners and biologists have contributed to a narrowing of human–nature relationships in India. Though human engagements with wildlife were historically multifaceted, contemporary conservation's limited perspective deems the use of most species of wildlife, however abundant, unacceptable. This appears rooted in the politics of social hierarchy, where the consumption of meat is considered as polluting by dominant vegetarian castes. Beyond the imposition of values, this has potential nutritional and health consequences for many communities, and therefore for their overall well-being.

THE POST-WAR DREAM

Through the lens of political ecology, these actions with regard to knowledge, money and space are typical of a political entity trying to garner control of resources through the exercise of power, namely imperialism.[79] Is conservation just another instrument in the race for power? And if so, how does one democratize conservation so that it can achieve its more utopian goals? We argue that the solution lies in the decentralization of conservation, no different from other spheres such as politics or economics. All three domains—knowledge, financial resources and control over land/water—need to be democratized both at global as well as at regional and local scales for greater equity in benefit. This is not a new idea. In the late 1980s, David Western stated that 'the best hope for all species is linked to a single, uncompromisable goal—the improvement of human welfare'.[80]

The first step towards this democratization is to acknowledge the lack of a simple dichotomy between indigenous and scientific knowledge.[81] The involvement of resource-dependent communities provides a pathway for more democratic knowledge generation and decision-making. For example, community-based resource monitoring can help bridge knowledge divides. It has been argued that modern science is the lingua franca of the state and therefore serves as a language of power that shapes discourses.[82] Thus, being able to use the language of science can empower communities to participate in dialogue and decisions about resource management and balance the influence of the authoritarian biologist.

Similarly, community ownership of land, particularly the commons, is receiving increasing attention, in no small part due to Elinor Ostrom's work.[83] These provide a pathway for the management of common resources, including land and biodiversity, that need not lead to depletion or degradation. Notwithstanding problems in implementation, the FRA does provide a model in community ownership that has potential positive outcomes for both people and the environment. In principle, this could be extended over even larger landscapes for joint ownership and stewardship that has material and cultural benefits for local communities, while providing provisioning services and accommodating the deep ecology aspirations of biocentric conservationists.

Conservation may best be served by a philosophical approach that lies between pure biocentrism and anthropocentrism, and stresses cultural values.[84] This approach is embodied in the *Millennium Ecosystem Assessment Report*'s definition of ecosystem services, which includes cultural services in addition to the supporting, regulatory and provisioning services of nature.[85] Many conservation organizations have now explicitly incorporated sensitive approaches, but these may be more instrumental, i.e. purely for conservation benefits, than for rights-based concern for communities. We find that while the movement as a whole has begun to pay lip service to social concerns, there are a range of worrying signs that, globally, conservation continues to be an ideological and spatial stronghold created by and for the privileged. The change in discourse does offer some hope that the conservation will be more inclusive, but the voices of protectionism remain.

In closing, we would argue that while the battlefields have been transformed, the terms of engagement have not. Authoritarian biologists and deep ecologists continue to attempt to influence conservation disproportionately but the resistance narrative has grown stronger. In addition to social scientists, human rights campaigners and community spokespersons, many biologists and ecologists have become strong supporters of community rights. Guha's classic essays were simultaneously a critique and a call to action. Both remain deeply relevant today and critical to the future of conservation.

4

NATION'S BODY, RIVER'S PULSE: NARRATIVES OF ANTI-DAM POLITICS IN INDIA

AMITA BAVISKAR

RAMACHANDRA GUHA'S WRITINGS on ecology and environment have shone a light on a neglected, yet vital, field of research, inspiring others to venture into its tangled thickets. Guha combined a formidable talent for capturing the salient contours of landscapes of struggles with bold theorization, evoking admiration as well as provoking engagement. Three decades after he began, environmental scholars still wrestle with his analysis of colonial forestry, peasant politics, caste and tribe, and the future of this fissured land. To be read, quoted and argued over long after one has stopped writing on a subject is perhaps the best compliment a scholar can receive.

Guha's relevance to contemporary environmental studies is also evident in the epistemological frames that structure inquiries. Our understanding of collective action attends to cultural histories while remaining conscious of the transformative role played by particular leaders.[1] We recognize the complexities of caste and class underlying tactical solidarities and how they shape the scale of political concerns and the substance of popular perceptions.[2] More generally, we acknowledge the pre-eminence of *political ecology* as an approach for apprehending environmental change and contestation in India. As Guha pointed out in 1988,

> There are three solid reasons why economic growth in India will continue to use resources both wastefully and unsustainably. The *economic* system of capitalism is inherently expansionist; fuelled by narrow criteria of profitability, it is completely insensitive to the questions of relative factor endowments and ecological stability. *Ideologically*, this wasteful and destructive economic system is buttressed by the seductive hold of modernisation theory on the minds of our elite. Our present *political* system is hardly equipped to serve environmental ends either. Five years (the time horizons of our most enlightened politicians) is too short a period for ecological reconstruction. Moreover, the links between big business and the state, and the centralising tendencies in the present constitutional set-up, further shrink the space for dissent and debate.[3]

Today, these constraints not only continue to prevail but have become crippling. That is why, even as we fan out into new areas of research—animal-human relations, climate change, pollution and health—Guha's opus serves as a compass to steer by, reminding us where lie North and South. This essay reflects my great debt to Guha's pioneering work, his approach and his insights. It builds on those insights to incorporate recent social and political developments, especially ideologies and institutions, that have altered environmental politics in India in ways that Guha could not have anticipated.

In the 1990s, social movements against large dams in India were celebrated for crafting a powerful challenge to dominant policies of development. These grounded struggles were acclaimed for their critique of capitalist industrialization and their advocacy for an alternative model of socially just and ecologically sustainable development. Twenty years later, as large dams continue to be built, their critics have shifted the battle off the streets to new arenas—to courts and government committees, in particular—and switched to a techno-managerial discourse of maintaining river health. What accounts for this change? This essay traces the trajectory of cultural politics around Indian rivers within the larger imagination of the nation, the rise of economic liberalization and Hindu nationalism, and the emergence of environmental bureaucracies. It argues that, while being shaped by this context, current anti-dam campaigns also contend with the legacy of earlier social movements, including their gains as well as losses. This political field has narrowed the potential for radical critique, large-scale collective mobilization and, ultimately, keeping rivers alive.

On 6 December 1959, Budhni Mejhan, a fifteen-year-old worker, was invited by Prime Minister Jawaharlal Nehru to switch on the turbines in the powerhouse of the newly built Panchet dam in the state of Bihar (now Jharkhand) in eastern India (Fig. 1). Nehru was to inaugurate the dam but, as the *Statesman* newspaper reported, he said that 'it was right that those who had worked on a project should have the honour of declaring it open'.[4] The prime minister's presence at the commissioning of the dam signalled its importance. The Panchet dam was part of a multi-purpose river valley scheme to harness the 'Sorrow of Bengal'—the river Damodar—for flood control, irrigation and electricity. Modelled on the Tennessee Valley Authority in the US, projects such as this were meant to deliver India from hapless poverty into prosperity and modernity.[5]

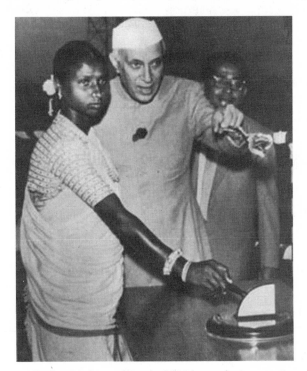

Fig. 1: Budhni Mejhan and Jawaharlal Nehru at the inauguration of the Panchet dam, 6 December 1959 (Source: *The Hindu*)

Those were heady times for a young nation. Accomplishing feats of engineering that matched the Western world was a challenge for the newly independent country and required skills and material resources on an unprecedented scale. Each completed project was an achievement to be celebrated. In 1955, from the site of another dam on the river Krishna, the prime minister declared, 'When I lay the foundation stone here of this Nagarjuna Sagar, to me it is a sacred ceremony. This is the foundation of the temple of humanity in India, a symbol of new temples that we are building all over India.'[6] At the opening of the Nangal canal on the Bhakhra dam in north-western India, Nehru was moved to remark, 'Where can be a greater and holier place than this?'[7] These temples of modern India were part of a vision of development where large, capital-intensive projects represented economic progress. And, in turn, the strength of the economy represented the country's well-being. This was Nehru's distinctive contribution to the nationalist project of imagining India. As a socialist impressed by state-led industrialization in the USSR, and as a secular politician appalled by the Hindu–Muslim killings that accompanied the partition of India, Nehru believed it was crucial to unite the nation in striving for shared economic goals that would overcome the centrifugal spin of disparate religions, castes, languages and cultures. Each citizen's contribution counted, including that of Budhni Mejhan, the poor young Santhal adivasi whose labour helped build the Panchet dam.[8]

NATIONAL DEVELOPMENT: PRODUCER PATRIOTS AND SACRIFICIAL VICTIMS

Dams, steel plants, fertilizer factories, nuclear reactors and planned industrial cities were sites of development where citizens were invited to see themselves reflected in the mirror of technological change. This imagined community of 'producer-patriots',[9] whose hard work and frugality were geared to meeting the Five-Year Plan targets for economic growth, was central to Nehru's vision of a self-reliant and prosperous nation, freed from a century of colonial exploitation. And to realize this vision, more than 50 million Indians were displaced and dispossessed to make way for development projects in the first fifty years of Independence.[10] Large dams alone took away the lands of at least 16.4 million people. And though adivasis constitute only 8 per cent of India's population, they figure disproportionately among those displaced by development: an estimated 50 per cent of the dispossessed belong to the Scheduled Tribes, residents of forested hills where dams and mining projects were most often located. For people with a strong attachment to ancestral lands and near-absolute dependence on localized natural resources, displacement is virtually a death sentence.[11] Until 2013, the government could forcibly evict people in the 'public interest' by using a convenient colonial-era law—the Land Acquisition Act of 1894. This Act only compensated for privately owned land. In many cases, adivasis did not have legal title to the land that they had lived on and farmed for generations. Failing to qualify as 'Project-Affected Persons' or PAPs, they were denied even the meagre monetary amount allowed by the law. The commons that were vital to their survival—forests, pastures, rivers and ponds—were not taken into account. Money received as compensation was not enough to buy land elsewhere and nor were small farmers knowledgeable in the ways of investing in a trade or running a business. Most were rendered destitute, wage-labourers scrabbling for a living at the very bottom of the economic heap, their close-knit communities scattered and shattered. These were not 'producer-patriots'. They were sacrificial victims on the altar of national development.

But Budhni Mejhan, the young Santhal woman with whom we began this story, *was* a producer-patriot. After all, she worked on the Panchet dam. Surely she must have had a share in the glory and success of India's industrial growth? Not so. The journalist Chitra Padmanabhan who traced Mejhan's story describes a darker end.[12] After the dazzle of flashbulbs as she was photographed switching on the power with Nehru at her side faded, her life took a bizarre turn. On returning home, Mejhan was told by village elders that since she had garlanded Nehru at the inauguration ceremony, she had in effect married him.[13] And since the prime minister was not a Santhal, she was no longer a part of the community. Mejhan was told to leave the village. Excommunicated and isolated, Budhni Mejhan struggled along, only to lose her job with the Damodar Valley Corporation three years later. She surfaced again in the archives after more than twenty years when she travelled to Delhi to meet the then prime minister, Rajiv Gandhi, grandson of the man she had garlanded, with the request that she be reinstated in her job. No more was heard of her in the media. Padmanabhan conjectures that she probably died around 2002, poor and alone. Meanwhile, the reservoir of the Panchet dam is now dry and produces no power. From its silt have now risen again the ruins of old Santhal villages and historic temples, while the people who lived and worshipped in them have sunk without a trace.

It bears repeating: 50 million people displaced by development projects between 1947 and 1997; 16 million dispossessed by large dams alone; 8 million of them adivasis, among the poorest and most vulnerable sections of Indian society. Yet, despite the scale of these evictions—project-specific as well as cumulative—there was little public attention to the fate of those affected. Such was the aura of the developmentalist vision, the power of the technological spectacle that was the large dam, the promise of the good things that gushed forth from it—irrigation for the Green Revolution that made India self-sufficient in foodgrains, electricity for industry and lighting up homes, relief from the scourge of floods—that no one was counting the costs. Even those parameters of a proposed project that could be assessed with some reasonable degree of accuracy—its economic and financial viability—were found to be greatly exaggerated when independently evaluated after completion.[14] For many officials in India's notoriously corrupt construction bureaucracy, such blithe optimism was no doubt lubricated by considerations of the illicit gains to be made from commissions and kickbacks, but there were enough upright administrators and engineers who also believed that large dams would deliver the nation from want. For planners, these benefits far outweighed the social and ecological costs of such projects. That is, if they thought of these costs at all. Given the sharply unequal social landscape that divided decision makers from those adversely affected by their actions, the destruction of adivasi lives and the loss of their riverine ecosystems barely registered as public concerns. Puny subjects of a giant nation, adivasis could do little but resign themselves to the inevitability of a state-ordained fate. Theirs was the painful duty of making the nation great. Despite their distress, it is notable that there were hardly any protests against displacement until the 1970s.[15] And so it went on for more than twenty-five years after Independence. Colossal, eye-wateringly expensive projects were built. Millions of the most vulnerable people in the country were displaced. Hundreds of thousands of square kilometres of forested and farmed hills, valleys and rivers, and their distinctive flora and fauna, were destroyed forever.

From Dams to Development: The Changing Contours of Challenge

The first stirrings of protest against damming a river occurred in 1973, when the state government of Kerala proposed a hydroelectric project on the river Kunthipuzha. The reservoir of the dam threatened to submerge an area of primary rainforest known as Silent Valley, habitat for the endangered lion-tailed macaque and other rare species. Scientists and wildlife conservationists wrote to Prime Minister Indira Gandhi about the need to preserve the unique biodiversity of the valley but, until 1983, the government was inclined to allow the project with some modifications. What eventually persuaded Indira Gandhi to change her mind was the determined campaign launched by the Kerala Sastra Sahitya Parishad (KSSP), a left-affiliated people's science organization, that mobilized its network of school and college science teachers as well as its supporters among the intelligentsia to keep the issue in the media spotlight. The KSSP succeeded not only in stopping the dam but also eventually getting Silent Valley designated as a National Park.

In the years that the Silent Valley controversy simmered, 'the environmental crisis' had begun to be discussed internationally. The first United Nations Conference on the Human Environment was held in Stockholm in 1972, the same year that the Club of Rome published its report on *The Limits to Growth*. In India, the press reported on Chipko, a remarkable movement of village women who were hugging trees to stop government contractors from clearing deciduous forests in the foothills of the Himalaya.[16] The Chipko movement brought a new dimension to budding environmental consciousness: if Silent Valley highlighted the importance of conserving biodiversity, Chipko made visible the concerns of rural communities confronted with ecological change that threatened their livelihoods. As young activists and intellectuals travelled to the hills and talked to villagers involved in the movement, they forged a distinctive understanding of ecological crises and their solutions. *The State of India's Environment* report declared that poverty and environmental destruction were two sides of the same coin.[17] Social justice and environmental welfare must be pursued in tandem. This perspective, that Guha labelled 'environmentalism of the poor',[18] was to prevail and become the hallmark of Indian environmentalism through the 1980s, a time when environmentalism in the affluent Global North was primarily preoccupied with post-industrial concerns around the preservation of clean air and green spaces, where equity in the control and use of natural resources was not a fundamental issue.[19]

This emergent understanding of Indian environmental politics was part of a growing human rights discourse that burgeoned in the late 1970s in the aftermath of a two-year Emergency when, faced with student protests and trade union-led strikes, Indira Gandhi had suspended civil liberties, imposed press censorship and jailed critics and political opponents. After the Emergency was lifted, disaffection with the state was at its peak. So was mobilization by women, Dalits or Scheduled Castes, farmers and workers, in small and large action groups and social movements.[20] The ideological inspiration of these groups ran the gamut from Gandhi to Mao, with a good deal of hybridization in between.[21] These 'grassroots groups' or 'people's organizations'—so-called because of their direct engagement with the subjects they represented and their lack of affiliation with mainstream political parties—were also increasingly encountering a new entity: the NGO. Urban-based NGOs, many of which were regarded with suspicion by leftists as agents of American imperialism that aimed to undermine the revolutionary potential of Indian social movements,[22] gradually came to be incorporated into the flourishing ecosystem of social advocacy, protest and organization. This period was also marked by the rise of public interest litigation as the Supreme Court tried to redeem itself after its quiescent complicity with the Emergency regime by taking up the cause of citizens victimized by the state, such as poor people imprisoned without trial and pavement-dwellers evicted without a hearing.[23]

It was in this vibrant political landscape that Kalpavriksh, a Delhi-based group of environmentalist students, undertook a journey along the Narmada to investigate the likely effects of a series of large dams that were planned along this central Indian river.[24] Its report, *Development or Destruction?*, outlined for the first time the wide-ranging social and environmental impacts of thirty large dams and as many as 3000 medium and small dams on the tributaries of the river.[25] Activists from Arch-Vahini and Multiple Action Research Group (MARG) who began working in the area to be submerged by the Sardar Sarovar dam's reservoir focused on securing legal rights to compensation for the people to be displaced. However, one of them, Medha Patkar, a social worker from Mumbai, soon realized that the resettlement package offered by the government was not only grossly inadequate but, in fact, impossible to implement for the estimated affected population of 2,50,000 in 245 villages. Patkar started organizing villagers in the submergence zone of the dam and, with a team of activists, launched the Narmada Bachao Andolan (Save Narmada Campaign). The Andolan accomplished a remarkable political feat by bringing together two disparate and generally antagonistic constituencies: well-to-do upper-caste Hindu farmers in the plains and adivasis who lived in the forested hills.[26] In particular, the campaign drew attention to the vulnerability of this latter group who regarded the Narmada as the source of all life. For these communities of small upland farmers, their villages along the river anchored them to their ancestral spirits, their cultural identity and social being. Displacement would mean dismemberment, and no money or land elsewhere could heal that wound.

The first critical evaluations of the Sardar Sarovar Project (SSP) focused on reviewing the cost-benefit analysis used to justify the project. Economists showed that the social and environmental costs of the dam were severely underestimated while its potential benefits were greatly exaggerated.[27] As the struggle in the valley gained momentum, these technical arguments against the project were augmented to include the issue of social justice. Activists demanded a 'class-benefit analysis' of the dam. If the SSP stripped away the meagre assets of impoverished adivasis to further enrich well-off farmers with irrigation, how could it be described as serving the public interest, they asked. A state project that did not first serve the poorest and most oppressed and that irretrievably destroyed the country's natural wealth was neither 'national' nor 'development'. The Andolan gradually became the epicentre of increasingly deep fissures that cracked the consensus around the dominant model of development. From questioning the distributional aspects of the project, the movement began to challenge the logic of large dams itself, asking whether this capital-intensive technology was appropriate for Indian conditions. The protest in the valley now attracted not only human rights supporters but also disenchanted engineers looking at alternative technologies for decentralized water management, power generation and agriculture.[28] The Chipko movement had agitated for local control over forests as opposed to centralized state-led decision-making. The Narmada Bachao Andolan raised those stakes to demand an overhaul of the entire project of development.[29]

Social justice was at the heart of the Andolan's critique of development. Instead of the abstract 'Nation' conjured up by technocratic planners, the movement drew a different picture of a society divided between rich and poor, city versus village, India against Bharat,[30] that was only growing further and further apart. While this discourse drew upon the Indian Constitution's list of the fundamental rights guaranteed to each citizen, especially to those who had been denied these rights so far, it focused in particular on the question of *cultural rights*, and whether the distinctive beliefs and practices of a vulnerable minority could be crushed in the course of pursuing the greater common good.[31] The movement emphasized the sacredness of the river Narmada for those who lived along its banks, choreographing protest events where hundreds of adivasis standing by the water vowed to save their beloved mother from being killed. Although the majority of affected villagers who were active participants in the Andolan consisted of relatively prosperous upper-caste farmers from the fertile plains, the image of the movement as disseminated by its metropolitan supporters and the media was of hill adivasis, picturesque in their traditional clothing, holding bows and arrows, defending a lifestyle based on benign coexistence with nature. These performances portrayed adivasis as 'ecologically noble savages' such that saving them was coterminous with saving the river and forests. Despite the problems with such strategic essentialism, the movement came to be firmly associated in the public imagination as protecting a fragile and valuable culture.[32]

To a large extent, this celebration of adivasi culture brought into the mainstream what had until then been a marginal perspective. For the most part, the Indian state and dominant society regarded adivasis as 'backward' people who needed to be modernized and assimilated into 'civilization' or urban, middle-class, upper-caste Hindu life, aspiring towards ever-increasing consumption and accumulation. As Guha's biography of Verrier Elwin shows, those who argued in favour of adivasi culture, not only defending their right to self-determination but also discerning in their heritage an alternative model of living in harmony with nature, were sneered at as naive romantics.[33] The Andolan, too, faced this charge and, on this issue, found support within the country from only a tiny minority within the intelligentsia. However, this perspective on adivasis was far more sympathetically received among international supporters of the movement. From the late 1980s, grassroots protests in the Narmada valley had been supplemented by organizations such as International Rivers Network, Friends of the Earth and Cultural Survival. Based in the US and Europe, these NGOs targeted the World Bank for funding the Sardar Sarovar dam, pointing out that the institution was violating international conventions on the rights of indigenous people.[34] While the claim of indigeneity was difficult to sustain in the Indian context, and was indeed officially refuted by the Indian government, it figured centrally in the World Bank's decision to withdraw from the project in 1993.[35]

After more than a decade of protests that included hundreds of marches and demonstrations, and protesters being harassed, intimidated and assaulted by the police, when even extreme actions such as indefinite hunger strikes only resulted in the government setting up toothless commissions of enquiry, the Andolan decided to take its case to the Supreme Court. Taking heart from several progressive judgments passed by the court in public interest litigation, in 1994, the Andolan filed a comprehensive petition asking for the project to be stopped. Construction on the dam was halted but this reprieve proved to be temporary. In 2000, the court delivered its final orders, declaring that dams were good for the nation. In September 2017, the gates of the dam were closed, bringing about full submergence and ending what had been an inspiring and exhilarating chapter in river-related politics.

GROWTH, GODS AND BUREAUCRACIES: ACCELERATING ACCUMULATION BY DISPOSSESSION

By 1994, much of the Andolan's electric charge had ebbed away. Indeed, much had changed in India in the last decade of the twentieth century. In consonance with the global turn towards neoliberalism, India too adopted policies of economic liberalization, inviting foreign investment and encouraging Indian capitalists by offering land, minerals and other resources, tax concessions and a 'business-friendly' regulatory environment. Economic growth was the prime goal of government, and the Nehru-era notion of inclusive development to be achieved through redistributive policies was replaced by the trickle-down theory of prosperity. Although this rising tide did float many boats, it also left the smallest stranded. For small farmers, sharecroppers and agricultural workers whose lands and homesteads were acquired for dams, mining, industrial estates, real estate ventures and Special Economic Zones—and the pace of dispossession speeded up since the government undertook to broker land for private businesses as well as public-sector projects—the growth of the Indian economy was bad news.[36]

Several of these turn-of-the-century land grabs resulted in pitched battles between the state and those resisting 'accumulation by dispossession'.[37] Private security personnel now augmented police forces in violently suppressing protests and undertaking the daily work of intimidation and attrition. The development map of India was dotted in red: Kalinganagar, Kashipur, Jagatsinghpur and Niyamgiri in Odisha,[38] Nandigram and Singur in West Bengal,[39] as well as proposed Special Economic Zones in Goa and Maharashtra,[40] were among the many sites of strong resistance. Faced with mounting anger that could result in electoral losses, the government in 2013 passed the Right to Fair Compensation and Transparency in Land Acquisition, Rehabilitation and Resettlement Act (called the LARR) which raised rates of monetary compensation among other provisions. However, despite having been consulted in the drafting of this legislation, movement activists were disappointed to find that the LARR failed to specify 'public purpose' in a manner that would exclude land acquisition for private, profit-oriented projects. While this Act largely permitted business as usual, a previous piece of legislation, the Scheduled Tribes and Other Traditional Forest Dwellers (Recognition of Forest Rights) Act, 2006 (called the FRA) which was chiefly intended to grant small plots of forest land to adivasis for cultivation, came to be used for challenging land acquisition in forested areas. However, even in the limited number of instances where the FRA is applicable, activists have to engage in protracted bureaucratic and legal wrangling to implement the law.

For Indian rivers, the single-minded pursuit of economic growth has brought new challenges: more dams and inter-basin water transfer projects propose to change rivers beyond recognition.[41] Touting hydel power as renewable energy, all the more attractive in an age of fossil fuel-driven climate change, the state is building a string of high dams across the Himalayan mountains. The vast basin of the river Brahmaputra in north-east India, where wild rivers cascade through forests dense with biodiversity, is to have dams on every tributary, on a scale that will double India's entire hydelpower capacity.[42] The steep gradients that these tributaries traverse enables them to gather energy, picking up and breaking down rocks that they deposit as mineral-rich sediment in the Brahmaputra's floodplains in Assam. Hundreds of upstream dams would not only impound water, they would hold back the silt that keeps Assam's farms and fisheries alive.[43] The situation is equally worrying in north-west India where the proposed Pancheshwar dam on the Mahakali river is slated to be the highest in the world. It will displace an estimated 30,000 people and destroy forests and riverine ecosystems in an intensely active seismic zone.[44]

If Himalayan rivers are to be dammed within an inch of their lives, peninsular rivers are being treated little better than drains in a megalomaniacal plumbing system. A grand project of interlinking rivers envisages 'a garland of canals' ringing the country and diverting water from 'surplus' rivers to 'deficit' ones. This at a time when fluvial flows have become highly stressed because of over-extraction and are likely to become even more uncertain because of climate change. There is little environmental and social assessment of the impacts of such spectacular projects, but their enormous technical and economic scale helps explain why politicians and their construction industry funders love them. The proposed link between the Ken and Betwa rivers is already in process despite strong objections from conservationists alarmed that the reservoir will drown a large section of Panna National Park, habitat of critically endangered tigers and vultures,[45] and general puzzlement from farmers and agro-ecologists about the rationality of linking one water-scarce area with another.[46]

To observers of the 1990s anti-dam campaigns, it is striking that there is hardly any visible opposition to these projects from affected communities. In the case of the Brahmaputra dams, downstream farmers *have* challenged the projects but their distance from the construction sites has diluted the strength of their demonstrations and calls for action. In large part, the absence of collective mobilization by proximate populations can be traced to the legislative changes produced by the anti-dam campaigns of the 1990s. Those legally defined as 'Project-Affected Persons' or PAPs, because their lands will be acquired for building the dam, now stand to gain substantial monetary compensation due to the LARR 2013. These payouts are especially handsome in the Brahmaputra basin since the numbers of families to be displaced are small and builders are willing to offer large sums to pre-empt protest.[47] With a limited local grassroots base, anti-dam campaigners find it hard to muster the political legitimacy that the Narmada Bachao Andolan and other mass-based campaigns could claim.

The other notable difference from the 1990s is in the 'repertoire of contention' deployed by anti-dam campaigns,[48] or what Guha and Joan Martinez-Alier call the 'vocabulary of protest'.[49] In the last two decades, the notion of cultural rights to place has been monopolized by Hindu nationalists demanding that Muslims vacate centuries-old mosques and shrines because they were built on the site of previously existing temples.[50]

Claims about ancestral attachment—the indissoluble links between blood and soil—have been mobilized to disenfranchise non-Hindu minorities, even if they have lived in India for generations, as 'matter out of place'.[51] The suspicion and animosity engendered by Hindu nationalists has created a systemic shift towards treating Muslims as second-class citizens and regularly triggers violent clashes. This growing communal tension now extends into some adivasi areas too, where not only Muslims but also Christians have been attacked and killed.[52] In this context, progressive movements are wary of voicing claims about cultural rights because that strategy may potentially play to the Hindu nationalist gallery. In recent campaigns against displacement, the argument about defending a unique cultural attachment to land has only been used by the movement against bauxite mining by Vedanta corporation in the Niyamgiri hills in eastern India.[53] The tiny community of Dongaria Kondh adivasis, only 8000 in number, who regard the Niyamgiri hills as sacred, unitedly defended their forests against land acquisition. Their distinctive dress and self-sufficient mode of living made this group a poster child for organizations like Survival International that took up their cause in the London headquarters of Vedanta (see Fig. 2). While these culturalist claims had some traction in the Indian media, the instrument that actually enabled the Dongaria Kondh to eventually stop the project was the Forest Rights Act of 2006.[54]

Fig. 2: Dongaria Kondh women (Source: Amita Baviskar)

It should be emphasized that the Niyamgiri campaign remains somewhat exceptional, both for its ability to fuse cultural and legal rights and for its success. In an overwhelming number of cases involving land acquisition, there is no grassroots collective action at all, for the reasons outlined above: the hardened hegemony around economic growth-at-all-costs and the increase in compensation rates for land. These factors are compounded by the scale and complexity of new river projects that stretch across and between basins, large landscapes where it is hard for localized communities to come together for sustained periods. Under these circumstances, campaigns to save rivers have shifted their organizational form as well as their repertoire of contention. Instead of Narmada Bachao Andolan–style mass movements, campaigns tend to emanate from networks of NGOs, where technically trained and media-savvy activists proficient in legal and bureaucratic procedures analyse data in official documents in order to file objections and petitions before government committees and courts. The South Asia Network of Dams, Rivers and People (SANDRP) is an excellent example of such environmental and social justice advocacy.[55] While it supports local mobilization and works closely with grassroots organizations, it often finds itself the sole actor commenting on and intervening against mega-projects that, cumulatively, have landscape-level impacts.

As collective action by affected populations has become harder, voicing concerns in the vocabulary of human rights has become rarer. Increasingly, NGOs draw upon a discourse of *environmental health*: safeguarding the integrity of rivers by maintaining minimum flows, protecting complex and fragile ecosystems, and cautioning about climate change–induced uncertainties. Hydrology, biology and climate science now carry more weight with the bureaucracy and the courts than sociology and anthropology. Environment trumps social justice, a far cry from the Andolan's insistence on the inseparability of the two. A troubling corollary to this—which may either reflect Hindu nationalist thought or be a strategic response to it—is the move to recognize rivers as 'living human entities', as the Uttarakhand High Court declared in March 2017 for the Ganga and Yamuna, taking inspiration from New Zealand's legislation to grant legal rights to North Island's Wanghanui river which is sacred to the Maori. The Uttarakhand state government successfully challenged the high court's order in the Supreme Court.[56] While the divinity of Indian rivers has never been an impediment to polluting them, the attempt to grant them the legal rights due to living beings poses a new challenge. Who will speak for rivers? Will environmentalists who claim to speak on their behalf respect the rights of citizens who are as much a part of riverine ecosystems as its water, rocks and sand, flora and fauna? People whose life depends on the fate of rivers and the landscapes they sustain were earlier trapped in the body of the Nation. Will they now be swallowed by the 'living being' that is the River? As Guha pointed out, when it comes to recognizing human rights, Indian conservationists have an abysmal record.[57] The likelihood that they will strive for ecological *and* social justice seems remote. And the prospects for poor citizens to represent themselves seem equally dim. While, at first glance, the zoo-centrism underlying the grant of 'living entity' status to rivers appears to be a radical critique of the dominant capitalist model of exploiting and destroying nature, in practice it may further marginalize vulnerable people. This debate, however, has only begun. And, considering the challenge of stopping the surge of projects relentlessly rolling in, it may not even be relevant. What *is* evident is that the future for Indian rivers and those who live by them is bleaker than ever before.

5

WEAVING OUR WAY THROUGH ENVIRONMENTAL JUSTICE MOVEMENTS IN INDIA

BROTOTI ROY AND JOAN MARTINEZ-ALIER

India today is an environmental basket case; marked by polluted skies, dead rivers, falling water tables, ever-increasing amounts of untreated waste, disappearing forests. Meanwhile, tribal and peasant communities continue to be pushed off their lands through destructive and carelessly conceived projects. A new Chipko movement is waiting to be born.

Ramachandra Guha (2013)[1]

IN THE RICH history of environmentalism in India since the 1970s, one could ask which are the most important environmental justice movement(s) of the country. Indeed, there are certain environmental justice movements which have captured national and international attention, such as the Chipko movement which was a peasant initiative against commercial forestry in the valleys of Uttarakhand; the Narmada Bachao Andolan against the construction of the gigantic Sardar Sarovar dam; the movement following the Bhopal Gas Tragedy against industrial pollution and lack of environmental liability (the polluter does *not* pay principle); the Silent Valley movement for the protection of forests in Palakkad district in Kerala (a successful case of convivial conservation); and, in recent years, the Niyamgiri Bachao Andolan against bauxite mining in the tribal regions of Odisha.

While these movements are internationally well known, we argue that there are others which are no less significant. There are many Indian environmental justice movements with landmark successes (and failures) which in turn have inspired countless local movements and are relevant for the growing global movement for environmental justice within and beyond India, a subject which has also been of long-term interest to Ramachandra Guha.[2]

Using evidence from the EJAtlas, an international atlas of environmental justice movements, we explore a few of the significant, but lesser-known cases of environmental justice movements in India, though the examples are far too diverse and growing to be summarized in a handful of movements. The EJAtlas is a tool for collaborative research on ecological distribution conflicts with a global perspective and a theoretical framing rooted in activist knowledge.[3] It was launched in March 2014 with 920 cases from around the world.[4] By January 2020 it has documented more than 3000 cases, of which about 324 are from India.[5] The motivation behind documenting these cases is to understand whether there is a global movement for environmental justice that is helping to push society and economy towards environmental sustainability.[6] Although the conflicts involving different commodities and communities might seem dissimilar at first glance, more so when they are from various parts of the world, the research with EJAtlas data hypothesizes that the root cause of such conflicts is the growth and changes in the social metabolism. The economy is not circular;[7] it is entropic. Hence, there is a relation between the growth and changes in the social metabolism and the rise of the number of ecological distribution conflicts.[8] Such conflicts often involve contradictory, incommensurable languages of valuation.[9]

THE CONFLICTS

Using the categories of conflicts of the EJAtlas (summarized in Fig. 1 along with the percentages of cases in each category),[10] we describe a few lesser-known ones.

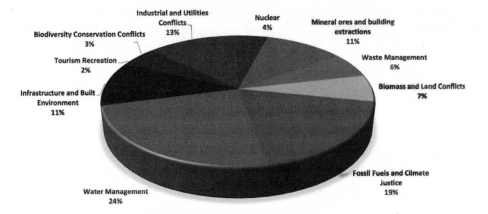

Fig. 1: Share of cases in each of the categories in the EJAtlas from India till December 2018 (Roy, 2018)

Biodiversity Conservation Conflicts

The recent Supreme Court case in 2019 against the Forest Rights Act (FRA) is a classic example of the conflict between conservationists and ecosystem people. There has been an ongoing debate on whether the people who live in and from the forests harm or help in preserving the forests.

One site which exemplifies this debate is the Kaziranga National Park in Assam[11] which houses two-third of the global one-horned rhino population. It was notified as a wildlife sanctuary in 1950, established as the Kaziranga National Park in 1974 and declared a UNESCO Heritage Site in 1985. Due to the barbarous market for rhino horns, poaching is a serious issue here. Between 2006 and 2016, 141 rhinos were poached.

The main reason for the conflict is that the forest guards, in an attempt to combat poaching, often see (and shoot at) local villagers living in and around the national park as alleged poachers. This became more commonplace after 2013, when the Assam government amended the provisions of Section 197 of the Code of Criminal Procedure granting forest officials immunity from prosecution if they attack poachers. Consequently, forest department officers shot twenty-two and twenty-three suspected poachers in 2014 and 2015, respectively. This went in parallel with a Public Interest Litigation (PIL) filed for removal of human habitation in and around Kaziranga following wide media coverage on poaching of rhinos. On 9 October 2015, the Guwahati High Court directed the district administration to evict the human inhabitants from Kaziranga, and from adjoining villages—Deurchur Chang, Banderdubi and Palkhowa. During the eviction drive carried out on 19 September 2016, two people were killed and seventeen injured. Both the evictions and the shootings of villagers, often adivasi, have created conflicts and protests and have been taken up by human rights organizations.[12] One of the local organizations involved in the movement asserting the rights of the local people living in and around Kaziranga is the Greater Kaziranga Human Resource Development and Environment Protection Committee. In July 2019, the committee, in association with many regional and political organizations such as the Gorkha Students' Union and Asom Jatiyatabadi Yuba Chatra Parishad, organized a meeting against the proposed eco-sensitive zone to be constructed within a 10-km radius of the park, which would lead to further displacement of the local people.[13] This meeting was a continuation of a long list of protest rallies and mobilizations which have erupted in the region since the Supreme Court passed an order on 13 December 2018 to build eco-sensitive zones around twenty-one national parks and wildlife sanctuaries, which would adversely affect the local population in and around Kaziranga.[14] This movement in Kaziranga is in response to the attempts at 'militarized conservation' in multiple tiger reserves and national parks in the country while defending local populations' role in 'convivial conservation'.[15]

Biodiversity conservation conflicts, although largely focused on conservation of emblematic endemic species such as tigers and rhinos, also occur around waterbodies. The Bhitarkanika National Park, in the Kendrapara district of Odisha containing India's second largest mangrove forest, is one such example.[16] It has a high-density population of adivasi communities dependent on the biodiversity-rich forest, which is a source of triangular dispute between conservationists, small paddy farmers and inland fisherfolk, and the illegal prawn industry.

Each year there is a ban on fishing in a 20-km radius from the coast for a period of seven months (1 November–31 May) coinciding with the breeding period of the Olive Ridley turtles, which is enforced by the forest department to protect these endangered turtles, and affects nearly 20,000 traditional fishworkers in the district every year, who are often arrested for alleged trespassing. The conflict with the shrimp mafia is harder to document. Illegal shrimp farms not only pose a direct threat to the mangrove forest but also to the fertility of the agricultural land and the groundwater table due to discharge of toxic effluents.

These two major conflicts that the traditional fishworkers face, one with the forest officials around livelihood and land rights, and the other about the illegal shrimp farms controlled by the shrimp mafia, have given rise to multiple street protests and blockades over the years. In June 2019, around 3000 hectares of illegal shrimp farms were demolished in Kendrapara following a protest staged by the villagers by blocking the Kharinasi-Ramanagar main road.[17]

Biomass and Land Conflicts

The Chipko Andolan often seen as the first environmental justice movement of India, which has inspired many contemporary environmental movements, is a biomass and land conflict.[18]

A contemporary of this movement was the Appiko Movement.[19] It started in 1983 in the Uttara Kannada district in Karnataka and spread awareness about biomass and land conflicts across southern India. It was a spontaneous movement started by the local communities struggling to retain control over productive natural resources and to defend their livelihoods and lifestyles in the Western Ghats. The protest to stop the felling of the trees lasted for thirty-eight days where more than 160 women, men and children from different castes united in protest. There was a direct influence or confluence with the Chipko movement as Sunderlal Bahuguna was invited in August 1983 to Gubbigadde, where he described the movement taking place in the Garhwal Himalaya.[20] Although orders for felling the trees were withdrawn, the struggle endures. The movement continues under the banner of Save the Western Ghats.[21]

A second more recent movement, also influenced by Chipko and in which women were the main protagonists, was in Balarampur village in Dhenkanal district of central Odisha against an industrial brewery project that would destroy the Jhinkargadi forest.[22] This protest had a very short lifespan when the state government decided to take quick action due to a strong media frenzy in favour of the people protesting. Although this particular conflict had a short lifespan, the nurturing of the forest has a long history. The trees of the Jhinkargadi forest have been nurtured for three generations by the villagers of Balarampur. Not only are the forests a source of livelihood to the villagers, it is also an important elephant corridor. Not surprisingly, when the state government decided to allocate this land for a commercial brewery company, it erupted in an ecological distribution conflict, with protests to prevent the felling of trees for the project.

Amidst the protests, the ceremony for laying the foundation stone of the project was conducted on 3 November 2018. On 17 November 2018, hundreds of villagers of Balarampur village clashed with the police to prevent the felling of sal trees. On this day, according to local reports, three platoons of police personnel entered the forest area early morning, at about 4 a.m., and cordoned the entire area. Once the villagers were made aware, they immediately rushed to stop the cutting of the old trees by hugging the trees. However, they were pulled away forcibly and close to 1000 trees were felled by the local administration, amidst protests, scuffles, arrests and live media coverage. Throughout that day and the next, the incident garnered a lot of media, activist and political attention. Eminent social activists, including Prafulla Samantara (a Goldman Prize winner), addressed the villagers and expressed their solidarity. Many forest rights and tribal rights activists and advocacy groups also reported about the incident on social media. Due to the visibility of the protests, Chief Minister Naveen Patnaik ordered a probe into the matter by the Revenue Divisional Commissioner and cancelled the brewery project. This case can be considered as a swift success of environmental justice.

However, this category in the EJAtlas called 'Biomass and Land Conflicts' doesn't solely concern terrestrial conflicts. One example is that of the Kerala Fishworkers' Struggle[23] which has a rich and complex, albeit perhaps lesser-known, history than the Chipko and Narmada movement. It was a case of working-class environmentalism defending the commons. This movement developed out of the crisis in the traditional fisheries sector due to the introduction of mechanized fishing in the sixties as a result of the promotion of export-oriented fisheries.[24] Traditional fishworkers felt an acute need to organize themselves against increasing threats to their livelihood, especially during the fish-breeding season in monsoon. The attack was two-fold: a reduction in the immediate catch and a threat to the stability of future resources. This created what John Kurien (1996) called an 'enclosure movement' or a 'tragedy of enclosure' (explicitly criticizing Garrett Hardin's misnamed tragedy of commons).[25]

The Kerala Swathantra Matsya Thozhilali Federation (KSMTF) formerly known as the Latin Catholic Fisherman's Federation (LCFF), was created in 1977 as a state-level organization to answer this call. A well-known leader was Thomas Kocherry. One of the first tasks of LCFF was to submit a memorandum to the chief minister of Kerala demanding that mechanized boats be only allowed to operate beyond 5 km from the coast. This was followed by a second memorandum demanding a ban on monsoon trawling and for the curbing of pollution of inland water resources. It also demanded a comprehensive Marine Regulation Act. In November 1978, the LCFF called a relay hunger strike in the district of Alappuzha when this demand for an Act was not met. This hunger strike went on for fifty-nine days with four people fasting in front of the district collectorate each day. Yet, the mechanized boats continued to operate.

To ensure that fishworkers across religions could unite, on 20 March 1980, LCFF was renamed Kerala Swathantra Matsya Thozhilali Federation (KSMTF)—translated as Kerala Independent Fishworkers Federation. This was done to ensure that the union remained independent from both political and religious influence. The main aim of KSMTF was 'to work for the socio-economic and political development, and education of fishworkers who are involved in fishing and marketing of fish in inland and coastal waters, and to work to get the rights and benefits of fishworkers from the government'.[26]

From then till the mid-nineties, there were multiple marches, hunger strikes, rallies, demonstrations, blockades, torchlight processions and 'fill the jail' campaigns, to organize people not just against monsoon trawling, but also for demanding welfare programmes, which were mostly met by silence on the issue of the ban of monsoon trawling from the government for a long time, as well as arrests and intimidation.[27] Finally, after years of protest, the Kerala High Court ruled in favour of the fishworkers' right to demand a ban on monsoon trawling in 1989, which was followed by the Supreme Court issuing an order in 1993 stating that the government had taken the correct decision to ban the trawling in the monsoon. This was considered a huge victory for KSMTF.

The struggle of the Kerala fishworkers eventually merged with the struggles of fisherfolk in Goa, Tamil Nadu and Karnataka, and today is a powerful voice basing itself on workers' solidarity while incorporating environmental concerns. On a worldwide scale, the Fishworkers' Movement is linked to the Via Campesina movement. In November 1997, the World Forum of Fisher Peoples was founded in Delhi. They convened again in Delhi in 2017 for their Seventh General Assembly to demand international support for small-scale fishworkers.

INDUSTRIAL AND UTILITIES CONFLICTS

The case of the Sterlite copper smelting unit in Tuticorin, Tamil Nadu,[28] spanning more than two decades, is a protracted example of industrial pollution involving both naked direct violence and slow murder.[29] This has gained recent attention due to the killing of thirteen protesters in May 2018. However, it has a long history spanning more than two decades.

The Sterlite copper smelter plant had begun operations in January 1997 after receiving a licence to operate in 1996. Protests against the plant began almost immediately after environmental clearances were granted, in March and October 1996, with hundreds of fishermen blockading the port with their boats, to create hindrance for the unloading of copper ore. Since then—over a period of more than two decades—villagers and local residents have been protesting against noxious sulphur dioxide leaks and poor effluent management with two major milestones in 2013 and 2018. On 23 March 2013, the 'Anti-Sterlite People's Committee' started protesting following a gas leak, when many people from the neighbourhood fell sick. More than 5000 people participated in the protest, and a strike was called shutting down the city for several days. Due to this, the Tamil Nadu Pollution Control Board issued a notice directing the Vedanta group company to close the plant. However, the Supreme Court of India eventually permitted the plant to restart operations under the condition of a payment of Rs 100 crore (15 million USD at the time), to compensate for polluting the surrounding land and water sources since 1997 and for running the smelter without various environmental clearances for a few years.

In September 2017, the National Green Tribunal (NGT) found that the Sterlite plant, between 2013 and 2017, was responsible for blocking the river stream by dumping copper slag in the Upper Odai river, as well as operating without authorization under the Hazardous Wastes (Management, Handling and Transboundary Movement) Rules, 2008, and ordered compensation for the affected villagers.

Since then, although there had been eruptions of occasional resistance, it was not until the announcement for expansion of the plant that public anger revived strongly. The smelter capacity was set to increase from 4,00,000 tons to 8,00,000 tons per year within the next twenty-four months. In corporate statements, Vedanta-Sterlite stated that this expansion would make the Tuticorin smelter, 'one of the world's largest single-location copper smelting complexes'. Protests re-emerged with residents calling for an indefinite dharna (protest) and hunger strike on 12 February 2018. It was reported that in the beginning of February, villagers had petitioned the district collector several times seeking closure of the unit, but no action had been taken.

Eventually, after top district officials failed to reach an understanding, around 250 people began an indefinite fast. Over 500 people, including many women and schoolchildren, blocked the company gates until they were rounded up and arrested on 14 February 2018. Since then, protests had been ongoing day and night, especially in the villages—which were the most affected by the expansion—surrounding the plant. On 22 May 2018, which coincided with the hundredth consecutive day of the peaceful protests, more than 20,000 villagers marched to the collector's office demanding the closure of the plant. Police shot at the protesters, killing thirteen of them. Due to a lot of public and international pressure following this incident, when claims were made on crony capitalism and industry-government collusion, the plant was finally ordered to be shut down.

A second industrial conflict from Tamil Nadu is on mercury poisoning. It is the notorious case of Unilever's thermometer plant in Kodaikanal[30] which has gained media attention due to a couple of viral songs about the conflict.[31] The conflict began in 2001 after public interest groups unearthed a pile of broken glass thermometers with mercury content from the interior of the *shola* forest, suspecting the involvement of the company. In March, the company was forced to shut down owing to a public protest led by the local workers' union and international environmental organization Greenpeace. However, many workers who weren't given any protective equipment or information about the disastrous health effects of toxic mercury had already been exposed to mercury poisoning.[32] The company had also dumped toxic waste around the factory and in forests, which continues to contaminate soil and groundwater, affecting thousands even today. Yet, the company tried to avoid responsibility for many years by trying to persuade the authorities that its responsibility was limited to cleaning the factory site and no further.

The protests found renewed strength in 2015 when a protest song about this conflict went viral. The song by Sofia Ashraf as well as a petition asking Unilever to face liability was signed by over 1,00,000 people and led to a public apology by the company.

This was followed by the agreement to financially settle on 9 March 2016 for an undisclosed sum with a group of 591 workers who had sued the company for health damage. However, the fight is not over yet. Unilever is yet to clean up its mercury contaminated sites. Such high levels adversely affect the environment and the densely forested Kodaikanal Wildlife Sanctuary. The clean-up campaign is being spearheaded by the People's Union for Civil Liberties under the banner Campaign to Cleanup Kodaikanal Mercury Pollution. In September 2016, they started an online petition for writing to the environment minister to not accept the sub-standard clean-up proposal by Unilever. In December 2016, fish samples were collected and tested from the Kodaikanal lake and the surrounding Periyakulam pond by researchers from the Indian Institute of Technology, Hyderabad. In November 2017, in a press conference, academics and activists associated with the Campaign to Cleanup Kodaikanal Mercury Pollution urged the district administrations to advise people to limit their fish consumption, and instruct Tamil Nadu Pollution Control Board to tighten clean-up standards for Unilever's contaminated site remediation. As of early 2021, Unilever has not taken any responsibility to clean up.

INFRASTRUCTURE AND BUILT ENVIRONMENT CONFLICTS

Conflicts around infrastructure and built environments revolve around special economic zones, big real estate developments, airports and expressways, many involving land acquisition conflicts. We briefly describe one case from Tamil Nadu.

Ennore creek, a sacrifice zone situated in the north of Chennai, bounded by the Korttalaiyar river and Bay of Bengal, can be seen as an example of ecological violence.[33] The case was the topic of a study by environmentalist Nityanand Jayaraman that was later converted into a Carnatic song by T.M. Krishna. The song explains that Ennore creek (with its mangroves and fishing grounds) was a true *poramboke*, a 'commons', although the word poramboke is now used in the sense of 'wasteland' or even 'waste-people'.[34] This industrial area consists of three operational state-owned coal thermal power plants, next to the Ennore Port where the coal comes in. The site hosts several other polluting chemical industries, including painting, fertilizers, cement and pharmaceutical ones, as well as a landfill. This is a case combining coastal protection and enormous damage by industry and utilities to the environment and can be considered a clear case of ecological violence against nature and humans.

Workers employed to construct the power plants are all casual labourers, many from Odisha and Jharkhand, living with their families in miserable huts on the toxic fly ash dumps without any facilities (water, sewage or electricity). The nearby inland fisherfolk villages have been devastated by pollution, ill health and dwindling catches. There are hardly any fish in the creek now, villagers report. Those with boats sail to less-polluted waters to fish. The rest with hand-cast nets can only walk with uncertainty along the banks to the river mouth 8 km away.

Recently, locals started to notice the encroachment of wetlands. There are signs such as 'This land belongs to TNECL' (Tamil Nadu Energy Company Ltd). Nityanand Jayaraman explains that these signs are a lie, as this was never land but water and wetlands. In November 2015, the port authorities faced similar allegations when activists claimed that about 400 acres of hydrologically sensitive wetland area was being dumped with the spoils of dredging as part of the port's development activities. The port authority claimed otherwise and claimed that the natural flow of the creek wasn't being disturbed due to the dredging. The conflict is ongoing.

Mineral Ores and Building Material Extraction Conflicts

Every long-drawn movement witnesses a few deciding moments which define its course. In many cases, unfortunately, these moments are marred by violence and deaths, which capture media attention and sometimes result in swift judgements in favour of the movements. The next movement is one such case.

In 1993, the Utkal Aluminium Industrial Limited (UAIL) was formed as a consortium, originally as a joint venture between ALCAN, Canada, Hindalco of Birla Group, India, Tata, India and Norsk Hydro, Norway with the motive to mine bauxite from the Baphlimali Hills of Kashipur block in Rayagada district in Odisha and construct an alumina refinery, also in Rayagada, to refine it for export. The project, however, was resisted since its inception by the local adivasi people. Although they were able to delay the operationalization of the plant, they were unable to stop the project in the end.

Commonly known as the Kashipur anti-bauxite movement, it has a long and violent story, and is one of the historic environmental justice movements of Odisha.[35] The reason why people resisted the project since its inception is because they were aware of the false promises of employment, basic amenities and infrastructure and development which National Aluminium Company Limited (NALCO) had made in the early 1980s in the neighbouring regions for the creation of the biggest bauxite mine and refinery of the country. Opposition to the Kashipur bauxite mine was spearheaded by the Prakrutik Sampad Surakshya Parishad movement and several adivasi–Dalit movement organizations in south Odisha, in addition to various national and transnational solidarity groups.

These non-violent forms of protest systematically met with violent repercussions from the state—be it the police force, or the goons employed by the mining companies. The most memorable one is the police firing on adivasis on 16 December 2000 in Maikanch village of Kashipur block, killing three protesters (grassroots environmental defenders, as they would be called today), permanently disabling six and seriously injuring thirty. Although this incident was successful in delaying the project, the work was finally taken up in 2008. Despite reports of violation of mining and environmental laws, the mining continues.

Nuclear Conflicts

India has been pushing for nuclear energy, with the usual mixture of reasons in most large countries—increasing electricity supply and serving military purposes. In this section we briefly consider one nuclear conflict case in Tamil Nadu, out of the twelve recorded so far in the EJAtlas for India.

The construction of the Kudankulam nuclear plant in Tamil Nadu has been contentious.[36] On 20 November 1989, a deal was signed between the Soviet premier Mikhail Gorbachev and the then Indian prime minister Rajiv Gandhi, for the construction of two nuclear power plants. It is notable that the deal was signed within just two years of the Chernobyl nuclear disaster.

In 1989, more than 10,000 people gathered under the banner of the National Fishworkers Union and other organizations to register their anger against the proposed nuclear plant. The project was in limbo for almost a decade. In March 1997, the then Indian prime minister, H.D. Deve Gowda, and Russian president, Boris Yeltsin, signed a supplement to the 1989 agreement and commissioned a detailed project report on Kudankulam. According to the revisited agreement, two Russian high standard pressure VVER-1000 (PWR) water-cooled and water-moderated reactors that would produce 1000 MW per unit were to be delivered to India.

In 2001, when the Government of India planned to further extend the plant by adding four more nuclear reactors within the premises of Kudankulam nuclear power plant, the public was tremendously distressed. The people resorted to a huge demonstration against the denial of comprehensive environment impact assessment and staged public hearings under the banner of People's Movement Against Nuclear Energy (PMANE). Between 2001–2011, various protests and demonstrations were organized by PMANE. Later, after the Fukushima disaster in 2011, the protests intensified because people were deeply frightened with the idea of nuclear disaster of such a great magnitude.

The villagers went on a hunger strike in mid-2011. At the time of the local body election, for which the strike had been suspended, the police entered into the villages at the forefront of the protests. They started a blockade that would last almost a year, stopping the inflow of milk, water and food. This led to a reaction at the national level, with solidarity groups emerging all over India. The villagers, mainly fisherfolk, resisted. They decided that the men would keep on fishing while the women would be the protagonists of the struggle. However, ultimately, in 2012, the protests began to diminish in intensity. At least one fisherman was killed in police firing in September 2012.[37]

The Chennai Solidarity Group for Koodankulam Struggle was among the most active. It published a pamphlet in November 2011 titled *Koodankulam and Nuclear Power*. The pamphlet presented 'Some myths, realities and answers to frequently asked questions' about this case, answering common doubts about the protesters and their claims. The authors claimed that 'India's chest-thumping "nucleocracy" wants to play the death game with peasants and fisherfolk as the pawns in the gamble.'

A PIL was filed in 2011 with the Supreme Court asking for nuclear power development to be delayed until safety concerns were independently assessed. In May 2013, the Supreme Court ruled in favour of the plant, stating that the nuclear power plant was in the larger public interest. In June 2013, the first reactor went critical and production supposedly started in late 2013. However, this unit shut down in June 2015 for maintenance. The second unit was supposed to become operational. The construction of the third and fourth units was to start in 2016. Negotiations are on with Russia for the fifth and sixth units. Both the protests and technical problems seriously delayed the project. Environmental justice activist Nityanand Jayaraman believes that 'uneasy questions about the damaged and poor quality of components, including the steam generators, in Koodankulam's Units 1 and 2, have resurfaced. It is not just the safety, but the very viability of Units 1 and 2 to produce electricity consistently and sustainably that is being questioned.'[38]

Water Management Conflicts

Among the multiple controversial dams and anti-dam movements in India,[39] we describe a lesser-known conflict surrounding a smaller dam in Arunachal Pradesh in the north-east of India, which presents certain novel elements. There are grandiose plans for 50,000 MW worth of hydroelectric power to be produced in the state; little of which has been built. Protests driven by both environmental and religious concerns started in 2011 when the state government announced plans to construct multiple dams.

The Nyamjang Chhu dam in Tawang[40] is a proposed 780-MW project with an investment of Rs 6400 crore. Tawang is the last Indian district bordering China. Historically, it had links with Tibet. It is home to the Monpa people and is a tourist destination. To stall this spree of dam construction, people from the Monpa community joined hands with local Buddhist monks in 2011 to form the Save Mon Region Federation (SMRF).

On 7 April 2016, the NGT suspended the environmental clearance of the project in response to an appeal filed by the SMRF, ordering fresh impact assessment studies, public hearing for local people and appraisal by the Expert Appraisal Committee on River Valley and Hydroelectric Projects and the ministry of environment, forests and climate change. A major issue was the impact on the wintering habitat of the black-necked crane, a vulnerable bird considered sacred by the Monpa people, an embodiment of the sixth Dalai Lama who was from Tawang and wrote about the bird in his poetry.

Following this, SMRF general secretary, Lama Lobsang Gyatso, was arrested twice due to alleged corruption for reasons, according to him, 'linked to not only the NGT decision but also to our plan to take legal recourse for other hydel projects'.[41] After his second arrest on 28 April 2016, he was denied bail by the court of the district magistrate. A number of villagers and lamas came together seeking his release. After hearing of the bail rejection on 2 May 2016, they started moving towards the police station and were fired on, leading to two deaths—a woman and a student of the Tawang monastery. By mid-afternoon, orders under Section 144 were clamped on Tawang town, and the army was called in to stage a flag march. The then chief minister Kalikho Pul, who was in New Delhi, ordered a judicial inquiry into the firing, and Rs 5 lakh ex-gratia to the family of those killed. The National Alliance of People's Movement demanded an official commission of enquiry.

CONCLUSION AND FUTURE RESEARCH AGENDAS

Although all the environmental justice movements discussed above have been sourced from the EJAtlas, the need for documentation of environmental conflicts is not a new one. Since the 1990s, the Centre for Science and Environment (founded by Anil Agarwal in 1980, with Sunita Narain as the current director general) has been preparing a monthly selection of newspaper clippings on the environment in India, South Asia and on a global level. Each Green File was divided into ten sections (dams, water, forest, pollution, land, health, people, pesticides, energy and habitat) and came with an executive summary. This was later complemented by the India Environment Portal, which is an online open-source platform with vast information on environment and development issues. In recent years, the Land Conflict Watch, which is a project to map, collect and analyse ongoing land conflicts in India has also been doing incredible work of highlighting ecological distribution conflicts in the country.

There is then ample documentation in India to do research in comparative political ecology, beyond single case studies. In the recent past, the EJAtlas has been utilized for such comparative analysis in India[42] and globally.[43]

Looking at our sample of cases mentioned above, we find many of them have long histories, uncertain outcomes and are marred with violence, both direct as well as structural, ecological and slow (which is harder to document), and can be understood using a multidimensional violence framework.[44] There are multiple intriguing aspects which could be further studied to understand better the environmental justice movements in India and worldwide. We list below such potential research areas.

One of the interesting aspects which could be studied is a region-wise enquiry about movements. Questions such as why certain regions have more conflicts than others or how do certain regions manage to stop conflictive projects better than others could be analysed within this scope of enquiry.

A second interesting research area for the study of environmental justice movements is a global thematic coverage of conflicts around commodities, such as copper, eucalyptus, gold, shrimp, iron ores, etc. Comparative research on impacts, forms of mobilization, outcomes, etc. could enrich the understanding of the global movement for environmental justice and its manifestations in India. Are there transnational organizations fighting in certain conflicts, such as, for instance, coal mining, nuclear power, aviation, ship-breaking, incineration of waste, and how are they represented in India? The EJAtlas also provides information on different social actors, including social class, caste, ethnicity and gender aspects, as well as multiple forms of mobilization. Research could be carried out to better map and analyse the common and distinctive forms of mobilizations in India.

A third research focus could be the cultural expressions of environmental justice movements. This essay highlights the power of protest songs in Ennore creek and Kodaikanal. There is a distinctive vocabulary in the movement for environmental justice in India (sand mafia, *kolya satyagraha*, etc.) and a rich multicultural history of artistic expressions of protest through music, dance, painting, theatre, documentaries or banners. One aspect to study could be how cultural expressions (including music, slogans, murals, etc.) travel and alter through time and space.

A fourth focus could be on the past and distant influences on environmental justice movements. This would deal with drawing the connection between present-day movements and historical ones such as: What has the role of Appiko been in the subsequent organized protests in south India? How influential are the Chipko movement strategies in current contexts? How much of the current call for fisheries justice against 'ocean grabbing' around the world is rooted in the Kerala Fishworkers' Struggle of the 1980s? A potential research line could also focus on how events occurring outside India shape the movements within the country. A clear example is the nuclear accident of Fukushima in 2011. Research could focus not just on events but also on international NGOs such as Friends of the Earth or Greenpeace, and how their influence shapes mobilizations. A hypothesis (to be tested by network analysis) could be the relative isolation of the environmental movement in India.

PART II

THE MAKERS OF INDIAN DEMOCRACY

6

TRAVELS WITHIN THE SELF: M. LAKSHMI AND HER LETTERS FROM LONDON

A.R. VENKATACHALAPATHY

RAMACHANDRA GUHA HAS been the strongest critic of the Bengal-centredness of much of Indian historiography. While being in agreement with his call to provincialize Bengal, this essay on a personal narrative by M. Lakshmi, a Tamil woman in the early twentieth century, begins by contrasting her story with the Bengal scenario. The first autobiography by a Bengali woman—*Amar Jiban* by Rashsundari Devi, published in 1868—Tanika Sarkar observes, was 'probably the first full-scale autobiography in the Bengali language itself'.[1] Malavika Karlekar notes that there is 'a record of at least fifty autobiographies and autobiographical sketches' by Bengali women in the nineteenth century alone.[2] To add to this richness is also the diversity. While elsewhere in India most narratives of female writers in the nineteenth century were by upper-caste/class women, in the case of Bengal, we even have an autobiography by an actress.[3]

In my many years of rummaging through the Tamil cultural archives, I have not come across any nineteenth-century autobiographical narrative by a woman. Arguably, the earliest full-fledged personal narrative is an epistolary travelogue published in the early 1920s. Through the recovery of this fascinating text I explore the life of its author and the articulation of her self, and reflect upon the genre of autobiography as practised in colonial Tamil Nadu.

Both feminist and cultural historians of India have used the term 'autobiography' in a capacious sense to include a wide range of personal narratives such as dairies, memoirs, reminiscences, letters, etc. I expand this range by the inclusion of travelogue as well. My choice is dictated not just by the sparseness of the literature in the autobiographical genre—I suggest that travelogue can be a form of life writing. In subtle and indirect ways it can narrate the self-reflection and transformation of the self as well as be a comment—by silence and by contrast—on the social world, which is the staple of autobiography.

Antoinette Burton, in her engaging study of three narratives by women in colonial India, has argued that 'house and home are central to the social identities' of colonial Indian women, and that they are 'the cultural forms through which they experienced both family life and national belonging'.[4] In contrast to this formulation, M. Lakshmi Ammal,[5] the protagonist of this essay, makes no mention of home and house at all in her writing: instead, she articulates the realization of her self and its transformation through a travel narrative. Before I explore this narrative, an introduction to Lakshmi and her milieu is in order.

I

M. Lakshmi was no ordinary woman. She was the daughter of A. Madhaviah and Meenakshi. Madhaviah (1872–1925)[6] was one of the foremost bilingual intellectuals of colonial Tamil Nadu and is celebrated to this day for writing the earliest Tamil novels.

Despite this distinguished pedigree, little is known of her. Lakshmi is a rather common name among Tamils, especially upper castes. Many parents fondly name their girls after 'the goddess of wealth' and rejoice at the fortunes that would result after their birth. Ironically, in this case, Lakshmi caused much grief to her parents. This essay is about a narrative that stands testimony to her, and her father's, resolve not to be cowed by adversities.

Lakshmi was born in Narasinganallur, Tirunelveli district on 12 April 1896. Despite her father's social reform zeal and enlightened views on the age of consent, she was married off in 1905 at Ramanathapuram to Salem Krishnaswamy Sastrigal Venkatarama Sastry—she was barely nine then. But Madhaviah showed greater courage when she was neglected by her in-laws during her illness (smallpox)—he brought his ailing daughter home and refused to send her back even after she recovered. (This illness left permanent scars on her face.) Instead, he gave her a good education, trained her as a teacher and taught her to be independent. Lakshmi received a BA (Honours) in English from the University of Madras, and also acquired an LT (Licentiate in Teaching). Later, during 1923–24, she went to study at the Bedford College, an all-women's college of the University of London. English literature was her discipline, and not unsurprisingly, she specialized in Shakespeare. On her return, she taught for many years at the premier women's college of Chennai, Queen Mary's College. After serving as principal for some months, she retired in 1950 due to a heart attack. After her father died, in 1925, it was she who ran the family. A close friend of the women activists Sister Subbalakshmi,[7] Lady Andal[8] and Mary Clubwala Jadhav,[9] she contributed to the Madras Seva Sadan girls' school. Little else is known of her accomplishments. We know that, in 1944, she published two short stories in an anthology consisting exclusively of contributions by Madhaviah's children![10] I have also traced three other pieces that she published.[11] Lakshmi died on 6 December 1958. Her niece recalls that she was of medium build, her wavy grey hair braided into a single plait and pinned up in a figure of eight. Her flaring nostrils resembled her father. She wore saris of a traditional pattern and instead of matching blouses, which were already the vogue in those days, she chose to buy shirt material, white with stripes or checks, picking up the colours of the sari. Another niece confirms that she was a quiet woman who dressed simply.[12]

Lakshmi's was no ordinary family. The family was distinguished but in a way very unlike other Tamil Brahmin families. Her father, as we noted, was one of the towering figures of modern Tamil literature. Madhaviah's novels are marked by the challenges that colonial modernity posed to the emerging middle-class intellectuals and the radical positions that he took in relation to social reform.

Madhaviah's *Padmavathi Charithiram* (1898), considered to be the third Tamil novel—after S. Vedanayakam Pillai's *Pratapa Mudaliar Charithiram* (1879) and B.R. Rajam Iyer's *Kamalambal Charithiram* (1896)—is a classic and continues to be in print and read to this day. In a life cut short at the age of fifty-three, he wrote prodigiously.[13] Madhaviah studied at the Madras Christian College in Chennai where, like many of his contemporaries, he was influenced by William Miller, Scottish missionary, educationist and Shakespeare teacher. Like most colonial intellectuals, 'crushed by English poetry'[14] he began his writing career by composing English verse. Thankfully, he gave it up but produced a prodigious amount of work in other genres: novels, short stories, essays, poetry, plays, reviews and criticism in Tamil. He also wrote in English. His novels in English include, *Thillai Govindan* (published by Unwin of London), *Satyananda* and *Clarinda*. His name continues to occur in standard histories of Indian writing in English even if only as a footnote.[15] He also attempted translation and adaptations of Tamil classical literature.

Madhaviah retired as the assistant commissioner of the salt and excise department of the Government of Madras, not an insignificant position. The family itself was not rich—Madhaviah preferred to spend on books rather than on land and jewellery. His eldest son, M. Ananthanarayanan was an Indian Civil Service officer who later became judge at the Madras High Court and was a writer himself. But the most distinguished member of the family was M. Krishnan, the legendary naturalist. Lakshmi had an elder sister, Meenambal (Meenakshi), and three younger sisters, Visalakshi, Muthulakshmi (Mukta Venkatesh)[16] and Dr Saraswathi.

Madhaviah was the primary influence on Lakshmi. From the sparse biographical sketches and memoirs that we have it is not difficult to figure out that, heavily influenced by Western cultural norms of conjugal and familial life, Madhaviah attempted to fashion a companionate marriage and a convivial family for himself. Ninety years after his death, members of the extended family[17] recollect how he taught his young wife to read and write (an inevitable vocation for all colonial Indian social reform intellectuals who were pulled between their convictions and the reality of Indian social life) and built a library rather than accumulating wealth.

Madhaviah was born and raised in the Tirunelveli district in southern Tamil Nadu. It was here that protestant Christianity made deep inroads into Tamil society. Christian missionaries not only successfully proselytized some upper-caste Vellalars but more importantly large numbers of lower-caste Nadars—probably the most important social churning in nineteenth-century Tamil country. From among the Vellalars, referred to as Murugankurichi Vellalars, emerged H.A. Krishna Pillai, the poet, translator of *Pilgrim's Progress*, and the author of one of the earliest Tamil autobiography/conversion narratives, *Palayamkottai Henry Albert Krishna Pillai Kristhavanana Kathai* (How Henry Albert Krishna Pillai Became a Christian).[18] Tirunelveli was the site of the missionary activity of Clarinda, a Brahmin widow who was dramatically saved by a British military officer from her husband's pyre, and converted to Christianity. She later worked as a missionary. Madhaviah wrote a novel in English, *Clarinda*, which draws both on historical and local lore.

Madhaviah's writings show a lifelong intellectual and social engagement with Christianity and conversion. And his negotiation and engagement with Brahminical religion and Hinduism was refracted by this engagement. His many novels, stories and essays stand testimony to this engagement. In one of his novels, the eponymous Muthumeenakshi's complaint that 'We have ruined all our practices—eating, dressing, sleeping, etc. by entangling them with religion. Christians do not do so. Religion is one thing. The rest entirely another. Therefore, if this wretched world should torture us like this it's quite right to become a Christian', is indicative of his thinking about Christianity. While Madhaviah was not unfamiliar with theological and philosophical issues, his engagement with Christianity and conversion was primarily social. He was so critical of Brahmins and their social practices that two senior Tamil writers and historians of the Tamil novel remark: '[He] wrote as though he wanted to wreak vengeance on his own community'.[19]

Madhaviah was a forerunner in the genre of autobiographical narrative as well. At a time when the autobiography as a genre was little known in Tamil, Madhaviah embarked on a very novel attempt. In June 1892, in the newly launched monthly journal of the Society for the Diffusion of Useful Knowledge, *Viveka Chintamani*, he began a novel called *Savitri Charithiram*. Structured as the autobiography (it is likely that he was the first to coin in Tamil the term '*swasarithai*' to refer to autobiography) of a Brahmin widow, it was signed 'Savitri'—evidently an attempt to create a real-life feeling. For reasons unknown, probably a disagreement with the editor, on its reformist content, the serialization was discontinued after a few months. Ten years later, in 1903, Madhaviah rewrote and published this fragment as a separate book under the title *Muthumeenakshi: Oru Brahmana Pennin Swasarithai* (Muthumeenakshi: The Autobiography of a Brahmin Girl).[20]

This short novel describes in the first person the everyday persecution of a young Brahmin girl by her widowed mother-in-law—in what was to become a staple theme of social reform novels in the coming decades. Muthumeenakshi remarries a young man, and the novel ends on a positive note as the married couple defiantly set up house in the Brahmin quarters. In this novel, critical remarks on the regressive nature of Hindu Brahmin life and society are articulated through Muthumeenakshi. It is poignant that the sufferings that Muthumeenakshi undergoes at the hands of her mother-in-law anticipate the travails of Lakshmi, who could not but have read this novel. Indeed, according to a recent biographer of Madhaviah, Sita Anantha Raman, Lakshmi herself translated this novel into English and serialized it in the *Social Reform Advocate*.[21] As indicated earlier, Lakshmi was also mistreated by her in-laws and was rescued from their clutches by a firm father. But unlike Muthumeenakshi, she did not remarry but led an independent life of her own.

The genre of autobiography was thus very much available to Lakshmi, and one wonders why she did not try her hand at it. However, in not exercising this choice, she was by no means unique. As I have argued elsewhere, autobiography was a new genre in Tamil, and few Tamil intellectuals experimented in any form of life writing.[22] As late as 1910, when Subramania Bharati attempted a short autobiography in verse, he wrote a defensive preface.[23]

> This little book of poems is written in a novel manner. Some poems may give pleasure. There could also be a lot of chaff. Its feature is that of the protagonist speaking his own words—that is, the hero narrates his own story directly . . . I am publishing this little book to test if it is worthy of the recognition of learned Tamil scholars. If these scholars test and approve this, I will publish more in the same fashion. Scholars should bear with flaws born out of lack of experience and talent.

Autobiography's progress in Tamil literary culture was very tardy. It took off in the Tamil literary culture only towards the end of the interwar period. If few men wrote autobiography virtually no woman attempted any form of life writing. My archival search has yielded a very small crop. I have been able to identify and trace the following autobiographical narratives by women—many of these remain scattered in various journals—and I am involved in compiling these narratives: a short narrative by Pandita Asalambikai, a prolific versifier, nationalist activist, conservative Brahmin child widow (1931); a brief autobiographical sketch by C. Saraswati Bai, the first woman Harikatha exponent (1935); an autobiographical serial by Sister R.S. Subbalakshmi, possibly the first full-length autobiography in Tamil by a woman (1951).

The narrativization of the formation of a unique and unfolding individual self, which is the core of the autobiography, posed certain insurmountable challenges to the Tamil self. The unfolding of the self involves, in the words of Sudhir Kakar, 'the scrutiny of the life in terms of a ruthless examination of motives and feelings'.[24] Indian autobiographers have found this almost impossible. As Kakar argues, Indian autobiographies tend to be 'evocations of places and accounts of careers, records of events from which the self has been excised'. Tamil autobiographers too have turned their narratives into a record of a world lost to modernity. There is little exploration of the self, the psychological tensions of family life, the loss of innocence, the awakening of sexuality and the like. Except in the case of Brahmins, caste too has been pushed under the carpet rather than foregrounded—exceptions are narratives by lower-caste personalities such as Rettaimalai Srinivasan (1860–1945).[25]

If this was the case with men, women wrote their autobiographies under even more dire circumstances. As Tanika Sarkar points out, writing about one's own life was an 'audacious act'.[26] In their essentials, women's autobiographies have tended to be accounts of their struggle to enter social life.

In this context, Lakshmi may be excused for not attempting an autobiography. It may have given her only pain. But what she did write was a travelogue to which we now turn.

III

Lakshmi would have been about twenty-eight when she went to London and wrote this series of letters. She was a mature student and not an impressionable young girl. As mentioned earlier, she was then studying at Bedford College. It was certainly unusual for young Tamil women to go abroad to study at that time—not one of the many women students she met in London seems to have been from the Tamil country. We have no information at all on how Lakshmi made it to London. Until then, no member of the family had travelled abroad. It must have come at great financial cost to the family, and one can only imagine that Madhaviah must have strained every resource to make this possible. The series of letters Lakshmi wrote was titled 'Seemai Kaditham' (Letters from a Foreign Land). This series of ten epistles, plus an essay on her sea voyage to England, constitutes a travelogue where she describes in some detail her life and travels in England and Europe. It includes a great deal of subtle self-reflection. These epistles were originally published in the rich literary monthly review, *Panchamirtam*, edited by her father Madhaviah between April 1924 and April 1925 before his sudden and untimely death in October 1925. (It was left to Lakshmi, along with her younger brother, M. Ananthanarayanan, to bring out the final issue of the journal.) These remain to be published as a stand-alone book.

The first instalment of the travelogue was published in the inaugural number of *Panchamirtam*. Describing London's weather in some detail, it begins with Lakshmi's observations about the worst winter in ten years. Though Lakshmi uses a controlled prose, the excitement of seeing the first snow in her life is palpable. The narrative presupposes an audience which is completely unfamiliar with the West, i.e. Europe. Nowhere in the text does she explicitly compare or contrast her experience in India. Observing that buses are no longer driven by women, she states that this practice stopped after the war (World War I), but adds that it was now quite common for women to earn a living by their own labour. In commenting on this—of women earning their own bread and living on their own—she writes that this was not the case in their grandmothers' times. And in a sentence pregnant with meaning, evidently talking about herself, she states, 'Even women from abroad who have no special skills can live here without fear!' The first chapter thus sets up her narrative with a broad-brush view of the city.

Lakshmi continues her description of London in the second epistle. This paints the bustling activity in the city with its extensive market streets. Clearly, she was excited by what she saw and commented that such activity could scarcely be seen anywhere else in the world. Little is known of how much Lakshmi might have travelled in India—not much I would surmise—for her father set up his family in Chennai and lived on his own in his various transfer postings. The family first lived in the Chennai neighbourhood of Triplicane before moving to adjacent Mylapore. As such, it is unlikely that the family, especially Lakshmi, travelled much. There's a reference to Bangalore in this narrative in relation to the time it took to reach the city from Chennai (about eight hours then, according to her).

What was soon to become the standard cliché that anything from 'a pin to a motor car' could be bought crops up in the narrative. Shops, salons, promenades, musical events dominate the scene. Lakshmi was particularly fascinated with the electric elevators. The neon-lit advertisements caught her eye, and when she added that the city shone splendidly only in the night, she was perhaps making a statement about her participation in London's nightlife, something that would have been out of bounds for women in India. She did not fail to note that three-quarters of the shopping crowd consisted of women. Even while she was constantly alert to the presence of women, the standard Indian nationalist response to Western material wealth is articulated at the end of the second epistle.

> Is this what is called civilization? Mannequins, which anyone would mistake for real women, strike a pose in shop windows; advertisements—now in green, now in blue, and now in red—glow in mid-air like an astral sign. Are these the signs of civilizational progress! The foundation of this civilization rests on the accumulation of wealth.

After a description of London and its glittering wealth, Lakshmi then moves to Europe. It is May, and Bedford College is on summer vacation. Lakshmi sets out on a tour of Europe, accompanied by a female friend and her parents. Their names are not mentioned, nor does she discuss her relationship with them. One is able to surmise that they were Indians.

Crossing the English Channel on the ferry, they arrive in Paris. One of the first comments that she makes is about 'the ample facilities for people to travel *independently* without troubling others' (emphasis added). This is one of the many comments that she makes which implies a criticism of the Indian situation though she makes no explicit contrast. This is a strategy that is employed throughout the text.

Interestingly, in describing her Parisian experiences the contrast is with London and not India. Lakshmi and company follow the usual touristy route, and there are funny moments with their broken French that doesn't take them far. After the incessant chattering of the guide, she jokes that she would be happy to see even a ruined wall as long as no one was dinning information into her ears. After visiting the Palace of Versailles, she astutely observes that, unlike what the English said, the Orient was not the only place to be marked by extravagance.

From Paris they proceed to Switzerland. Lakshmi eagerly looks forward to seeing the Alps. At the Grindelwald Glacier, she hires skiing equipment. Lakshmi was possibly the first Tamil women to ski. The blue light in the resorts that shone on the snowy slopes remind her of fantastic descriptions from *The Arabian Nights*. All through the text Lakshmi tries to relate her experiences to her own reading.

When Lakshmi reaches Zurich, after travelling to Berne and Lucerne, the spring festival is in progress. In a Zurich bookshop she espies a book on Gandhi on display. It further pleases her that the local guide was familiar with the Mahatma's name and reputation.

The group then proceeds to Munich. Visiting cathedrals, chapels and museums form the staple of their tour. But in Munich Lakshmi is wonderstruck to meet an Orientalist—unfortunately he is not identified—well versed in both Tamil and Sanskrit. Being interested in folklore, he enquires if such oral traditions were available in print—a question only her father could have answered.

From Munich they move on to Vienna. Lakshmi is impressed by the palaces of the erstwhile Habsburg Empire which now functioned as museums. From there they travel to Italy where Lakshmi feels very much at home. The sights and the people remind her of India. At Venice she goes rowing on a gondola. The places she travels to include Milan, Florence, Naples and Pisa. On visiting Mount Vesuvius, she peers into the volcano, and takes a tour around Pompeii. The text is peppered with gentle but astute comments. Lakshmi expresses annoyance at the guides who repeated memorized lines. The rest of the tour takes her to Genoa, Nice and Monte Carlo. As she takes the train from Naples to Nice, the scenic beauty of the mountains reminds her of descriptions from *Nala Venba*, a medieval Tamil poem narrating the story of Nala and Damayanti. From Nice they return to London as her summer vacation comes to an end. I am unable to calculate how much time she may have spent on the continental tour—it was probably more than a couple of weeks.

In subsequent epistles Lakshmi provides vivid and happy descriptions of summer in London. Commenting on the English response to the summer and sunlight, she compared them to camels that store up water when available; the people could never have enough of the summer and the sun. Lakshmi also played golf, tennis and went punting. During the weekends, in the company of her female friends, she visited Cambridge, Windsor and Canterbury.

Lakshmi devotes one epistle to the British Empire Exhibition at Wembley, the over a year-and-a-half (April 1924–October 1925) event planned to herald a great imperial revival. Once again, in an implied contrast to India, she noted the orderliness with which the huge, milling crowds conducted themselves. On this occasion, a British friend accompanied her. At the India stall there was reason for mirth as her companion misread the significance and function of many of the artefacts. Inevitably, there was an argument about the state of industry and enterprise in India. The latent nationalism in her burst out. When Lakshmi emphasized the achievements of precolonial Indian industry, her friend was least impressed. She also visited the funfair, and took a ride on the rollercoaster train and enjoyed it 'to her heart's content'. At the end of a long and tiring eight-hour day, she promised herself that, in order to avoid the crowd, she would return to the Wembley Exhibition when it rained.

In a separate letter Lakshmi provides a full account of the daily life of a college student in England, observing that it was little different from her Chennai experience, even as she noted that all generalizations had an element of falsehood. Unlike Tamil women who were raised to believe that eating frugally was their duty, she noted that English girls ate excessively and with relish; she was amazed that four heavy meals were served in the college. She also thought that Englishwomen were stronger than even Indian men, not to mention women.

Women in her college were aged between eighteen and twenty-five. They hailed from modest middle-class families. They were not, Lakshmi observed, characterized by modesty and restraint—this she stated in a non-judgemental, if not in an approving, manner. Rather than being slim and full of beauty, they were well built and had an upright gait (a posture, one may add, disapproved strongly for women by Indian tradition). They possessed a glowing face. She noted approvingly that Englishwomen demonstrated unlimited enthusiasm and energy for studying and playing. Showing interest in wearing fashionable clothes, they loved to dance and visit the theatre. She also contended—with admiration, one could say—that their hearts were unsullied by fear, falsehood and hypocrisy. Though having a deep love for their family, they nevertheless looked forward to the day when they would leave their homes and lead an independent domestic life. They were also moved by compassion and displayed considerable broad-mindedness. Deeply patriotic, they believed that no nation in the world equalled theirs.

Though written in a gentle prose that reveals no emotion, Lakshmi is clearly making a criticism of her fellow Indian/Tamil women rather than providing an objective description of Englishwomen. Was she also expressing her desire to emulate them? One must emphasize that her positive comments on young Englishwomen are in marked contrast to the then current Indian stereotypes about them as permissive, uncultured and materialistic.

As her many friends went off to Europe on a holiday, Lakshmi now desired to spend some time in the English countryside. Browsing through newspaper advertisements, she hit upon a village called Vantage. This would surely have been unthinkable in her home in Chennai. The village had never seen an Indian woman, and she was at first mistaken for a Chinese or a Japanese woman. Lakshmi was amused by the prejudices and stereotypes that the local villagers harboured about Indians: as a people who were only interested in and wasted time on luxuries and who used cheap labour. The villagers believed that India survived only through the industriousness of its white masters.

Lakshmi lodged with an elderly woman, with teatime providing the occasion for jokes and laughter. Lakshmi was impressed that this woman was interested in books and reading. As it proved to be a rather rainy summer, on the advice of the landlady, Lakshmi visited Oxford and Stratford-upon-Avon. Not surprisingly, given her interest in English literature, the visit to Shakespeare's birthplace left her deeply impressed.

At the beginning of her new academic year, it was now Lakshmi's turn to act as guide to the women students arriving fresh from India. She counted forty such students living in London, and noted that many of them had earlier lived as *purdanashin* (secluded) women in India. She guided them through the major tourist spots, and oriented them to living in London. This provided an occasion for self-reflection. She recollected that, on arriving in London a year earlier, she had been bombarded with such questions as 'How do you like England?' 'Does London look like what you had imagined?' 'What do the sights here remind you of?' Disoriented by her displacement, and confused by anticipation and longing, she had been unable then to respond clearly. Keeping this in mind, Lakshmi sensitively remarked that she desisted from inflicting such questions on the newly arrived students.

This also provided the occasion for Lakshmi to give practical tips for living in London. Among the many sentences that she wrote, tucked away in a matter-of-fact tone, is the statement: women can live in London on their own without any fear. Here, in one of the very few references to missionaries, she mentions the assistance provided by some Christian agencies to Indian women.

But her year-long sojourn in England left Lakshmi with mixed feelings. While she conceded that she had learnt a lot from London, visiting its many museums and studying in the college and travelling across Europe, she stated that she still longed to return to India.

The last instalment of her travel narrative ends with the year-end Christmas celebrations. She joined the Christmas party hosted by fellow Indian students—whether the party included men or it was an all-woman affair is not clear. Thirty poor children had been invited to the party. Lakshmi recounted the comment of one of the Indian girl students who played with them by cuddling and lifting some of them: 'I'm a Christian, and I do not entertain caste differences. But until coming to England I had never mingled with lower-caste and poor children. Henceforth no Christmas would be festive without playing with poor children'. Once again we find Lakshmi recording remarks and statements without a gloss or comment. But it is evident that these are conscious recordings written with intent.

The narrative ends on a rather symbolic note. One of her companions at breakfast commented that she could smell spring in the air. Lakshmi and her friends rushed out for a stroll in the garden but could only experience a cold wind. Lakshmi remarked wryly, 'Spring will come in its own time, but it won't be late'.

* * *

I argue that the traditional Western understanding of the autobiographical narrative is limiting. In fact, even the manner in which Indian men 'Indianized' the autobiographical form was inappropriate for Indian women to describe and construct the realization of their self. While the few autobiographical narratives by Tamil women written a few years later were largely records of their struggle to come into the larger social world, and as a chronicle of events in their life, we find that Lakshmi, even though desisting from making a single observation about her own life, was providing a subtle account of other possibilities for women. Lakshmi might not have written about her painful experiences as a young and abused wife. But a keen contemporary reading of the narrative would have easily revealed the desires of a young woman who wanted to live on her own without fear; who could travel with friends in far-off lands; enjoy playing golf; punt on the river; ski on the snow; experience the thrill of a rollercoaster ride to her heart's content; seek board and lodging in the countryside by herself; who could guide fellow women in finding their feet in a distant land; who could relate her experiences to her reading; come to her own judgement about fellow human beings, without falling into the trap of nationalist stereotypes; and ultimately hope that spring would come.

In the three or so decades that Lakshmi lived following her return to Chennai, she might not have become a celebrity but evidently she lived a purposeful life independently and on her own terms.

7

THE SINGING SATYAGRAHI: KHURSHEDBEN NAOROJI AND THE CHALLENGE OF INDIAN BIOGRAPHY

DINYAR PATEL

IN RECENT YEARS, the 'bare cupboard' of Indian biography, identified nearly two decades ago by Ramachandra Guha, has begun to slowly fill up. But Indian biography still remains remarkably underdeveloped—no doubt due to extant challenges. A biographer in India, for example, needs proficiency in several languages to do justice to particular individuals. Current-day political sensitivities render some subjects, such as Aurangzeb or Shivaji, out of bounds or hazardous to undertake. A whole new crop of challenges occurs within archival facilities. Modern India's track record of archival preservation has been quite abysmal. Bureaucratic obstruction, archival incompetence and paranoia-induced restrictions on access throw up further obstacles to the researcher. It is hardly surprising, therefore, that so many scholars of South Asia eschew solid empirical research in favour of easier paths, such as reliance on arcane theory.[1]

In this article, I draw on the life of Khurshed A.D. Naoroji (1894–1966?)[2] to illustrate a set of particular challenges for writing Indian biographies. Khurshedben, as friends and associates knew her, was the granddaughter of Dadabhai Naoroji (1825–1917), the early Indian nationalist leader. A Parsi Zoroastrian, she was a member of a tiny, affluent and westernized minority community. She grew up around wealth and privilege. While in her early thirties, nevertheless, she sacrificed a promising career as a classically trained soprano to join Mohandas K. Gandhi (1869–1948), exchanging the concert halls of Paris and Bombay for the rigorous, ascetic life of a satyagrahi. In time, she became one of Gandhi's most tireless and fearless associates. She promoted women's involvement in the Civil Disobedience Movement, served as an emissary between Gandhi and the Pashtun leader Khan Abdul Ghaffar Khan (1890–1988) and undertook a remarkable mission in the North-West Frontier Province (NWFP) to promote non-violence and stop a spate of kidnappings of Hindu villagers.

And yet, hardly anything is known about her life. Such is the consequence of the first and greatest challenge in Indian biography that I would like to identify: gender. Most biographers have undertaken work on Indian men, resulting in an astounding lack of scholarship on prominent female leaders. Much of this has to do with an inherent gender bias in the archival record. There are relatively few rich archival collections of Indian women—Sarojini Naidu's papers at the Nehru Memorial Museum and Library, for example, are disappointingly thin—and the papers of Indian men oftentimes make scant reference to their female counterparts. In a country where the papers of so many prominent men are missing or disintegrating into moth-eaten heaps, it should be of little surprise to us that the written records of significant women leaders have long ago turned to dust. Khurshedben and three of her sisters, popularly known in Bombay as the Captain Sisters, were prominent Gandhians and close friends of the Nehru family. They would have had the historical sensitivity, financial resources and personal contacts to ensure that their correspondence was properly preserved. In spite of this, their letters and papers have entirely disappeared.[3]

Denied intact collections of personal papers, the biographer encounters further challenges. As is the case with Khurshedben, one has to write life stories indirectly, through the lives of better-documented family members and friends. A wealthy American heiress living in Greece, Eva Palmer-Sikelianos, therefore becomes a critically important figure for understanding Khurshedben's shift from music to Indian nationalist activity: Sikelianos preserved her correspondence with Khurshedben. There is also the acute challenge posed by chronological unevenness of material. While much of Khurshedben's life remains a blank slate, there is an overabundance of material for a two-year period in the early 1940s—from letters stashed in Gandhi's correspondence—before she once more fades from view. Reconstructing Khurshedben's nationalist career with this short burst of material is much like trying to approximate a great painting with only a few surviving tatters. It requires constant guesswork.

Yet the rewards of Indian biography are legion. There is the thrill of unearthing completely forgotten episodes of history, such as acts of bravery and sacrifice that propelled the nationalist movement. In Khurshedben's case, this involved long years in jail, hazarding death by negotiating with Pashtun dacoits and launching salvos of unrestrained criticism against Gandhi and his policies. There are fleeting glimpses of a remarkable personality, someone who evoked feelings of both consternation and admiration amongst her British colonial interlocutors. 'You could see nationalism oozing from her eyes,' remarked the Gandhian scholar Ushaben Mehta, who was jailed in the 1940s alongside Khurshedben. For our eyes, unfortunately, only brief snippets of her nationalist career are visible.[4]

I

Khurshedben Naoroji was born on 27 June 1894 to a family in mourning. Nine months earlier in October 1893, her father, Ardeshir Naoroji, a doctor in the princely state of Kutch, passed away from a sudden heart attack. From faraway London, a grief-stricken Dadabhai Naoroji, then in the middle of his parliamentary term, reached out to Kutch officials to ensure royal support for Ardeshir's widow, Virbai, their four daughters, three sons and the new addition to the family.[5]

We know hardly anything about Khurshedben's youth. Her mother and siblings moved between Bhuj, the seat of the Kutch darbar, and Bombay, where the rest of the Naoroji clan dwelt, while Dadabhai Naoroji remained ensconced in imperial politics in London. In family letters dispatched from Bombay to London, which Dadabhai preserved, we find Khurshedben's earliest writings: a childhood scribble in Gujarati from April 1906, for example, where eleven-year-old Khurshedben excitedly informed her grandfather about the upcoming Easter school holidays. Otherwise, few sources within India tell us anything about the first three decades of her life.[6]

For more clues about Khurshedben's formative years, it is necessary to interrogate the archival records of family members and friends. The lives of her elder sisters, in particular, offer us valuable clues on how Khurshedben grew up in a home environment that was remarkably forward-looking in terms of social norms and political activity. Dadabhai Naoroji was a committed supporter of female education, and he therefore ensured that his granddaughters received the same educational opportunities as his grandsons. Meher (1881–1974), the eldest of Virbai and Ardeshir's eight children, earned a medical degree at the University of Edinburgh in 1906 and quite likely became the university's first female Indian graduate. Around the same time, Meher's two younger sisters travelled to Europe for education. Gosi (1884–1976) studied at Oxford while Perin (1888–1958) pursued a degree in French literature at the Sorbonne in Paris. Khurshedben's elder sisters therefore enjoyed a degree of emancipation unheard of for most elite Indian women of the time—and also set a very high bar in the family for achievement.[7]

Additionally, Khurshedben's sisters took up nationalist politics. Dadabhai requested Bhikhaiji Rustomji Cama, the Parsi revolutionary nationalist, to look after Perin while she was in the French capital. Cama did much more than supervise the Grand Old Man's granddaughter: she introduced Perin to fellow Indian radicals based in Europe and a wider circle of exiled revolutionaries from around the world. By 1910, British intelligence picked up reports that Perin was eagerly learning the art of bomb-making from a Polish radical. Of equal worry to intelligence officers was Perin's close relationship with V.D. Savarkar. She accompanied Savarkar to London in August 1910, where he was arrested at Victoria Station, and later greeted the incarcerated radical with a hearty 'Bande Mataram' before his bewildered jailers. By this time, Perin seems to have pulled her sister Gosi into revolutionary nationalist circles. In the Indian subcontinent, government sleuths followed the movements of the two women and made plans for Perin to be 'watched on her arrival in India most discreetly and carefully'.[8]

Their revolutionary zeal was not to last. Instead, once Mohandas K. Gandhi returned to India in 1915, Perin and Gosi—now back in Bombay—undertook a dramatic transformation in their political demeanour, renouncing the cult of the bomb for the creed of non-violence. It is here that Khurshedben briefly re-enters the historical record. While she does not seem to have gone through a revolutionary stage, she evidently did arouse the interest of intelligence officers. In 1919, she wrote to a young Jawaharlal Nehru (a close friend of her brother, Jal), informing him of French authorities' efforts to gather intelligence on her after she tried to get in touch with women leaders in Indochina. And she shared her sisters' pluck and their enthusiasm for the nationalist cause. Khurshedben appears to have joined Gandhi on a tour through Gujarat in 1920. It is quite likely that she took on the mantle of a satyagrahi during the Non-Cooperation movement, joining Perin, Gosi and another sister, Nurgis (b. 1887), who popularized khadi production in Bombay and mobilized women volunteers by helping found the Rashtriya Stree Sabha. Gandhi took note of their exertions. Speaking about Dadabhai Naoroji at an event in Colombo in 1927, he remarked that 'today his grand-daughters are a tower of strength to me in my khadi work'.[9]

Khurshedben simultaneously took on another vocation: singing. Once more, there were family antecedents. Dadabhai Naoroji had been an enthusiastic member of Bombay's Gayan Uttejak Mandli, an organization that promoted Indian classical music. Earlier British intelligence files had noted Perin's penchant for singing nationalist songs at gatherings of revolutionaries in Paris. Instead of the Indian tradition or patriotic numbers, Khurshedben concentrated on European classical music. A music critic for the *Times of India*, reviewing her debut performance with the Bombay Chamber Orchestra, where she sang arias by Puccini and Offenbach, observed appreciatively that 'the range of her voice is wide and the tone of her upper register is specially pleasing'.[10]

In her mid-twenties, Khurshedben was on the cusp of a promising career as a soprano, a full-time occupation that would leave little time for political work. She earned the moniker 'Bul' (nightingale) amongst family members and friends, including the Nehru family. This prompted a life-changing event. Following in the footsteps of her sisters, she sailed to Europe sometime before 1924 for higher education, taking up classical music lessons in Paris with the acclaimed teacher Claire Croiza. We do not know if she met Bhikhaiji Rustomji Cama while in the French capital. But she did meet an equally remarkable woman: Eva Palmer-Sikelianos (1874–1952). Sikelianos, a wealthy American heiress who had relocated to Athens, was one of the most fervent architects behind the revival of classical Greek culture and tradition in the early twentieth century. She was best known for staging the Delphic festivals of 1927 and 1930 with her husband. As Cama had done for Perin, Sikelianos would help Khurshedben navigate between her studies and political activity.[11]

It is difficult enough to reconstruct Khurshedben's early life through her sisters. Doing so through Sikelianos, a New York blue blood married to a Greek poet, is even more challenging. Yet, it is through Sikelianos that we hear Khurshedben's own voice for the first time, thanks to sustained correspondence that survives in a library in Athens—recently discovered by Sikelianos's biographer, Artemis Leontis—and passages in the American's autobiography. The two women met through music. Sikelianos had spent nearly two decades as a student in Athens, absorbed in the world of Greek musical traditions, when, in 1924, she visited Paris as part of an attempt to procure a pipe organ. Here, she somehow befriended Khurshedben, finding the aspiring musician to be mired in frustration. As Sikelianos noted in her autobiography, Khurshedben was now attempting to use her classical musical training to notate traditional Indian music, passed down orally and in danger of disappearing due to Western influence. 'But, I must be very stupid,' she confided to Sikelianos, 'for I still cannot play the simplest Hindu melody on the piano, nor can I write any song of my own country.'[12]

Sikelianos 'jumped a foot' when she heard of Khurshedben's troubles. She explained that she had been studying Byzantine musical notation in Athens to save Greece's own oral tradition of music—and that this system of notation could be easily deployed in the Indian context, as well. After a successful attempt to notate and recite one Indian melody, Khurshedben exclaimed to her new friend, 'You are singing my songs.' She immediately took up Sikelianos's invitation to join her in Greece to study Byzantine notation and help Sikelianos establish a special school of non-Western music.[13]

In the warmer and sunnier Hellenic climes, Khurshedben flourished. Dispensing with her training in Western classical music, she demonstrated her fluency in the Indian tradition. 'We had the joy of seeing her,' Sikelianos recalled, 'seated on a pillow, with her little Indian drums, one between her knees, and one on the ground beside her; and her tiny hands and delicate wrists would bring out extraordinary resonance from these fascinating instruments.' She stayed with the Sikelianoses for several months, gaining some proficiency in Byzantine notation and acquiring a range of musical and cultural contacts—one visitor invited Khurshedben to travel to Persia to document oral musical traditions in villages. And she was absorbed into the family of her American friend. Khurshedben referred to Sikelianos as 'Mummy', while the latter's family adopted her pet name of 'Bul'.[14]

The true significance of Khurshedben's time in Greece lay outside the realm of music. Unexpectedly, 'Mother Greece', as she referred to it, drew her closer to Mother India. Amidst the rugged Greek landscape, Khurshedben was reminded of her home and the nationalist political struggle. A railway trip from Patras to Sykia, Sikelianos recalled, caused her to make 'the statement that she felt as if she was seeing India, but India "all joined together," as if she was seeing North, South, East and West, all in one. "A sort of essence," she said, "of India."' Khurshedben set aside her Western attire, which she had adopted in Paris, and resumed wearing traditional Parsi saris. As was the case with her sisters Perin and Gosi, time in Europe evidently stirred Khurshedben's feelings of national identity and patriotism. It is notable that this occurred in Greece rather than Paris—the French capital, after all, hosted a large number of politically minded Indian students and revolutionaries. In later correspondence, after she returned to Paris from Greece, Khurshedben spoke of Gandhi and her desire to 'take the "khadi" vow', signalling a definite transformation of interest from music to anti-colonial activity. This was confirmed when Khurshedben turned down Sikelianos's request to come back to Athens and help her plan the first Delphic Festival. Khurshedben instead made plans for her return voyage to Bombay.[15]

An American in Greece, therefore, played an unintentional but instrumental role in forging a Parsi Indian woman's nationalist convictions. Even by the standards of the Indian nationalist movement, which spun complicated webs of personalities and ideas around the world, this was a uniquely transnational episode.

II

Khurshedben Naoroji returned to India in March 1925. She was not pleased with what she saw. 'India is unhappy,' she told Eva Palmer-Sikelianos. 'The poor are poorer than before.' Her observations of Indian poverty were coupled with a dawning realization of her own wealth and privilege. Writing to Sikelianos from her family's bungalow on Bombay's posh Nepean Sea Road, Khurshedben confessed, 'I hate to live in the house I'm living and hate to see so much waste of food and to go about in a car when millions are starving.' All of these emotions and experiences fired remarkably strong sentiments against Western cultural influences. She was disheartened to find an influx of automobiles and 'cheap European finery' in Bombay, signs of a foreign-imposed modernity. Virbai, her mother, had 'noticed indifference and a certain hardness towards European civilization in my letters', and had 'spoken to Gandhiji about it'. In one of her last letters to Sikelianos, written in Bombay's intense April heat in 1925, Khurshedben stated her resolve to establish an Indian music academy, something that could counteract the inroads Western music had made through the proliferation of radios and phonographs.[16]

This did not come to pass. In spite of some soprano performances in Bombay, Khurshedben seems to have fully renounced her musical ambitions by the late 1920s, instead pledging all her energies to Gandhi and his movement. It is extremely difficult to reconstruct the next few years of her life, but Gandhi and his associates offer us some clues. The Mahatma took an evident interest in Khurshedben's musical talents. After she visited him at Sabarmati Ashram in the second half of 1928, Gandhi encouraged her 'to add Indian music to your accomplishments' and held out hope that she would eventually 'be able to take to the Ashram life.' A few months later, Khurshedben acted as an interlocutor between Gandhi and an Indochinese delegation visiting Calcutta, while Gandhi invited Khurshedben to join him on a proposed tour through Burma. Steadily, it seems, Khurshedben was drawn to Gandhi's work that involved foreign relations or, like Burma, affairs on the very peripheries of the Indian empire. By 1931, Pyarelal Nayyar, one of Gandhi's secretaries, was relying upon Khurshedben to translate incoming correspondence from Europe.[17]

Within a remarkably quick period, Khurshedben began moving closer to Gandhi's inner circle. During the Civil Disobedience Movement, while Perin remained in Bombay and commandeered women volunteers of the newly ordained Desh Sevika Sangh, Gandhi ordered Khurshedben to train female satyagrahis in Sabarmati Ashram. She coordinated activities in villages surrounding Ahmedabad, sending regular dispatches to Gandhi on their progress: sanitation programmes and the picketing of stores selling liquor and foreign cloth, including the thorny question of how to picket a liquor store owned by a fellow Parsi.[18]

From correspondence and speeches that Gandhi delivered during the Salt March, it is clear that Khurshedben played a small but definite role in changing the Mahatma's attitudes towards women's broader involvement in nationalist work. Gandhi had originally insisted that women play a visibly second-tier role in the Civil Disobedience Movement, one limited to picketing and weaving khadi. But Khurshedben's forthrightness and leadership impressed the Mahatma. She might have issued a strongly worded protest against Gandhi's exclusion of women in the Salt March.

Later, Gandhi surveyed how Khurshedben and Mridula Sarabhai had encouraged proper sanitation in a village along the Salt March's route. 'In this campaign of swaraj by self-purification,' he pronounced following his visit, 'it will be nothing surprising if the women outdo the men.' Gandhi subsequently tried to involve Khurshedben in a special conference in Dandi for defining women's roles in the Civil Disobedience Movement. As importantly, Khurshedben specifically saw the movement as an opportunity for female empowerment. The *Bombay Chronicle* reported her saying that Gandhian activity allowed for 'the great awakening of women'—and that women were 'not going to stop their work so well begun'.[19]

In rapid-fire succession in early October 1930, Khurshedben was appointed as secretary of the Ahmedabad District Congress Committee and arrested. This was likely the first of her many stints in jail through the 1930s. Some two years after her release in Ahmedabad, a brief telegram from Gandhi indicates that she was behind bars again, this time in Lahore, where her failing health necessitated a medical operation. What was she doing in Punjab? As we have seen, Khurshedben was continually attracted to foreign or frontier locales in relation to her nationalist activities. Her stint in a Lahore jail cell was likely the result of work that she began in the NWFP. Here, the Civil Disobedience Movement had thrown up a remarkable leader, Khan Abdul Ghaffar Khan, who preached non-violence to his fellow Pashtuns. It is not possible to determine whether Khurshedben went to the NWFP on her own accord or as an ambassador of the Mahatma, who took great interest in the 'Frontier Gandhi' and his body of non-violent volunteers, the Khudai Khidmatgars. Regardless, Khurshedben, along with Gandhi's son Devadas, became early intermediaries between the two leaders. By June 1933, Gandhi could use Khurshedben's reports from the NWFP to reassure his old friend, C.F. Andrews, about Ghaffar Khan and his movement. Although she and Devadas had found him 'hot-tempered' and 'hasty in action', they were 'convinced that there was no guile about Abdul Ghaffar Khan'. Khurshedben helped rubbish the rumour that the Frontier Gandhi was an agent of King Amanullah of Afghanistan.[20]

Gandhi urged Andrews to rely upon the young Indian woman's testimony, as she was 'free of hysterics, full of faith and spirituality', and had come 'in intimate touch with the people' of the NWFP. An undated letter from Khurshedben to Devadas might offer more clues for precisely how she established relations with Pashtuns during one of her first visits to the Frontier. With remarkable vigour and candour, Khurshedben spread Gandhi's messages of non-violence and constructive work to anyone she came across. She hectored local Congress workers about their pace of activity, asked members of the Hindu minority to volunteer and make financial contributions to the Congress, appealed to the local police force and 'rubbed it in as to how Bapu loves them' and gave 'a short but stiff dose of advice to Government officials from magistrate downwards'. Copies of Gandhi's writings, she informed Devadas, were cyclostyled and distributed across Peshawar. There is little information about how Pashtuns received Khurshedben, but she undoubtedly created quite a stir in a region unaccustomed to political campaigns being waged by an unaccompanied, independent-minded woman.[21]

Inevitably, she was arrested. Yet, within the confines of the Peshawar prison, 'where the fleas & I kept each other warm', Khurshedben found new candidates for her appeals. She spoke to fellow inmates in the criminal ward, 'shook hands with them' and 'blessed them & other criminals, between 5A.M. & 7A.M'. Her jailers, no doubt perplexed and worried about the activities of their inmate, felt it would be wiser to wash their hands of her. They put her on the next Frontier Mail to Lahore under police escort. Writing from Lahore, Khurshedben told Devadas that she was now free from police custody and, therefore, plotting ways to return to the NWFP—perhaps repeating the cycle of agitation and incarceration once more. But Khurshedben's dogged insistence on returning to the Frontier had a clear purpose. She stressed, above all, the need for Gandhi and the Congress to augment support for the Khudai Khidmatgars. She was visibly impressed with their sacrifices, noting that Frontier jails were bursting with members of Ghaffar Khan's non-violent organization, who were being subjected to awful tortures in a vain effort to coax them to violence. 'We *must* keep on sending people to keep up their spirit,' she implored.[22]

Through the 1930s, Khurshedben continued to champion the political interests of the NWFP. There were, however, moments of doubt about herself, her political work, and Gandhi. For example, in December 1932 she took issue with Gandhi's insistence on undertaking a fast out of a sense of disappointment. 'Have you been disappointed in us?' Khurshedben asked Gandhi accusingly. 'I gave up my artistic aptitude on the altar of service just for your sake and your cause. Why are you still disappointed?'

Gandhi assured her that his planned fast was inspired by 'hope eternal'. But Khurshedben's own sense of hope and resolve seemed to be faltering. A major health setback during one prison stint no doubt further dampened her spirits. Indeed, in an attempt to rekindle correspondence with Eva Palmer-Sikelianos in the mid-1930s, she recounted to her old friend that 'years of prison life, coupled with solitary confinement has left me weaker in body'. She sent a meandering note to Gandhi in June 1935 that was permeated with self-doubt and self-criticism. 'How can I search for Truth when I evade Truth in my daily existence,' she asked rhetorically. 'I am a coward.' To cite an example, Khurshedben noted that, the previous day, she had encountered a wounded panther outside of the Gujarati town of Bhilad but did not have the courage to comfort and treat the animal. 'We are a long way from fraternizing with panthers,' Gandhi retorted. Eager to help, the Mahatma contemplated dispatching her to another frontier region, somewhere in the fastness of the Himalayas, for work. He ultimately encouraged her to find solace at Sri Aurobindo's ashram in Pondicherry.[23]

A spiritual restlessness stalked Khurshedben into middle age, which perhaps limited further opportunities to return to the NWFP. In 1937, she threatened to fully withdraw from society and cut off all human contact. Gandhi presciently warned her against such a move. 'You may run away even from those who love you. But what about them?' he counselled. 'You can no more run away from men than you can from your own body.' But he ended on a pleading note, indicating his deep reluctance to lose a trusted and loyal supporter. 'Oh, do please wake up from your sleep. You may forget me, disown me, [but] I simply cannot forget you,' he wrote. 'What shall I do?'[24]

III

So far, Khurshedben Naoroji's life has unfurled in snippets—some long and detailed and others tantalizingly vague, requiring significant guesswork and conjecture. However, for a two-year period—from April 1940 until the eve of the Quit India Movement in summer 1942—the archival record is unusually rich. Within Mohandas K. Gandhi's papers is a trove of letters from Khurshedben, many brimming with details about her political ideas and work in the Frontier during the remainder of 1940. Even the ever-prolific Gandhi remarked about the scale of this correspondence, wryly noting that she was 'raining letters' on him.[25]

Khurshedben returned to the Frontier to promote Hindu–Muslim unity and Congress support amongst Pashtuns. Her letters provide remarkable insight into the courage and determination that fired her work and the utter perseverance with which she carried out her duties. By 1940, she had established exceptionally strong relations with Abdul Ghaffar Khan and other prominent figures in the NWFP. In her first surviving dispatch to Gandhi from her 1940 tour, she outlined an ambitious agenda of visiting villages between the distant towns of Bannu and Dera Ismail Khan, attending Congress meetings, encouraging spinning of khadi and, above all, speaking with locals. 'I am cultivating the art of listening,' she stated. On these 'wanderings', as she termed them, she was likely alone or accompanied by a few men. This was an extremely risky endeavour. Not only was the NWFP a deeply conservative society, but it was also a region plagued by armed bandits and kidnappers. In a later missive to Gandhi, Khurshedben offhandedly noted an occasion where 'bullets hissed in the sand near me'.[26]

She persisted. Under scorching summer sun and fierce pre-winter gales, Khurshedben made increasingly lengthy tours on foot, living off 'dirty' food and water that was 'tea coloured'. Bouts of malaria did not slow her down. In November, against the express wishes of local Congress workers, she set out on an approximately week-long tour of Waziri-inhabited regions, which involved 60 miles of walking through around forty villages. But first, she confessed to Gandhi, she had to 'rest my feet for a couple of days' since 'they are cut open with the sand and wet and cold'.[27]

How precisely did she undertake her tours? A few factors worked in Khurshedben's favour. Firstly, she reached out to women. Amongst the women of the Frontier, she found friends and fervent supporters—who no doubt influenced their menfolk to greet her with hospitality rather than a loaded gun. On her tour through Waziri villages, she wrote that 'the women are wonderful & enthusiastic'. There were, however, unique challenges to working with women. Due to prevailing social norms, reinforced by strict orders issued by Ghaffar Khan, Khurshedben knew that it was impossible for them to join her as itinerant political activists. She therefore limited her outreach to matters of sanitation and self-help, although she felt that 'the women all over are better equipped for a non-violent struggle' than the men.[28]

Secondly, Khurshedben had an uncanny ability to judge the character of local leaders and identify promising foot soldiers in the local Congress branches. She recommended a handful of outstanding volunteers to Gandhi, such as Fateh Chand, 'a young Hindu student full of zeal & devotion'. Fateh Chand would later distinguish himself in nationalist politics in the NWFP—and a thin, uncatalogued file of his papers at the Nehru Memorial Museum and Library testifies to his enduring work with Khurshedben. Amongst these papers is a Pashto-language speech, written in Roman script in Khurshedben's distinctive hand, with occasional transliterations in Gujarati script. The speech indicates a final factor behind Khurshedben's success: her steady mastery of local languages. She modestly acknowledged possessing 'halting Pashtu' and 'bad Urdu'. However, given the sheer scale of her outreach and speaking activities in the NWFP, it is likely that Khurshedben was more fluent in these languages than she cared to admit.[29]

Traversing the arid valleys and hills of the Frontier, Khurshedben realized that she had to take on an added, weightier responsibility to her political work. The local Hindu population had been terrorized by dacoits—bandits who streamed in from Waziristan, part of the 'unsettled' tribal territories that was largely autonomous of British control, to conduct kidnappings and raids. Consequently, Hindus had retreated from the political sphere and had been extremely reluctant to work with the Congress or Ghaffar Khan, instead seeking the protective embrace of British authorities. In order to convince Hindus to join the Congress, and in order to achieve true Hindu–Muslim unity in the Frontier, Khurshedben knew that she had to intervene. She decided to preach non-violence to the dacoits. This was an understandably difficult task: in spite of the best efforts of the Khudai Khidmatgars, the NWFP was still a place largely defined by violent discord rather than peace. Khurshedben also realized that her particular political message sounded strange to many locals. 'It is amusing to see the surprise of the Waziris; because they're not in the habit of hearing that people without arms, guns & the like can be brave,' she wrote to Gandhi during her November tour through Waziri villages. 'They do not know or understand such words as soul-force. We have to explain to them that violence is man & gun & non-violence is man & God.'[30]

Such words might sound a little patronizing today—and Khurshedben did occasionally indulge in stereotypical assessment of Pashtuns as an innately martial, warlike people. But it is clear that she understood the real reasons for violent crime in the region, such as extreme poverty and unemployment. The tehsil most plagued by dacoities, Khurshedben explained to Gandhi, had experienced famine-like conditions for the past four years. She therefore urged Congress leaders to promote locally produced cloth 'to give the starving weavers a chance to survive instead of turning [into] dacoits'. In addition to economic factors, Khurshedben came to the unsettling conclusion that local British authorities had a hand in promoting 'badmashi' in the Frontier. Colonial officials could control cross-border raids from Waziristan to their advantage: they vigorously pursued a few raiders to woo local Hindu support, and then looked the other way to ensure that the fear of kidnapping prevented political consolidation between Hindus and Muslims. Although Khurshedben offered no direct proof to Gandhi of government connivance, she asserted that a wide spectrum of locals—both Hindus and Muslims, pro-Congress and anti-Congress—agreed with her assessment.[31]

In spite of incredible odds, Khurshedben achieved some tangible success in her crusade against dacoity. She certainly helped change the mindsets of local people. In early May, for example, she actually sallied into a camp of raiders and, appealing to the 'ancient Pathan code of honour', urged them to free some kidnapped Hindus who had been sold in Waziristan. It was 'difficult for them to realize that they had no right to sell those whom they had kidnapped', Khurshedben recounted, but through gentle counsel, she tried to convince her listeners of their misdeeds. Her audacious diplomatic efforts ended with her interlocutors promising 'to carry the Congress message of peace & good will to all raiders'. Aside from approaching kidnappers, she also pursued slightly less death-defying avenues for her work. During her outreach to women, Khurshedben specifically sought out the female relatives of well-known dacoits: mothers, sisters and daughters. One mother of a dacoit was so moved by her appeals that she 'swore that she would not cook for him' or let him 'lay his head under her roof till he gave up being a dacoit'. Khurshedben was particularly successful in linking the immorality of dacoity with the broader anti-colonial struggle. Kidnapping and raiding, she claimed, were forms of dishonesty that helped perpetuate foreign rule. She also met with local Muslim clerics and pirs, urging them to counter the prevalent sentiment that kidnapping kaffirs was a religious duty.[32]

By the time that winter descended on the Frontier, Khurshedben had become a much-admired figure in the province, widely credited for a steady drop in kidnappings. A barrister in Bannu wrote to Gandhi in December

1940, praising her 'iron will, indomitable courage and transparent sincerity'. 'That she carried on her good work for over 8 months without any molestation,' he stated, 'in an area which could not be called very peaceful, is a clear indication of the popularity Ben ji enjoyed.' The decrease in kidnappings strengthened the Congress. Hindus became less ambivalent towards the party, and Muslim Congressmen became more committed towards stamping out the practice. Khurshedben even received an unexpected letter of praise from the British deputy commissioner of Bannu.[33]

And yet she was not satisfied. Word reached Khurshedben that dacoits were holding eight Hindu captives in Walo Tangi, a scorched valley just across the border from 'settled' tribal territory in Waziristan. British authorities had been unsuccessful in freeing the captives and, in spite of their praise for Khurshedben's work, they categorically refused to let her cross the border. It was far too dangerous—and they worried about her Congress propaganda amongst the Waziris. Characteristically, Khurshedben resolved to defy government orders and make an attempt to set the captives free. Local Congress officials balked. Four steadfast volunteers, including Fateh Chand, agreed to join her, but she ultimately went alone, refusing to even hire a coolie to carry her bedding. Khurshedben was fully aware that, by attempting to reach Walo Tangi, she was risking grave personal injury or death. She warned Gandhi that, if dacoits captured her alive, they 'would occasionally chop off a finger or a[n] ear or even the nose & send it to you asking for my ransom'. This did not seem to faze her. On 3 December 1940, Khurshedben dispatched one final letter before she tried to cross the Waziristan border and proceed to Walo Tangi. 'God has been good to me,' she stated. 'This will be done.'[34]

She never reached there. British officers arrested her at the border the following day, sentencing her to a Rs 100 fine or three months in jail. Khurshedben, of course, chose the latter. After releasing her from the Bannu jailhouse, Frontier officials deported her to Bombay with a warning from the Government of India not to leave the city. It took Khurshedben little time to compose a series of polite letters, informing Bombay's police commissioner and other authorities that the internment order 'insults my intelligence' and that she intended to disobey it. On 1 August 1941, while attempting to travel to Sevagram to visit Gandhi, she was arrested and jailed without trial at Yerawada. Gandhi issued a notice to the press, protesting that this crusader against dacoits had finally been 'kidnapped', albeit by the British.[35]

It is difficult to say what, precisely, happened from this point onward. In December 1942 she was arrested again, this time in Bihar, along with the wife of Jayaprakash Narayan. Despite the pleas of her sisters Perin and Nurgis as well as Gandhi—who lobbied on Khurshedben's behalf while interned at the Aga Khan's palace—she languished in Bihari jails until March 1944, when she was transferred to Yerawada jail and released a few months later. The British government, however, kept alive an order prohibiting Khurshedben from the NWFP, Punjab and Baluchistan until May 1945: colonial authorities were deeply worried that her activities in these provinces could prejudice the war effort. Such was the threat posed by a middle-aged, classically trained female singer to the mighty British Empire.[36]

* * *

While in the NWFP in 1940, and before her long incarceration in Bihar, Khurshedben did much more than just campaign for non-violence and against dacoity. She became an astute commentator on India's political dilemmas. In the Frontier, for example, she developed her long-standing interest in foreign affairs, formulating nuanced views on India's future border and foreign policy. Via numerous letters to Gandhi, she implored Congress leaders to devote more resources to Frontier affairs, including dispatching a high-ranking Working Committee member, such as Rajendra Prasad or C. Rajagopalachari, to be a border emissary. Such an emissary could hammer out an understanding with tribes for the NWFP's future: whether the province would remain within India, or whether Pashtuns would elect for a federated tribal state. Whatever the outcome, the Congress's policy needed to be dictated by border security concerns. 'We should be more realists in our outlook in foreign affairs,' she lectured Gandhi. This was especially the case during wartime. Throughout 1940 and 1941, as Axis forces came within closer proximity to the subcontinent, Khurshedben urged the Congress to develop a defence policy in case Britain suffered defeat. She expressed worry that Germany could stir up trouble through Afghanistan, encouraging secessionist sentiment in Baluchistan and the NWFP, or that Great Britain would concede these two provinces to the Afghan emir, 'with probably Karachi thrown in', in a last-ditch attempt to secure India's borders from a German onslaught.[37]

By delineating these wartime scenarios, Khurshedben also revealed her growing scepticism about political prospects in the Frontier. In spite of her success in fostering some trust between local Hindus and Muslims, communal tensions remained high—and she claimed to be uniquely qualified to judge the situation on the ground. 'The Hindus do not trust the Mohammedans & vice versa & it needed a Parsi to show that to both,' Khurshedben declared to Gandhi. Worryingly, there was rank discord between Hindus and Muslims in local police forces, something that exacerbated the incidence of dacoity. As she surveyed the widening communal divisions across the subcontinent, Khurshedben urged the Mahatma and Abdul Ghaffar Khan to 'act as one person, without any reserve': only their example and joint leadership could salvage Hindu–Muslim relations. But the Frontier Gandhi was also a source of concern. He had 'no plan and Satyagrah [sic] has fallen flat'. Bogged down by factional disputes within the Khudai Khidmatgars, Ghaffar Khan was no longer in close contact with the people, which had damaged his standing amongst Pashtuns. 'Khan Sahib has not the same influence he had in 1930 & even the Government officials say the same,' Khurshedben related. A further complication was that the provincial Congress ministry in power during 1937–39 had 'not been very brilliant'; indeed, it had 'left its mark of disillusionment' upon locals.[38]

All of these factors led Khurshedben to question the long-term prospects of the Congress in the Frontier. Writing to Gandhi a year after the Lahore Resolution brought the issue of Pakistan to national prominence, she worried about the Muslim League's growing influence amongst Pashtuns. 'Some Muslims are waiting for Jinnah to pull the chestnuts out of the fire & then they will change their political allegiance,' she warned. A far more immediate threat was posed by Mirza Ali Khan, better known as the Fakir of Ipi. He was a violent Waziri rebel whose daring raids and guerilla manoeuvres had utterly terrorized British forces, which had been pulled into a wider insurgency in Waziristan during the late 1930s. Khurshedben repeatedly urged Gandhi to reach out to the wily Fakir and make the simmering conflict in Waziristan an 'all India question'. When this did not come to pass, she despaired, predicting that the Fakir would soon steal momentum from Ghaffar Khan and that the Congress would be 'finished'. He was a 'rising power' across the Frontier, calling for the violent delivery of an independent Pashtunistan, and not even the Frontier Gandhi could prevent his own Khudai Khidmatgars from defecting to the Waziri rebel.[39]

Amidst these worries and concerns, Khurshedben singled out another source of disappointment: the Mahatma. As a political leader, Gandhi was unique in the sense that he heartily welcomed criticism from allies and subordinates. And, during the first half of 1940, Khurshedben emerged as one of the most vocal and fearless critics within his camp. Her protests centred on the Congress's ongoing negotiations with the Raj. In the months following October 1939, when the Congress ministries had tendered their resignations, Gandhi struggled to formulate a wartime policy that balanced sympathy for the Allied cause with growing impatience for independence. Khurshedben quickly identified herself as a supporter of sustained wartime confrontation with the Raj, and thus savaged Gandhi for supposedly weak-kneed prevarication. The tone of her letters is quite remarkable. In a May 1940 dispatch to Gandhi, she ridiculed him as a 'Generalissimo . . . waiting for the inner voice & like the proverbial Nero fiddling away while Rome is burning'. The next month, she remarked with frustration that 'the revolutionary urge has gone out of you'. According to Khurshedben, Gandhi had surrounded himself with acolytes and politicians in Sevagram and was now out of touch with his foot soldiers, who were eager for the commencement of a new campaign. She therefore pleaded with him to 'cease to be a Mahatma' and 'be truly one with the poor'—a particularly stinging rebuke given the persona Gandhi had cultivated.[40]

Khurshedben's frustrations extended to other Congress stalwarts—she called for a general 'change of leadership' and did not seem to care much for the new party president, Maulana Azad—but her candour with Gandhi, specifically, tells us much about how she had evolved into an inspired, self-confident leader of men and women. She felt qualified to judge the consistency of Gandhi's politics and his commitment to overall nationalist objectives. 'You are not negotiating for yourself or your pet theories,' she hectored him in the summer of 1940, when Gandhi was still conversing with the British viceroy in order to avoid a political impasse, 'but for the lives & dignity of 35 crores of people.' Hiding none of her innermost feelings, she accused the Mahatma, a leader who claimed intimate association with the most humble and destitute of his political volunteers, of profound betrayal. In fact, Khurshedben felt herself to be a spokesperson for ordinary Congress volunteers—the 'under-dog' with whom 'I work & whose minds & wishes I represent'—who were now anxiously waiting for their leader to make up his mind about civil disobedience. Gone was the self-doubt and spiritual torment that stalked Khurshedben in the late 1930s. In its place was bold conviction and moral certitude. She threatened to resign from the Congress if Gandhi ruled that her demeanour was out of line, although she held out hope that 'someday Congress will take back its rebels with pride'.[41]

None of the Mahatma's replies, if any were written, survive. It is therefore difficult to judge how Khurshedben's forceful criticisms were judged in Sevagram. They produced no rupture—indeed, from the scanty evidence available, Gandhi's ties with his vocal critic seemed to only strengthen through the early 1940s. After Khurshedben's arrest at the Waziristan border, one of her supporters in Bannu wrote to Gandhi, claiming, 'We Indians need not be pessimistic about our future freedom, when Mother India can give birth to such brave daughters.' As the Mahatma especially knew, that sense of bravery was well apparent in both Khurshedben's deeds and words.[42]

IV

After her release from prison in the twilight months of the Second World War, the narrative thread of Khurshedben Naoroji's life once again becomes obscure. A sheaf of letters from the files of the Bombay Pradesh Congress Committee indicates that, in late 1944 and early 1945, she played an important role as one of Gandhi's secretaries in Sevagram, scrambling to help restart the Congress machinery once its leaders had been released from wartime incarceration. The Mahatma's correspondence from late 1945 reveals some of her work in Delhi on behalf of the defence committee for soldiers of Subhas Chandra Bose's vanquished Indian National Army, who were being tried by British authorities behind the sandstone walls of the Red Fort. A few months before Independence, Khurshedben's interests swerved back to Indochina, when she offered her services as a French-language translator for an Indian medical mission to war-ravaged Vietnam. Finally, by January 1948, as is revealed in Gandhi's last-ever surviving letter to his long-time friend and associate, Khurshedben was in a girls' school in Jalandhar in Punjab, perhaps assisting Partition refugees.[43]

Jalandhar was as close as Khurshedben got to the NWFP after she was released from prison. She was no doubt anguished to watch, from afar, as her beloved Frontier slipped into chaos and was relinquished by the Congress to Pakistan, and as Abdul Ghaffar Khan expressed the heavy weight of betrayal from his former Congress colleagues. A heartbreaking letter in the papers of her former associate from Bannu, Fateh Chand, reveals that she did not forget her friends. In the letter, Khurshedben appealed to an associate to help Fateh Chand, 'who has suffered for the cause we held so dear' and who was now, along with his family, a penniless refugee in a Delhi camp. Partition is also the final challenge for Indian biography that I would like to identify in this article. The bloody vivisection of the subcontinent, and decades of bitter India–Pakistan relations, scattered historical records between two hostile powers. In order to thoroughly investigate Khurshedben's life story, an Indian scholar would need to cross the border and visit the archives of the erstwhile NWFP in Rawalpindi.[44]

As with the first decades of her life, Khurshedben's last years are largely a blank slate. She disappears from archival records and newspaper columns. So complete is this disappearance, in fact, that it has been impossible for me to verify when she died. While some sources claim, without attribution, that she died in 1966, one author improbably asserts that she survived until 1996. We cannot rely on any family accounts for a definite answer. Khurshedben never married and none of her siblings had any children. When her last surviving brother passed away in 1980, Dadabhai Naoroji's line came to an end, a trove of lived memory vanished, and any family papers and belongings were likely relegated to the scrapheap. This is hardly a unique fate for an individual of historical importance in India. And the lack of evidence about Khurshedben's death poignantly illustrates the argument I wish to make about the difficulty of Indian biography. When it is not possible to ascertain such a vital detail, how can we expect to adequately weave together the various surviving strands of Khurshedben's life and career?[45]

Amidst the paucity of evidence on Khurshedben's last years, there is only one thing that we can definitively establish, which is conveyed through a few scattered newspaper articles. It is this: the singer-turned-satyagrahi rediscovered her musical talents. In January 1952, she relaunched her career as a classical soprano in Bombay's Sir Cowasji Jehangir Hall, where she had performed in the 1920s. Before a packed audience which included Jawaharlal Nehru as the chief guest, she sang a mix of French, Spanish and Italian pieces. The *Times of India*'s music critic noted that 'the timbre of her voice may have lost a little in flexibility, but it is courageous of her to appear in public after sacrificing 20 years of hard labour of love for the country'. On a stage before a genteel Bombay audience and the Indian prime minister, Khurshedben continued to exhibit her characteristic bravery.[46]

Gandhi, too, had been fortunate to witness Khurshedben's renewed musical interest. In September 1944, an American journalist for *Time* witnessed her trying to cheer up the Mahatma, weary from protracted talks with Muhammad Ali Jinnah. She sang a parody of Gilbert and Sullivan's tune 'On a Tree by a River', from the opera *The Mikado*:

> A Mahatma sat singing on top of a fence
> 'Quit India, quit India, quit India.'
> He would pause for a while, then again would commence
> 'Quit India, quit India, quit India.'
> And I said, 'Oh Mahatma, I fear I am dense
> But your song doesn't seem to make very much sense.'
> His reply was to chant in a tone more intense.
> 'Quit India, quit India, quit India.'

The Mahatma, the *Time* journalist reported, 'was amused'.[47]

ACKNOWLEDEGMENTS

During the past ten years, Ramachandra Guha has been an important mentor and guide for me. I am deeply indebted to him for his generous support, which has included critical evaluations of my dissertation and other publications, fulfilment of far too many of my pesky requests for letters of recommendation and constant encouragement in my research endeavours.

I must thank Murali Ranganathan for his comments and suggestions for this essay. I am deeply grateful to Artemis Leontis for providing me with photographs of letters from Khurshedben Naoroji which she located in the Eva Sikelianou Papers at the Benaki Museum Historical Archives in Athens.

8

'GROCER, TAILOR, CHAMPION WRESTLER': THE TRANSNATIONAL CAREER OF BUTTAN SINGH, c. 1900–1912

PRASHANT KIDAMBI

I

THE FIRST SATURDAY of November 1904 saw a packed house at the Wirth Brothers' Circus in Melbourne. The audience that evening was treated to 'an all-embracing and comprehensive' programme of entertainment. They witnessed daring equestrian feats, thrilling performances by acrobats and contortionists, and variety acts featuring baboons, bears, camels, elephants, lions, tigers, and 'the only football dog in Australia'.[1] As the show moved towards its finale, two Indian men bounded on to the stage. One was a lithe Sikh, and he offered ten pounds to anyone who could last fifteen minutes in the ring against him or his companion. Even as he scanned the audience, a murmur arose in the cavernous canvas tent. A tall, 'symmetrically built' young man in the audience announced that he would accept the challenge on behalf of 'White Australia'.[2] A follower of the world-famous strongman Eugen Sandow, the twenty-two-year-old Clarence Weber was a physical culture enthusiast. Once the terms and conditions of the bout were agreed on, the Australian found himself pitted against the Sikh's companion. The fight did not last very long. The Indian—a man known as 'Gunga Brahmn'—

proved too canny for his stolid White opponent, who tripped and lost his bearings. Undaunted, Weber demanded a second match. This time, it was the Sikh fighter who stepped on to the mat. The two men proceeded to grapple fiercely in contrasting styles. Weber, a relatively inexperienced wrestler, relied on his great strength to stymie his opponent. The Punjabi, more skilled and dexterous, sought to use his vast experience to bring down the Australian. As the wrestling became more frenzied, the Sikh suddenly deployed a stranglehold that choked Weber. Within seconds, the burly challenger was spreadeagled on the floor, apparently rendered unconscious.[3]

The press reports of the sensational fight presented utterly divergent versions of what transpired next. According to one Melbourne newspaper, the 'White Australian' spectators were incensed by what they saw as the unfair tactics of the wily 'Asiatic'. They advanced towards the ring, bent on thrashing the Sikh wrestler. The victor of the fight, 'still in his abbreviated wrestling costume, fled up St. Kilda road, with the shouting crowd on his heels, around the Homeopathic Hospital and back to the city, where hunted, trembling and scared, he secured the assistance of two constables, who escorted him back between them to the circus'.[4] But a rival newspaper pooh-poohed this story. 'Nothing of the kind happened at all', contended its reporter; the Indian wrestler 'needed no protection at all'. Furthermore, 'He never fled along the St. Kilda road, nor went a yard in the direction of the Homeopathic Hospital. That is the cold fact'.[5]

That two newspapers in early twentieth-century Australia should squabble at length over an incident featuring an Indian circus performer is in itself astonishing. But what renders the event even more extraordinary is that the Sikh at the heart of the controversy claimed for himself the title of Australia's 'national wrestling champion'. Buttan (Bhuttan) Singh had arrived in the country some years earlier. Soon, he began to make his presence felt on the wrestling circuit. By the time he performed at the Wirth Brothers' Circus, Buttan had become one of the best-known sportsmen in Australia, renowned both for his wrestling and his exhibitions with Indian clubs. Remarkably, he achieved fame at a time when the newly formed Commonwealth of Australia had introduced racially discriminatory laws that targeted 'Asiatic' immigration into the country. In June 1909, Buttan set out for Britain. In London, the capital of the wrestling world, he held his own against an assortment of fighters from across the globe. Two years later, Buttan moved from Britain to the United States in order to pit his skills against the champions of that country.

Buttan thus belongs to a small band of Indians who attained international recognition for their sporting accomplishments in the two decades preceding the First World War. Of these, the most written about is Kumar Shri Ranjisinhji ('Ranji'), whose dazzling batting exploits made him a cricketing superstar in the decade between 1895 and 1905. His sporting celebrity enabled Ranji to become the 'Jam Saheb' of Nawanagar.[6] In the early 1900s, another 'Jam' appeared on the imperial sporting scene. This was Jamsetji Marker, a gifted Parsi racquets player from Bombay, who was crowned world champion in London in 1903, a title that he held until 1911.[7]

Unlike Ranji and Jamsetji, the two other internationally renowned Indian sportsmen of that era were both plebeians. Gama Baksh (born Gulam Mohammed) hailed from a family of wrestlers in North-west India.[8] Although his origins were humble, Gama acquired social respectability on account of his service at royal courts. Following a series of famous victories over his rivals in the subcontinent, he led a team of Indian wrestlers who travelled to London in the summer of 1910. The following year, the first 'All-India' cricket team travelled to the imperial metropolis. The best bowler in this team was the extraordinary Palwankar Baloo, who overcame the stigma associated with his caste status as a Chambhar (Chamar) to become the first great 'Indian' cricketer.[9]

Although he belongs to this illustrious group of sportsmen, Buttan Singh has languished in obscurity. In the first instance, then, this essay seeks to reconstruct the career of a long-forgotten Indian champion. However, this foray is neither an exercise in sporting antiquarianism, nor a celebratory chronicle. While it dwells on the agency and experience of a remarkable individual, the essay seeks to frame Buttan Singh's life story against the broader historical currents on which it was borne aloft.

I set Buttan's career in Australia within the larger context of transnational mobility across the Indian Ocean. The migration of Indians to Australia was one strand in the flows of people within this vast oceanic zone in the 'long nineteenth century'. It was a world peopled by convicts, indentured labourers, sailors, saints, soldiers, slaves, traders and travellers.[10] By the end of the nineteenth century, it was also a world in which the racial anxieties and prejudices of European colonizers resulted in new barriers to the free movement of non-Whites. In a context marked by pervasive racial discrimination, Buttan's status as a sporting champion set him apart from most of his immigrant compatriots and allowed him to construct a public profile.

At another level, the essay shows how Buttan's trajectory was part of a novel trend in the 1900s that saw plebeian strongmen traverse the globe in search of riches and fame. In turn, the mobility of boxers and wrestlers across national boundaries triggered intense debates about masculinity, race, and national identity. Buttan's peripatetic sporting career, this essay suggests, was the product of a singular—and short-lived—conjuncture in the age of empire-driven 'globalization' prior to the First World War.[11]

II

From the mid-nineteenth century onwards, a growing number of Indians went abroad in search of work and wages. A number of factors triggered this vast churn. Imperial conquest and the expanding frontiers of agrarian and industrial capitalism drew millions out of their rural homesteads to work in plantations, mines and infrastructure projects in the Indian Ocean world. The revolution in transport and communication ushered in by the railway, the steamship and the telegraph rapidly enhanced the scale of migration.[12]

Rural migrants who departed Indian shores did so because of the growing precariousness of their existence in their regions of origin. Impoverished peasants ravaged by debt, drought and disease moved to regions within the British Empire, often—though not inevitably or always—in circular patterns. Indentured labour from eastern India travelled to the Caribbean and Mauritius. Labourers from south India travelled to Burma, Ceylon (Sri Lanka), Malaya and South Africa.[13]

In the late nineteenth and early twentieth centuries, the Jat Sikhs of central Punjab represented a significant strand within these broad patterns of overseas Indian migration. Members of this community had begun to move abroad in the three decades between 1880 and 1910. Some went to the newly built canal colonies to the west, where an ambitious experiment in social engineering sought to transform the desolate pastoral highlands beyond the Sutlej into a productive agrarian zone.[14] But others sought pastures abroad, travelling to South East Asia, East Africa and North America. By 1910, the income from overseas migration was 'the greatest source of new wealth in Punjab'.[15]

Significantly, too, the movement abroad of Jat Sikh migrants was shaped by the British construction of this community as a 'martial race'. They were regarded by their imperial recruiters as natural soldiers: hardy, valorous, disciplined and loyal. As a result, Sikhs travelled abroad as part of the British Indian army units deployed in an arc extending from East Africa to the Far East. Their reputation for martial prowess also led to their recruitment as policemen in Hong Kong, Shanghai, Malaya and the Straits Settlements.[16] From there, Sikh migrants moved to other overseas locations. One stream made its way, through transcontinental transport networks, to Canada and California. Another—less numerous—strand headed to *Telia* (as Australia came to be known among Sikh migrants).

It is not entirely clear by what route Buttan Singh made his way Down Under. In his press interviews in Australia, he seldom dwelt at length on his previous life in India. Stray references in contemporary Australian newspapers to Buttan's military record suggest that he might have served in a British Indian regiment stationed in South East Asia. But it is equally possible that he travelled directly from Punjab to Australia.

It is also likely that Buttan hailed from Jalandhar, the home district of most of the Sikhs and Hindus in Australia.[17] In the early 1890s, one historian has noted, 'a few adventurous spirits' travelled from Jalandhar to Australia and returned 'with substantial proof of the fact that money could be made there'. Soon thereafter, it was said that it 'became common for villagers from Jullundur district in particular to go to Australia in search of their fortunes'.[18]

What we can venture with more certainty is that Buttan travelled to Australia sometime in 1899 or early 1900. He could not have chosen a more fraught moment to migrate. In the years immediately preceding his arrival in Australia, a viciously xenophobic campaign—waged by right-wing ideologues as well as socialist trade unions—had relentlessly targeted 'Asiatic' immigrants. Advocates of a 'White Australia' policy repeatedly called for Chinese and Indians to be kept out of the country in order to maintain its racial purity. The downturn in the Australian economy during the 1890s—a decade marked by trade depression and droughts—served to intensify the hostility directed at non-White immigrants.[19] Their presence in the country was decried by White nationalists as a threat to the 'Australian way of life'. In this racially charged atmosphere, many Australian colonies introduced immigration laws that sought to exclude Chinese and Indians from their territories.

To a large extent, the drive to construct 'White Australia' was 'an essential condition' of the Commonwealth that was proclaimed at Centennial Park, Sydney, on 1 January 1901. Among the first pieces of legislation passed by its newly constituted federal Parliament was an Immigration Restriction Act (IRA), which was explicitly designed to prevent the free movement of non-Europeans into Australia. Acting on the advice of the Colonial Office in London, which recommended Natal's linguistic test (introduced in 1897) as a model, the framers of the Act deployed language rather than colour to achieve their desired goal.[20] Its key feature was a fifty-word dictation test—in *any* European language chosen by the immigration official—that had to be taken by every non-European immigrant seeking to enter the country.

The dictation test was a powerful deterrent in keeping out non-European migrants to Australia. Migrants from China and India, in particular, were immediately affected by the move. In the years spanning 1902–05, only fifty individuals out of a total of 975 managed to clear this taxing test.[21] News of the stringent restrictions reached India, and reduced migrant flows from Punjab.[22] For their compatriots in Australia, the tightening of immigration laws made it harder to travel in and out of the country. They had virtually no hope of bringing over their wives and children. Unsurprisingly, many chose to return home. The number of Indian migrants in Australia was dramatically reduced from an estimated 7637 in 1901 to 3698 a decade later.[23] Those who chose to remain were forced to survive in a deeply racialized environment, in which they were constantly the objects of surveillance. Their occupations only served to accentuate the suspicion with which White Australia viewed immigrants from the subcontinent.

At this time, most South Asians in Australia earned their livelihood in one of two ways. In the first category were those designated 'Afghans', an elastic term that included predominantly Muslim migrants from the North-West Frontier Province, northern Punjab, Baluchistan and Sind. The male migrants who came from these regions were employed as camel owners or drivers. They had first arrived in the country in the 1860s and played a pioneering role in bringing the infrastructure of modernity to the interior of Australia. Leading lives defined by constant movement, they set up camps—dubbed 'Ghantowns'—on the outskirts of towns and cities.[24] The second category of South Asian migrants was also defined by its peripatetic lifestyle. Sikh and Hindu hawkers bought goods from wholesalers in the cities and travelled the Australian outback selling their wares. They carried clothes, cosmetics, utensils, medicines and other items of domestic consumption. Unlike the cameleers who tended to travel in small groups, most hawkers operated on their own, leading a solitary existence on the road.[25]

But 'White Australia' made no distinction between the 'Afghan' cameleers and the Sikh and Hindu hawkers. In their writings in the press and in their debates in the legislatures, White Australian publicists and politicians constructed fearful images of these immigrants. Their 'filthy habits' were seen as flagrant violations of modern norms of public health and sanitation. Their neighbourhoods and settlements were seen as squalor-ridden 'slums'. Their presence in the Australian outback was perceived as a threat to White women and children who lived in isolated rural homesteads. The brutal images of violence associated with the Great Uprising of 1857 were liberally invoked to impress on the public mind the dangers of allowing Indians into the country.[26]

III

As with many of his Punjabi compatriots in Australia, Buttan quickly took up hawking. A newspaper report in July 1903 noted that 'his beat' was in the Western District of Victoria, 'where he runs rather a good turn-out—a big wagonette and two horses'.[27] But he also seems to have simultaneously taken up a career as a wrestler. According to one reporter, he kept himself 'in constant training by lifting a couple of huge stones that he carts about in his waggon'.[28] It would also appear that the income Buttan earned as a wrestler allowed him, for a while, to set up shop in one place. In August 1905, a number of Australian newspapers carried a snippet in their miscellany columns about a 'quaint sign' that was displayed over a Melbourne shop. It read: 'Buttan Singh, Greengrocer, Tailor, and Champion Wrestler'.[29] The news item was even circulated in the metropolitan press in Britain.[30]

The fame that Buttan earned in the imperial public sphere was, of course, entirely on account of his career as a wrestler. Indeed, in June 1900 one newspaper informed its readers that he had come to Australia 'with the reputation of having, in his own country, "held the belt" against all comers for many years'. The report added that in his career as a wrestler in India he had 'won eighty-two out of eighty-five matches'.[31]

Wrestling was well established as a popular sport when Buttan arrived in Australia. Although the sport had been pursued in the convict era, it was the Australian gold rushes of the late nineteenth century that transformed it into a source of popular entertainment. European migrants drawn to the continent by the prospects of riches brought with them the wrestling traditions of their home countries. As in America and Europe, the prevailing format was 'catch-as-catch-can'. This was a hybrid 'freestyle' that combined old folk wrestling and new grappling techniques that were developed in North America and western Europe in the late nineteenth century.[32]

As a mass sport, modern wrestling in Australia was shaped by the conjunction of industrial urbanization, the advent of electricity and the shortening of working hours. Notably, it was in the major Australian port cities—Sydney, Melbourne and Perth—that the sport was most keenly followed. By the early 1900s there had also emerged a thriving wrestling culture in the gold-mining towns—especially Coolgardie and Kalgoorlie—of Western Australia. Like boxing, wrestling was notable at this time for the variability of its rules, standards and practices. There was no central organizing body, and the sport was driven largely from below by the activities of wrestlers and their impresarios, as well as a popular press keenly attuned to its value as a source of sensational stories. Wrestling's close association with the world of theatrical entertainment meant that its competitive character was frequently open to question. Many exhibition bouts featuring international strongmen appear to have been fixed beforehand.

Buttan made his public debut as a wrestler in Australia sometime in the early months of 1900. Notwithstanding the racial prejudice against 'Asiatics', he swiftly broke through into a sporting realm dominated by European fighters, agents and trainers. Significantly, too, at a relatively early stage in his wrestling career in Australia, Buttan was able to draw on the support of White promoters and publicists. In turn, these men facilitated his access to the sporting press, and the terms and conditions of his fights were settled in the offices of various Australian newspapers.

Remarkably, Buttan was thirty-seven years old when he began to take part in wrestling matches in Australia. His sporting career took off at an age when most athletes are well past their prime. But going by the newspaper accounts of his bouts, Buttan appears to have been in superb condition. 'He weighs 12st.7[lb] in trim, strips lithe and sinewy as a panther, with hard bunches of muscle on arms and back. Buttan Singh looks the catch-as-catch-can wrestler all over', wrote an admiring reporter in June 1900.[33]

These remarks were made shortly after Buttan achieved his first major triumph as a wrestler in Australia. On 9 June 1900, he defeated Wilhelm Pagel, a twenty-two-year-old Teutonic strongman dubbed the 'German Hercules'. The fight was staged at the Victoria Hall in Melbourne in the catch-as-catch-can style for a £50-a-side wager.[34] Press reports of the encounter—couched in the prevailing racist language of the time—highlighted the stark difference in the physique of the two men; 'a German sausage to a black pudding', sneered one writer.[35] 'Pagel looked as if he could catch hold of the darkey and tear him to bits,' noted another White Australian. 'But the Hindoo [sic] was too wily, and his cat-like play ended in his cleverly twisting the German to the floor'. By the end of the fight, Buttan had conclusively demonstrated his superiority over his gargantuan opponent.[36] In doing so, he dramatically undermined the dominant notions about European racial superiority. Notably, too, the 'Hindoo [sic] hawker', as the press described him, was quick to trumpet his victory. 'The conduct of both Buttan and the hundred or so turbaned barrackers who turned up to support him belies the general belief in the placid fatalism of the Oriental. Instead of murmuring "kismet", Buttan whooped wildly and danced about the middle of the ring, while the Hindoos [sic] in the body of the hall arose, waving their turbans and howling with glee,' noted one account of the extraordinary scene at the Victoria Hall.[37]

This report also noted that 'Indian wrestlers are becoming thick'.[38] The statement alerts us to the fact that Buttan was by no means the first or only South Asian wrestler in Australia. He was one of a number of Afghan, Sikh and Hindu grapplers at that time who paraded their skills on the wrestling circuit. One well-known Afghan fighter was a man named Abdul Kader, who was involved in wrestling matches in Western Australia. We also hear of Massa Singh, who made a name for himself as a wrestler at the same time as Buttan. And above all, there was Gunga (Ganga) Brahmn (Brahmin), who was for some years Buttan's fiercest challenger. Because their fights in the early 1900s were publicly billed as contests for the status of Australia's 'national wrestling champion', it is worth dwelling on this extraordinary rivalry and intriguing relationship.

Gunga, who also hailed from Punjab, appears to have arrived in Australia a couple of years before Buttan. He had certainly begun to take part in wrestling matches before the latter did so. According to one—almost certainly apocryphal—story, Buttan had been summoned to Australia by his Sikh compatriots to take on Gunga in the ring.[39] They first wrestled each other at the Democratic Club in Melbourne on 7 January 1901. After three thrilling rounds, Buttan was declared the winner. Gunga took the result badly and claimed that his Sikh opponent had used unfair tactics.[40]

Over the next two years, both wrestlers enhanced their sporting reputations by defeating a succession of European rivals. 'These two Indians have completely outclassed all aspirants who have met them in Australia, and are themselves about equally matched in strength and skill,' noted the *Age* before their second fight at Wirth's Circus on 30 April 1903. As a result, the second face-off between the two wrestlers was billed as a battle for the 'championship of Australia'.[41] This did not go down well with sections of White Australia. 'The casual and tired Australian evidently thinks that wrestling isn't within his ability, and it's hardly a policy for athletic bodies to recognize championships which can only be won by aliens to their country', complained one writer.[42]

But clearly many Australians were not put off by the spectacle of two 'coloured' wrestlers vying with each other to be the 'national champion' of their country. The Buttan–Gunga fight attracted well over 3000 spectators to Wirth's Circus, among them the Lieutenant-governor of Victoria, Sir John Madden, and 'several hundreds of ladies'.[43] Against all expectations, it was Gunga—ten years younger and half a stone heavier than Buttan—who carried the day, winning the closely fought contest by two falls to one.[44]

The Hindu wrestler's triumph was short-lived. A month after the match at Wirth's Circus, Buttan defeated Gunga at the Queen's Club in Melbourne and reclaimed his status as the 'national wrestling champion' of Australia.[45] The two Indians went on to fight each other four times over the next six months. On 1 October 1903, the owners of Wirth's Circus, noting their box office draw, invited them to grapple once again for the 'national championship of Australia' at their show in Sydney. The match ended in a draw. Four weeks later, the Indians squared off at Sydney's National Sporting Club. On this occasion, it was Buttan who was declared the winner. On Boxing Day 1903, the match between Buttan and Gunga was one of the principal attractions at the 'Coolgardie Week' celebrations. And the following February, they were pitted against each other at Freemantle.[46]

But by the time the last of these fights was staged, the relationship between Buttan and Gunga had changed. Although they continued to wrestle ferociously in the ring, the later fixtures were no longer marred by the acrimony and antipathy of the early encounters. The two men now began working with, rather than against, each other. The adversaries appear to have buried the hatchet during their tour of the Western Australian goldfields in 1903–04. Buttan even acted as Gunga's manager when the latter defeated a European fighter named Jack Perryman at Perth on 29 December 1903.[47] Some months later, Buttan and Gunga were jointly hired to perform regularly in Wirth's Circus. That is how the foes-turned-friends came to take on Clarence Weber on that notorious November evening in Melbourne, when Buttan unleashed his deadly headlock against the young Australian strongman.

An equally legendary encounter—this time to their detriment—occurred three months later when both Indians went up against George Hackenschmidt, the globally renowned wrestling star of the 1900s. The 'Russian Lion', as he was known, had established his reputation with a series of spectacular triumphs in Europe. In November 1904, the 'champion wrestler of the world' arrived in Australia for a four-month tour arranged by a private theatrical company. As was the case with such commercial ventures, almost all the matches featuring Hackenschmidt were fixed beforehand.[48] However, his encounter with the two Indian wrestling champions was a notable exception. This eagerly anticipated fixture was staged at the Exhibition Hall in Melbourne on 11 February 1905. It turned out to be a rather damp squib for the 5000-odd spectators (including scores of women) who had gathered to watch the match. Hackenschmidt, a classical 'Graeco-Roman' wrestler by training, had agreed to fight, in the catch-as-catch-can style, both the Indian champions in succession. First, Gunga came on to the stage, 'gorgeously attired in a cloak of red velvet, profusely ornamented with gold braid'. But, one Australian reporter noted, with more than a hint of schadenfreude, 'Its wearer failed most egregiously to justify his startling get up'. Hackenschmidt, whose 'large wash towel, worn toga-wise' made him look like a 'Roman Senator', used his massive strength to bring down Gunga within seconds. Buttan now stepped on to the stage and 'made up for his countryman's easy capitulation by putting up a really first class resistance, during which he displayed a wonderful scientific defence'. But it was to no avail and, after nine intense minutes of wrestling, Buttan yielded to the Estonian.[49]

The unalloyed joy with which the audience greeted Hackenschmidt's victory over his Indian opponents was as clear a manifestation as any of the 'colour line' in sport. Although Buttan and Gunga were 'British' subjects in Australia, it was Hackenschmidt—technically a 'foreigner'—who was the crowd favourite. It is worth noting, too, that years later this fight was recalled with glee by many White Australian sporting journalists and former wrestlers. For these veterans, Hackenschmidt's victory was a moment to savour because it had restored what they regarded as the natural state of affairs: a White man putting the 'darkeys' in their place.

After Hackenschmidt's departure, however, Buttan quickly regained his status as Australia's premier wrestler. In July 1905, he defeated Clarence Weber, who had sought to avenge his humiliation the previous November. However, Weber, whose wrestling skills had improved after training with the 'Russian Lion', finally had his revenge in November 1906. In a brutal fight for the 'Australian championship' at the Cyclorama in Melbourne, he used his immense physical strength to batter his Indian rival.[50] With his mission to defeat the Sikh accomplished, Weber announced his withdrawal from wrestling. This allowed Buttan once again to proclaim himself the national champion of Australia. His hold on the title remained secure until 1908, when he was confronted by two White challengers—George Dinnie, a 'red-haired' Scot, and Peter Bannon, a Lancastrian—who inflicted defeats on him. Alongside these well-publicized fights, Buttan continued to perform with Gunga at Wirth's Circus. He also appeared in music-hall entertainments in which he displayed his prowess with heavy Indian clubs.

By 1909, the forty-six-year-old Buttan was well established as a box office draw in Australia. But he had begun to harbour greater ambitions. London in the Edwardian era was the capital of the sporting world. Buttan's European contacts on the Australian wrestling circuit would no doubt have told him about the riches that awaited him in the imperial metropolis. Astonishingly, the intrepid Sikh wrestler decided to try his luck at the very heart of empire. On 29 June 1909, he sailed—as a third-class passenger—from Fremantle on board *SS Pericles*, an ocean liner bound for London via South Africa.[51]

IV

Buttan arrived in London on 6 August 1909.[52] Four weeks earlier, his more famous Indian compatriot, Mohandas Karamchand Gandhi, had arrived in the capital to represent the political demands of Indian immigrants in South Africa. Unlike the future Mahatma, whose visit attracted some attention in the British press, the Sikh wrestler's presence in London was barely registered by the city's sporting newspapers. 'We are asked to mention the arrival in England of the celebrated Hindoo [sic] wrestler, Buttan Singh,' said a terse snippet in the *Sportsman*.[53]

It was not the most opportune time for an Indian to be present in the 'city of the world'. On the night of 1 July 1909, a twenty-five-year-old Punjabi student named Madan Lal Dhingra had assassinated Sir William Hutt Curzon Wyllie, aide-de-camp to the Secretary of State for India, and also accidentally killed a Shanghai-based Parsi surgeon called Kavasji Lalkaka. The assassin was swiftly arrested and convicted. At the time of Buttan's arrival, Dhingra was imprisoned in London's Pentonville Prison, awaiting his execution on 17 August 1909. The sensational assassination of Curzon Wyllie crystallized sharply in the public consciousness the problem of 'Indian sedition'. London's tabloids indulged in lurid speculation about fanatical Indian terrorist cells that were supposedly plotting to wreak havoc in the capital.[54]

When he had first landed in Australia, Buttan had contacts in the Sikh community who eased his path in the new country. But it is not quite clear if he had any acquaintances or friends in the small, but thriving, South Asian community in London. The evidence suggests that Buttan drew on the European sporting connections that he had forged in Australia. He swiftly acquired a British manager called Jack Neill in whose company he made the rounds of newspaper offices in Fleet Street. One journalist who met Buttan in September 1909 described him as 'a tall coloured man of priestly mien, clad in a garb altogether drab and European'. But there was one 'brilliant exception' to his attire: 'a highly-coloured turban', which 'at once gave him the distinction of a label'. Interestingly, this reporter noted that Buttan spoke 'very good English'; a result, no doubt, of the decade he had spent in Australia. Equally noteworthy is the way Buttan presented himself in his new setting. He told his British interlocutor that 'his forebears were concerned on the English side in the Indian Mutiny, and he had served himself in the Bengal Infantry, and that he had eventually turned his attention to wrestling'.[55] Loyalty to the empire, military service and a commitment to physical culture: these were themes calculated to appeal to a British audience, especially one that was unnerved by the spectre of 'Indian sedition'.

During the autumn and winter of 1909, Buttan spent much of his time touring English provincial towns. Interestingly, however, his public performances did not involve any wrestling. Instead, Buttan gave 'athletic displays' with Indian clubs at variety shows in Plymouth, Devonport and Margate. Both the public and the press were taken with this aspect of the Sikh's oeuvre. 'His powers as a club swinger are astounding,' reported *Health and Strength*. 'He commences with two 45-pounders, studded with nails, and swings them for an hour at a time. His 79-pounders he swings about fifty times without a break, and his 100-pounder about twenty. He challenges any weight lifter or club swinger in the world to lift his clubs against him'.[56] The challenge was never taken up. This is unsurprising: insofar as British strongmen used clubs, these seldom weighed more than 10 pounds.[57]

While the British public marvelled at his extraordinary dexterity with the 'Singh clubs', Buttan was more keen to establish his credentials as a wrestler. Shortly after his arrival in the country, the Sikh fighter's manager issued challenges on his behalf to prominent European wrestlers. Only one opponent stepped forward: an Anglo-Austrian middleweight named Henry Irslinger, who was twenty-seven years younger than Buttan. The fight was arranged via the *Sporting Life* and staged at the Theatre Royal in York on 23 December 1909. It turned out to be a four-hour affair, spread over two days, at the end of which Buttan was declared the winner.[58]

The following month, Buttan finally had his chance to make his presence felt on the British wrestling scene. The occasion was an international tournament organized by the National Sporting Club and staged at the Alhambra Theatre in London's Leicester Square. This competition had been initiated to revive a sport that was seen by many to have been corrupted by its association with 'music hall' entertainment. In particular, those who preached the gospel of amateurism alleged that wrestling in Britain had declined in popularity because of pervasive match-fixing and gambling. The 'Alhambra tournament', as it came to be known, was started in 1908 to stem the rot by promoting 'clean' wrestling. Significantly, the competition attracted wrestlers from across the world: Lancastrian wrestlers from Wigan, Icelandic *glima* exponents, Swiss *schwinger*, Turkish *yagh güres*, Japanese *sumotori* and *jujutsu-kai*, and an assortment of 'catch-as-catch-can' wrestlers from Australia, North America and the Caribbean.[59]

Stepping into this extraordinary global melange, Buttan immediately made his mark. Defeating a series of rivals, he swiftly advanced to the middleweight semi-final, where his opponent was a Black Jamaican wrestler named Frank Crozier. The bout was widely criticized in the British press because Crozier, one observer complained, offered 'a perfect example of still life'.[60] Clinging to the mat, the Jamaican frustrated Buttan's strenuous efforts to shift him. After a 'monotonous fight', the Sikh finally secured the falls that took him to the final. Here, Buttan's adversary was Bob Berry, an ex-miner from Wigan. There was a large attendance at the Alhambra when the two men fought for the championship on 3 February 1910. Berry, who was half Buttan's age, was known to use his immense physical strength to rush his opponents off the mat. True to form, after twenty minutes of fierce grappling the Lancastrian charged at Buttan. Tightly clutching each other—'like trussed turkeys'—the two men plunged headlong over the footlights, into the orchestra pit.[61] In the second round, Berry once again used questionable tactics to bring down his tired rival. Although he lost the fight, Buttan won the unstinted admiration of the watching press corps. 'He is an extraordinary man, all wire and whipcord, with an altogether puzzling mastery of his limbs', gushed one reporter after the fight.[62]

Buttan was stung by his defeat against Berry. He issued a fresh challenge to the victor of the Alhambra tournament. This was accepted and a rematch was fixed for 16 July 1910 at the Manchester United football club in Old Trafford. Shortly after the arrangements had been fixed, Buttan fell out with his manager. He successfully sued Jack Neill in the Manchester City police court for 'the recovery of certain goods, including clothing, letters of introduction to music hall managers, wrestling records, an iron bar for weight-lifting, and a gold ring'.[63] Under the watchful eye of Herbert Turner, his new British manager, Buttan prepared strenuously for the face-off with Berry. When the two men stepped into the ring, the Sikh 'resembled a fighting fit grey-hound'. Berry, who was hampered by an injured arm, stood no chance. After barely twenty-five minutes of wrestling, he withdrew from the contest. 'Fastening on his prey like a suckling tigress, Singh administered the gruelling of his lifetime to the Wiganer, who sat in his dressing room, a picture of consternation', reported one observer. But Berry 'was chivalrous enough to acknowledge that the veteran was a wonder even in this athletic era'.[64] It was a sentiment shared by the large crowd that watched the contest and gave Buttan a prolonged ovation at the end.

Buttan's victory over Berry allowed him to claim the title of the middleweight wrestling champion of the world. 'It is no exaggeration to say that the name of Buttan Singh is a household word in India, Australia, and the Mother Country', noted *Health and Strength*.[65] And across the Atlantic, at least one sportsman would have received with pleasure news of Buttan's triumph. On the eve of the Berry–Singh fight, Jack Johnson, the world's most famous African-American boxer, had sent the Sikh wrestler a telegram wishing him success.[66] It is more than probable that their paths crossed in Australia, where Johnson wrested the world heavyweight wrestling championship in December 1908 by demolishing the Canadian Tommy Burns at Rushcutters Bay, Sydney.

Buttan Singh's triumph was also greeted with delight by an extraordinary group of Indian wrestlers who were present that summer in Britain. Led by Gama Baksh, the 'Lion of the Punjab', these men—Imam Baksh, 'Champion of Lahore'; Ahmed Baksh, 'Champion of Amritsar'; and Gamu, 'Champion of Jullundhur'—had been camping in London since April, waiting for European wrestlers in the city to take up their challenge.[67] But they waited in vain, for word had spread within the highly international wrestling community in London that these earnest newcomers could not be persuaded to engage in the 'match-fixing' that had become an integral feature of the sport in the imperial metropolis. The *Sporting Life* remarked on the curious fact that 'Gama's advent has synchronised with an extraordinary exodus of champions from England'.[68] Eventually, an American wrestler—Benjamin Franklin Roller—agreed to take on the 'Lion of the Punjab'. On 8 August 1910, the two men squared off at the Alhambra Theatre. In front of a packed house, Gama briskly demolished 'Doc' Roller. In the audience that day was Stanley Zbyszko, one of the best-known European wrestlers of the day. It soon transpired that a match between Zbyszko and Gama was to take place the following month. The widely anticipated fight generated massive public interest both in Britain and India.

At this juncture, R.B. Benjamin, Gama's Jewish manager, sought Buttan Singh's help in preparing his fighter for the most important match of his career. The 'Grand Old Man', as the British press had begun to refer to Buttan, moved to the Royal Hotel in Surbiton (a suburb in south-west London), which had served as the Indian wrestlers' base since their arrival in the country. The Sikh veteran became Gama's trainer and partner, using his experience to guide the younger man in devising stratagems to counter the wily Zbyszko. The wisdom of Benjamin's move in hiring Buttan became evident when Gama finally confronted his Polish opponent on 10 September 1910 at London's Olympic stadium. From the outset of the contest, Zbyszko refused to make any moves, preferring instead to cling tenaciously to the mat. Buttan was in Gama's corner throughout the controversial fight, urging him on with advice and encouragement. After two and a half hours—during which the recumbent Zbyszko frustrated Gama with his tactics—the contest was abandoned. Irate spectators jeered Zbyszko, and the police were called in to protect the wrestler. The match was rescheduled for the following weekend. But while the Indian contingent showed up at the Olympic stadium, there was no sign of Zbyszko. Gama was declared the victor and awarded the cash prize of £250 and a gold belt.

Shortly thereafter, the Indian wrestlers departed for home. But on the eve of their departure from Britain, they expressed their gratitude to Buttan in a letter whose contents were made public in *Health and Strength*. The letter read as follows: 'Dear Buttan Singh—We are leaving for India to-night, and all of us wish you good luck and a happy career. We shall be very glad to hear from you now and then. May Providence always crown your efforts with success. Ours salaams to Mr. Thana (Turner) and his sons.— Sincerely yours (Signed), Gama, Gamu, Imam Bux, Ahmad Buksh'.[69] Gama also 'presented Buttan with his lovely silk turban' and 'offered to defray the expenses of his old friend and trainer for a trip to India'.[70]

Buttan did not take up the offer and continued to reside in Britain. But the autumn and winter of 1910 appears to have been a difficult one. He had sustained a severe knee injury while training with Gama.[71] His manager told the press that Buttan had refused to undergo surgery, preferring instead to 'adopt an Indian cure for sprains'.[72] The setback prevented him from taking part in competitive wrestling or club swinging. Instead, Buttan seems to have devoted his energies to the school for physical culture that he had set up in Manchester. Inevitably, this meant withdrawing from the public eye. It is not surprising, therefore, that Buttan's name does not appear in any contemporary British newspapers after September 1910.

The following summer, Indian wrestlers were once again in the news in Britain. R.B. Benjamin brought over, in two batches, a much larger contingent from the subcontinent, including Imam Baksh and Ahmed Baksh.[73] The highlight of their tour was a highly publicized fight between Ahmed Baksh and Maurice Deriaz, a Swiss strongman, which took place at the Crystal Palace on 24 May 1911. Baksh reaffirmed the superiority of Indian wrestlers over their European adversaries by easily vanquishing

Deriaz. As they had done the previous summer, the Indian wrestlers stationed themselves in London and issued challenges to other wrestlers in the country.

Meanwhile, Buttan re-established contact with his old friends and it is likely that he spent much of his time that coronation summer with his compatriots in London. It is during these weeks that Buttan became part of Benjamin's plans to take some of his wrestlers across the Atlantic to challenge Frank Gotch and George Hackenschmidt, the two pre-eminent grapplers of the day, who were scheduled to fight on Labor Day in Chicago. The group—comprising Benjamin, Ahmed Baksh, Kala Pertapa and Buttan—sailed on 25 August from Liverpool to New York on board the *Virginian*.[74] By 4 September, the men were in Chicago, where Benjamin hoped to entice the winner of the Gotch–Hackenschmidt fight to take on one of his men.

Buttan's trip to the United States turned out to be a disappointment. Benjamin mostly promoted Kala—who was referred to in the American press as 'Karla, the Indian Panther'—and Ahmed Baksh. Although neither Gotch or Hackenschmidt could be persuaded to take up the challenge of the Indian wrestlers, 'Karla' secured matches against the two other ubiquitous figures on the international wrestling circuit: Stanley Zbyszko and 'Doc' Roller. Buttan, it would appear, was largely relegated to the status of Kala's trainer.[75]

What accounts for the change in Buttan's circumstances in the United States? For one, Buttan was not one of Benjamin's protégés. Throughout his career, the Sikh had steered clear of the impresarios that dominated the wrestling world. Even when he had taken on European managers and trainers, he had retained a considerable degree of independence in conducting his affairs. Although he travelled with Benjamin's men to the United States, it is likely that Buttan sought at the outset to rely on his own contacts to arrange fixtures for himself. However, the Indian veteran did not have the connections in North America that might have enabled him to operate on his own. This may well have forced him to stick with Benjamin's group and accept a diminished status within it. There may have also been another factor that affected Buttan's ability to secure fixtures for himself. He was a middleweight, whereas most of the prominent wrestlers in the United States were in the heavyweight category. Buttan was thus confronted with a paucity of well-known wrestlers in his category against whom he could pit his skills.

Had he more time in his new setting, Buttan's ingenuity might perhaps have enabled him to find a way around these obstacles. But as the months went by in the United States, the clock was ticking on his three-year Australian certificate of exemption from the dictation test. Accordingly, Buttan made the decision to return Down Under. He landed in Fremantle on 17 June 1912, eleven days before the expiry date on the certificate.

V

In recent years, scholars have explored cultures of mobility within the increasingly globalized world of sport in the decade and a half that preceded the First World War. Their accounts have focused on the role of sportsmen—White and Black—from the anglophone world who earned their livelihoods by parading their skills in Europe, America and Australia. As one historian notes, 'Connected through international circuits constructed and consolidated by managers and entertainment entrepreneurs, and via the circulation of numerous press reports and still and moving images, these men constituted a significant, but largely neglected, transnational popular cultural network during the so-called "first wave" of modern globalization'.[76]

Buttan was an unlikely figure in this world, which was largely dominated by Europeans and Americans. As a migrant from a colonized society, he had far fewer resources than many of his White peers. And yet his exceptional skills and extraordinary self-confidence enabled him to become one of the most well-known sportsmen of his time. In breaking through into the world of professional sport, Buttan also managed to overcome many of the constraints that shackled the lives of his Indian compatriots in Australia and Britain.

At the same time, Buttan's celebrity was a product of the historical context of the 1900s. There was a new interest in the West at this time in 'Oriental' sportsmen. Buttan's career suggests that sport was a sphere in which the 'Oriental' was supported and savoured because he was regarded as an exotic—and, importantly, commercially profitable—artefact of empire.[77] Equally, the attention that Buttan received in Australia and Britain shows how physical culture became the site of intense, and increasingly anxious, debates about the comparative racial vigour of Europeans and non-Europeans. Men like Buttan were subjected to close scrutiny in the colonial and imperial press precisely because their bodies were seen to furnish the clues to how European dominance might one day be overturned by the 'Oriental' races.

As for Buttan, 1912 did not mark the end of his astonishing career. But what happened to him after his return to Australia is a tale for another occasion.

ACKNOWLEDGEMENTS

For their comments and suggestions on an earlier version of this essay, I thank Radhika Chadha, Samanth Subramanian, Nandini Sundar, Srinath Raghavan and Samira Sheikh. The usual disclaimers apply as regards any errors in the text.

9

AGYEYA: HINDI LITERATURE'S FIRST FREETHINKER

AKSHAYA MUKUL

BY THE WINTER of 1954, Sachchidananda Hirananda Vatsyayana Agyeya had arrived in the world of Hindi literature. Agyeya was forty-three at the time, but had already led a hundred lives. The previous years, considered his 'great decade', saw him churn out *Shekhar: Ek Jiwani I* and *II* (Shekhar: A Life I and II), *Tar Saptak* (String Septet), *Dusra Saptak* (Second Septet) and *Nadi Ke Dwip* (Islands in the Stream) in quick succession. He had published other notable collections, too, as well as started the bimonthly publication *Pratik*. Apart from his literary genius, Agyeya was also by then a revolutionary, short-term peasant leader, editor, an acolyte of the communist leader M.N. Roy and an officer in the British Army in the Indian north-east during the Second World War. One bad marriage and a passionate love affair gone awry had turned him melancholic.

At the height of his fame, the literary journal *Naya Path* (New Path) did the unthinkable. In its November 1954 issue, it wrote about something that was only so far spoken of in hushed tones in the Hindi world. It addressed Agyeya as the 'Indian sheet anchor of American Imperialism-fed CCF' (the Central Intelligence Agency [CIA]–funded Congress for Cultural Freedom) and a 'prominent Royist who fed on the money of British imperialists during the war'.[1] A year earlier, he had received a letter from a well-wisher, an unnamed lady, who worked in the Indian embassy in Beijing asking if the magazine *Thought* that Agyeya worked for was funded by the CIA.[2] Averse to writing letters at the best of times, Agyeya ignored the serious attack on him in *Naya Path* and, as was typical of him, did not even reply to the woman. At any rate, it did little to change his mind about his firm position that it was not the job of a writer to usher in political change. For far too long he had explained his political positions through essays, interviews and even a novel.

It is difficult to square Agyeya's very real political engagement with his stand that writers need not subscribe to any particular ideology. The very addition of '*Agyeya*' (Unknowable) to his name by Premchand was the result of his revolutionary politics. The writer, Jainendra Kumar, had brought Vatsyayana's story 'Amar Vallari' (Immortal Twiner) to Premchand for publication in his magazine *Jagran*. On realizing that the writer was in jail, Premchand carried it under the alias 'Agyeya'. But Agyeya's politics did not fit a particular pattern and he had no enduring association with any group or ideology. An enigma to the Hindi literary establishment, and at the receiving end of the leftist group dominant at the time, he was nonetheless among the most political writers of his time. At various stages, Agyeya had been a member of the Hindustan Socialist Republic Association (HSRA) founded by the revolutionary Bhagat Singh and others, the Congress and M.N. Roy's Radical Democratic Party. Knowingly or unknowingly, he had also been part of the CCF. Never though, in his long and chequered career, was Agyeya an establishment stooge.

A revolutionary—he preferred the term anarchist—of the 1930s, and an alleged collaborationist of the 1940s and 1950s, Agyeya was the Hindi literary world's first freethinker. This was not an easy thing to be at a time when Marxism was the dominant ideology among writers. As in life, Agyeya remained a *yayavar* (itinerant) in his ideological persuasions. His politics was shaped by lived experiences and not by hitching his wagon to an elite literary group to further his writing career.

A major part of Agyeya's latter-day personality was developed by what flowed from experiences in his early domestic life—a life constantly on the move, a house full of books, homeschooling and a culture of *vad-vivad* (debate). This cosmopolitan upbringing set him apart from his contemporaries, most of whom came from rural backgrounds, and had made intellectually robust towns like Allahabad, Patna and Banaras their home. These were the places where the Hindi world's schisms, ideological battles, pettiness and grand debates played out. An illustrative survey of his political journey will explain his independent mind, free of all *vad* (ideology).

EARLY EDUCATION

The son of noted archaeologist–epigraphist Hirananda Sastri, Vatsyayana was born on 7 March 1911 in an open field outside the tent Sastri had pitched for himself and his family near the Buddhist excavation site of Kusinagar in the United Provinces (present-day Uttar Pradesh). This was Hirananda's second trip to Kusinagar; the earlier one was as an assistant to Jean Philippe Vogel in 1904. On the day his fourth child was born, Hirananda discovered a copper plate,[3] 'consisting of Nidana-Sutra in Sanskrit, the first line engraved and the rest written in black enamel',[4] a gift from 'Haribala, the chief superintendent of the viharas'.[5] According to family lore, some local lamas visited the Sastri family with a request to adopt the child and turn him into a monk.[6] Hirananda and his wife Vyanti Devi declined the request.

Hirananda was a follower of the Arya Samaj movement. He owed his school and university education to the Samaj's vast network in Punjab. Like his son, Hirananda had literary interests, becoming the second editor of the small magazine, *Swadeshi Vastu Pracharak*.[7] In his later years, he developed a keen hatred for Muslims. Yet, when it came to his children, Hirananda was a liberal, letting them find their own way, both politically and personally. He disagreed with, protested against and regretted his favourite son Agyeya's tryst with revolutionaries. But this was not so much because of a difference of opinion as it was for the love of a child of whom he had high expectations.

Hirananda's frequent transfers to places as diverse as Patna, Srinagar and Ootacamund, and his habit of taking his sons on long excavation tours helped Agyeya create a world of his own. Amidst historical ruins, nature and silence became the boy's constant companions. Being his father's favourite, Agyeya was taken on these tours more than his siblings. Incidents from his childhood, silence and isolation running through them, were frequent themes in his writing. His deeply autobiographical and intensely political novel, *Shekhar: Ek Jiwani*, perhaps the most iconic Hindi novel of the twentieth century, is a testimony to this.

While politics was always discussed at home, Agyeya's first encounter with resistance was at the age of eight or nine in Srinagar, in 1918. A visit by Lord Chelmsford had been scheduled and thousands had lined the streets, ostensibly to greet him. But as his cavalcade passed through, a collective roar of '*Mat khudaya*' (Oh God no! or you are not God) rent the air, making it amply clear that the people of Kashmir were not one with their maharaja in welcoming the viceroy. When Agyeya travelled with his mother and sister from Jammu to Lahore in 1919 after the Jallianwala Bagh massacre, the young boy witnessed arson and rioting all the way, especially in Sialkot. It was on this trip when for the first time Agyeya heard the name Mahatma Gandhi and also developed a keen interest in reading newspapers.[8]

Gandhi always remained an enigma for Agyeya, though, and never a rallying point, ideologically or intellectually. He considered Gandhi an astute politician who could get anyone to do anything. But he did not consider the Mahatma an ethical politician. It was only after Noakhali and the partition of India that Agyeya revisited his views on this. What impressed him was Gandhi's relentless pursuit of peace and communal harmony in the face of strong opposition from all over.[9]

Since Agyeya was homeschooled—two attempts to send him to schools in Lucknow and Srinagar had failed miserably—and spent the better part of his childhood in remote places, his first encounter with caste politics was in Madras Christian College (MCC) which he joined in 1925 for the intermediate course. That same year, E.V. Ramasamy had left the Congress and launched the self-respect movement. Though Agyeya's father would talk of their Brahmin identity at home, he and his siblings were not brought up with the attendant markers of that identity. Therefore, what Agyeya saw in MCC was shocking and unpalatable. He remembered how in the First Student Home, a hostel exclusively for Brahmins, whenever a man of lower caste passed by the dining hall and happened to look at their food, Brahmin students would rise and leave without eating.[10]

Agyeya wanted to move to a place where 'this evil spirit of caste does not rave maniacally'.[11] Within two months of taking admission, he shifted to the relatively new College Park Hostel, 5 miles from college. It was a mixed residence for Brahmins and non-Brahmins, with another wing exclusively for Christian students. However, it had three different messes for Brahmins, non-Brahmins and Christians run by the students themselves.[12] Agyeya moved to the non-Brahmin hostel and ate in the mess run by them. He was happy that at last he did not have to meet 'caste snobs' and could rub shoulders and exchange plates not only with low-caste folk but with 'untouchables'.[13] Staying with 'untouchables, even miserables' in Madras leavened Agyeya's personality. It was an experience he treasured: 'Some of the noblest characters I have known, some of the truest and most lasting friendships I have formed were among them'.[14]

Later, Agyeya moved to Lahore's Forman Christian College (FCC) for his undergraduate degree, and it was here that he got involved with politics and politicians. His first love was physics. His favourite teacher, J.M. Benade, involved him as a research assistant on a prestigious global project on cosmic rays, initiated by Benade's Princeton classmate, the Nobel-winner Arthur H. Compton, then teaching at the University of Chicago.[15]

Agyeya's career in physics could not take off, though. A serious bout of typhoid before the final university examination meant he could not appear for the physics practical examinations and an honours degree eluded him. Keen to top the university examination, he wanted to take a year off. But Benade prevailed upon him to appear and got the university's permission for a scribe.[16]

Between assisting Benade and the failure to get an honours degree in physics (he graduated with a second division), much had happened in Agyeya's life. He had excelled in English, coming first among the members of the fourth-year class, for which he was awarded a scholarship.[17] For his master's, he enrolled in English—a move that did not go down well with Benade, who was confident Agyeya had a future in physics. The two argued and eventually Benade relented.[18]

Agyeya was in favour of letting his 'vagrant intelligence choose its own path' since he felt if it was put in 'chains', it would 'lose its vigour and be half-dead as if drugged'.[19] He chiefly turned to art and poetry. He was spending all his money and time on this, building a collection of prints and books on art, and occasionally dabbling in painting. There were good days when drawings and verses would come together. On bad days, he would take refuge in the verses of his favourite poets, Rabindranath Tagore, Christina Georgina Rossetti and Percy Bysshe Shelley, his 'beacons in the dark moments of soul'.[20]

But this soon changed. The all-pervading poverty and suffering—employers betraying poor labourers, youth dying for a cause and grown-ups letting them perish—filled him with an 'irrepressible disgust'. 'Rossetti was forgotten, Tagore set aside, art neglected and its message of peace died into the restlessness of a desire to remodel society on a better basis'.

Robert Browning and Romain Rolland were the new heroes that gave rhythm to his restlessness. Their works did not drown him but washed him into a new colour, gave him the hardness he thought he lacked. 'And the hardness was steel and the colour was red . . .' He would often feel his soul wake up to Rolland's words—'Young men, with hearts strong and well-tempered in battle, who among you is ready to challenge the march of Destiny?'—with the answer 'I'.[21]

BECOMING A REVOLUTIONARY

The historic annual Congress meeting in Lahore that began on 29 December 1929 gave him 'that tiny particle of ice, that weight of the feather'. He had enlisted himself as a volunteer for the Congress Seva Dal and it is this experience, of 'short-duration but complicated', that turned him into a 'piece of organized resistance'. His diary provides one of the most vivid descriptions of the inner world of annual Congress meetings.[22]

By the time the Lahore Congress concluded in January 1930, Agyeya was convinced that India needed a revolution and revolutionaries. He had found his true calling: 'I made a great decision that I would train and discipline myself, any others that I could acquire, a sense of honour and duty, find and follow a capable fighting head to a noble goal'. 'Inertness of forbearance had perished' and he became a votary of the undying flame of a revolutionary ideal.[23]

It would still be a while before Agyeya turned into a full-time revolutionary. During the first year of his MA, he had joined the revolutionaries part-time: student by day and underground activist by night, writing and distributing pamphlets. But writing and literature was never left behind. The FCC magazine published his first poem, a lyrical rhyming pining ode to a woman's beauty, heavily influenced by Tagore's *Gitanjali*. Agyeya included it in *Chinta*, his first poetry collection, and would often ask readers and friends to identify his first poem just like his hero Tennyson did with his poem 'Birds in the High Hall Garden'.[24] Prior to joining the HSRA, a few of Agyeya's friends from the FCC had set up a service that would churn out thousands of cyclostyled pamphlets exhorting youth to become revolutionaries. The pamphlets selected interesting extracts from books. News of the seizure of at least one of the pamphlets made it to the pages of the daily *Tribune*.[25]

Soon this motley group hit the revolutionary big league, merging with the HSRA. The HSRA was a formidable group; names that Agyeya had only read about and heard of were now his comrades. Chandrasekhar Azad, Bhagwati Charan Vohra, Vishwanath Vaishampayan, Yashpal and Dhanwantri were core members of the team, while Bhagat Singh was in Lahore jail awaiting his death sentence. Azad and Agyeya got along well. Azad's organizational skills, his sense of humour and extraordinary intelligence impressed Agyeya. Though Azad's bearing was rustic given his rural background, the manner of which he had not lost, he commanded immense respect from his colleagues.[26]

This group of anarchists had in their initial days 'more or less consciously' modelled themselves on Russian nihilists. They were also reading a lot, which suggests a strong ideological grounding. *The Career of a Nihilist* by Stepniak was a kind of Bible to them. During this time Agyeya would read Boris Pilnyak's *The Naked Year* and the Irish revolutionary Dan Breen's *My Fight for Irish Freedom*. But his favourite was Mikhail Alexandrovich Bakunin whom he preferred over Trotsky.[27]

Called 'Scientist' by his HSRA comrades, Agyeya was asked to move to Delhi by the organization by the end of July 1930.[28] He was described by Girwar Singh, who turned approver, as a man of fair complexion and stout build. His age, Girwar thought, was twenty-four or twenty-five though Agyeya had just turned nineteen in March that year. The Scientist's job, he reported, was to prepare picric acid to make victims unconscious.[29] By the end of 1930, HSRA was thrown into disarray. Azad was killed and the overground members were on the run. By November 1930, Vatsyayana aka Scientist was arrested in Amritsar, and tried under the Arms Act and later brought to Delhi to face trial in the Delhi Conspiracy case.[30] It took more than four years and lengthy legal procedures for him and others in the Delhi Conspiracy case to be released from jail in March 1934. He had to spend two more years in Lahore under strict police supervision, and was only allowed to go as far as Dalhousie and Mussoorie for vacation. Even a journey to Banaras for admission to Banaras Hindu University (BHU) was denied.[31]

Agyeya's politics took a different turn after the acquittal. Unlike many of his revolutionary comrades, he did not turn to communism. He moved to Agra to help edit *Sainik*, a weekly edited by Krishna Dutt Paliwal. But not everyone was convinced he would survive *Sainik* or Paliwal. Jainendra, still trying to get Agyeya to *Hans,* was not in the least hopeful. Even before

Agyeya left Lahore, Jainendra warned him, 'Go to *Sainik* if you want but be prepared to break away'.[32]

AGYEYA THE EDITOR

Sainik, claiming to be a 'high-class illustrated weekly', was a political and literary journal. In his short stint, apart from several editorials and signed articles, Agyeya wrote under various pen names and, most notably, commissioned M.N. Roy to become a regular contributor for the journal. In an article about India's role in international politics, *Sainik* described Roy as a man of international fame, who achieved national popularity after the Faizpur Congress.

Roy and Agyeya were in jail around the same time. It is possible they met after Roy's release in 1936 in Faizpur or Meerut, where Agyeya was getting seriously involved with peasant movements. But Roy and his philosophy of radical humanism left a permanent mark on Agyeya. Despite Agyeya's stated policy that writers should not get enmeshed in any political ideology, he maintained he was 'closest to people who called themselves Radical Humanists'.[33] While India was one in its fight for freedom, Roy said, political freedom alone would not suffice.[34] Both Roy and Agyeya opposed the Congress joining the government after its victory in the 1937 elections, fearing it would be corrupted or rendered powerless by the bureaucracy and provincial governors.[35]

Agyeya's foray into political journalism was under the name of Dr A. Latif, a curious moniker, the antecedents of which are unknown. One reason for using a pseudonym could be that articles published under that name were generally critical of the government, and Agyeya had promised the colonial government he would keep away from politics when he was released from jail. He was now writing on the rise of fascism, and had translated two of the Nobel laureate Romain Rolland's letters on this, prefaced with a small introduction. In India too, he wrote, several attempts had been made to start a fascist party as a panacea for all problems. Agyeya aka Latif argued that communism, even if young, had a bright future, whereas fascism was an attempt to resuscitate an ageing capitalism.[36]

As expected, *Sainik* did not live up to Agyeya's expectations, or to the journalistic standards it professed. It turned out to be a sham, a contest between the ideals that had led him to *Sainik* and Paliwal's political ambitions. It is believed that in Agyeya's absence, Paliwal managed to sneak in an article in his own praise. Agyeya got wind of it, came to the office and took it off.[37] Agyeya was also disgusted with the advertisement of Chinese aphrodisiacs. He had protested against their inclusion and was told that after the existing contract was honoured, the advertisements would not be renewed. He doubted the promise would be kept.[38]

After he quit *Sainik* Agyeya was interested in getting his prison poems published. While still in jail, he had reached out to the Anti-Imperialist League of the United States with a request to look at his manuscript, but not much came of this association. Although the league was keen to know more about Indian independence, for some reason their reply on the fate of his manuscript was never dispatched.[39]

Agyeya now turned to C.F. Andrews, who had played a big role in the removal of restrictions on him in Lahore for a foreword to his prison poems. Andrews responded saying that poems that 'came out of such an intense experience of imprisonment' were 'the best', and wanted Agyeya to send more such poems.[40] But for some reason there was no foreword forthcoming from him. Agyeya also wanted to approach Sarojini Naidu for a foreword, which was surprising as he did not 'think highly of her critical faculties and words'.[41]

Jawaharlal Nehru, Agyeya's hero since the Lahore Congress, was also sent the manuscript for a foreword. It was the peak of campaigning for the 1937 elections and Nehru was on whirlwind tours. He was in Allahabad when Agyeya's request reached him. Nehru read the poems immediately, 'liked some of them very much' but added the caveat that he was 'not a competent critic of poetry'. All the same, he agreed to write a foreword.[42] However, it would be a long time before Nehru delivered on his promise.

By the time Agyeya took over as editor of the Calcutta-based magazine *Vishal Bharat*, which was a bigger platform, he had an enviable reputation. Months before he moved to Calcutta, the twenty-six-year-old had already stirred up the Hindi world with his audacious English essay in the *Visva-Bharati Quarterly* on post-war modern Hindi poetry. He criticized the poetic oeuvre of a giant like Suryakant Tripathi Nirala, asking: 'Does Hindi poetry, then, tell us of the joys and sorrows and perplexities of this most complex age?'[43]

As editor of *Vishal Bharat*, Agyeya wanted to make a quick mark. He took strong positions on issues related to language politics, not sparing even the owner Ramananda Chatterjee, nor did he let his deep-seated doubts about Gandhi come in the way of bringing out a first-rate special issue on him, drawing in scholars, writers and poets from all over the world. But it is his run-in with Chatterjee that became the most memorable event of his Calcutta stay.

The magazine's sister publication, *Modern Review*, carried a report on a symposium on a national language organized by Rabi Basar, an exclusive fifty-member club of Calcutta intellectuals that included Tagore and Chatterjee. The symposium had two 'main trends' of argument: Hindi did not have a superior claim to Bangla in becoming the country's national language; neither Hindi nor Bangla ought to be accepted as the national language of India.[44]

Agyeya decided to take on Rabi Basar in *Vishal Bharat*, forgetting that Chatterjee was a member. He argued that the outcome of the symposium reflected animosity against Hindi and asked a serious question: 'At a time when the divisive agenda of "religion in danger" is being propagated, is it beneficial to the nation to spread the destructive fear of "language in danger". Can we hope that Bengal's prestigious literary institutions will oppose this mindset?'[45]

If Agyeya thought he was upholding the highest traditions of journalism by attacking a sister publication and its editor, he was inhabiting a make-believe world. Chatterjee was no pushover. A former president of the Hindu Mahasabha (1929), who had established and was editing *Modern Review* and *Prabasi* and had opened its pages to ideologically opposed politicians like Nehru, Gandhi and others, Chatterjee could not take this offence. What had particularly irked him was *Vishal Bharat*'s criticism of *Modern Review*. Chatterjee felt Agyeya had created the impression that his two magazines were the 'greatest enemies of Hindi'.[46]

Dripping in sarcasm, he said he should be 'pardoned' for saying that a 'very insignificant proof of Bengal's *udarta* (large-heartedness) was a Bengali financing a Hindi magazine and in the process losing thousands of rupees'. Chatterjee said he was not a 'linguistic imperialist' and added that a reply was not expected.[47]

Agyeya's reply was testy. He conceded Chatterjee had given his editors a free hand, but said he 'would have appreciated it as a personal obligation to have been spared the reminder'.[48]

His editorship ended within a year, but this had little to do with it. Agyeya's predecessor, Banarsi Das Chaturvedi, who was micromanaging the affairs of *Vishal Bharat*, convinced the owners that he needed to return as the supervising editor with two deputies to run the journal.

SHEKHAR

Not long after, with the publication of *Shekhar* I (1941) and II (1943), Agyeya was caught in political cross hairs. His two-part novel about the life of a revolutionary took the literary world by storm. It came at a time when Hindi prose was shifting overwhelmingly towards 'presentism in the form of *Nayi Kahani* (new story)'—a deep interest in psychological moods, in the alienation of the subject from the patterns of social life, and a resistance to social and socialist realism.[49] 'Impersonal' was being replaced by the 'personal'.

This new wind had a political context. The 1930s saw the Gandhian value system under great stress within the Congress and outside. The chosen counter-path was 'armed opposition' to the colonial power. Hindi literature reflected the complexities of its time. Instead of a duel between the 'good' and the 'bad' as in the novels of the 1920s, or 'writers hoping for a rebirth of a cooperative society based on reformed Hindu ideals', the focus shifted to individuals, and the family was 'pushed far into the background'.[50] The protagonists of the novels of that period were a bit like 'Nietzsche's Ubermenschen (superman), created in reaction to the passive acceptance of destiny or this new dogmatism of materialistic dialectics'.[51] *Shekhar* fits right in, its political imagination drawn from the 'disenthralled decades of the 1930s and 1940s', its protagonist's life 'seamlessly transitioning between the personal and the political'. [52]

Vatsaraj, Agyeya's younger brother, was prescient in his prediction of 'extravagant praise and extreme vilification' for *Shekhar*.[53] Even before critics could take it up for serious reviews, the new novel had achieved something unthinkable: readers on the left and right were united in their anger and denunciation of it. Agyeya remembered there were meetings (sometimes jointly organized by left and right) to condemn and burn copies of the book, especially in Agra and Delhi. What had riled the conservative set was *Shekhar*'s alleged obscenity, the 'incestuous relationship' with his cousin.[54] The left was angry about the derision of Trotsky and Stalin. Thus, the 'two extremes combined' to burn the book in a public meeting and wanted it banned too.[55]

The ordinary reader was not outraged. Women readers, especially, were not bothered by the 'incest' or so-called Stalin-bashing. They were caught up in the grand sweep of the story. The mystique around Agyeya, the writer with a revolutionary past, deepened further. One Kumari Sarla

Chandel, a student, wrote from the cantonment town of Mhow about how her life had changed after reading *Shekhar*. It had taken Chandel years to get Agyeya's address, and now she desired to hear from him with an autographed picture. Until she read *Shekhar*, Chandel had a low opinion of Hindi novels. She wrote that she was confident there would be no other work like *Shekhar* in the future.[56]

The writer Maithilisharan Gupt, *dadda* (a term of endearment for elder brother) to Agyeya, was from an earlier generation and represented different literary sensibilities. Gupt was up till two in the morning, finishing the first volume in one sitting. But he was angry too, and troubled. He immediately shot off a letter telling Agyeya that *Shekhar* was unacceptable to him, was against his *sanskar* (upbringing and culture) but also that he could not help finishing it in one go.[57] Not far from Gupt's Chirgaon, in Agra, young writer Nemichandra Jain read *Shekhar* twice in a single day. By his own admission, Jain was not easily agitated by what he read, but *Shekhar*, he said, 'shakes you from the very depths'.[58]

Shekhar generated a lot of discussion everywhere. Some reviewers would send Agyeya a copy of their article. As did Onkar Shankar Vidyarthi, son of legendary editor-politician Ganesh Shankar Vidyarthi. Onkar was a regular writer for *Pratap*, the Kanpur daily established by his father in 1913. He had written a scathing review of *Shekhar*. But on finding out that another volume was lined up, he regretted his review. Onkar tried to make amends by telling Agyeya the first volume was a complete novel in itself, and even if there was no sequel, it would not detract from the beauty and importance of the published one. He requested Agyeya to not take some of the criticism seriously.[59] Agyeya appears to have responded to Onkar, suggesting that the review was an insult and asking him to read *Shekhar* again.

In the intense ideological battle in the Hindi literary world, leading critic Shivdan Singh Chauhan had established himself as the spokesperson of the Progressives. He and Agyeya shared a formal but cordial relationship. Chauhan reviewed Premchand's *Godan* and Agyeya's *Shekhar* together. *Shekhar* was a psychological study of a man whose consciousness was that of an anti-social. Chauhan felt that after *Godan*, a novel was needed to take forward the tradition of farmer Hori, its protagonist, or some middle-class character, either psychologically or socially.[60] Between Hori and Shekhar, Chauhan made it clear that he preferred Premchand's farmer. With Hori's decline, he said, we see the decline of society, and his rise shows society's inherent ability to revive itself. On the contrary, Shekhar was a personification of discontent and struggle.[61]

Modern Review said that through Shekhar's life, one witnessed the 'drama of all the conflicting currents and cross-currents of our age'. Calling it an 'earnest novel, impassioned though restrained', reviewer Mohanlal Bajpai liked the way sex was 'subconsciously introduced' and the role it played in the development of the 'hero's character'. He also praised the way Agyeya had consciously avoided identification with any isms. But Bajpai could see the book would attract both 'approbation and wrath', leaving very little place for the opinion of the common reader.[62]

Agyeya's depiction of incest particularly offended Delhi University's Nagendra. He wrote derisively, 'It must have required immense goodness (*satogun*) of character in Agyeya to depict a relationship that is considered a despicable crime in both east and the west.'[63]

Meanwhile, Agyeya was trying to move beyond the laurels and intense criticism that *Shekhar* received. The period after *Vishal Bharat* was melancholic. He was working for All India Radio (AIR) in Delhi, had drawn close to M.N. Roy's Radical Democratic Party and embarked on a passionate affair with Kripa Sen—an artist with AIR and a schoolteacher—who came from an elite Indore family. Sen was waiting for the dissolution of a bad marriage, just as Agyeya's own marriage with Santosh Kashyap was on the rocks.[64]

AGYEYA'S ANTI-FASCIST PERIOD

Meanwhile, a serious anti-fascist movement had started in 1940 and Agyeya was in the thick of it. Roy was the key organizer of the two-day conference in Calcutta, and Agyeya was also invited. Roy's public appeal clearly stated: 'Non-cooperation with the war should not be the badge of Indian patriotism, no pacifism can be a practicable ideal. In the midst of a world enslaved by triumphant fascism, the chances of India attaining her freedom will be even more remote than ever. Herself conquered by this or that fascist power, India will lose the very possibility of carrying on her struggle for freedom.' The fifty-four signatories to this appeal consisted of some formidable names, the majority of them opposed to the Congress, like Syama Prasad Mukherjee, B.R. Ambedkar, Humayun Kabir, Tej Bahadur Sapru, H.L. Kunzru, Sir J.P. Srivastava, Master Tara Singh, Sikandar Hyat Khan, R.M. Palat, N.B. Khare, M.S. Aney and others.[65]

These events helped firm up Agyeya's allegiance to anti-fascism. It was a strong personal belief he wanted to translate into action. At thirty-two, with a colossal literary reputation, a revolutionary past, and a marriage on its last legs, Agyeya was embarking on a new path, a journey that would change his life and reputation forever. He joined the army.

It was an unimaginable metamorphosis: a former revolutionary, involved in armed insurrection against the colonial government, taking up arms to defend the empire. His detractors, most of whom were a part of the left camp, labelled him a collaborator. Agyeya's lucid writings arguing that fascism was the bigger foe were totally disregarded. The army sojourn became part of a larger war within the left camp: between the Communist Party of India (CPI) and M.N. Roy's Radical Democratic Party, each of whom accused the other of ideological distortion from the Marxian path. Although Agyeya was a keen votary of Roy, it is unlikely the former was involved in the ideological debates within the larger left fold. He often argued with Roy, though—and remembered how Roy would mercilessly demolish his arguments.[66]

Agyeya was assigned to Assam, and was waiting to join. There were rumours he was having second thoughts.[67] Kripa too was worried. She was not in favour of Agyeya becoming a 'military man in Assam'. Her reasons were not selfish. 'For one thing, you sell yourself to our Rulers and above all, you go into a life devoid of any intellectual or even intelligent outlet', she told him. Agyeya's present life in which he could choose his 'environment to keep aloof, to write, to read, to go out' whenever he felt like, was dear to Kripa. In Assam, she feared, he would be part of the military crowd, 'dull, stupid and mercenary'. Kripa wondered if there was 'anything worth killing yourself for'.[68]

Her letter stayed in Agyeya's mind. He did not want to leave it unanswered, and responded with a tediously long missive, taking many days over it, explaining himself. Agyeya said he was not peeved with her but stood his ground. The war he was about to join was 'war worthy' even though, he agreed, war in general was an unsavoury, brutal act. He did not care about remaining impartial, and left it to Kripa to decide if he was taking himself too seriously and feeding his own ego. She had warned him about living with people of less intellect in the army. He believed there would be much to learn from interacting with lower-rank officers and non-military personnel. 'Therefore, my death will not be as quick as you fear, I mean the intellectual death', he assured her.[69]

The fundamental question, he believed, was how India and Indians should respond to Japanese aggression in the North-east, even if India had no role to play in the war. He also dismissed the argument that helping Japan could have resulted in an easy Independence. As for the inherent incongruity of a revolutionary-turned-soldier, Agyeya was often at a loss to understand how literary critics could criticize contradiction as a negative strand in any personality.[70]

Literature did not take a back seat while Agyeya was in the army. The *Tar Saptak* project, an anthology collecting the work of seven poets, was gathering momentum. It turned out to be a manifesto of modernism in Hindi literature. Consisting of poems by Agyeya, Nemichandra Jain, Bharat Bhushan Agarwal, Prabhakar Machwe, Ramvilas Sharma, Girija Kumar Mathur and Muktibodh, *Tar Saptak* was self-published in 1943. From its very conception to after-life, the *Saptak* series (four volumes) has been one of the most discussed and controversial anthology series of Hindi poetry. And like everything that Agyeya touched, there continue to be detractors, even though it is established that the anthology heralded a new era in Hindi poetry—the literary movement of *Prayogvad*, experimentalism, paved the way for *Nayi Kavita*, the new poetry. For German scholar Lothar Lutze, 1943 was the year of the birth of 'Hindi literariness' and Prayogvad was the first literary movement in Hindi poetry.[71]

The significance of the collection is well laid out in Agyeya's sharp introduction. He said the poets in the collection see poetry as a 'sphere of experiment . . . [they] do not claim that they have found the truth of poetry; but consider themselves to be mere seekers'. He talked of poets not belonging to any school, not serving any ism (vad), as mere travellers, or not even travellers, but seekers of a path (*rahon ke anvesi*). However, the collection fell foul of the left-dominated Hindi literary establishment. The Hindi Sahitya Sammelan of Uttar Pradesh (UP) held a meeting and its subject committee prepared a resolution for the plenum to ban the volume on the ground that some of the poems were obscene. But Purshottam Das Tandon as president did not allow censure and the resolution was dropped.[72] Interestingly, most poets in the group, like Muktibodh, Jain, Sharma and Agarwal, were Marxists, and Agyeya was a Freudian.[73] This alone was proof that the charge—of *Saptak* being a well-devised assault on the Marxist-led Progressive school—did not hold water.

Agyeya alleged that, in the 1950s, while he was editing the literary journal *Pratik* in Allahabad, the Progressive Writers' Association (PWA) discussed how he was public enemy number one, and that it ought to be official policy, both for the party and PWA, to try and first isolate and then to liquidate him.[74] He blamed Nemichandra Jain, a friend and then a member of CPI, and Bharat Bhushan Agarwal, also a Marxist, for sabotaging *Pratik*, and alleged Jain was sent by the party to do so.[75]

The ICCF Incident

While the Hindi literary world was still grappling with Agyeya's so-called collaborationist act of joining the British Army, he distanced himself from the debates. He had met Jayaprakash (JP) Narayan after the latter's Hazaribagh jailbreak and the two hit it off instantly. In the 1940s, JP was already disenchanted with the Congress, but Agyeya joined an editorial board—that also had Rajendra Prasad, S. Radhakrishnan, K.M. Munshi, Seth Govind Das, Vishwanath More, Nandalal Bose, Lanka Sundaram and Purshottam Das Tandon—that was planning a commemorative volume to celebrate Nehru's sixtieth birthday. Being the youngest member, Agyeya was doing the bulk of the work. Reluctant to praise Nehru in print and probably trying to wriggle out, M.N. Roy demanded remuneration for his article. Agyeya promised to take up this demand with the editorial board, and suggested Roy should write on New Humanism. In any case, Agyeya had very little hope from the book, not only because it was heavily priced but also because there was 'considerable general disillusionment and perplexity' in society.[76]

Soon, however, Agyeya became part of something Nehru abhorred. The anti-fascist, anti-communist movement had taken a new turn in the 1950s with the emergence of the CIA-funded CCF. Agyeya and many acolytes of M.N. Roy—Abu Sayed (editor of *Quest*), K.K. Sinha, A.B. Shah, J.B.H. Wadia, Nissim Ezekiel, Philip Spratt—became part of it and so did JP, Ashok Mehta, Minoo Masani and others. CCF was funding *Freedom First* and *Quest*. Agyeya was the first secretary of the Indian CCF (ICCF) and also the literary editor of *Thought* magazine from Delhi.

The Nehru government did not take kindly to the formation of the Indian chapter of CCF. It was suspicious of its intentions and felt the forum would attack the government's neutral foreign policy. It was with great reluctance that the Nehru government gave permission to the CCF to hold its second international conference in Delhi in 1951. However, with just a week left for the conference, permission was withdrawn. One of the reasons given was that it was less a meeting of CCF and more of an American Congress, forcing Agyeya and others to shift the venue to Bombay where Minoo Masani's Democratic Research Service took over the task of organizing the event. Celebrated international writers, scientists and poets like Stephen Spender, W.H. Auden, Denis de Rougemont and H.J. Muller attended the meeting. Nehru's bête noire K.M. Munshi, a member of the cabinet, was also present and made the inaugural speech.[77]

For Agyeya, the conference became a huge personal embarrassment. Neither he nor his authorized biographer mentioned this incident in their writings. However, the James Burnham Papers in Stanford's Hoover Institution have all the details. A bank draft of $1000 sent by James Burnham, the CIA's pointsman for CCF, went missing. Burnham thought that Agyeya, as secretary of ICCF, had diverted the funds to the bank account of *Thought* magazine. On close scrutiny of the magazine's accounts, it turned out that he had indeed diverted the funds. Masani called him a thief and suspended him from ICCF. The ICCF office was moved to Bangalore and Philip Spratt was asked to run it. All documents were also shifted from the *Thought* office to Bangalore. The Indian committee also found other financial discrepancies in *Thought*'s bank balance, like Agyeya not having accounted for a part of an expenditure that was incurred. One grant from the Tata Trust could also not be sufficiently explained.[78]

Though Agyeya's relationship with ICCF formally ended with this unsavoury incident, he kept a close eye on its activities and maintained a good relationship with many of its members. In later years, ICCF became a one-man show run by Masani. Agyeya took the opportunity to get back at him. He said ICCF had become too partisan and suggested it should 'devote itself to the promotion of culture in all aspects'.[79] This incident—the diversion of funds—caused much heartburn in the *Thought* editorial board. Martin Russell, a board member, offered to sever the relationship between the weekly and ICCF. He also requested that the board itself be dissolved.[80]

1960s AND THE EMERGENCY

In the 1960s, Agyeya's frustration with the road independent India had taken, a tale of corruption and poverty, resulted in poems like '*Azadi Ke Bees Baras*', a searing indictment of missed opportunities and the growing social and economic divide.

Agyeya's tryst with politics peaked in the years before the Emergency. At the request of JP, he took up the editorship of the newly established *Everyman's* which also had S. Mulgaonkar in the editorial board. It was Agyeya's eighth job as editor, a testimony of his independent mind and politics. *Everyman's* came at a time when JP was under relentless attack from what he called the 'tycoon press', 'pro-Soviet press of different hues' and '*Patriot-Link* and *Blitz*' variety of journals.[81]

Everyman's called itself a 'non-partisan journal of public affairs—national and international'. 'It is not wedded to any ism or ideology, whether of the Left, Right or Centre. It will examine public issues dispassionately to offer constructive criticism in the light of the broad ideals, values and principles to which it is dedicated', JP wrote as *Everyman's* statement of policy.[82] It was highly critical of the government, Congress culture and Indira Gandhi's totalitarian streak. It mapped Cold-War politics incisively, and also seriously covered human rights, the application of Gandhian principles in day-to-day life, books, music, culture and the environment. When news of the imminent arrest of Russian physicist Andrei Sakharov broke, *Everyman's* did a story on dissent in Soviet Russia and issued a public statement signed by Agyeya, M.C. Setalvad, J.P. Narayan, M.C. Chagla, V.M. Tarakunde, S. Mulgaonkar and Asoka Mehta.[83]

But *Everyman's* gave JP no respite as *Blitz* and *Patriot-Link* continued to attack him. But it was not until the *New York Times* did another exposé of CIA funding for the CCF that JP responded with a centre-spread article with this resounding headline: 'The Day Jayaprakash Narayan Turns a Foreign Stooge, There Will Be No Patriot Left in This Country'. He gave a point-by-point rebuttal of the allegation but his defence was meek. JP contended that except Mike Josselson of CCF and perhaps one or two others, 'no one else had known the real funding source of the American foundations that ostensibly financed the Congress'. 'All of us in the Congress felt cruelly deceived and let down. I immediately resigned my honorary presidentship and cut off my relations with the international organisation', he wrote.[84] Like in 1954, when it was first alleged that the CCF was CIA-funded, Agyeya chose to remain silent.

By the 1970s, Agyeya had clarity about what constituted a political act. He was opposed to writing that only served a political cause. He argued that what a writer really does is enlarge or deepen human sensibility and if they succeed in that then their readers become different social entities, and in that sense there is social change. But social change is not what the writer works for. He often referred to the writer Yashpal, his comrade during the revolutionary years, as an example of how writing might suffer when it is written around an ideology.[85]

So where did this leave Agyeya? He defended his contradictions and would often cite Walt Whitman's 'I am large, I contain multitudes'.[86] But at a serious level he argued that training as an anarchist, and the experience of being thrown into sometimes compulsory and disagreeable company helped. 'I still tend to think differently and I may say so, without self-praise, a little more consistently than many of my contemporaries'.[87] It is only after his death in 1987 that some of his detractors changed their position and made an attempt to understand his works. The left critic Namvar Singh not only edited a volume of Agyeya's poems but even acknowledged 'Asadhya Veena' (Unmastered Lute), a long court poem, as among the three best Hindi poems of the twentieth century.[88] There have been several such U-turns about Agyeya and his modernist ethos. But his 'multitudes' are still viewed through the Hindi world's grand conspiracy theories, leaving him more unknowable than Premchand could have imagined while giving him the name Agyeya.

10

ALONE AT HOME, AMONG FRIENDS ABROAD? B.R. SHENOY FROM AUSTRIAN SCHOOL MONETARY ECONOMIST TO COLD-WAR PUBLIC INTELLECTUAL

ADITYA BALASUBRAMANIAN

DISCUSSION OF THE late Indian economist B.R. Shenoy's (1905-78) life and career seems to be characterized by a focus on his isolation. Ramachandra Guha's *India after Gandhi* refers to Shenoy in the 1960s as a 'lone free-marketeer drowned out by a chorus of social democrats and leftists'.[1] His contemporary, the veteran Indian policymaker I.G. Patel, observed that Shenoy was 'not heard, not listened to, and not even respected'.[2] Aware of his marginalization, Shenoy complained to the eminent American free-market economist Milton Friedman in 1959 of 'how lonely I am in India advocating the viewpoint I have been doing' and that 'hardly any of the senior Indian economists . . . have found reason to agree with me'.[3] On his deathbed, Shenoy confessed to a former student and friend his regret about being unable to persuade policymakers to accept his free-market views.[4]

If alone at home, Shenoy was among friends abroad. His relationships to a network of Western free-market economists and publicists whom he met through involvement in the Mont Pelerin Society or MPS helped him remake himself as a Cold-War public intellectual after a career as a monetary economist. Membership in the society created the possibilities for mutual publicity; Shenoy could become visible abroad, and he helped to popularize ideas of MPS economists and publicists in India. The esteem and indeed lavish praise of senior thinkers abroad served as a form of legitimation for Shenoy that helped him overcome long-standing professional disappointment. Crucially, the interactions and exchanges that these connections spawned invigorated Shenoy and helped make possible his transition from a largely technocratic economist into a public intellectual of the early right.

Because Shenoy did not leave any papers behind and had a peripatetic career making any institutional collection only partial, this essay has used a combination of published writings, newspapers and multiple archival fragments to reconstruct the salient aspects of his intellectual biography. The motivations of such an exercise are threefold. The first is to underscore how transnational networks serve not merely in facilitating the co-production or flow of knowledge and capital but also help to satisfy more basic human needs like emotional support and fellow feeling. Next, Shenoy was not merely useful for Western free-market economists in constructing narratives of the failure of scientific planned development, as recent work has contended; this was a two-way street.[5] Finally, this essay points to a cultural Cold War in India, more or less ignored in literature that has focused on war, diplomatic or foreign policy history.[6] By drawing attention to Shenoy, the essay underscores the polyphony of economic ideas in India during an era typically associated with Nehruvian hegemony.[7]

Becoming the Lone Indian Free-Market Economist

Shenoy's professional career traced an alternative trajectory from most of his contemporaries, reflected in his institutional training, academic field of study, and early political influences. From the town of Bellikoth in South Kanara district of Madras Presidency (today's Karnataka), he ran away from home to take part in the nationalist movement. He was imprisoned during the Non-Cooperation movement of 1921-22, where he encountered Madan Mohan Malaviya. In jail, Malaviya was not in the best of health, and Shenoy helped the senior nationalist leader in basic tasks. The two established some kind of relationship. Shenoy followed Malaviya to the Benares Hindu University (BHU), where the latter was the founding vice-chancellor.[8]

BHU was the country's first Hindu university. Most of its funding came from Hindu upper-caste families in north India rather than the colonial state. Unlike the presidency universities established in the aftermath of the 1857 uprising to train Indians for administrative office, training in the Hindi language was emphasized.[9] BHU was unmistakably nationalist. Here, Shenoy encountered the Hindu revivalist strand of Indian nationalism as opposed to the Gandhian or Nehruvian varieties. This brand of nationalism had a more individualist current and was religiously communal.[10] When he would later speak of the perils of socialist planning, he would single out the dangers of a life without culture. The revival and modernization of Hindu culture was one of BHU's founding aims.

Shenoy received both bachelor's and master's degrees in economics during the period between 1924 and 1930, performing at or near the top of his class in his examinations and taking part in student government. Shenoy's politics and economics were parts of a whole from his early days as a student. He read for a master's under Professor Pran Nath, who held both a DSc in economics from London and a PhD from Vienna. Austrian economics was rooted in methodological individualism, consistent with the individualism of Malaviya's brand of Hindu revivalism. Most recently, economists working in the Austrian tradition had linked monetary theory to issues of production and consumption.[11] In contrast to their rival German historicist school, this school of thinkers sought to develop universally valid theories. Nationalist interest and the political economy being practised in Vienna and London, which focused on monetary theory, overlapped.

While Shenoy studied in Banaras, an intense debate broke out about the independence of the rupee from the pound and the prospects for an independent central bank. Indian nationalists and business came together to protest the British proposal to peg the rupee at the pre-World War I exchange rate. This measure was being undertaken in the aftermath of the restoration of the pound to its pre-war rate exchange and the resumption of convertibility to gold.[12] This overvalued rate of exchange would bring about deflation and economic distress. The idea of bringing India back to the pre-war exchange rate, which was too high, was in part to help Britain deal with its gold shortages.[13] There were two major lines of argument adduced by Indians. The first was that this peg was too high and would diminish export prospects. The second, consistent with broader demands for self-government being made by nationalists, was that colonial monetary affairs should be independent from those of the metropole and India required an independent central bank.[14] It was small wonder then, that Shenoy's proposed research topic when he applied for further studies at the London School of Economics (LSE) after passing out of Banaras was monetary economics. But this was an unorthodox interest. While economists of the previous decades from India like B.R. Ambedkar studied monetary affairs like Shenoy, contemporaries like V.K.R.V. Rao studied national income accounting and D.R. Gadgil studied industrial development. As time wore on, those influenced by the socialist intellectual currents of interwar Britain would gravitate towards the study of economic planning.[15]

Shenoy proceeded to the LSE in late 1930, as Great Britain was beginning to experience the pain of the Great Depression. He completed coursework exclusively on problems of currency and finance, and at least one of his teachers was a laissez-faire economist.[16] Shenoy graduated with an MSc with a thesis on 'Some Aspects of a Central Bank for India', a rather topical subject given the 1931 publication of the *Report of the Indian Central Banking Enquiry Committee* recommending the establishment of the Reserve Bank.[17]

Shenoy experienced academic and financial hardship in London. His coursework examination was unsuccessful the first time, and it was only after a second examination conducted six months later that he was awarded the degree. Although he had hoped to receive a doctorate, lack of funds forced Shenoy to cut short his studies. He wrote wistfully in a letter requesting remission of his examination fee that 'I came to this country partly on borrowed money and partly on a scholarship which was a loan scholarship. I did a thing which I could not afford, and therefore a thing which was wrong. I am now called upon to pay a penalty for it!'[18] One should not read too much into this anguished statement or draw analogies from the context of the individual to the state carelessly, but in light of Shenoy's later aversion to public deficits, his equation of indebtedness with immorality and ultimate punishment is noteworthy.

Shenoy's time at the LSE was punctuated by an intense debate raging about the origins of and methods to overcome the economic slump. The Austrian F.A. von Hayek arrived at the LSE to deliver lectures which would form the foundation of a book called *Prices and Production*.[19] This work synthesized previous work in the Austrian tradition, which Shenoy would have encountered in Banaras. Hayek argued that business cycles originate from excessive credit creation by the central bank. He opposed the use of monetary policy to decrease interest rates at a time of downturn, suggesting that it interfered with the natural adjustment processes of the market. Deficit spending by governments would merely prolong this process by artificially increasing prices and stimulating unproductive investment. On Hayek's theory, the origins of the British economic slump were excessive credit creation in the past. The lectures were a major success; LSE offered Hayek a chair.[20]

By contrast, the influential Cambridge economist John Maynard Keynes was building upon his recent *Treatise on Money* (1930) to argue that it was the return to the gold standard at an overvalued rate of exchange of the pound that had forced down wages and savings and resulted in credit contraction that arrested productive investment in the economy. When savings exceeded investment, the economy went into recession. He argued for public works to help combat the slump by raising investment, suggesting that they would generate further spending from the newly employed through a multiplier effect. As these views were not politically acceptable, he later suggested introduction of protective tariffs to stimulate domestic industry.[21]

Keynes and Hayek squared off against each other in the pages of the *Economic Journal*. Their quarrel was the beginning of one of the biggest rivalries in twentieth-century economics. This sharpened after Keynes took aboard Hayek's criticism about having no theory of capital and interest by developing one as part of his magnum opus, *The General Theory of Employment, Interest and Money*.[22] It was also indicative of political differences. Keynes believed in an active role for the government in economic life; Hayek was deeply sceptical of its possibilities. Although in the early 1930s the British government would not take on Keynes' prescriptions, a broader Keynesian paradigm shift would take place, lasting most of the next three decades. Demand management through public spending and the manipulation of interest rates through central banks became a standard feature of economic policy, especially in the Western world. Elsewhere, a related phenomenon took place, as state interventionism in the economy, particularly in the form of central planning, became the modus operandi of the new 'development economics' that sought to lift poorer and decolonizing nations out of poverty.[23] The intellectual ballast to central planning was provided by the Soviet Union, which had used these techniques to convert itself into a major industrial power.

Two articles he published in Harvard's venerable *Quarterly Journal of Economics* during the early 1930s suggest strongly that the young Shenoy was more aligned with the Hayekian vision. In the first, Shenoy built on equations featured in Keynes' *Treatise on Money* to argue that the price level of investment goods was solely based on efficiency earnings of the factors of production used in making them added to the profit per unit output of new investment goods. But unlike Keynes, Shenoy felt that this price level could not be influenced by liquidity and credit in the banking system 'in whatever way it may behave', but only by the rate of efficiency of the earnings of the factors of production.[24] Two years later, in the second article, Shenoy argued that the price levels of investment goods and consumption goods were interdependent, contesting Keynes' assertion in the *Treatise* that these prices were independent of each other.[25] Both showed Shenoy's mistrust of the efficacy of creating high liquidity in the banking and credit system, something that a Keynesian monetary policy would prescribe in a period of slump. Shenoy's willingness to take on Keynes foreshadows his later works' unambiguous disagreement with certain tenets of Keynesian economic policy. His early academic output reveals the influence of price theory, the notion of market efficiency, and an almost exclusive focus on questions of finance.

Shenoy went on from the LSE to a peripatetic career as a monetary economist. He became respected in his field of monetary policy but was not in the inner circles of planning policymaking. He moved from the obscure Rajaram College in the princely state of Kolhapur, to the Ceylon University College and Board of Commissioners of Ceylon Currency in in Colombo, to SLD Arts College in Ahmedabad, to the Reserve Bank of India in Bombay, to the Indian Mission of the International Monetary Fund (IMF) in Washington.[26] He was also prolific and published a number of books. These ranged from the monetary history of Ceylon to prescriptions for Indian economic policy to overcome the post-war slump.[27] These books were chiefly concerned with issues of currency and finance and informed by a classical view of monetary theory that saw price as solely determined by the forces of supply and demand.

Shenoy's books underscore his departure from mainstream views. After the war, he suggested that credit expansion would create an inflationary boom followed by a bust rather than help to combat the shortfall in demand for goods because of the destruction of peacetime productive capacity during the war. He therefore suggested avoiding a boom by continuing wartime command and control policies.[28] He further believed that India was not in a creditor position to the United Kingdom despite having accumulated sterling balances for contributing to the war effort, by incorrectly valuing all foreign investment in India as a liability.[29] The sterling balances had been seen as a key source of finance for development planning, particularly by the authors of India's 1944 Bombay Plan that formed the foundation of the First Five-Year Plan. In a book reviewing the financial provisions of the plan, Shenoy argued that using the sterling balances would undermine the currency stability of the rupee. By spending the sterling balances and raising deficits by printing money, he felt that India would not be creditworthy enough to raise the capital required to meet the plan requirements.[30] Moving from institution to institution with such ideas, Shenoy won little sympathy for his views.

A major professional disappointment occurring during these years came from Shenoy's three unsuccessful attempts to secure a doctoral degree from London by submitting published work for a DSc (Econ).[31] The first time, his manuscript on the history of Ceylon currency and finance was turned down because it was unpublished, rejecting his request for the relaxation of the publication requirement in view of wartime paper shortage. The second time, after publication by the Indian branch of Oxford University press, it was rejected for the degree of DSc for being too narrow and limited in scope. Shenoy was advised that he might have been more successful in applying for the external PhD, a lower degree. However, there was a technicality that prevented this from taking place. According to the rules for the external PhD, the applicant was required to have a first degree from the University of London. Furthermore, the economics department was beginning to bring its policies in line with other faculties and discourage published work from being considered for the PhD. Shenoy's request for an exception in light of the circumstances was turned down. After the war, Shenoy submitted two additional books to make a fresh application for the DSc (1946). However, the archival trail runs cold here, and he never listed this credential in subsequent works like he did his others. Shenoy's tenacity in keeping up his publication record and submitting multiple applications for the DSc indicated how important this recognition was to him. Being denied the doctorate was being denied a kind of legitimacy as an economist.

The period 1954-55 was a turning point for both Shenoy and Indian economic policy. Shenoy moved from relative obscurity at the IMF and into the public eye. He left Washington for Gujarat University in Ahmedabad to take up a position as director of social sciences in 1954. Shenoy's new role, which was not specifically focused in economics like his previous positions, allowed him to stop working on policy questions or for an academic audience and move into publishing for the reading public. It also meant that he would extend his ideas from monetary economics to the economy at large. The next year, he was invited on to the panel of economists on the Second Five-Year Plan frame in 1955 as its sole monetary expert.

The plan frame aimed at establishing a heavy industrial base for India through capital goods-led import-substituting industrialization.[32] It was part of a broader programme of state-led development that sought to bring about what was described by the Congress Working Committee as a 'socialistic pattern of society'. Notably, state-directed planning sought to invert historical processes of development by bringing about industrialization before agricultural self-sufficiency. What particularly concerned Shenoy was that the plan frame left approximately 8 per cent of the budget unfunded and involved substantial foreign aid.

'Probably the greatest enemy of the Kuomintang in China was the printing press', Shenoy warned in his 'Note of Dissent' submitted to the panel. He warned of the 'over-ambitious character of the Plan Frame which would unleash "uncontrolled inflation"'.[33] He also felt that statistics from communist economies like the Soviet Union, Poland and Bulgaria had given the panel false impressions of how quickly the Indian economy could grow. Unlike these countries, the Indian government could not count on 'the efficiency of totalitarian devices' to bring about such rapid change.[34] Democracy occupied a central position in Nehru's conception of the planning enterprise. As a result, the optimistic projections for savings to be invested in the plan overstated their true values. In reality, procurement of the funding required for a plan of the envisioned size would involve running large deficits. 'No plan can be bigger or bolder than the available real resources', Shenoy wrote, and this one was striving for the impossible.

Shenoy was the only dissenter in the panel of economists and his strident tone indicates a penchant for hyperbole. While this would not have endeared him to his colleagues in India, it was the kind of rhetoric that would be noticed in the press and did well with the media. Ultimately, it helped Shenoy court a new audience. Over the next fifteen years, he would continue to adopt this tone as he transitioned into the role of an economic commentator and adviser.

Legitimation and Mutual Publicity: Shenoy and the Mont Pelerin Society

The appearance of Shenoy's Note of Dissent as part of a set of papers relating to the formulation of the Second Plan ensured that it would be read by those interested in Indian economic development all around the world. Among its readers was development economist Peter Bauer (1915-2002), then lecturing at Cambridge. Bauer was the rare pro-market-development economist of his day and established himself as the most forceful critic of foreign aid. He believed that aid essentially funnelled resources into the hands of government and created incentives for corruption rather than productive investment. More broadly, Bauer considered private entrepreneurship as the engine of economic development rather than central planning. As he was learning about the Second Plan, he came across Shenoy's note.[35] Bauer would draw upon Shenoy's work a few years later when he wrote a report for the American Enterprise Institute seeking to discourage the United States from increasing its foreign aid contribution to India.[36]

The note's publication coincided with the Chicago economist Milton Friedman's visit to India to advise on the Second Plan. Whereas most of the galaxy of esteemed economists that descended upon India during the formulation of the Second Plan were enthusiastic about its outline and prospects, Friedman expressed considerable reservation.[37] His confidential note submitted to the Government of India criticized the over-emphasis on heavy industry and the neglect of small- and- medium-size enterprises. Too much was being attempted by the public sector, and the attempt to control the private sector was too rigid, it suggested. Like Shenoy, Friedman also raised the concern that deficit financing would stoke inflation. He further suggested, as he did irrespective of the country, that India should abandon its fixed exchange rate. This, he reasoned, would create a depreciation of the currency that would stimulate exports and raise foreign exchange earnings to finance development.[38] Friedman would have first encountered Shenoy at this time.

Both Bauer and Friedman were part of Hayek's Mont Pelerin Society. This organization was convened in 1947 in response to the rising tide of statism and the influence of collectivist ideologies in economic policy. It was 'an international gathering place for leading philosophers, economists, journalists, politicians, and philanthropists who supported the market mechanism', and members played a decisive role in bringing market economics back to the mainstream of public discourse in the second half of the twentieth century.[39] Bauer arranged an invitation and financing for Shenoy to attend the society's annual meeting at Oxford in 1959.

In a powerful, booming voice, the erstwhile member of BHU's student government addressed the body on 'Free-Market Economy for India'. He presented a binary between a communist and a free-market economy, rejecting India's 'mixed economy' model, comprising both state-owned and private enterprise, as disingenuous. He labelled its policymakers 'Neo-communist strategists' taking India on the path to serfdom and 'leftist dictatorship'. Even if it achieved its economic aims, Indian planning would result in 'totalitarian prosperity', 'a case of seemingly full, physical well-being without culture. And life of physical well-being without culture is not life worth living' (sic). Shenoy made a number of rhetorical leaps to get there, even conceding that further dirigisme might be successful. But it was a Faustian bargain. The international community was partially to blame for the trajectory of Indian development. Foreign aid, by helping to 'patch up policy aberrations', had 'an element of disservice in disguise'. Shenoy suggested an alternative:

> The greatest foreign aid India requires, is the philosophy of the Mont Pelerin Society. (applause). If this philosophy can be freely imported and freely used in the country, and if the country can be rescued from the policies that are now being pursued, and there is a changeover to the free market economy, we will have done more for speedy Indian economic development than all the foreign aid that is planned, and all the foreign aid that has come into the country.[40]

This rhetoric made quite an impression. The written text from which the speech had been composed lacked any reference to communism. Animated by the surroundings, Shenoy rose to the occasion and deviated from prepared remarks.[41] The following month, he wrote to Hayek that the meeting 'has reinforced my confidence in the importance of the free market economy for accelerated economic growth, in particular, of under-developed countries. I was also glad to see so many eminent people supporting my line of thinking on Indian economic issues.' He offered to send Hayek some of the books he had written.[42]

In his reply to Shenoy, Hayek wrote that 'your participation in our meeting was equally valuably fruitful to us and to me personally in particular'. Previously, Indian affairs seemed to Hayek 'a hopeless case', and the Indian students he had met at the LSE were 'intellectually not a very attractive type'. Now, however, 'my attitude to India has completely changed and . . . I do feel it again worthwhile to take an interest in developments in India'.[43] He offered the Indian economist membership of the society and replied that he eagerly awaited the receipt of Shenoy's books. Shenoy later tried to bring a panel of Mont Pelerin Society economists led by Hayek to speak in India. In 1965, he wrote to Hayek requesting permission for a student of his to translate Hayek's *Road to Serfdom* and *Constitution of Liberty* to Gujarati.[44]

Through membership in the society, where he became a director by the early 1970s, and these associations with leading Western economists, Shenoy experienced a form of legitimation he did not otherwise enjoy. In one letter, responding to some writings Shenoy had sent him, Friedman gushed that his article was 'magnificent', like all of Shenoy's writings on planning. He further praised Shenoy's erudition and courage to 'express himself despite the extraordinary weight of allegedly informed opinion on the other side'.[45] Bauer, who had just moved to the LSE, helped Shenoy get out of India by organizing the financing for sabbaticals. He invited Shenoy as a visiting professor back to his alma mater in 1963. The following year, he and another MPS economist, Magnus Gregersen, organized for a private foundation that supported conservative economists to bring Shenoy to the United States for a sabbatical year.[46] He spent time at Chicago with Friedman, who had recently visited India. The Chicago economist rolled out the red carpet for the Indian economist, throwing him a party attended by the who's who of the university. But this legitimation came not just in the form of being invited for academic visits or exchanging papers. It was also in the sense of being considered a fellow traveller or member of a community. This is evoked most clearly in Friedman's letters to Shenoy, where he referred to an economist who had recently visited India as one 'very much on our side', and described the society as 'our fellowship'.[47] For an economist who was ostracized by peers in his own country, this was friendliness he did not otherwise experience. Shenoy and his interlocutors lavished all kinds of praise upon each other, which would have reinforced this feeling of fellowship.

Another function of this network was mutual publicity. Shenoy intermediated between newspapers and organizations in India and the United States, courting economists and publicists of the society. This is evoked both in his interactions with Friedman, who was at the time reinventing himself as a public intellectual,[48] and in his contacts with middlebrow American publishers and newspapermen. All of them were associated with the post-World War II rebirth of political conservatism in America. Shenoy organized the publication in an Indian newspaper of an article 'Exchange Rate Policy' by Friedman, later republished as a pamphlet titled 'India needs a free market exchange rate' by the Bombay-based Forum of Free Enterprise.[49] He also organized for the forum to publish excerpts from Henry Hazlitt, a *Newsweek* columnist and co-founder of the first libertarian think tank, the Foundation of Economic Education. From his side, Hazlitt attempted to find an American publisher for Shenoy's book *Indian Economic Policy* and introduced him to the editor of *Fortune* magazine. This culminated in Shenoy publishing an article called 'The Right Road to Indian Progress' in the April 1960 issue of the magazine, which included a short profile of the author. In it, Shenoy argued that increasing foreign aid to India, as the recent Kennedy Cooper resolution had proposed, would merely subsidize the socialization of Indian economic policy and pave the way for communist ascent.[50] The West German economist Magnus Gregersen noted that Shenoy 'gives me good ammunition'.[51] In turn, Shenoy did the reverse in India.

Self-Refashioning in a Cold-War Public

By 1952, as the *Eastern Economist* noted, 'The Cold War has come to India. In Parliament it was only to be expected, but it is now seen increasingly in the corridors of buildings, in Club rooms and in every centre of discussion'.[52] Shenoy detached himself from the academy and refashioned himself as a Cold-War public intellectual through prolific media commentary on economic affairs, advising the right-wing Swatantra and Jana Sangh parties, and founding a short-lived think tank in New Delhi. In so doing, he helped bring economic policy into the sphere of contestation from a free-market perspective.[53]

Between 1954 and 1977, Shenoy wrote sixty-eight articles and thirty-seven letters to the editor in the *Times of India* alone. He was most prolific in the period 1960-61, directly after his induction into the MPS. At the time, the newspaper enjoyed the second highest circulation among English dailies, of over 1,00,000 copies.[54] Shenoy's name was reaching the reading public, and his articles drew critical responses nineteen times, apparently. He was also being noticed.

Shenoy's pieces in the *Times* and other periodicals, some of which have been compiled in an edited volume, are notable for their unswerving commitment to balanced budgets, devaluation of the exchange rate to promote exports, and minimal state intervention in the economy. He frequently raised the spectre of communism when discussing economic planning. He was especially concerned by India's food imports from the United States, which he believed prevented the country from addressing her productive capacity constraints and giving sufficient attention to agriculture. The other cause he championed was abolishing gold control measures which had been introduced to help India cope with foreign exchange shortages. Deploying the classic free-market argument against them, he argued that such measures essentially led to the hoarding of gold and facilitated a thriving gold smuggling industry. This was part of Shenoy's broader commitment to the idea that government allocation or control of resources led to the corruption of bureaucratic officials; therefore, allocation via the market was most efficient.[55] The Cold-War character is best brought out by an article that presented East and West Berlin as a natural experiment in 'free' vs 'controlled' economy and suggested that West Berlin's relative material prosperity was an indication of the wisdom of markets.[56] This was a slightly revised version of Shenoy's MPS speech from Oxford.

Shenoy told *Fortune* in 1960 that he had no political aspirations for himself. But he was by no means politically apathetic.[57] In late November 1964, with the US presidential elections just concluded, he wrote to Friedman that the conservative Goldwater's convincing loss to incumbent Lyndon Johnson was a 'great disappointment'.[58] On the eve of Indira Gandhi's thumping re-election in 1971, Shenoy warned Hayek that 'we are now facing what may turn out to be the most critical election as the party in office has extreme leftist bias bordering on communism',[59] But Shenoy was not just a partisan bystander. He played a crucial role in advising Chakravarti Rajagopalachari and Minoo Masani as the two formulated a political economy-based platform for the Swatantra Party, to date India's only secular party of the right.[60] The late S.V. Raju, the party's executive secretary, recalled that 'No parliamentary speech would be delivered by a Swatantra Party member without it being looked at by Shenoy first'.[61] While he ended up withdrawing his candidacy, Shenoy did submit papers to run for a seat in the Rajya Sabha as an independent from Ahmedabad in the 1968 elections.[62]

Most remarkably, Shenoy courted business and attracted private financing for an Economics Research Centre based out of Delhi.[63] This may well have been India's first right-of-centre think tank, and Shenoy commenced the process of establishing it almost immediately after he returned from his visit to the United States. It led him to resign his position at Gujarat in 1968 and operate from the Centre for the last ten years of his life. Although available details about this institution are scarce, it appears that Shenoy envisioned it to work like a comparable institution in the United States. He tried to organize funding from the MPS to bring Hayek to India for a visit and brought out an Indian edition of Hazlitt's *The Conquest of Poverty*.[64]

Shenoy's move into the public eye was a product of professional disappointment and an ideologically inflected turn in Indian economic policy. It is also in part due to his long-standing interest in political issues that dates back to his involvement in the nationalist movement as a youth. But this does not quite explain his tenacity. Here, two other factors are worth considering. The first is his strong anti-communism and acceptance of the idea that state intervention was always and everywhere bad for the economy, putting it on a path towards totalitarianism. He bought into the idea that the Cold War was a battle between good and evil, or free vs regulated markets. The second reason could be that the esteem and fellowship the MPS accorded him emboldened Shenoy as he remade himself as a public economist of the right. It gave a second wind to a career that was otherwise heading to obscurity. And although he did not officially join any party, his sympathy to the political right comes out clearly.

Conclusion

Hazlitt wrote a moving message of condolence to Shenoy's daughter after he passed away in 1978, recalling that 'I had a profound respect and admiration for him on both intellectual and moral grounds . . . The world can ill afford his passing at this time'.[65] Five years later, Peter Bauer declared Shenoy 'a hero and a saint', acknowledging Shenoy's personal influence on his thinking about India. Almost two decades later, the Centre of Civil Society in New Delhi, which aims to carry on Shenoy's line of thinking and work, published edited collections of his academic and journalistic writings, proclaiming him an apostle of India's post-liberalization economic policy.[66] The narrative, if advanced by a small constituency, was one of posthumous vindication articulated within the context of a stream of literature following liberalization regarding these measures as unshackling the chains of the Indian economy.[67]

In the aftermath of the 2008 global financial crisis, when faith in free-market economics is once again under attack across the world and India's market-based economic trajectory has hit more than a few developmental roadblocks, these assertions appear to be less complementary and this narrative more problematic.[68] Still, Shenoy's story is illuminating. At one level, it underscores how Indian nationalism gave rise to a plurality of views on political economy and how politicized Cold-War networks of expertise and publicity operated through strategic intermediaries in areas where one might not expect to find them. Further, it helps situate the first chapter of market advocacy in independent India in a broader global context, even as it emerged in the context of Shenoy's isolation. Building a transnational mosaic of the intellectual biographies of middling figures like Shenoy can help disentangle the complex strands of ideology comprising the ascendant right in India and indeed across the world.

PART III

THE MAKING OF INDIAN DEMOCRACY

11

THE ROAD TO SEVAGRAM

VENU MADHAV GOVINDU

ON 16 JUNE 1936, Mohandas Karamchand Gandhi walked through pouring rain from Wardha to the nearby village of Segaon. Sevagram—as Segaon was soon renamed—was to be his last home. Segaon had little to commend itself. It was a 'sickness-inducing, snake, scorpion and tick-infested summer inferno and winter swamp without road, railway station, shop or post office'.[1] This move to a remote and inhospitable village was seen by many people as yet another of Gandhi's perplexing gestures. They fretted at the inconvenience it presented to the Congress stalwarts who wished to meet him. But 'Gandhi liked the idea of living in an isolated hamlet'.[2] For him, Sevagram represented much more than its hostile environs or its isolation. The move to a simple hut in a remote village was the culmination of a series of measures that Gandhi undertook in the early years of the 1930s to underline the reorientation of his concerns.

While the literature on myriad aspects of Gandhi's life and work is voluminous, there is much to be gained in understanding Gandhi's motivations to move to Sevagram. In the compass of this essay, I will examine the primary political and economic forces at play in the first half of the 1930s and the nature of Gandhi's commitments and actions that—figuratively speaking—put him on the road to Sevagram.[3]

The 1930s began with the high point of the Indian nationalist struggle for freedom—the Salt March and the Civil Disobedience campaign.

This was followed by a severe political crisis as the Raj retaliated with a mailed fist. It is in this period of political and economic turmoil that we see the emergence of a distinct phase in Gandhi's life. He increasingly turned his attention away from the political questions of the day to the economic challenges faced by the ordinary masses. Since at that time the vast majority of Indians lived and worked in the rural areas, Gandhi's focus was on the village and its economy. Gandhi's championing of an agrarian economy had elicited responses that ranged from derision to bemused tolerance by India's intelligentsia and political class. Unfazed by the widespread disinterest amongst the educated, Gandhi sought to turn public attention to the economic welfare of the people in agrarian India. Arguing that the needs of the village could not wait any more and unable to find sufficient common ground with the rest of the Congress leadership, towards the end of 1934 Gandhi resigned from primary membership of the party he had helped build. In the years that followed, he devoted a considerable amount of time and energy to founding a number of constructive work organizations aimed at addressing the problems of the countryside. More broadly, throughout this period Gandhi's struggle was not so much with the British but with fellow Indians. Instead of the political campaign against colonial rule, he was engaged in a range of debates on the nature of freedom to be obtained in a future independent nation. All through this period, his actions were informed by an interpretation of ahimsa that widened it from non-violence to addressing all forms of injustice.

THE POLITICAL CRISIS

By using the symbolism of marching to Dandi with an intent to manufacture illicit salt, Gandhi galvanized a nation into action. Despite the demands for his arrest by the Bombay administration, the Raj stayed its hand and Gandhi was allowed to fulfil his objective. The Civil Disobedience campaign that followed was a major success in its ability to mobilize a large number of Indians for the cause of freedom. The colonial reaction was equally formidable in the use of severe measures of repression. It is estimated that as many as 90,000 Indians were imprisoned during this period.[4] Gandhi had been arrested in May 1930, but in early 1931 he was released along with the members of the Congress Working Committee. Soon Gandhi entered into parleys with the viceroy resulting in the well-known Gandhi–Irwin Pact.

At the time, the pact was seen by many Indians as a major victory for the nationalist cause as it put Gandhi at par with the representative of the British Empire. Certainly Winston Churchill agreed with this assessment although he objected to this parity in terms that have since achieved much notoriety. In recent decades, a number of scholars have arrived at a rather negative view of Gandhi's agreeing to end the Civil Disobedience campaign with no substantial gains in return. It has been argued, most notably by the historian Sumit Sarkar, that Gandhi signed the pact to uphold the interests of Indian big business. This belief that Gandhi was easily prevailed upon to uphold the interests of a single class has been challenged.[5] A more plausible explanation emerges if we take two factors into account. First, the suppression of the Congress and repression unleashed on the wider populace had taken a severe toll. The Congress organization was in poor shape and the people were longing for some relief. Second, Gandhi would have been concerned with the increasingly impatient voices demanding a violent response. Indeed, it is much more reasonable to argue that Gandhi 'wanted to consolidate the gains of his campaign before it ended in a violent rebellion which the British would have to crush with brute force'.[6]

Despite signing a pact with Irwin, Gandhi had argued that it was futile to attend the second Round Table Conference in London with no substantial measures up for deliberation. Nevertheless, he was outmanoeuvred by the Raj into changing his position and agreed to participate. Arriving as the sole representative of the Congress, Gandhi found a number of hand-picked individuals arraigned against him. They contested the claim of the Congress to represent all sections of Indian society. In any event, a combination of British strategy and a change in its domestic politics due to a general election led to the effective collapse of the conference. Gandhi did manage to reach out to the British people and make an impression but he returned home empty-handed.

The India that Gandhi returned to at the end of 1931 had undergone an enormous change in its political climate from the previous year. Earlier, although Irwin had no intention of granting any real concessions against the Congress demands, he was astute enough to recognize that the popular upsurge needed a calibrated response. Irwin's decision to hold talks with Gandhi and sign a pact was an act of mollification of public sentiment in India. But, even as Irwin did not yield ground to Gandhi on substantial issues, for many diehard colonialists back in Britain, the very act of speaking to Gandhi was unacceptable. Two months after signing the pact with Gandhi, Irwin's term as viceroy ended and he was replaced by an old colonial hand, Willingdon, who had served as governor of Bombay and Madras presidencies. In agreement with those back in London who had reposed their confidence in him, Willingdon firmly believed in the colonial idea of ruling with a heavy hand. In contrast with Irwin's dealings with Gandhi, Willingdon's strategy was one of 'no negotiation, no manoeuvring, no bargaining with [Gandhi], but go straight ahead on the line of policy we have laid down in the past'.[7]

In 1932 and 1933, India was to pay a heavy price for Willingdon's approach. Many of the Britishers who populated the provincial officialdom had disliked the restrictions imposed on them due to the Gandhi–Irwin Pact. They often violated the truce between the Congress and the government. Now, with a more favourable viceroy on the job, even the marginal restraint imposed from above was missing. The Raj set about exacting revenge against satyagrahis with evident glee. Upon arriving back home from the second Round Table Conference and learning of the grim situation on hand, Gandhi asserted the right to non-violent resistance and protested against what he called 'measures of legalized Government terrorism'.[8] Willingdon rejected a request for an interview and ordered Gandhi's arrest instead. Determined to finish off the Congress as an organization, Willingdon unleashed a series of repressive measures that went beyond those enacted by his predecessor. The Congress was banned, its offices were raided and almost all levels of its leadership were put behind bars. Street protests were met with lathi charges and police firing became a regular event. As a contemporary Western news report noted, there already were 60,000 officers and 1,65,000 Indian troops to keep India 'safe for Britain'.[9] But now Willingdon had 'stiffened his repressive ordinances still further' and 'special judges were empowered to pass any sentence including sentence of death on persons convicted of violating the emergency ordinances'. India was being ruled by Ordinance Raj.

The Raj had been rattled by the scale of mass protests during the Civil Disobedience campaign as well as the effectiveness of picketing of shops selling liquor or foreign cloth. It was further unnerved by the potential impact of agrarian no-rent campaigns that had begun in the United Provinces. Now, during the second phase of the Civil Disobedience campaign, as many as 75,000 were arrested in 1932. While all of these challenges were conducted within the ambit of Civil Disobedience under the aegis of the Congress, there were other groups in Punjab and Bengal who owed no allegiance to Gandhi's ideas of ahimsa and caused much anxiety for the officials. For instance, the Chittagong armoury raid and a series of assassinations of English officials in Midnapur instilled a sense of fear and foreboding amongst the European populace of Bengal. As a consequence, Bengal was subjected to a most brutal repression calculated to terrorize the populace and suppress any attempts at rebellion. The seriousness of British intent is evident in an official list prepared in 1934 that simply lists the 'Acts in force for dealing with subversive and revolutionary movements'.[10] Of the twenty-one Acts listed therein, seven were specifically enacted in 1932 to deal with Bengal.

Willingdon's inflexible approach of inflicting severe violence on an unarmed people and crushing any form of rebellion yielded results. Even before the year was over, he noted with grim satisfaction that 'the civil disobedience movement at present is quiescent, and conditions in this country are really quieter than they have been for a very long time'.[11] By the end of 1932, Civil Disobedience was effectively over. Willingdon also had an effective strategy to neutralize Gandhi in a cat-and-mouse game. He refused to enter into any negotiations with the Mahatma. Instead, every time Gandhi participated in civil resistance he was immediately thrown into prison, only to be released later. In May 1933, Gandhi was prematurely released from one of his stints in jail due to a fear for his life after a fast. Noting the parlous state of the Congress, he decided to suspend Civil Disobedience as a mass campaign for a period of six weeks.[12]

The year of 1933 was an *annus horribilis* for the Congress. Its organization was in disarray, its leadership was in and out of prison, and the rank and file were exhausted from the blows dealt by the government. The Raj matched its stick of repression with the carrot of a White Paper laying out measures for constitutional reform.[13] As a political entity, the Congress had always held a number of disparate elements together. Now in the face of severe repression and the prospect of political wilderness, the cleavages stood out in sharp relief. At this low point in its history, the Congress was a house divided on the way forward. Already weary from the demands of Civil Disobedience, the possibility of some devolution of power and governance acted as a precipitating agent. Reflecting the divisions of an earlier period, some were eager to revive Council Entry and participate in the legislatures. While these individuals desired an *entente* with the government, they were opposed by the more radical elements within the party. The Civil Disobedience campaign had also firmed up the socialist commitments of a number of younger leaders who formed themselves into a new group that soon emerged as the Congress Socialist Party.

For Jawaharlal Nehru, the suspension of Civil Disobedience and the desire to enter into negotiations with the government was an appalling climb down from the Congress objective of *purna swaraj* or complete independence.[14] While Nehru had his disagreements with Gandhi, he also had a sense of personal loyalty towards the Mahatma. This was not the case with many others in the Congress. In this period of deep discontent, Gandhi's leadership was increasingly and publicly questioned. Much of the Congress leadership had always held a limited allegiance to Gandhi's creed of ahimsa and largely accepted his leadership as a political necessity. Now his position was openly challenged. From the heights of Gandhi's power and popularity in 1930, this was a dramatic transformation. A case in point is this remarkable public statement issued by Vitthalbhai Patel and Subhas Chandra Bose in late 1933 arguing that:

> The latest action of Mr. Gandhi in suspending Civil Disobedience is a confession of failure as far as the present method of the Congress is concerned. We are clearly of the opinion that as a political leader Mr. Gandhi has failed. Time has, therefore, come for a radical reorganisation of the Congress on a new principle and with a new method. For bringing about this reorganisation a change of leadership is necessary . . .[15]

Along with the collapse of the second phase of Civil Disobedience, in late 1932 Gandhi was confronted with another major issue with enormous political implications—the announcement of the Communal Award. His subsequent fast, the Poona Pact, debates with Ambedkar and the question of untouchability have been the subject of significant historical analysis and argument. We will not consider this rather fundamental aspect of modern Indian history here except to make note of a point of relevance to our discussion. In much of the literature, the events of 1932 and their aftermath have been stylized as a debate between Gandhi and Ambedkar. This fails to take into account two other significant players in the story, i.e. the British government and its Indian counterpart as well as upper-caste Hindu India. More significantly in our context, Gandhi's decision to stake his life against the institutionalization of separate electorates upset and angered many within the Congress leadership. They felt that entering into the caste question was a major distraction from the task of achieving freedom and a hindrance to their cause. This was to lead to further alienation between Gandhi and the Congress.

THE ECONOMIC CRISIS

Following his return from South Africa in 1915, Gandhi's earliest campaigns included the Champaran satyagraha against indigo planters and against land taxation in the Gujarat region of Kheda. But Gandhi did not limit himself to protesting conditions in agrarian India. He also laid significant emphasis on social and economic transformation and building capacities of self-reliance through constructive work. In the 1920s this approach was exemplified through the khadi movement. By the early 1930s, addressing the economic question in agrarian India took on a greater sense of urgency. Indeed, in comparison with the Non-cooperation movement of the early 1920s, for the Civil Disobedience campaign of 1930 Gandhi laid emphasis on 'the economic grievances of the masses and the meaning of political freedom for them'.[16] Of the eleven demands Gandhi placed before the viceroy on the eve of marching to Dandi, a number of them were related to economic issues that affected Indians.[17] The demands to abolish the salt tax and halve the land revenue reflected the interests of the poor, especially the peasantry. Gandhi's inclusion of the demand of a tariff on foreign cloth as well as reservations favouring Indian shipping represented the interests of the Indian capitalist. Another important item that figured in Gandhi's list was a revision of the controversial sterling-rupee ratio. While such a revision had been an important demand of India's wealthy industrialists, in the 1930s the adverse implications of this ratio were devastating for the rural peasantry. A key measure of monetary policy, the sterling-rupee ratio conclusively demonstrated that as long as India was a subject colony, its interests would remain subordinated to those of British commerce.

Throughout the 1920s peasant discontent was high and land revenue was a major bone of contention. The crisis came to a head in Bardoli in 1928. During the preceding years, the Bardoli peasant had suffered from dwindling profits. But when it was time for a revision of the land revenue assessment, the Raj was unwilling to take such considerations into account. It viewed land revenue as a form of rent rather than a tax on actual produce. Spearheaded by Vallabhbhai Patel and advised by Gandhi, a large-scale satyagraha by the peasants of Bardoli forced the Raj to significantly reduce the rate of taxation. The nationalist movement had not tasted success in a long while now and Bardoli was keenly watched and applauded. But for Gandhi, the lessons of Bardoli were not limited to how to take on the might of the government in a political battle. Rather, it brought home the urgency of the need to understand and address the crisis of the Indian countryside. One direct outcome of this recognition was *An Economic Survey of Matar Taluka*, an important and authoritative nationalist assessment of the economic state of affairs in rural India.[18] More significantly, while the political crisis of the Civil Disobedience campaign occupied Gandhi's life for the next few years, the economic question remained foremost in his mind.

While the Bardoli satyagraha was a localized event owing to specific considerations, the problem was actually a global one. Although the Great Depression is popularly associated with the crash of Wall Street in October 1929, the economic crisis had been brewing for a while. Indeed, even before the crash, agricultural prices had taken a steep downward trend across the world. For instance, 'food prices had fallen by almost 30 per cent between 1925 and 1929'.[19] The agricultural depression was quickly transmitted globally, and in India agricultural prices collapsed to half their value in a short period. In other words, 'Indian agriculture was subjected to the forces of the world market without really participating in it'.[20] The causal reason for this anomalous situation was the fact that India's monetary policy was tightly controlled in favour of metropolitan interests in London, primarily through the instrument of the sterling-rupee ratio.

Shorn of much important detail, the problem of the sterling-rupee ratio in the early 1930s can be stated as follows: Following the end of the First World War, Great Britain eventually reinstated the gold standard in 1925. However, contrary to recommendations, the Indian rupee was pegged to the pound sterling at a fixed rate of 1s 6d (or 3/40-th of a pound). Indian opinion held that this was a high rate that worked against Indian exports and favoured the import of British commodities into India. The result was a deflationary tendency coupled with a balance-of-payments crisis. In 1931, owing to its own economic compulsions, Britain dropped the gold standard. However, India was not permitted to devalue its rupee which continued to be tied to the older 1s 6d ratio 'which required deflationary measures that greatly enhanced the impact of the Great Depression on India'.[21] Under these circumstances, the depression had a huge impact on India's countryside. In a context of crashing prices for their produce, peasants were faced with the prospect of parting with their land to service their debt. Naturally they chose instead to sell the bits of gold jewellery that Indian women traditionally held as an asset. Owing to higher prices for gold in London, much of this bullion was exported out of India. Such exports were enabled by British policy emanating from London that steadfastly ignored protests by Indian business as well as that of the Raj itself and simply refused to place any restriction on such exports.[22] The result was a huge wave of 'distress gold' that left Indian shores only to hugely benefit Britain by bolstering its reserves. As a contemporary report argued:

> The fulcrum of the Government's exchange policy of linking rupee to 18d sterling is deliberately designed to bring indirect support to the tottering pound sterling in terms of gold. Not only have exports of gold from India served to maintain the rupee at 18d sterling to provide remittances for Government in spite of our declining exports of commodities, but they have also succeeded in arresting the collapse of England's currency in terms of gold.[23]

The fact that the peasants had to part with their family gold was a pointer to the acute economic distress in the countryside. This was evident to anyone willing to take note. Thus, a newspaper reported the English clergyman and champion of Indian freedom C.F. Andrews as saying that 'by far the most important fact he had observed was that the economic crisis in India was now becoming even more serious than the political one. Indebtedness due to the low price of agriculture products had become so excessive that agrarian trouble might arise at any time'.[24] But throughout the 1930s, British officialdom remained inured to the suffering their policy was inflicting in India. As one historian noted, the 'flow of gold [out of the Indian countryside] was a windfall, but to sit back without making use of it for the benefit of India in a deep and prolonged depression was a case of criminal negligence'.[25]

Amidst the political turmoil of the period, Gandhi would have stayed abreast of the dismal news of India's economy. More importantly, in 1933–34 he got a first-hand experience of the state of affairs in the countryside.

In the aftermath of the Poona Pact, the campaign against untouchability was making slow progress, whereas the backlash from upper castes was growing in strength. With Civil Disobedience suspended, Gandhi needed a new approach to challenge Hindu conservatism without inviting a crackdown by the government. Consequently, between November 1933 and August 1934, Gandhi travelled across the country on a social reform campaign against untouchability. In keeping with the usage of the time, this was known as the Harijan Tour. During his travels, Gandhi covered more than 12,500 miles and collected around 8 lakhs of rupees for his cause. While a detailed examination of the Harijan Tour is outside our purview here, the poverty and suffering that Gandhi witnessed in this period made a deep impression on his mind. It helped firm up his understanding that the needs of the village could wait no more.

RETIREMENT FROM THE CONGRESS

Throughout his travels across India during his campaign against untouchability, Gandhi was met with hostility from the upper castes. He was repeatedly accosted by lathi-wielding groups threatening violence, and an attempt was also made on his life. Indeed, Gandhi's campaign 'revealed and manifested all the contradictions of our social reality'.[26] Here it is germane to reiterate that despite the personal loyalty he commanded from many of his colleagues, the relationship between Gandhi and the Congress had always been an uneasy one. If the Congress resented his fast in prison against the Communal Award, Gandhi's Harijan Tour evoked no response from the party. Rather the Congress continued to be mired in directionless infighting between factions professing opposing political ideologies.

The collapse of Civil Disobedience had provided an opening for the Swarajists to push for the Congress to enter the Central Legislative Assembly. Despite having little faith in the legislative process under a colonial dispensation, Gandhi approved of it as he recognized that the Congress did not have the organizational capacity to resist the Raj at that point. He would have also wanted to avoid a split in the party. However, the leftist elements of the party who organized into an All-India Congress Socialist Party saw the Swarajist move as a compromise with the government and a repudiation of the Lahore resolution that called for a boycott of legislatures. The new developments 'left a residue of bewilderment and disillusionment . . . and had inflamed smouldering doubts of the efficacy of Gandhian tactics'.[27] The socialists were a committed lot and were driven by a revolutionary zeal. But they tended to speak in airy generalities which had little reference to the ground reality of the poor health of the Congress. Thus, at the formation of the Congress Socialist Party, Acharya Narendra Deva observed that 'The *objective situation* in the country continues to be revolutionary and if we had achieved co-ordination of forces, all the dejection and despair so conspicuous today, would not have come upon us'.[28] On his part, Gandhi welcomed the rise of the Congress Socialist Party within the Congress although he disagreed with their programme as it seemed to him 'to ignore Indian conditions' and also did not reject violence as a political means.[29]

By the middle of 1934, Gandhi's parting of ways with the Congress was clear. While the Swarajists and Socialists disagreed on most ideological and strategic questions, they were equally disinterested in giving effect to Gandhi's commitment to non-violence.[30] Thus, Gandhi's attempt to change the Congress creed from 'truthful and legitimate' to 'peaceful and non-violent' failed.[31] Gandhi was also deeply unhappy with corruption in the Congress, especially in Bengal where factional shenanigans and manipulation of membership for winning internal power at the provincial level were a serious problem. On a visit to the province, he had stated that the Congress 'is reeking with corruption, and Bengal, I must confess to my sorrow, has been the worst sinner in this respect'.[32] Finally, Gandhi was acutely aware of the disinterest in his constructive programme involving khadi. Indeed, what Gandhi said publicly in 1940 would seem to have been valid much earlier as well. Congressmen, he held, 'believe in mass action but do not believe in the connection I see between it and the charkha, etc., if the action is to be non-violent'.[33] As he went on to add:

> They believe in my hold on the masses, but they do not believe in the things which I believe have given me that hold. They merely want to exploit me and will grudgingly pay the price which my ignorance or obstinacy (according to them) demands.[34]

In the face of the criticism of the end of Civil Disobedience and indifference towards his constructive programme, Gandhi remained keen on giving effect to his emphasis of addressing the needs of the village. Therefore, desiring 'complete detachment and absolute freedom of action', at the

Bombay session of the Congress in October 1934 Gandhi resigned from primary membership of the Congress.[35]

Even as he planned his exit, Gandhi recognized that he could not completely dissociate himself from the Congress for ever. In subsequent years, especially following the advent of the Second World War, he was pulled back into a position of political leadership. Perhaps, this fact has served to occlude the significance of Gandhi's resignation as historians have tended to view it as an insignificant episode in his life. However, if we were to look at the question from the vantage point of 1934, we can recognize that Gandhi's intent was serious. Indeed, along with resigning from the Congress, Gandhi also founded a new constructive work organization, the All-India Village Industries Association (AIVIA). The economic philosopher and constructive worker J.C. Kumarappa was given the task of building this organization.

In the preceding years, during the turmoil of the political events of the time and the impact of the Great Depression, Gandhi had come to a clear recognition that khadi was failing to satisfy the economic needs of many in rural India. During his travels in 1933, Gandhi had encountered 'multitudes of men with quantities of enforced leisure on their hands' who 'could never win swaraj'.[36] For such people, he reasoned, '[w]hether the exploiter was from outside or from the Indian cities, their state would be the same, they would have no swaraj'. In a broader sense, Gandhi argued that the economic relationship between the urban India and the rural areas was a form of 'organized violence'.[37]

Here we may contrast Gandhi's approach to the economic question with that of other Congress leaders. As noted earlier, the successful mobilization of the Bardoli Patidar peasants in the 1928 campaign against the Raj gave a fillip to the political ambitions of the Congress. The economic depression led to a rising tide of peasant discontent in the early 1930s, and leaders such as Jawaharlal Nehru saw a window of opportunity for their mobilization under the Congress banner. Strikingly, Gandhi saw things in a different light. He recognized that the consolidation of peasant support for the Congress in the ryotwari region of Bardoli was an outcome of special circumstances created by the groundwork of local activists over a period of time. Similar favourable conditions did not obtain in many other regions of the country, especially in zamindari areas where the local landlords were very directly aligned with the Raj and likely to inflict severe violence on protesting peasants.

More significantly, while the Congress was interested in using the question of revenue assessment as a tool for making political inroads in the countryside, Gandhi looked beyond such considerations. First, he was opposed to opening up multiple fronts of confrontation with the government without first building adequate local capacity to cope with the guaranteed backlash of the government and its coercive power. In the absence of adequate preparation, the chances of success were remote while the suffering due to state violence would be certain. Second, while a campaign for revenue remission would undoubtedly help the cause of the Congress and the peasants who would directly benefit from it, there were an overwhelming number of individuals in the rural economy who did not own any land. Such people would not benefit from the fruits of a political campaign against revenue demands. Third, and most importantly, Gandhi looked beyond political calculus and was concerned with the question of justice for the individual and building their capacities for self-reliance. At a time of great economic dislocation, the welfare of the ordinary individual was an urgent objective.

Thus, in a country where millions had limited or no education, skills or assets, the challenge was to build an economic order based on the labour of individuals. It needed to enable them to be productive agents, thereby preventing the loss of their economic autonomy. Indeed, under Indian conditions, addressing the challenge of economic empowerment and building capacities for self-reliance was a formidable task. And it could not be answered with conventional economic theory that advocated the use of technological advances and large-scale industrialization. As Gandhi wrote to a correspondent:

> The more I study of economics the firmer I grow in my belief that the methods suggested in these books for eradicating poverty are not at all efficacious. The method lies in working out a scheme wherein the production and consumption happen to be simultaneous and this scheme can work only with the revival of village industries.[38]

In other words, it was necessary to strengthen the economic capacities of ordinary Indians who were the primary producers in the countryside. It was also essential to build a sound local economy and prevent the drain of economic value to the more powerful urban areas. Towards this end, the AIVIA was tasked with the challenge of reviving and scientifically rationalizing viable traditional village industries that would allow the village to retain the economic and usage value of its own agricultural produce. In its early years, the AIVIA focused on inexpensive ways to address the problem of diet, nutrition and sanitation and also assemble and disseminate scientifically validated knowledge of relevance to the agrarian economy. The AIVIA also went on to develop a number of inexpensive technologies for the manufacture of edible oil using modified *ghanis*, jaggery from palms, unpolished rice and various other commodities.[39]

When Gandhi approached a number of public figures for their support in furthering his new cause of village industries, he was met with the expected indifference. Many held that 'in this age of mechanisation it is futile to revive village industries' and ridiculed Gandhi's approach as backward-looking and for his emphasis on human labour as a means of economic production.[40] An angry Gandhi answered the charge by asking if his approach was 'going back to the village, or rendering back to it what belongs to it?'[41] Gandhi was 'not asking the city-dwellers to go to and live in the villages'. Rather he was 'asking them to render unto the villagers what is due to them'.

Expectedly the socialists were amongst the strongest critics of Gandhi and the AIVIA. Their position is exemplified by Jayaprakash Narayan, popularly known as JP. While later in his life JP came to be seen as an advocate of Gandhian values, in the 1930s he was as doctrinaire a socialist as any. At the Bombay session, JP vehemently opposed the proposal to found the AIVIA. Subsequently, he continued to canvass extensively against the organization and the theory of economic decentralization it represented. JP, like many socialists of the time, argued that the problem of exploitation of the masses could only be addressed through large-scale industrialization and by socializing the ownership of the means of production. In response to Kumarappa's charge that economic violence was inherent to large-scale industrialization, JP argued that 'centralized production means exploitation and violence only when it is run on capitalist lines. Under a socialized economy it involves no violence and no exploitation and far from suppressing encourages initiative'.[42]

While Congressmen were unimpressed or opposed to Gandhi's turn to the village, the Raj had a better grasp of the subversive potential of the Mahatma's agenda. For instance, unwilling to take Gandhi's proclamations at face value, Willingdon argued that the 'real purpose in this village uplift scheme of his is to get the Congress ideas into the minds of all the agriculturists of the country and then . . . start again with redoubled vigour'.[43] Even as the AIVIA was being founded, the Raj advised local administrators to pay more attention to their rural development programmes and step up the propaganda machinery to present this work as a better alternative to the one presented by Gandhi. That the colonial regime was worried is evident in the alacrity with which it sanctioned 'one crore of rupees for village improvement'.[44] This led a member of the Bombay Legislative Council to describe the government's sudden solicitude for the welfare of the villager as an attempt at 'political contraception adopted . . . to prevent the growth of Congress influence in villages'.

THE MOVE TO SEVAGRAM

Since leaving Sabarmati Ashram for Dandi in early 1930, Gandhi had been caught up in the turmoil of the period. By the middle of 1933, with the government refusing to negotiate with the Congress, Gandhi recognized that the ongoing struggle called 'for much greater sacrifice than the people have hitherto undergone'.[45] Therefore, he argued, it 'follows that the greatest measure of sacrifice is to be expected of me as the author of the movement'. While the ashram did not directly take part in the politics of the time, Gandhi concluded that under the circumstances it could no longer exist along with the acts of civil disobedience of its residents. Hence, he decided to disband the ashram and asked the government to take it over. The government refused the offer, and eventually Sabarmati Ashram was disbanded and its assets distributed to a number of constructive organizations. By September 1933, Gandhi's break with his life in Ahmedabad was complete.

By the time Gandhi resigned from the Congress and founded the AIVIA, the question of the location of his residence remained unresolved. The man instrumental in Gandhi's decision to move to Wardha was Jamnalal Bajaj. A wealthy Marwari businessman from Wardha, Bajaj was personally devoted to the Mahatma and had thrown in his lot with the nationalist movement.[46] Bajaj had wished for the Mahatma to reside in his town and had offered to build Gandhi an ashram there. However, even a year after Gandhi had shut down the Sabarmati Ashram, it was not a settled matter that Wardha would be his home. In his September 1934 press statement announcing plans to retire from the Congress, Gandhi offered a tantalizing glimpse of his thinking at the time. Explaining his desire to work on village industries, he stated, 'I would like to bury myself in an Indian village, preferably in a Frontier village'.[47]

During the Civil Disobedience campaign of the preceding years, along with the growing sentiment of nationalism, India had also witnessed a widening of the gulf between Hindus and Muslims. Indeed, the lack of Muslim participation in Civil Disobedience was a worrying turn of events. The one exception was an unusual non-violent movement that emerged in the most unlikely of regions. This was the Khudai Khidmatgar, a group of Pathans led by Khan Abdul Ghaffar Khan in the North-West Frontier Province. If the Raj backed its rule over India with violence, it was paranoid about a possible Russian invasion of the Frontier Province as part of the 'Great Game'. Under these circumstances, while the adherence of Pathans to ahimsa was considered uncharacteristic, it was even more remarkable considering the brutality with which the Raj dealt with the general populace of the Frontier. The newly found adherents to his creed of non-violence pleased Gandhi. He also hoped to use the opportunity to build an alliance to tackle the problem of communalism in the country. But if Willingdon was unwilling to even meet Gandhi, it was obvious that he would never accede to Gandhi's request to be allowed to visit the politically sensitive Frontier region.

Thus, by the end of 1934, Gandhi was at a crossroads. His ashram in Ahmedabad was disbanded, and plans to move to the North-West Frontier Province were stymied. The newly founded AIVIA needed both funds as well as facilities to work out of. Vallabhbhai Patel had tried to persuade Gandhi to move to Bardoli. Instead, Gandhi accepted Bajaj's offer of land and a building in Wardha that was originally earmarked for a memorial to Gandhi's late nephew and the prime mover of the khadi movement, Maganlal Gandhi. The premises—now named Maganvadi—became the headquarters of the AIVIA, and both Gandhi and Kumarappa took up residence there. By early February of 1935, Gandhi had settled in at Maganvadi and worked on his village industries agenda. Soon, Gandhi ended up gathering about twenty people around him. Some were old Sabarmati hands, but others were 'a strange medley of various kinds of cranky people . . . all cheek by jowl in one building, there was no peace and no escape'.[48]

Although he was now living in Maganvadi, Gandhi felt that his 'heart is in the villages' and wished to 'settle in a village near Wardha'.[49]

His colleagues tried to dissuade him from making yet another move to a village, but Gandhi remained committed to his plans. Since the inception of the AIVIA, he had been asking constructive workers to 'go and settle in villages and to serve the villagers'. His message could only ring true if he was to do so himself. Gandhi's disciple Mira had been unhappy to live amidst the chaos of Maganvadi. She scouted for a nearby village to move to and work on its sanitation. The village Mira selected was Segaon, some 7 kilometres from Wardha. Jamnalal Bajaj owned much of the land in the village but Mira could not elicit much cooperation from its residents who remained hostile to Gandhi's campaign against untouchability. Although he suffered from poor health owing to high blood pressure and was faced with an indifferent village community, Gandhi persisted with the idea of moving to Segaon where a hut was erected for him within his specified budget of 100 rupees.

Gandhi had moved to Segaon to signal his commitments and also have a modicum of quiet to pursue his agenda of constructive work. But a move to a remote village would scarcely prevent others from invading his life. Even as he was settling in, Gandhi was lamenting that his new environs had 'become a confused household instead of a hermitage it was expected to be. Such has been my fate!! I must find my hermitage from within'.[50] A number of visitors frequently made their way to Segaon to meet him. Owing to the large volume of correspondence that he received, Segaon soon acquired a post office of its own. To avoid being confused for another village with the same name, Segaon was renamed Sevagram. This was to be his home for a decade.

Throughout his public life in India, Gandhi maintained a distinct identity in terms of his philosophical ideas, social, political and economic objectives and programmatic approaches. During the 1930s, Gandhi gave effect to many of his concerns by directly working on constructive work activities that looked beyond political campaigns. Although he was engaged in a number of public debates with fellow Indians on the road to the future, Gandhi signalled his commitment to the public weal through the force of personal example. By moving to a hut in Sevagram, Gandhi affirmed his simple and powerful credo—My life is my message.

12

FLIGHTS OF FREEDOM: GERMAN ÉMIGRÉS, AERONAUTICS AND SELF-RELIANCE IN INDIA

JAHNAVI PHALKEY

THERE ARE SEVERAL beginnings to this story. One could begin with the industrialist Walchand Hirachand who wanted to manufacture aircraft in India in the late 1930s. Or one could begin with the British Government of India that was at the same time struggling with permissions from London to manufacture aircraft in India should the Eastern front flare up. One could begin with the German aircraft designer Kurt Tank and his international journeys to build aircraft for different governments starting in the 1940s. No matter where we begin, this story retains three characteristics: first and foremost, it is inherently transnational. The story of aeronautics and aerodynamics is in many ways similar to the twentieth-century history of molecular biology, which, as historian Pnina Abir-Am shows, 'has primarily constituted itself in an international space' in the same time period because of the migration of scientists across national borders.[1] At the same time, this is an important story of Indian effort at self-sufficiency after Independence. Self-sufficiency, especially for defence-related procurement, was critical for a newly independent country with limited access, if any, to the tightly controlled market for defence and dual-use technologies, which often included equipment for research in physics and engineering. A comparable story can be told of Chinese efforts at the time as historian Sigrid Schmalzer convincingly argues: 'China's relative isolation during certain periods of the Cold War intensified the emphasis on self-reliance in science'.[2] Finally, this is a history of the military-industrial-academic complex as it took shape in India in the context of the global Cold War.

Let us begin in Germany at the University of Göttingen in the laboratories of Ludwig Prandtl—the physicist who is often described, against all historiographical instruction, as the father of aerodynamics. Ludwig Prandtl is credited with being the founder of the field of aerodynamics for his work (1904) on the boundary layer, which adjoins the surface of a body moving in air or water—in gas or liquid as physicists would put it. His work led to an understanding of skin friction drag and of the way in which streamlining reduces the drag of airplane wings and other moving bodies.[3] Two among his eighty-seven doctoral students were Indian. The first, Nolini Kanto Bose, ended up working with the British Government of India;[4] the second from Kolhapur, Vishnu Madav Ghatage, would play a significant role in the establishment of aeronautics research, education, as well as aircraft manufacturing in India.[5]

Ghatage completed his undergraduate studies in physics at Sir Parshurambhau College, or SP College as it is commonly known in Pune, followed by a master's degree at the Royal Institute of Science in Bombay.[6] In 1932, when he was awarded a merit scholarship, he took it to the University of Göttingen (Georg-August-Universität Göttingen) where he was awarded a PhD in 1936 for a thesis on *Modellversuche über die gegenseitige Bewegung von Luftmassen verschiedener Temperaturen* (Model experiments for the relative motion of air columns of different temperatures). His study, drawing on Prandtl's growing interest in meteorology and atmospheric flows, was considered to be of importance to gliding thus resulting in a sponsorship from the Gliding Society of Germany.[7]

Upon his return to India, Ghatage took appointments at the universities of Pune and Bombay to teach general physics. He would have continued so, but for the outbreak of WWII.

Hindustan Aircraft Limited (HAL)

Ghatage's expertise in aerodynamics would be called upon to lead Hindustan Aircraft Limited (HAL)—the aeronautics part of the Allied war effort in India once the Japanese occupied Burma. Alongside, he would lead the establishment of India's very first department of aeronautics and aerodynamics research at the Indian Institute of Science (IISc), also in Bangalore. But in order for all of that to happen, there were efforts afoot that he was not party to until well into 1940.

Narratives about the establishment of HAL have been but mentioned in passing by historians of technology and business. They tend to follow the narrative provided by Walchand Hirachand—the industrialist who invested in the establishment of HAL[8] and for whom HAL became a symbol of imperial priority undermining Indian industrial entrepreneurship.[9]

In the 1930s, Hirachand, who started out as a construction contractor and diversified into shipping and sugar, began to think seriously about automobile and aircraft manufacture in India. As the legend goes, the idea took root in October 1939 when he met the American industrialist William D. Pawley on a flight from San Francisco to Hong Kong. Pawley was the director of the Central Aircraft Manufacturing Company in Kuomintang China, building aircraft for the Chinese national government.[10] Enthused, Hirachand wrote to the imperial government suggesting that he could provide aircraft for the war that had just broken out in Europe, if they supported his enterprise.

He received a response about a year later. Historian Aparajith Ramnath in his recent study of the establishment of HAL suggests that the year-long silence was far from one of neglect. In fact, the imperial government had noted, a month before the Hirachand and Pawley proposal, the need to consider aircraft production in India.[11] Following a series of proposals that went back and forth, the secretary of state for India (and Burma), Leo Amery, appeared enthusiastic while the British Government of India remained cautious. A note to the British air ministry read:

> Mr Amery is of the opinion that the proposal should be considered on the assumption that the war may last for several years . . . In view of this possibility, and of the likelihood of a universal expansion of air services, both military and civil . . . the question should, in his

opinion, be studied from the point of view of considering a bold programme of all metal construction, including engine construction. The possibility of the use of plastic construction might also be investigated.[12]

The British Government of India came around in the end for two reasons: aircraft production soon became a strategic necessity, and it had become necessary to be seen as responsive to Indian demands. On 6 July 1940, Pawley was invited to India to hold talks with Hirachand and the imperial government. A few days later, the government agreed provisionally to support the factory and place an order worth 10 million dollars for trainers, fighters and bombers along with spare parts—all, of course, pending approval from London. In London, the project was discussed in the context of the larger war effort in China and Burma.

Hirachand, in the meanwhile, arrived at an agreement with the princely state of Mysore which provided land, power and water, held half of the shares issued, and waived tax on income from supplying aircraft to the British Government of India. In April 1941, the government also contributed an equal sum, and the board of directors of this private limited company was now reorganized with the British Government of India, Hirachand's agency and the Mysore government contributing three directors each. Pawley's role was crucial. His firm was to shape the 200-acre manufacturing unit and obtain the licences to produce American aircraft at HAL. Much of this came via Pawley's existing unit in China. In August 1941, the company was able to deliver their first aircraft to the government. Ghatage was one of the first recruits in the design section.

As of 1941, '300 Indian engineers highly trained in mechanics and nearly two thousand skilled workmen were working under the direction of 22 American technicians . . .'[13] With the establishment of the South East Asia Command, following the Japanese occupation of Burma, Allied warfare opened the Eastern war front. Bangalore, where HAL was located, was considered a good source of trained manpower. The IISc, the first advanced research university in the engineering sciences on the subcontinent, had been training engineers since 1911.

In fact, the establishment of HAL was seized upon as an opportunity to further advance the institute, and within two years after starting out at HAL, Vishnu Madav Ghatage was asked to serve as the officiating head of the newly established Department of Aeronautical Engineering at the IISc from 1942–45. In December 1942, they began training graduate students of the mechanical and electrical engineering departments to then qualify in aeronautics related to the wartime effort. Between 1942 and 1948, the department was led by engineers from HAL, which was established initially as an aircraft repair and maintenance unit for wartime needs.

At the end of the war, Ghatage returned to HAL, and R.G. Harris of the Royal Aircraft Establishment became professor and head of the department of aeronautics. Aeronautics as a field began to develop along two strong lines in Bangalore: one with indigenous aircraft design and manufacture at HAL; and the other at the department of aeronautical engineering with teaching and advanced research. These two were to come together again, in a strange way, in the late 1950s. Let us stay with the research and education side of the story for now.

Harris continued at the IISc until 1948. A number of young engineers and technicians who had worked energetically during the war across the boundaries of the HAL and the department of aeronautical engineering now decided to further continue their training in the field. The new department had hit the ground running and the energy was well-sustained by the departing Americans: William Pawley established scholarships for students at the IISc for further study at Caltech. A couple of them were later to become leaders of Indian aerospace research. More immediately, they were going to the California Institute of Technology (Caltech) where many of them were to come in to contact with Theodore von Karman, another Göttingen PhD (1923) and legendary aeronautical engineer, and his young colleague, Hans Liepmann. Those who stayed back would not escape the Göttingen school. Beginning 1949, Oskar Tietjens, a batch mate of von Karman, also with a PhD from Göttingen (1923) and a co-author of Prandtl's, took over as head of the department at IISc Bangalore.

A WIND TUNNEL AT THE INDIAN INSTITUTE OF SCIENCE BANGALORE

Ghatage built the first closed-circuit wind tunnel at the IISc and carried out interesting experiments inspired by Prandtl's experiments in 'drag crisis'.[14] The second tunnel came with the arrival of Oskar Tietjens.

Operation Paperclip (originally Operation Overcast) saw the transfer of manpower and materials from Germany to the US (and there was similar movement also to the Soviet Union) even as it became impossible to continue with aerodynamics and aeronautics research and manufacture in occupied Germany. The immigration of scientists and skilled technicians from Germany to the United States, as well as the USSR, and to some extent the United Kingdom and Latin America, has been studied by historians. It has inspired films and books including science fiction and spy thrillers.[15] Some, like Willi Messerschmitt (Messerschmitt) and Kurt Tank (Focke-Wulf) who had designed German bombers and fighter aircraft during the war chose to go elsewhere.[16] Both will return in this story. For the moment, we are interested in Oskar Tietjens, professor of fluid dynamics at the University of Vienna, who became the head of the aeronautical engineering department at the IISc.[17] A student as well as co-author of Prandtl, Tietjens was the first academic at the helm of the department. Among his colleagues was Hans A. Havemann, professor of combustion engines, a specialist in jet engines and who had spent time in Farnborough (United Kingdom) between 1946 and 1949.[18] Among Tietjens's immediate responsibilities was the establishment of research infrastructure that included a wind tunnel facility.

Tietjens met Otto Königsberger, a nephew of another Göttingen legend, the physicist Max Born, who came to Bangalore more than a decade before Tietjens. Max Born, a Nobel laureate of Jewish origin, who together with Werner Heisenberg, Niels Bohr and other physicists developed the field of quantum mechanics, did not survive long in India; he came following an invitation by the physicist and Nobel laureate Chandrasekhara Venkata Raman, and left within two years as things did not go very well for him.[19] His nephew stayed back. Königsberger had left Berlin in 1933 shortly after creating a prize-winning design for the Berlin Olympic stadium. He spent a few years in Cairo from where he went to Bangalore to join his uncle. He was soon in the employ of the maharaja of Mysore and stayed on in India for a couple of decades establishing what is now called a school of tropical architecture.

Within five years of his arrival, Tietjens, with Königsberger, was to embark on an ambitious project: a 30m-long elliptical low-speed closed circuit wind tunnel for research and development in aerodynamics and aeronautics. The wind tunnel loop, which has a test section of 2.2m x 1.5m, and a maximum wind speed of about 200mph, was cast in

concrete and partially embedded in the ground. Short granite buttresses
provided additional support. Instead of covering the concrete structure,
Königsberger, following his own goals of architectural honesty, exposed
it. Königsberger considered this construction, especially 'in light of the
limited resources and technical expertise available, a huge achievement'.
Indeed, at the time, the aeronautical engineering department at the
IISc was the 'only place in India where facilities existed for training
and research, both theoretical and experimental in Aeronautical
Engineering'.[20] The construction took four years starting 1954; the
former maharaja and now governor of Mysore state, Jayachamarajendra
Wadiyar, inaugurated the facility on 3 February 1959. This was less
than two years into the arrival of a team of thirteen Germans at the
HAL to build India's first jet fighter. Kurt Tank, a design engineer
at the German Focke-Wulf aircraft manufacturer during WWII, was
beginning work on the supersonic jet fighter HF 24 Marut. HAL would
go on to build 147 of these fighters that would be finally decommissioned
in 1984–85.[21]

A JET FIGHTER

Kurt Tank was an aeronautical engineer and test pilot with Focke-Wulf
Flugzeugbau, the civilian and military aircraft (one of the predecessors
of today's Airbus). Starting his stint there in 1931, Tank emerged as
an important figure in the Nazi aviation industry of the 1930s. He
designed the Fw 200 Condor, an aircraft that successfully completed a
non-stop transatlantic flight from Berlin to New York in August 1938.
During WWII, Tank designed the Fw 190, considered one of the most
'advanced fighter aircraft of the war' upon which many future designs
of the firm rested. With the end of war and the ensuing restrictions
on aviation design and industry, Tank first emigrated to Argentina
in 1948.[22]

At the end of the war, as the aeronautical spoils of war were being
discussed, Kurt Tank almost agreed to move to the Soviet Union.
Instead, we find him in Argentina with forty-five members of his team.
In Argentina, the team embarked on the design and manufacture of *Pulqui*
(arrow), a supersonic jet fighter, for the Juan Perón regime. The aircraft
was never manufactured, and the project stopped after the construction of
two prototypes. Jonathan Hagood has argued that, 'the lack of full-scale

aircraft production encouraged Tank to look elsewhere prior to the end of the Perónist government'. A little less than a decade later, in 1956, it was possible for the team to return to Germany and eighteen of them did. Barely a year later, Tank proceeded to Bangalore to build yet another supersonic jet fighter, this time for the Indians.

The historian Michael J. Neufeld suggests that Tank had 'direct access to President Perón, but nothing could compensate for the fact that when he built his Pulqui II swept-wing jet fighter, there was no industrial base in Argentina to deliver adequate components, so the prototype had to be hand-made'.[23] Nonetheless, the aircraft performed impressively and was certainly useful as propaganda. The aircraft was, however, considered not quite flightworthy because there was no wind tunnel to refine its aerodynamics. Building a jet engine in Argentina proved even more difficult than the body of the aircraft, as a result of which Tank likely re-engineered an existing British one. The funding ran out after the development of a couple of prototypes of the *Pulqui* right before the overthrow of the Perón regime in 1955.

In the meanwhile, in India, a suggestion from the Indian Air Force (IAF) for a home-produced fighter-bomber was forcefully promoted by Air Marshal S. Mukherji in 1956 and backed by the minister of defence organisation, Mahavir Tyagi. Tyagi, it is said, met Kurt Tank at a decadent party in a castle just outside of Munich in early 1957.[24]

In June 1957, Tank went to HAL, India, with a much smaller team of eighteen German engineers and technicians (compared to the team he worked with in Argentina), which dwindled to thirteen by the time HF 24 Marut, a 'twin-engine fighter-bomber' designed to reach supersonic speeds, took its maiden flight on 24 June 1961. Hagood and Neufeld both allude to but do not sufficiently develop on Tank's experience in India. Hagood argues that given the much smaller number of Germans in India, 'unlike the Argentinean experience, in India, local engineers and technicians took responsibility for production engineering, tool design, and manufacturing activity' leading to what he calls 'a successful international technology transfer'. The Indian plane, too, like the Argentinian one, was of a good design 'but was underpowered with the only engines available, an older British design'.[25]

Ghatage had established the design office at HAL with a plan to develop incrementally complex aircraft, 'step-by-step' as the aerospace scientist and fluid dynamicist, Roddam Narasimha, puts it.[26] However, with Tank's arrival the design team was split and some of the trained personnel would now work with the Germans. Moreover, at least initial aerodynamics work on the new project was carried out in the wind tunnel designed and built by Ghatage, but also the one built by Oskar Tietjens and Otto Königsberger, two other prominent Germans in the city. Just how they evaluated and related to each other is not easy to tell—they were migrants with remarkably different personal and career trajectories. All the same, the department of aeronautical engineering at the IISc had maintained close contacts with HAL, thus connecting Tank and his Focke-Wulf colleagues with Ghatage and Tietjens (with a rather brief overlap, if any) from Göttingen, and their Indian students and colleagues.[27]

Assembly of the first prototype airplane was started in April 1960, and it was finished in eleven months. Marut was, in fact, based quite closely on the Pulqui design. Marut never reached supersonic speeds in flight because of the inability of the British firm Bristol Siddeley to supply the required engines. The aircraft was instead underpowered by two Orpheus 703 engines manufactured under licence from Bristol Siddeley by HAL.[28] HAL's Aero Engine Division was the first organization in Asia—outside the communist countries—to manufacture an aircraft gas turbine. The Orpheus engine manufacturing licence was concluded in September 1956, and further discussions between Bristol Siddeley and the Indian government were held in 1960 and 1961 for completing development of the earlier discussed Orpheus 12 (which was not supplied), or for development of a superior engine. The talks did not come to much.

Following failed discussions with the British firm, the Indians approached the Soviet Union for an appropriate engine in 1961. The Indian government imported six RD-9F turbojets in 1961. By 1962, they concluded that these engines would not be the best answer as they, too, would not allow the aircraft to accomplish full potential (Mach 1.5 versus Mach 2). Additionally, the Soviet Union refused to provide the necessary level of detailed information on manufacturing the RD-9F without which the Indians could not have produced the engine themselves. Between 1965 and 1977, HAL went on to produce 147 exemplars for the Indian Air Force until the aircraft was decommissioned in 1985. Marut was 'emblematic of a Nehruvian emphasis on industrial and economic self-reliance, deemed especially important in the realms of defence industries'.[29]

In 1964, two years after the maiden flight and the aircrafts' slow induction into the Indian Air Force, the Indians who had experience with the Marut, went to Egypt to attend the test flight of the *Helwan*. Willi Messerschmitt had designed Helwan for the Egyptian government. A team led by the Austrian engineer Ferdinand Brandner designed the turbojet engine, which was especially of interest to the Indians. The plan was to initiate collaboration with the (short-lived) United Arab Republic (Egypt, Yemen and Syria)—they had the engine to help the Marut reach design potential, and the Indians had the design for a robust supersonic aircraft body. The Helwan was tested in flight but never proved reliable. That effort, too, came to nought.

In the meanwhile, the IAF was acquiring aircraft on license. The first of the production Marut trainers were delivered to the IAF in November 1964—a year before the 1965 war with Pakistan, when they were deployed. They were extensively used in the 1971 war that led to the creation of Bangladesh. The IAF has claimed that the aircraft was robust and met their requirements. Fan sites dedicated to the aircraft claim, 'No aircraft were ever lost in air-to-air combat. However, 4 were lost to ground fire and two were lost on the ground'.[30]

Epilogue

Marut was much celebrated in the Eastern Bloc, and models of the plane were popular in Poland and Czechoslovakia and can be seen in advertisements at the time. Kurt Tank left India in 1962 or 1963; from Germany to Argentina to India, with strong connections to Egypt and the Soviet Union, his journey makes for an interesting Cold-War story.[31]

The successful as well as the less successful aspects of developing Marut established the importance of education, and research and development in aeronautics first in Bangalore and later elsewhere in India. In the late 1950s, the goal to build a jet fighter led eventually to the establishment of the National Aeronautical Laboratory (now the National Aerospace Laboratory), the Gas Turbine Research Establishment and the Aeronautical Development Establishment, all in Bangalore. Within years of HF 24's maiden flight, a committee led by the Caltech-trained aeronautical engineer Satish Dhawan recommended the creation of Departments of Aeronautical Engineering at all five Indian Institutes of Technology.

The history of research and development behind India's first jet fighter raises important questions about the articulation of the Cold War within the process of state formation in India after Independence. And yet, Cold-War dynamics have rather little to do with technological development and the establishment of an advanced aircraft industry. This story of state-building around a high-tech platform brings together princely states, the Indian government, American entrepreneurs, a private company, highly trained Indian aeronautical engineers, Egyptian aircraft builders and Germans who had earlier built planes for the Nazis. As historians Mitchell Ash and Alfons Söllner have noted in the context of the forced migration of German-speaking scholars, 'To inquire only about losses and gains in this sense presupposes a static view of science and of culture, as though the émigrés brought with them finished bits of knowledge, which they then inserted like building-stones into already established cultural constructs (and one might add *scientific and engineering practice*) elsewhere'.[32]

As Michael J. Neufeld—in his major study of the global circulation of German aerospace engineers after WWII—has pointed out, 'Jet engines were the Achilles heel of advanced aircraft projects outside the leading powers, as they were complex, expensive and difficult to develop, and much easier to subject to export controls than airframe design expertise'.[33] These controls clearly played a role in limiting the power of the engines on the Marut, and so in limiting Indian autonomy in aircraft construction. No one wanted to share engine technology with a third country like India, neither the British, nor the Soviet Union and especially not the Americans. The United States was ferociously against sharing engine technology with others, constraining it by expert controls from domestic suppliers and by intense diplomatic pressure when a country like Britain sought to secure new markets in Asia, as Jeffrey Engel has shown.[34]

The short time that it took to build a supersonic jet aircraft, albeit one that was underpowered, should be astonishing to us in hindsight. The level of expertise of Kurt Tank and his German aeronautical engineers was at its peak during WWII and subsequently furthered in Peron's Argentina. In Argentina, they also gained experience of working with constrained resources, such that, once they were at HAL, a place primed through the experience of war, with scholarly connections to Göttingen, Kurt Tank and his team could produce the desired results fairly quickly. Hindustan Aircraft Limited was under the administrative control of the ministry of defence, Government of India, when Kurt Tank arrived in India. The state apparatus did not seem to have involved itself directly with the production process, but served as a client that guaranteed a market for the aircraft.

In August 1963, within a couple of years of the successful HF 24 prototype, Aeronautics India Limited (AIL) was established as a company entirely owned by the Government of India, for the manufacture of the MiG-21 aircraft under licence from the Soviet Union. Within a year, Hindustan Aircraft Limited and Aeronautics India Limited were amalgamated and the new company established was called Hindustan Aeronautics Limited. It produced Marut for the Indian Air Force *alongside* the licensed production of MiG-21, the first fully powered supersonic aircraft of the Indian Air Force in 1964.

Those familiar with Operation Paperclip and German Émigrés during the Cold War are unlikely to find the Indian story surprising in any way. However, the design and manufacture of an Indian supersonic jet fighter is a story of historical interest for several reasons. The story opens up the discussion on the practices of non-alignment in at least two important ways: on the one hand, we see that the Indian government was willing to negotiate with non-state actors with a difficult political history, to produce a military project of strategic significance. It was also a project at the frontiers of technology at the time—a supersonic aircraft was a challenging undertaking. Second, we see the Indians and Egyptians working together on a military project, both with German Émigrés aircraft designers—Tank and Messerschmidt. The alliance was driven as much by Indian (and Egyptian) non-alignment politics as it was by the reach of the German network that drew on each other's skills and energies. There is also the larger context of German-Indian networks within which this particular instance could be seen as unexceptional.[35] With the failure of British engines to deliver supersonic speed and the strict controls established by the Americans, the Indians then went to the Soviet Union, and to the Germans and Austrians in Egypt. This history opens to inquiry the claims to self-reliance of the Indian state, and its capacity and struggle to avoid the constraints of alignment with one superpower or the other.

I would like us, equally, to reflect on the aspiration to 'self-sufficiency', and 'demonstration of Indian independence' through a 'home-produced fighter bomber'. This characterization is exaggerated: the jet fighter is not indigenous, but is best understood as a transnational object embodying knowledge borrowed from multiple sources, as would be the case anywhere else. Consider the geography of these global networks with an aircraft factory as a hub: it is shaped by the dynamics of Cold-War rivalry and the existing structures of technological inequality that continuously differentiate the industrialized powers from the recently decolonized world. This project is not simply undertaken in India but in an India that seeks and is sought to be placed in the world, enmeshed in a network of dependent (and contested) relationships in the global politico-economic system and more so, of migrating global actors.

What does the appeal to self-reliance then mean? How do we unpack it beyond the rhetoric? The appeal to self-reliance stakes a claim on the present by building and extending technological capability to substantiate an imagined future. The appeal for self-sufficiency both recognizes that a project to manufacture India's first jet fighter is embedded in global systems of political and technological inequality and dependence; and at the same time contests the limits that that inequality imposes on India's freedom of action. By seeking self-sufficiency, Indian actors hold the technological powers accountable for *their* anti-colonial rhetoric, so creating the space for the young state to shape a new and more autonomous India. The jet fighter produced at HAL was not swadeshi or indigenous—but by affirming that it was, those claiming so could both affirm India's determination to achieve indigenous production and define the ground rules for a more equal relationship with its mightier techno-political partners in future.

To conclude, this is indeed a story of building state capacity, but one not reducible to its final stages. A systematic study of German Émigrés scientists in India or about German engineers and scientists in aeronautical engineering and related fields in India is likely to yield an interesting story, one that is not yet fully explored.[36] In the first instance, we learn that the story of German Émigrés to India is complex even when the motivation for emigration seems obvious. During the Nazi times, some fled from Germany because they were of Jewish descent or for political reasons. After the war, they came to India mainly for reasons of career: many could not get appropriate jobs as engineers in Germany; and then there were those like Tank, Messerschmitt and Brandner who could have built careers in the United States or the Soviet Union, but chose not to. Alongside, we find that German universities and Germans have been crucial in the various stages of capacity building: Ghatage trained in Germany and was important to the Allied war effort, and to the first indigenous aircraft developed at HAL—the HT-2 Trainer aircraft (1951) and the two-seater HUL-26 Pushpak (1958); he was also the first head of the department of aeronautics at the IISc. He was able to put his skills to use for the war effort that led to the successful establishment of HAL in the first instance—which is a story, as we have seen, not merely of imperial priority but of private enterprise and the role of princely states, especially Mysore, in the middle decades of the twentieth century. Tietjens and Königsberger take the story one step further: a German architect and a German aerodynamics engineer, one came to India to escape the Third Reich and another following the occupation of Germany and the subsequent impossibility of pursuing aeronautical research and education. Together, they prepared the ground for Kurt Tank and his team to execute their Indian project: a supersonic jet fighter.

Capability was built in stages, and choices were made along the way by Indians and Germans for very different reasons, often in morally contradictory camps. Immigration is at the heart of this story—for education on the part of the Indians, for political reasons of contrasting kinds for the Germans. This fully transnational story of Cold-War dynamics that constrained the possibilities of aircraft construction, for all its allure, opens up the complex moral landscape of science and engineering in India.

ACKNOWLEDGEMENTS

I wish to thank David Edgerton, David Engerman, John Krige, Michael Eckert, Nandini Sundar, Roland Wittje, Srinath Raghavan and V. Siddhartha for their comments; Helmut Trischler for his generous support; and the late Roddam Narasimha and Aparajith Ramnath for sharing their conference papers with me. This chapter is part of a larger project which started with a scholarship from the Deutsches Museum, Munich.

13

THE SUPREME COURT AND DEMOCRATIC CONSOLIDATION

MADHAV KHOSLA

WHEN RAMACHANDRA GUHA'S *India after Gandhi* was published over a decade ago, it quickly became the most important topic of conversation among those interested in India's postcolonial life. For students like me, the book was a mark of possibility. It revealed how the story of India might be told; how one could capture a nation's journey with excitement, judgement and courage. Guha had demonstrated the elegance and command with which one could engage with the past, and he had brought into sharp relief the magic that could be produced out of even the most prosaic events. Though *India after Gandhi* was striking for its narrative, it did contain an important argument pertaining to the unit of analysis. Guha's overall framing was around India's unlikely survival as a democracy. The improbable endurance of Indian democracy has puzzled many a political scientist and has been the subject of considerable study.[1] In *India after Gandhi*, Guha contributed one possible answer to this puzzle: the role of leading political actors. Much historical research had chosen to de-emphasize, if not ignore, the domain of the political, and instead attended to the social or economic spheres of activity. It had also paid limited attention to individual agency and had expressed greater interest in structural matters. Guha took a different approach, and placed individual political elites at the front and centre of the modern Indian tale.[2] In his study, select figures did not merely become living beings, with vivid and human personalities; they also became agents who shaped history. Their actions were the product of deliberate, individual behaviour, and had real and tangible consequences.

No serious contemplation of the durability of the Indian nation can ignore *India after Gandhi*. This chapter is no exception. I share enormous sympathy with Guha's overall sentiment, and his effort to rehabilitate figures such as Jawaharlal Nehru has been crucial for a fuller appreciation of our past. Yet, I also believe that in telling the story of democratic consolidation during the early years of the Indian republic, a wider net must be cast. My aim is not to identify matters that might have been covered in the book. Such an enterprise seems churlish. Any person who has read *India after Gandhi* can hardly leave with the thought that more remains to be done. Instead, I want to use Guha's text as the foundation for probing the phenomenon of democratic consolidation. If we consider the early years of the Indian republic—the initial period of existence when so many other postcolonial nations unravelled—what moments and themes shall we note in the cementing of the nation's political ethos? The success of a constitutional order rests in part on whether that order is embraced by political elites, and Parts II and III of *India after Gandhi* emphasize Nehru's commitment in effectuating India's transition from subjecthood to self-rule.

That transition required the building of conventions and norms, in which Nehru was of course actively involved.[3] These conventions and norms related, in part, to the creation of institutions. In the case of a great many institutions, their emergence was linked to the government of the day. But in the case of others—most notably and importantly, the judiciary—this was not the case. Institutions such as the Supreme Court operated at some distance from the nation's political leadership; they could not be an instrument of the Nehruvian government's will and vision. This naturally invites the question of what role, if any, institutions such as the Supreme Court played in cementing democracy during the fragile and formative period of the new Indian nation. What might we say about the Supreme Court if we were to give it space within Parts II and III of *India after Gandhi*?

Scholars of Indian law have spilt much ink on the relationship between the Supreme Court and Indian democracy, though relatively little has been said about this relationship in the 1950s. The bulk of the analysis, as is well known, has been on the post-Emergency phase, where the Court expanded locus standi, widened its reading of several rights, and began to acquire a prominent place within matters of political significance.[4] In recent years, studies on the place of the Supreme Court within the nation's larger democratic unfolding have attempted to grapple with how the institution negotiates the political currents of the day, the means by which it shapes and is shaped by the environment within which it operates, and the techniques that it adopts to preserve and manage its place in the broader setting that exists.[5] Such contributions have been crucial in helping us understand the Supreme Court as a public institution, but their temporal horizon has been limited to the last few decades.

Insofar as the Supreme Court of the 1950s has been studied—with attention to the question of democratic consolidation—two kinds of contributions are especially worth mentioning. The first is exemplified by Granville Austin's classic work, *Working a Democratic Constitution: A History of the Indian Experience*.[6] Austin's text, in its coverage of the initial sixteen years of the Indian republic, underlined two forms of constitutional contestation. The first pertained to conflicts between different political offices and actors, such as tensions between the President and the council of ministers, tensions between the central and state governments, tensions between the government and the opposition, and so forth. The second form of constitutional contestation was linked to specific substantive areas of law, most notably the right to property. Through his coverage of cases and disputes, his description of judicial decision-making and legislative and executive action, Austin captured how the early years of the Indian republic saw serious conflict between the elected and unelected branches of government, and ultimately led to the formation of important constitutional practices and conventions. In other words, select constitutional challenges paved the way for an understanding between the Supreme Court and Parliament and helped to define their respective institutional roles within India's democratic framework.

A somewhat different approach has focused on the Supreme Court's role in legitimizing a new constitutional order. The birth of the Indian Constitution was a dramatic and radical event: it brought into being a new language of politics, a distinct conception of the state and a specific model of representation.[7] For any constitutional order that aims to undo so much of the past, a vital challenge lies in its legitimization—a problem that is of salience during the new order's initial years. It is not sufficient, here, to simply point to the coercive power of the state. For such power to have legitimacy, there is further explanatory work required, such as assessing the use of that power. In understanding the legitimization of India's constitutional revolution during its early years, one can turn to the Supreme Court, and Rohit De's recent book *A People's Constitution: The Everyday Life of Law in the Indian Republic* provides us with one possible way in which to do so.[8] In *A People's Constitution*, De captures how a wide array of ordinary individuals embraced the new constitutional project with interest and enthusiasm. He reveals how the Supreme Court became a forum for decidedly non-elite actors—by figures who took the new constitutional order to be their own and made claims on its basis.

There is much to be said in support of each of these approaches. Though they have attended to the Supreme Court in important ways, however, there has been limited emphasis on the details of constitutional doctrine during the period under study. In this chapter, I hope to explicate some features of the Court's doctrinal stance, and thereby shift the attention towards the internal legal reasoning that characterized the early period of the institution. That is to say, rather than studying the Supreme Court through an external lens—by considering its relationship with other public institutions and with citizens at large—I shall instead unpack features of its doctrinal stance. I shall, in particular, gesture at ways in which constitutional doctrine can help to cement constitutional stability, and thereby allow us to form a fuller picture of the role of the Supreme Court in India's democratic consolidation.

Though constitutions have become increasingly familiar in the modern world, their endurance has proven to be no easy matter.[9] One can conceive of a range of factors that can throw a new constitutional order into crisis, from those relating to the text itself to those linked to institutional and practical realities. In a text such as the Indian Constitution, where the judiciary is explicitly empowered to review decisions by the elected branches of government, there is considerable potential for a clash between elected and unelected institutions. This is likely to be especially so in the instance of a constitutional transition where, as in the case of India, the political forces that occupied the elected institutions at the time enjoyed enormous popular legitimacy. This places institutions such as the Supreme Court in a delicate position. On the one hand, their behaviour will have path dependence and form the basis for a set of constitutional conventions and baselines. On the other hand, their response to matters of controversy can threaten the stability of the constitutional order at precisely the very moment at which it is being formed.

Given these factors, the early jurisprudence of the Supreme Court is revealing. Across two domains which posed tricky constitutional questions and carried extraordinary political significance—the place of the directive principles of state policy within the constitutional framework, and the validity of land reform measures—the Court's stance demonstrates how potential constitutional tensions can be managed. In the first instance, we notice how tensions can be managed by, quite simply, being avoided. In the second case, we see that what are widely regarded to appear as tense contests between the judiciary and other branches are in fact means through which constitutional norms come into being. If the Court's approach towards the directive principles was an example of how potential clashes can be kept to one side, its orientation towards land reform was narrower and far less dramatic than conventional accounts suggest. Both cases suggest a strong emphasis on maintaining the constitutional order, rather than allowing it to spiral out of control.

The directive principles of state policy are among the more peculiar features of India's Constitution. As per Article 37 of the Constitution, 'The provisions contained in this Part shall not be enforceable by any court, but the principles therein laid down are nevertheless fundamental in the governance of the country and it shall be the duty of the State to apply these principles in making laws.'[10] Given their unenforceable character, and the contrast between this set of provisions and the enforceable fundamental rights, the status and meaning of the directive principles has been a source of considerable confusion and debate. In particular, courts have had to struggle with the question of what role, if any, the directive principles should play in constitutional interpretation and in determining the validity of state action. Can such principles override the fundamental rights? Are the fundamental rights to be interpreted in light of such provisions? Do they exclusively speak to the non-judicial branches of government and citizens rather than to courts? As scholars of Indian constitutionalism are aware, these questions assumed considerable importance in time. But what is striking is that the controversy and uncertainty over the directive principles lay, by and large, silent during the Constitution's initial years. How did this state of dormancy come about? What approach to constitutional interpretation made this possible? The answer is not that there was no occasion for such a conflict, something that might have occurred if no legislation had been enacted that could reasonably have involved a conflict between the directive principles and fundamental rights. On the contrary, the avoidance of conflict was enabled by an interpretive outlook that distracted the problem away. The possibility of a major constitutional breakdown was internalized by the Court's approach.

A good example of this is the case of *Champakam Dorairajan*, which appeared soon after the Constitution came into force.[11] The case related to colleges in the state of Madras, and in particular the validity of an admissions policy that reserved seats for select communities on the basis of caste. The state of Madras's defence of the policy was partly based on Article 46 of the Constitution, a directive principle that speaks to the promotion of disadvantaged sections in society. In fact, the state went so far as to argue that Article 46 took precedence over Article 29(2)—which prohibited caste-based discrimination—and thus suggested that the directive principles were to supersede the fundamental rights. The Court rejected this argument, and it affirmed the place of fundamental rights under the constitutional schema—these rights could not be conveniently displaced. What is interesting, however, is not this specific conclusion but the Court's reasoning. The Court did not provide any account for why the fundamental rights were inviolable even in the face of the directive principles. Instead, it claimed that no conflict could exist between both sets of provisions. The directive principles and the fundamental rights were, it claimed, entirely different in character. The difference was so fundamental that there could not be any conflict. Even disagreement, after all, requires some shared understanding upon which people can disagree.[12] Thus, the Court was able to avoid explaining how a conflict between the fundamental rights and the directive principles should be mediated—a matter of deep controversy and serious political ramifications—by denying that any such conflict could exist.

But was this the consistent approach throughout the 1950s? Consider a case where the Supreme Court took a somewhat different stance, such as *F.N. Balsara*.[13] Here, the Court dealt with the meaning of the word 'liquor' in the course of a challenge to the Bombay Prohibition Act, 1949. In interpreting this word, the Court placed some reliance on the directive principles, and held that 'the word "liquor" covered not only those alcoholic liquids which are generally used for beverage purposes and produce intoxication, but also all liquids containing alcohol'.[14] The question was relevant for the purposes of determining legislative competence. The Court needed to ascertain whether the legislature was empowered to not only limit intoxicating beverages but also medicinal and other products that might use alcohol. The Court's reliance on the directive principles here— on Article 47 that spoke of the need to advance public health—did not play any dispositive role. In fact, the Court suggested that the conclusion that prohibition was permissible could be arrived at by a careful reading of the relevant legislative entries. All one needed to do was to read Entry 14 of List II of the Constitution that dealt with public health. Similarly, in a different challenge to the Bombay Prohibition Act, the Court dealt with the right to property, and the question was whether the prohibition, sale etc. of 'liquor' would infringe this guarantee and should be seen to be a reasonable restriction on the right. Again, the Court placed reliance on Article 47 in the directive principles chapter and observed that general restrictions on alcoholic drinks were clearly permissible; the question was whether one could restrict substances that are not drunk but can be abused (such as toilet and medical preparations).

The short answer was that the law under challenge was severable. As in other countries, medicinal uses of alcohol could be distinguished from ordinary consumption. Article 47 itself expressly pointed to the possibility of severability by excluding medicinal uses in its general call for prohibition. Even though the directive principles were, as we can see, referenced by the Supreme Court in *F.N. Balsara*, a few points are worth noting. First, there was no account offered of the place that the directive principles occupied within the overall constitutional framework. The Court seems to have consciously sought to avoid confronting this question. Second, *F.N. Balsara* did not engage with *Champakam Dorairajan* in any fashion and it did not address its apparently divergent approach towards the directive principles. These facts might be explained by the nature of the reliance on the directive principles in *F.N. Balsara*. The reliance occurred on two occasions. In the first case, the Court relied on the directive principles to interpret the competence of the legislature. Here, the Court referred to several sources in support of the same conclusion, and thus the principles were merely confirming an outcome. In the second case, the reliance seems to have been greater, for the suggestion was that the scope of the right to property in the fundamental rights chapter should be determined by reference to the directive principle Article 47.

But this reliance needs to be probed. In *F.N. Balsara*, there was no strong version of the claim that the fundamental rights must conform to the directive principles, and that the latter can supersede the former. Rather, Article 47 was deployed to understand one simple issue: the application of a constitutional guarantee (right to property) to a specific factual scenario (prohibition). Article 47 was useful because it showed that the Constitution had envisaged the kind of state regulation that was in dispute, and it had regarded such regulation (prohibition) to be permissible. In other words, this was equivalent to an illustration that revealed how to apply a law. There was no broader suggestion whatsoever by the Court in *F.N. Balsara* that the fundamental rights are subservient to the directive principles, or that this is even an interpretive goal that must be aspired towards. Thus, though a case such as *F.N. Balsara* seems *ex facie* to be somewhat different from *Champakam Dorairajan*, it continued the trend of denying any possible tension between the directive principles and fundamental rights.

In *Hanif Quareshi*'s case, that came up at the end of the 1950s, we see a similar logic at work.[15] The case dealt with legislation banning cow slaughter, and the state defended the impugned legislation on the ground that they were based on the directive principles. More substantially, the state argued that the principles should override the fundamental rights. This Court rejected this argument and held that no law could violate the fundamental rights, whether or not it was in furtherance of the directive principles, even though it did eventually uphold the impugned statutes in considerable measure. The Court did award some interpretive place to the directive principles, as in *F.N. Balsara*, but did not gesture at the fact that there could be any tension or contest between the directive principles and fundamental rights. Indeed, it is only in *In Re the Kerala Education Bill, 1957*—a case dealing with the regulation of minority educational institutions—that a change in an interpretive outlook occurred.[16] Here the Court's very framing of the matter at hand, its suggestion that a conflict needed to be resolved between Article 30(1) that grants minorities the fundamental right to administer educational institutions and Article 45 in the directive principles chapter that sets out the goal of free and compulsory education, marked a major departure from cases throughout the 1950s. It signalled the first occasion where the Court recognized the possible tension between the directive principles and fundamental rights.

The Supreme Court's approach to the directive principles during its early years was subject to considerable criticism. Scholars desired a more affirmative role for the principles during the process of constitutional interpretation.[17] More recent scholarship has similarly characterized the Court's initial stance as one of 'judicial minimalism' in making the case for why the directive principles should play a greater role in our understanding of the fundamental rights.[18] Whether or not we find merit in the Court's early approach, it did not last for very long. What is notable for our purpose is not whether the Court has succeeded in forging the best relationship between both sets of constitutional provisions, but rather that its very endeavour to even address this relationship—let alone to grant the directive principles a major role as it has done—marks a major turn from its early approach.[19] Scholars of Indian constitutionalism have seen the Court's initial interpretive attitude as mistaken. It has been felt that, even though the directive principles are an important part of the Constitution, they were de-emphasized by the judiciary. Regardless of what we make of the Court's early approach, it is worth noticing that this approach avoided a doctrinal minefield. It prevented the emergence of tensions over potentially conflicting segments of the Indian Constitution and discouraged constitutional crises over the matter. The Court's approach revealed, in other words, how judges can manage potential tensions by downplaying the very fact that such tensions exist.

One tension in a new constitutional order that is often observed is that between the transformative and preservative features of the order. Many constitutions, and most certainly the Indian Constitution, put forth radical goals that threaten to upset established and settled relations of power. How do transformative elements of a new constitution get negotiated within existing social structures? In thinking more about this, one can consider efforts at land redistribution during India's early years. As per the 1950 Constitution, citizens were granted the right to hold and transfer property; acquisition could only occur by legislation, for a public purpose and with compensation. The incorporation of the right to property in India's Constitution was a tense matter, and the eventual set of constitutional provisions expressed a kind of compromise: compensation would need to be provided, but the quantum of compensation would fall outside the power of courts.[20] The legal history over land reform is widely known. Certain high courts struck down land acquisition, Parliament responded with a change in the Constitution in 1951, the amendment itself became a subject of challenge, the Supreme Court eventually adopted the line followed by the high courts, and so forth. There was a subsequent amendment in 1955, and the question of land acquisition is, even today, the site of considerable development.[21] Indeed, a total of ten constitutional amendments have taken place with regard to the right to property.

For our purposes, we need not delve into the long and complex history of jurisprudence surrounding the right to property in India. Instead, we can focus on the earliest portion of this history—that is, the period involving the first challenges to land reform in the high courts to the First and Fourth Amendments to the Constitution in 1951 and 1955 respectively. This period has been widely seen as a series of confrontational episodes between the legislature and judiciary, a period of ideological disagreement between judges and popular representatives.[22] This narrative captures some features of the truth, but it also leaves out a great deal. If we focus on democratic consolidation and turn our attention to the emergence of norms and conventions, the period appears differently. It can be understood as one involving judicial discipline, and as one that enabled a serious constitutional conversation over the respective roles of Parliament and the Supreme Court in India's democratic framework. On every occasion that the judiciary struck down a land acquisition measure, it located independent grounds for doing so—that is, grounds which fell outside the contours of the measure itself. At no stage did the judiciary either challenge the legislature's power to enact the measure or indeed the measure itself. We thus find that there was a remarkable degree of judicial deference towards the legislature, and no real clash between conservative and radical forces. The popular mythology, in part encouraged by scholars such as Austin—surrounding the contest between Parliament and the Supreme Court, that the former was committed to land redistribution, and the latter was committed to private property—gravely mischaracterizes the doctrinal truth of the time. The contest was an attempt at laying down the principles that govern lawmaking and captures a crucial period in an effort at democratic consolidation.

The 1950 Constitution attempted to secure early land reform measures through provisions in Article 31 that protected measures in operation when the Constitution came into force. Yet, all laws could not satisfy the conditions of the savings clauses and, moreover, there were points of challenge outside the savings clauses themselves. This led to numerous challenges to the land reform measures across India—the most significant being a challenge that led to the Patna High Court's decision in *Kameshwar Singh*.[23] In this case, the Bihar Land Reforms Act, 1950 that altered the rights of certain proprietors and tenure-holders and modified land holding in favour of those persons actually cultivating the land was called into question. The Patna High Court struck down the law, inviting a legislative reaction in the form of a new constitutional provision, Article 31A. This provision declared that 'no law providing for the acquisition by the State of any estate or of any rights therein . . . shall be deemed to be void on the ground' that it violated the fundamental rights. Further, the amendment introduced Article 31B and the Ninth schedule to the Constitution, which immunized laws placed in this Schedule from judicial challenge on the basis of a fundamental rights violation.

Though this history is by and large familiar, the reasoning in *Kameshwar Singh* has been relatively understudied. In the decision, the Patna High Court openly accepted that Articles 31(4)–(6) protected the law on the matter of compensation. It also rejected the suggestion that the acquisition was not for a public purpose. The applicable constitutional provisions meant that the judiciary was 'estopped from saying that the acquisition of estates and tenures is not an acquisition for [a public purpose]'.[24] The Supreme Court entirely deferred to the state on these matters, and the law was found to be wanting on a different basis, namely the equal protection guarantee in Article 14. The compensation scheme in the law, the Court observed, created a classification model that was discriminatory. The division between different individuals in the law, and the compensation that they would receive, was found to be without a rational basis. Thus, the Court did not find the compensation inadequate but rather probed the logic by which different levels of compensation were structured. In doing so, it made a key point regarding lawmaking and the institutional roles to be performed by Parliament and the Supreme Court: even though the quantum of compensation was outside the domain of judicial review, the legislature still needed to come up with a scheme that had internal coherence for it to be regarded as a valid law.

The remarkable First Amendment to the Constitution was itself challenged, though the judiciary refused to intervene and held that courts could not review an amendment on substantive grounds.[25] Again, this decision laid down an important principle about the respective demarcation of power between the legislature and judiciary. By the time the Patna High Court decision reached the Supreme Court, the First Amendment had altered the applicable legal reality. Again, the judiciary accepted this and held that the Article 14 argument could no longer be used, and that 'the impugned Acts [could] no longer be attacked on the ground of alleged infringement of any of the rights conferred by the provisions of Part III'.[26] But Articles 31A and 31B only protected the impugned laws from rights-based challenges. They did not protect a law from other possible challenges, such as those based on legislative competence. The relevant legislative entries permitted the state to acquire land, and they empowered it to determine compensation and the meaning of a public purpose. The argument therefore ran that such entries necessarily imposed two conditions on any law acquiring land—that compensation must be paid and a public purpose for acquisition must exist. But, if this was so, could the compensation be merely illusory and therefore be no compensation at all? Similarly, if a law merely altered a land-holding pattern, such as by substituting previous landlords for the government and not distributing the land, could such a law be challenged as not being for a public purpose?

Chief Justice M. Patanjali Sastri rejected such a challenge, seeing the matter as not truly involving legislative competence. Justice Mehr Chand Mahajan shared this view when it came to the payment of compensation but held differently with regard to the public purpose requirement. The Constitution did not prevent courts from examining the reason why property was being acquired. For example, there was clearly no legislative power to acquire property for any purpose whatsoever. The power to acquire property for a public purpose was essential to the nature of the law itself. 'The exercise of the power to acquire compulsorily,' he noted, 'is not an express provision of Article 31(2) but exists *aliunde* in the content of the power itself and that in fact is the assumption upon which this clause of the Article proceeds'.[27] But though Justice Mahajan did feel that courts could look into the matter, he rejected the challenge in this instance, even though the state had only transferred land to itself and not provided any redistribution proposal. For Justice Mahajan, the law was clearly meant for a public purpose even without such details.

Justice Mahajan did, however, find two provisions to be unconstitutional. The first pertained to the acquisition of arrears of rent. As per the law, half the rent to be paid to landlords was transferred to the state. This was thus a way for the state to increase its revenue and pay for the land acquisition. Justice Mahajan struck this down, taking note of a central principle of acquisition that it cannot occur exclusively for increasing the state's revenue. The second provision was one that, for all practical purposes, enabled the non-payment of compensation by artificially creating deductions that had no factual basis. Justice Mahajan declared this to be a case of confiscation, which was clearly beyond the power of the legislature. Justice Bijan Kumar Mukherjea and Justice N. Chandrasekhara Aiyar held similarly to Justice Mahajan, striking down the two aforementioned provisions. By holding that there were independent grounds of challenge outside of the fundamental rights chapter—such as legislative competence—the Supreme Court highlighted the kinds of constitutional challenges that could impact legislation.

We can notice how narrow the Supreme Court's judgment was. There was complete deference on all rights-related questions, there was a rejection of the argument based on illusory compensation and only two provisions of the impugned legislation were struck down. Further, in other cases decided at the same time, the Supreme Court upheld similar land reform legislation.[28] Subsequently, Parliament would enact a constitutional amendment altering the text of a relevant legislative entry (Entry 42, List III), and in the interim further tussles would occur over land reform between the judiciary and legislature. The meaning of compensation, and the differences between the acquisition and regulation of property, became major matters of controversy, eventually leading to the Fourth Amendment to the Constitution in 1955 that radically reduced the power of judicial review over legislation involving property interests.[29]

Scholars who have studied the early years of the Indian Constitution often portray this period as one of deep conflict between the legislature and judiciary. The Supreme Court's attitude, Granville Austin had once observed, placed 'the social revolution' that the Constitution had envisaged in trouble.[30] More recently, it has been noted that the Ninth Schedule and savings clauses including Articles 31A and 31B 'should be seen as a legislative reaction to judicial overreach reflected in an overzealous protection of the erstwhile fundamental right to property against legislation aimed at socio-economic justice'.[31] Yet, a careful reading of the cases at the time presents us with a different account. The consolidation of a constitutional democracy at least partly occurs by the cementing of constitutional argument. The initial period of Indian constitutionalism should not be viewed as one involving a major clash of ideology. Rather, it was one in which judicial review was exercised narrowly and carefully, a culture of constitutional argument and engagement was initiated and the role that legislatures and judges should play was forged into existence.

As we reflect on the early years of Indian democracy, it is worth thinking more carefully about areas of constitutional tension and the overall project of entrenching democracy. One way to think about the relationship of the trajectory of legal doctrine to the more materialist criterion of consolidation is to consider how the Supreme Court's approach in India's early years generated norms and conventions that had a long-term stabilizing effect. In the case of land reform, the Court's careful approach was not an instance of ideological conflict but rather an effort to take constitutionalism seriously and see that the contest occurred in the least ideological of ways. It is thus hardly surprising that the subsequent institutional crises in Indian political life, including in the judiciary, would occur alongside the collapse of norms relating to legal reasoning and judicial lawmaking. In the case of the directive principle and fundamental rights, on the other hand, the Court sought to limit its engagement with matters of potential conflict; here, doctrine was deployed to see that the constitutional project is allowed to stabilize. Needless to say, early periods of constitutional engagement do not settle constitutional controversies. In both of the areas explored in this chapter, the issues were not fully resolved, and may come to invite further contestation in future years. But this should hardly be seen as a failure. The absence of permanent answers may, in fact, be a sign of success. After all, one way to think about a functioning and robust constitutional culture is that it permits and allows constitutional conversations to take place, so long as they take place within constitutional limits.

14

FROM AUTONOMY TO INSURGENCY: JAMMU AND KASHMIR IN THE LONG 1970S

SRINATH RAGHAVAN

I

IN THE SUMMER of 2004, Ramachandra Guha published an essay titled 'Opening a Window in Kashmir'.[1] It focused on a long-forgotten episode in the troubled history of the state: Sheikh Abdullah's visit to Rawalpindi and Muzaffarabad in 1964—an attempt to find a lasting solution to the dispute that was scotched by the death of Jawaharlal Nehru. The essay offered a tantalizing preview of Guha's ongoing work on the history of independent India. This episode would figure prominently in the book he would publish three years later, *India after Gandhi*. There, Guha would argue that this interlude threw interesting light on the life and work of Nehru, who had valiantly sought to uphold democracy and secularism after Gandhi's death, but failed to live up to his own commitments in Kashmir.

The essay of 2004 is also interesting because here the historian sought to draw 'lessons' for the policymaker. Any solution of the Kashmir dispute, he wrote, would have to satisfy the conditions outlined by Sheikh Abdullah forty years earlier: 'that it must not lead to a sense of victory for either India or Pakistan; that it must make the minorities more secure

228

in both countries; and that it must satisfy the aspirations of the people of Kashmir themselves'.[2] This essay was written against the backdrop of a recently declared ceasefire on the Line of Control in Kashmir and the kindling of hopes of a renewed peace process under a new Congress-led coalition government.

Sixteen years on, these hopes have curdled. On 5 August 2019, the Government of India issued a presidential order under Article 370, nullifying the constitutionally guaranteed autonomy of Jammu and Kashmir. The same day, the Bharatiya Janata Party (BJP) government led by Narendra Modi tabled and passed a bill dividing and reducing the state into two union territories of Jammu and Kashmir and Ladakh. In ramming this legislation through the houses of Parliament, the government advanced several specious historical claims: that Article 370 was a 'temporary' provision; that by preventing the complete 'integration' of the state, the article had fostered separatism and terrorism as well as creating a corrupt political class that had thwarted the development of the state.

The history of the Kashmir problem, however, suggests that these hopes are likely to prove unfounded. For it was not the grant of autonomy that set the stage for organized violence, but the abandonment of constitutional pledges and the hollowing out of the state's autonomy. The crucial period in this turn from quest for autonomy to the onset of insurgency were the long years stretching from the mid-1960s to the mid-1980s on which the hinge of India's contemporary history turned. Kashmir, of course, had its own peculiarities. In the years after his visit to Pakistan, Abdullah remained important to Indian governments, especially under Indira Gandhi, in their quest at once to congeal the status quo and cement New Delhi's legitimacy in the state. The eventual outcome was not predetermined, but rather shaped by conjunctures and choices. Examining these is important not just to understand the history of Kashmir, but to sharpen our judgements about its potential futures.

II

We pick up the story of Kashmir from 1967: three years after Sheikh Abdullah's trip to Pakistan and during his subsequent spell of incarceration. By this time, Kashmir's autonomy had been substantially whittled away.

A capsule history of these developments is essential context for the subsequent period.

The maharaja of Jammu and Kashmir acceded to the Indian Union in October 1947. The Instrument of Accession specified only three subjects for accession: foreign affairs, defence and communications. In March 1948, the maharaja appointed an interim government in the state, with Sheikh Abdullah as prime minister. The interim government was also tasked with convening an Assembly for framing a Constitution for the state. Meantime, the Constituent Assembly of India was conducting its deliberations. Sheikh Abdullah and three of his colleagues joined the Indian Constituent Assembly as members in May 1949. Over the next five months, they negotiated Kashmir's future relationship with India. This led to the adoption of Article 370 in the Indian Constitution.

Article 370 restricted the Union's legislative power over Kashmir to the three subjects in the Instrument of Accession. To extend other provisions of the Indian Constitution, the state government's prior concurrence would have to be obtained. Further, this concurrence would have to be upheld by the Constituent Assembly of Kashmir, so that the provisions would be reflected in the state's Constitution. This implied that after Kashmir's Constituent Assembly was convened, the state government's concurrence would not suffice. Further, once the Kashmir Constituent Assembly met, framed the state's Constitution and dissolved, there could be no further extension of the Union's legislative power. It was thus that the state's autonomy was guaranteed by the Indian Constitution.

The Constituent Assembly of Kashmir met for the first time in November 1951. Even as it got down to its work, Abdullah wanted to depose the maharaja and end dynastic rule in Kashmir. Nehru had no love lost for the maharaja. But the move to depose the ruler raised serious constitutional issues; for the maharaja was recognized by the president of India. More importantly, it underscored the need to settle the broad principles governing the relationship between Kashmir and India. This was necessary to ensure that Kashmir's Constitution consorted smoothly with that of India. Following intense negotiations, Nehru and Abdullah concluded an accord in July 1952.

Under the 'Delhi Agreement' the Union's authority would be confined to the three subjects of accession; the residuary powers would be vested in the Kashmir government. The residents of the state would be citizens of India but the state legislature would define and regulate their rights and privileges. The head of the state would be recognized by the president of India on the recommendation of the state legislature. Delhi could only exercise emergency powers on the request of the state government. These were the contours of the 'pre-1953' autonomous status for Kashmir.

Unfortunately, the accord failed to hold. The Delhi Agreement came under intense attack by the Bharatiya Jana Sangh (precursor to the BJP) and the Praja Parishad in Jammu (a Dogra Hindu organization), both of which demanded complete integration of the state into India. Painted into a corner by these forces, Abdullah began toying with a variety of alternatives, including independence or a condominium of India and Pakistan for the whole state or the Valley. This set the stage for his dismissal, with Nehru's own approval, and imprisonment.[3]

Thereafter, successive Indian governments sought to shore up their slipping hold on Kashmir by planting pliant governments in Srinagar and by creatively undermining the state's autonomy. In May 1954, the Indian government issued an omnibus presidential order extending several provisions of the Indian Constitution to Jammu and Kashmir. At this point, there was at least the fig leaf of 'concurrence' of the state's Constituent Assembly. In November 1956, the state Constituent Assembly adopted a motion dissolving itself from 26 January 1957. Yet the Indian government continued to use presidential orders under Article 370 to apply more provisions of the Indian Constitution to the state. In November 1963, Nehru himself told Parliament that Article 370 and Kashmir's autonomy 'has been eroded . . . and many things have been in the last few years which have made the relationship of Kashmir with the Union of India very close . . . So we feel that this process of gradual erosion of article 370 is going on . . . We should allow it to go on'.[4]

After Nehru's death and Abdullah's abortive trip to Pakistan, the Lal Bahadur Shastri government took further steps to tighten New Delhi's grip on the state. In November 1964, Article 356 (imposition of President's Rule) was applied to the state via Article 370. During the Durgapur session of the Congress in 1965, three prominent leaders of the National Conference (NC) (the party led previously by Abdullah)— G.M. Sadiq, Mir Qasim and D.P. Dhar—sought and obtained Prime Minister Shastri's permission to form a branch of the Congress party in the state. Soon after, they announced the dissolution of the National Conference. Sadiq, it bears emphasizing, was the chief minister of the state. Later, in November 1966, Sadiq also introduced a bill amending the state's Constitution to replace the elected Sadr-i-Riyasat with a governor nominated by the central government. New Delhi could now go for the jugular of any government in Kashmir.

III

The 1967 elections in Kashmir were hardly free or fair. In almost a third of the constituencies, Congress candidates won unopposed—after their rivals' nominations had been rejected.[5] The Plebiscite Front backed by Abdullah and led by Mirza Afzal Beg stayed out of the elections. Although the polls were not marred by protests or violence, the simmering popular anger in the Valley bubbled up that summer in the shape of anti-India sloganeering and stone-pelting in Srinagar. The journalist J.J. Singh, who had long known Abdullah and Indira Gandhi, wrote to the prime minister with a first-hand account of these events. India was sitting atop a volcano in Kashmir, he warned: 'You never know when it will burst'. Only Sheikh Abdullah could help regain their credibility with the people. Singh implored Mrs Gandhi to release Abdullah, 'Please act in your forthright and fearless manner notwithstanding the cautious approach that your advisers are advocating'.[6]

As Sadiq's government scrambled to rein in the situation, troubles flared up on another front. In August 1967, a Kashmiri Pandit woman and a Muslim man—colleagues in a cooperative—announced their wedding as well as the woman's conversion to Islam. The Pandits in the Valley framed it as an assault on their community and launched an agitation demanding that the woman be placed in the custody of her parents. The chief minister initially sought to dissuade the couple, but gave up after ascertaining that the lady was acting of her own volition. This lit the touchpaper. Soon, the Hindus of Jammu began mobilizing in protest. The communal edge of the situation was sharpened by the Jana Sangh leader Balraj Madhok's visit to the state and his incendiary statements.[7]

The protests also underscored the regional divide between Jammu and the Kashmir Valley. This dimension of the problem had been impressed upon the prime minister by Karan Singh, the former Sadr-i-Riyasat and governor of the state and a minister in Mrs Gandhi's cabinet since the 1967 elections. Karan Singh held that the state of Jammu and Kashmir comprised three distinct regions—Jammu, the Kashmir Valley and Ladakh—with their own identities and interests. The dominance of the Kashmir Valley since accession to India, he maintained, 'was as unfair and unacceptable as the earlier position' when the ruling class came from Jammu. The 'predominant feeling' in that province was that 'if the State is to remain as one unit this can only be on the basis of both provinces getting a fair deal'. His own preference was for a 'linguistic reorganization of the State as had been done elsewhere in India'—a euphemism for the trifurcation of the state into separate entities. This naturally raised a host of thorny questions about the integrity and autonomy of Jammu and Kashmir.[8]

A third and neuralgic aspect of the situation was the persisting factionalism in the state unit of the Congress party. Since the Congress had come to power after subsuming the National Conference, the rivalry between Sadiq and Mir Qasim had sharpened. It was entirely in keeping with New Delhi's approach to Kashmir that even as it deplored this disunity, the Union government and the Congress party stoked the embers of factionalism. As Mir Qasim would rue: 'Whenever New Delhi feels a leader in Kashmir is getting too big for his shoes, it employs Machiavellian methods to cut him to size. This it does by projecting a lesser leader as an alternative'.[9]

By the end of the summer of 1967, it was evident to the prime minister's secretariat that these three dimensions of the Kashmir problem could no longer be ignored. The question of subregional autonomy in the state was handed over later that year to a commission led by the former chief justice of India, P.B. Gajendragadkar. The commission's report released in January 1969 recommended, among other things, setting up regional development boards for Kashmir and Jammu to ensure equitable distribution and effective use of government expenditure, appointing a deputy chief minister from another region, and allocating equitable share in government employment, judiciary and education to the regions and communities.

More nettlesome were the problems of dealing with factionalism and Sheikh Abdullah. P.N. Haksar, the influential principal secretary to the prime minister, was convinced that the situation in Kashmir had reached a 'critical stage'. The vision that had bound the state to India, he wrote to Indira Gandhi, had 'dimmed'. She must strongly convey to Sadiq the importance of a getting a grip on the situation and ensuring that he and Mir Qasim pulled together. As for the future of Abdullah, it was admittedly 'a difficult question, but we have to face it and Shri Sadiq and his colleague [Mir Qasim] will have to face it also. Even if we do not face it today, we shall have to do so tomorrow or the day-after'.[10]

Haksar had been pondering the future of Abdullah through the torrid summer of 1967. He had asked Home Secretary L.P. Singh as well as D.P. Dhar to assess the merits of setting Abdullah free. Unsurprisingly, both of them had argued 'heavily in favour of continued detention of Sheikh Abdullah'. The only question, it seemed, was whether it should be ordered by the state government or the central government. Haksar had felt that 'if the recrudescence of violence . . . is any indication of the state of public opinion, it would indeed be perilous to let Sheikh Sahib into the state'. Yet after the elections the question would have to be considered again.[11]

Meanwhile, Haksar starkly outlined the framework that would guide the government's efforts at a rapprochement with the Sheikh. First, New Delhi would 'resist every attempt' by Abdullah and his followers to impart to the issue an international dimension. Indeed, negating this aspect of the dispute was important in India's dealings with Pakistan too. Second, Abdullah had to understand that 'we are determined to keep as part of India the territory of J&K, irrespective of the wishes of the people'. Third, once the Sheikh accepted this premise, 'we would be prepared to consider refashioning the autonomy of J&K, provided of course our overall interests and security of India are kept in mind'. Finally, as this process unfolded, 'we should not . . . even remotely undermine the authority' of the present government.[12] In short, Abdullah would have to be brought back into the picture but entirely on New Delhi's terms. This defined the contours of engagement over the following decade.

In late September 1967, Indira Gandhi decided to reach out to the Sheikh. Her emissary was neither a friend of Abdullah, such as JP or Mridula Sarabhai, nor one of her usual advisers on Kashmir affairs. Rather she tasked the diplomat T.N. Kaul with this delicate assignment. A Kashmiri Pandit from Baramulla, who had joined the Indian Civil Service under the Raj before moving to the foreign ministry, Kaul had known Sheikh Abdullah since his days as a student in the early 1930s. Kaul would later be appointed foreign secretary and count as a member of the 'Kashmir mafia' that occupied senior positions in Mrs Gandhi's government. On 3 October 1967, Kaul wrote a short letter to Abdullah, inquiring if they could meet. The Sheikh readily agreed.[13]

In their first meeting on 10 October, Abdullah observed that 'the gradual whittling of Article 370 of the Constitution with regard to Kashmir was unfortunate. It showed a lack of faith in secularism and the ability of Hindus and Muslims in Kashmir to get along with each other'.[14] A couple of days later, he spoke more pointedly. He began with the external dimension of the dispute: 'the salvation of the people of Kashmir' lay in forging peace and understanding between India and Pakistan. 'It was too late in the day,' he said, 'for India to take the position that Pakistan had no locus standi in Kashmir'.[15]

There were two further complications. In the first place, the autonomy of Kashmir had been eroded since his arrest in 1953. 'The people of Kashmir had lost faith in the sanctity of Article 370 and would ask for firmer guarantees about the autonomy of the state.' Yet it might not be easy to go back to the status before 1953. For the situation within Kashmir had also changed during these years. The restoration of autonomy would be opposed by three distinct regional groups. There was a 'pro-Pakistan element' in the Valley apart from the Plebiscite Front, while groups in the Jammu province wanted 'complete integration with India' and some in Ladakh wanted to become a separate union territory.[16]

When asked his considered opinion on a feasible solution, Abdullah suggested that the government could place the issue before 'a small body of leaders of public opinion', including some leaders of the Opposition parties in India as well as Jammu and Kashmir. Such a body could consider various options and recommend a course of action to the government. Abdullah refused to comment on who might be invited to such a group or his own preferred solution. He indicated that if such a group recommended reverting to the status before 1953, it might be workable. 'However, there would have to be firm guarantees that Government would not whittle down Article 370 as it had done'. Abdullah said that he had 'confidence in the bona fides of the Prime Minister', but was unsure if political parties would support a quest for a reasonable solution.[17]

Kaul concluded that Abdullah had realized that an independent Kashmir was inconceivable—neither India nor Pakistan would countenance it. Nor could any government in India afford to let go of the Valley. Abdullah was 'probably reconciled' to the idea of autonomy for Kashmir with guarantees and safeguards. At the same time, he seemed unsure if he could carry the people of Kashmir with him.[18] The prime minister and Haksar asked him further to probe Abdullah's mind.

The third meeting was testy. The Sheikh observed that reverting to pre-1953 status might have been possible had the Indian government not eroded Article 370. 'They had only played into the hands of anti-secular and pro-Pakistani elements thereby'. He also let fly against New

Delhi's 'stooges in Kashmir', whose corruption and repression further incited popular passions against India. Abdullah said that while he was not a member of the Plebiscite Front, it was an influential body and the Indian government should talk to them: 'Their stand on plebiscite was not rigid. Its leaders had repeatedly declared their willingness to consider any alternative method of ascertaining the will of the people of Kashmir'. He further argued that 'it was very strange that while Government of India had no hesitation in talking to the Underground Nagas who had opened armed revolt against her, they should refuse to meet the real representatives of the people of Kashmir'. Asked if he would like to meet the prime minister, Abdullah said that his affection for her had not dimmed: 'when he was free from detention he would be glad to meet her'.[19] At a final meeting in the new year, Abdullah told Kaul and Haksar that he stood by the ideals of Jawaharlal Nehru: 'Let Shrimati Indira Gandhi give the lead on the right lines and I will go along with her'.[20]

IV

Sheikh Abdullah was released from prison in March 1968. Later in the year, he convened the Kashmir People's Convention in Srinagar—an event to which he invited all parties from the state and the rest of India. Although the Congress and the Jana Sangh kept out, some 250 delegates attended the conclave. Among those who spoke was Jayaprakash Narayan, the Gandhian socialist who had long championed the cause of Kashmir.

In his address, Jayaprakash Narayan maintained that a solution could be found within the bounds of accession to India, that there was no question of a plebiscite being held, and that Pakistan had no locus standi after its resort to force in 1965. Narayan's claim was strongly contested by certain groups. The Young Men's League claimed that it was 'absolutely incorrect and far from the reality'. With a third of the state under Pakistan's control, the latter was a party to the dispute.[21] The Sheikh had to intervene to ensure that the situation did not turn uglier.

After the convention, Abdullah broached the matter with Narayan. 'Permit me to say,' he wrote, 'that it did surprise, and even shock many of your admirers to hear from your lips that Indian Government would not keep their pledge by the people of Kashmir as Pakistan has made war on India in 1965'. This was continuous with the Indian government's policy of using Pakistan as an excuse to deprive the people of their rights.

Abdullah insisted that the will of the people and amity between India and Pakistan remained the keys to resolving the dispute.[22]

Narayan replied that no 'responsible person, either in Pakistan or in India, has thought for many years now that plebiscite in J&K was a practical solution of the problem anymore'. Even President Ayub Khan of Pakistan had told him in 1964 that if India was unwilling to consider a plebiscite, they could explore other modes of resolution. The only possible solution was, first, an accord between the state and the Indian government—one that could be placed before the people in the assembly elections. And second, a settlement between India and Pakistan. Even if the latter were elusive, the former was imperative.[23]

Abdullah, for his part, maintained that 'no canons of justice, morality or law can justify bypassing the pledges solemnly given to the people of Kashmir in regard to their right of self-determination'. If the Indian leadership believed that a plebiscite was impracticable, then 'the onus is on them to suggest a reasonable alternative, which would, in the circumstances, be—by and large—fair and equitable to all the concerned parties'. Abdullah hoped that there was 'still a chance of finding a lasting and honourable solution to this vexed problem'.[24]

By this time, Indira Gandhi was preoccupied with the struggle for power in her own party, which would fissure the Congress in November 1969. Her main interest lay in retaining control over the party organization in Kashmir and checking its fractiousness. The rift between Sadiq and Mir Qasim had opened into a crevasse, with the latter and his supporters unwilling to continue under the chief minister's leadership. In the event, the prime minister managed to persuade Mir Qasim to return to his position as president of the state Congress unit. Visiting Srinagar in July 1970, Mrs Gandhi bluntly stated in a public meeting that the issue of Kashmir had been settled once and for all. There was no question of reopening it; the course of the state's history could not be changed. 'We will build a new Kashmir', she asserted, 'quickly if you help, slowly if you don't, but build it we will!'[25]

Yet, once Indira Gandhi decided on early national elections in February–March 1971, the problem surfaced again. Karan Singh had told her that unity in the state Congress party was 'still only skin deep'. Allowing Abdullah and the Plebiscite Front to operate without restraints might prove a grievous mistake.[26] Haksar advised her that they had to prepare 'the political atmosphere and political justification for what might follow'.[27]

What followed were orders to keep Abdullah and Mirza Afzal Beg out of the state during the general elections. Jayaprakash Narayan had requested Mrs Gandhi and Haksar to desist from any such course. Now he issued a public statement calling the move 'foolish and cowardly'.[28] On 26 March 1971, Narayan wrote yet again to Indira Gandhi. 'I do not know what your long-term policy in Kashmir is,' he observed, 'but if it is anything like conciliation and winning the hearts and minds of the people, the externment order should be allowed to lapse after its term is over'. Now that she had returned to power with a strong majority, 'there should be no inhibition in acting according to your judgement'.[29]

Narayan erred in imagining that Mrs Gandhi had any interest in the 'hearts and minds' of the Kashmiris. As Haksar had pointedly noted, the sole objective was to tighten their grip on the state irrespective of popular opinion. In hindsight, Narayan also underestimated the balance of power between the two sides. Even as he penned his letter, a crisis erupted in East Pakistan which would culminate in an independent Bangladesh and an unprecedented Indian military victory with the surrender in Dhaka of 93,000 Pakistani soldiers.[30] The war not only left India in a strategically superior position to a bisected Pakistan, but it also enormously increased its leverage on the Kashmir issue. In the Simla conference of July 1972, India forbore from imposing a punitive settlement on Pakistan but ensured that Kashmir would thenceforth be treated as a bilateral issue to be settled without the use of force. This strategic and diplomatic context tremendously strengthened New Delhi in its dealings with Sheikh Abdullah. Indeed, the latter was left with practically no cards to play.

In early February 1972, Mirza Afzal Beg issued a press statement pointing out that the Plebiscite Front had never questioned the accession of Jammu and Kashmir to India and had always stood for Article 370 as the constitutional link that bound the state to the Union. The next month, Abdullah himself told the *Times* (London): 'There is no quarrel with the Government of India over accession; it was over the structure of internal autonomy'.[31] Radhakrishna Patil, an associate of Jayaprakash Narayan, met Beg and 'found him [Beg] a completely changed man, anxious to come to a settlement of the Kashmiri question . . . he repeated time and again they were prepared to advise the people of Kashmir to finalise the accession, if the status quo ante, as prescribed at the time of the accession was restored'.[32] Abdullah and Beg had evidently assessed their position anew, though they still overestimated their hand in any future negotiations.

In the run-up to the Simla conference, Haksar too began to pick up the pieces on Kashmir. On his instruction, the Intelligence Bureau (IB) had conducted a survey in rural Kashmir, especially Baramulla and Anantnag, of popular opinion about Sheikh Abdullah. The IB reported that 'Sheikh Sahib was held in high esteem and affection by the peasantry. He symbolises Kashmir to them . . . there was a feeling of sadness that India should deal with a true Kashmir patriot in so harsh and unjust a manner'. Haksar agreed with this assessment. He also felt that it would be unwise for the prime minister to meet her Pakistani counterpart, Zulfikar Ali Bhutto, with Abdullah languishing in her prisons: 'Our moral and political position would be very weak indeed if we negotiated with Bhutto with Sheikh Sahib in our custody'. So, Haksar asked D.P. Dhar—an architect of 'the original sin of what was done in 1953'—to ponder on how they should deal with Abdullah. Dhar spoke to Mrs Gandhi as did the new chief minister of the state, Mir Qasim. They agreed that Abdullah must be released. Haksar told the prime minister that 'it was imperative to make a fresh start and lead him by hand on the difficult and tortuous road whose ultimate destination would be reconciliation'. For a start, she must meet Abdullah before he left for the Valley.[33]

On 10 June 1972, Indira Gandhi met Sheikh Abdullah. No record of the meeting is available in the archives, but we do have a letter from Mridula Sarabhai, a long-standing associate of Abdullah, thanking Haksar for enabling this meeting. Sarabhai also suggested that 'today's meeting should lead to widening the door for exploring the various possibilities'. She had found no rigidity in Abdullah's stance and had urged him to allow Beg to meet Haksar and consider possible pathways to reconciliation.[34] Two days later, Haksar advised the prime minister to commence a dialogue—'rather than a "negotiation"'—which would be conducted away from the glare of publicity. Haksar was also clear that the 'dialogue should be a prolonged one'. At his suggestion, Mrs Gandhi tasked the diplomat and administrator G. Parthasarathi to represent her in these discussions.[35]

As designed, the talks between Parthasarathi and Beg proceeded at a stately pace. On substantive issues, Abdullah attempted to hold his own. In August 1974, he wrote to Parthasarathi that 'I have made it abundantly clear to you that I can assume office only on the basis of the position as it existed on 8th August, 1953'.[36] In other words, Abdullah wanted the repeal of all provisions of the Indian Constitution extended to the state under Article 370 since his dismissal as well as restoration of the old model of an elected Sadr-i-Riyasat. Subsequent negotiations between Beg and Parthasarathi resulted in a set of 'agreed conclusions' in November 1974.

These were far from the restoration that Abdullah sought. Article 370 would remain in place with residuary powers of legislation vested in the state. But the Indian Parliament would continue to have powers to make laws against secessionism. Provisions of the Indian Constitution that had been modified when extended to the state could be revised, but all provisions applied in toto would be unalterable. In an unprecedented move, the powers of the state legislature to amend the state's Constitution was curbed in two crucial areas: the appointment and powers of the governor, and the superintendence and control of elections—both issues that had determined New Delhi's ability to undermine democracy in the state. Any amendment to the state's Constitution on these subjects would need the prior assent of the president of India. This was justified as a 'reciprocal' arrangement to the powers granted to the state's Constituent Assembly and legislature—a mockery of the original intent of the framers to ensure the autonomy of the state.

Beg's attempt to discuss provisions of fundamental rights or to modify Article 356 (applying President's Rule) to require prior concurrence of the state legislature failed to make any headway. The facade of autonomy was kept up, however, by assuring the state the freedom 'to have its own legislation on matters like welfare measures, cultural matters, social security, personal law, and procedural laws'. The state government could review any provision extended to the state on the concurrent list.[37]

Abdullah wrote to Mrs Gandhi expressing hope for a satisfactory and amicable settlement of the persisting disagreements. But the prime minister was unwilling to concede anything: 'I doubt whether anything will be gained by our discussing these matters again.'[38] The Sheikh wrote a lengthy missive recounting the history of the dispute and the injustices meted out to him: 'in case you wish to help in rebuilding the faith and confidence that the majority community in the State has lost in India, I can only start from the point where I left off in August, 1953.' Abdullah perceptively added, 'For me to take even this position is not going to be without difficulties, and I shall be faced with many a doubting mind. But I would nevertheless give it a try'. But if the prime minister was unwilling to discuss disagreements, he was willing to walk away from the negotiations.[39]

Indira Gandhi and Abdullah met in Pahalgam on 11 February 1975. It was evident to the Sheikh that there was nothing more on offer. So, Abdullah elected to clinch the accord on the basis of the 'agreed conclusions' and return to power after twenty-two years in the political wilderness. The accord was signed in New Delhi by Beg and Parthasarathi on 24 February. It placed Abdullah's stamp of approval on the hollowing out of Article 370 and the evisceration of Kashmir's autonomy.

V

From a political standpoint, too, Abdullah's return to the helm was rife with contradictions. Mir Qasim agreed to step down as chief minister and Kashmir Congress legislators decided to elect Abdullah as the leader of the House. But Indira Gandhi personally intervened to ensure that they did not also choose Abdullah as the leader of the Congress party in Kashmir.[40] Her insistence on this arrangement underscored two key and related objectives that she sought to pursue in the wake of the accord. While she needed the Sheikh at the helm to secure popular legitimacy in Kashmir, she also wanted to ensure that he remained dependent on the Congress party's political support. Placing the party under his leadership would result in his taking control of it sooner rather than later. Further, Mrs Gandhi believed that the Congress party had to maintain its independent identity and remain a long-term political player in the state.

On 25 February 1975, Abdullah was sworn in as chief minister of Jammu and Kashmir. Along with him, three of his associates, including Beg, were sworn in as ministers. Mrs Gandhi was keen that the Congress should hold two cabinet positions. Abdullah was initially amenable to this power-sharing arrangement, but changed his mind owing to the popular response to the accord. The announcement met with a chorus of protest in the Valley that the Sheikh had sold out Kashmir's interests to secure power. These voices were amplified after the Union government tabled the details of the accord, including various exchanges, in Parliament. These substantiated the prime minister's statement in the House that the accord sealed the status quo and no substantial suggestions had been accepted. The All India Radio's report triggered protests across the Valley with slogans decrying the 'Sheikh-Indira accord'. A grand public reception in honour of the Sheikh had to be cancelled. Although Abdullah had anticipated some criticism, he had failed to gauge the depth of his people's discontent.

Indeed, he was so taken aback that he refused to attend his oath-taking ceremony—until Mir Qasim prevailed upon him.[41] So, from the outset, Abdullah was keen to assert his independence from the Congress party and the Indian government.

The context in which he sought to do this was hardly propitious. Four months after he became chief minister, Indira Gandhi imposed the Emergency on India. By dramatically centralizing power and crushing the opposition, she acquired a formidable position of authority. Never one to shirk political combat, her ability to take on recalcitrant state governments was stronger than ever. By the same token, Abdullah's room for manoeuvre shrank; though he continued to play on the weaknesses of the Congress party in Kashmir.

The central point of contention was the sharing of power between Abdullah and the Congress party. The Sheikh demurred against a swift expansion of his cabinet. Worse, when he agreed he sought to poach Congressmen as his own representatives in the cabinet. Within a couple of months of his elevation to power, Mrs Gandhi realized that 'new and complex problems' had arisen in Kashmir. 'I had envisaged such a situation', she observed, 'though not so soon'.[42] After a protracted tussle lasting over a year and a half, the matter came to a head. In a meeting on 17 October 1976 with the Congress president, Karan Singh and Mrs Gandhi's advisers, Abdullah agreed that his cabinet should have four Congressmen as well as four of his own associates. On the night before the new cabinet was to be sworn in, Mrs Gandhi took umbrage at Abdullah inducting an erstwhile Congressmen, Abdul Ghani Lone, as his nominee in the cabinet. At her instruction, the Kashmir Congress backed out of the agreement.[43]

Equally galling to the prime minister was Abdullah's decision to revive the National Conference. Since the party's absorption into the Kashmir Congress in 1965, Abdullah's organizational base lay in the Plebiscite Front. In the aftermath of the accord, Abdullah converted the Front into the National Conference. In October 1975, he held a public meeting of the NC and formally became a member. Soon he was the party's president. In April 1976, he organized a massive convention of the NC in Srinagar—a show of strength that did not go down well with the Congress. The Kashmir Congress's waning organization, drew the prime minister's ire. She would later reproach Mir Qasim that the accord 'turned out to be a patched up settlement which left the Congress without any significant representation in the Cabinet and virtually led to the exit of our party from the J&K political scene . . . For me the Accord was, and remains, a method of fruitful cooperation among all the secular and patriotic forces in the state. It certainly did not mean that the Congress should fade into oblivion. I did not and can not accept this interpretation of the Accord'.[44]

These issues apart, Indira Gandhi also resented the Sheikh's stance on the Emergency. By late 1976, the state had become—a bit like Tamil Nadu—a sanctuary for dissenters against the Emergency regime. After the infamous shooting and killing of protesters at the Turkman Gate in Delhi on 18 April 1976, Abdullah visited the area and met with the residents. When reports trickled in of his expressing 'great displeasure at the government's actions', the prime minister's son, Sanjay Gandhi, as well as her secretariat were not pleased.[45] It is not surprising, therefore, that in late October 1976 Mrs Gandhi told a confidant, Inder Kumar Gujral, that Sheikh Abdullah was now 'a pain in the neck'. Gujral learnt that she was seriously contemplating dismissing him from office.[46]

In the event, it was Indira Gandhi who was stripped of power when she called for elections in March 1977. Even as she was voted out of office, Mrs Gandhi instructed the Kashmir Congress unit to withdraw its support to the Sheikh Abdullah government, so wrecking an accord that had taken years to craft. In the state elections held in June 1977, the National Conference took forty-seven of the seventy-six assembly seats, winning forty of forty-two seats in the Valley but only seven of thirty-two in Jammu. The Congress won eleven seats in Jammu and drew a blank in the Valley. Abdullah's hold on the state seemed secure.

VI

This proved only a reprieve. In June 1980, Indira Gandhi returned to power with a strong majority. Soon, her attention was drawn to Abdullah's statements criticizing the Union government. Karan Singh wrote to her that 'the Valley is seething with secessionist and anti-Centre feelings, to which the Sheikh himself, through his public speeches and private conversations, gives a boost from time to time'.[47] In fact, Abdullah was struggling to contain the bubbling unrest among Muslim youth, which took the form of protest against the central government. Ironically, his own acquiescence in the destruction of the state's autonomy had sown disaffection.

Abdullah was in trouble on another front. Having promised regional devolution of power in 1975, he resiled from this pledge and sought to concentrate power in Srinagar against the machinations of New Delhi. In 1978, Poonch erupted in protest over subregional autonomy and access to government employment. The government responded with force, leaving one student protester dead and many injured. As the regional divide grew, the Congress party sought to secure its own hold on Jammu by branding the Sheikh a 'Muslim communalist'. Indira Gandhi played on this fault line. Visiting the state in July 1981, she publicly claimed that minorities in the state were feeling insecure.

The NC hit back with an editorial in its official weekly, *Nawa-i-Subh*. Abdullah, it claimed, had restored the 'emotional integration' of the state with the Union: 'Now it is the centre which is reversing the process.' The editorial observed that things were reaching 'a point of no return': 'Discontent is piling up among the youth. Those who hailed the Accord in no uncertain terms, are now openly saying that Kashmiris have no future in India. A reaction to the Prime Minister's speech in Jammu, in which she said that minorities were not feeling safe in the state, has been that certain youth have started thinking aloud about the two-nation theory'. A senior Kashmir hand and former adviser to the prime minister, K.N. Bamzai, conveyed this as well as popular concerns about Abdullah's imminent dismissal. Bamzai agreed that the Sheikh was in his autumn, but cautioned against 'an erroneous impression of his being reduced to a spent force'. He remained a 'legendary figure', and removing him at this stage would consecrate his image as a 'Martyr in defence of "so-called Kashmir Autonomy"'. Abdullah's sole desire was to secure the political future of his son, Farooq. So, New Delhi should leave well alone.[48]

Sheikh Abdullah died in harness on 8 September 1982. When state elections came around in a few months, Mir Qasim advised Mrs Gandhi to form an unofficial coalition with the NC as a secular front. But the prime minister was in no mood to cede much ground to young Farooq Abdullah. Nor could the latter carry his supporters with him for an alliance. The NC won forty-seven of seventy-five seats, the bulk of them in the Valley, and the Congress won twenty-three of thirty-two seats in Jammu but none in the Valley. Mrs Gandhi's focus on the regional and religious divide had paid off, though she continued to delude herself with avowals of secularism. 'The BJP [Bharatiya Janata Party, successor to the Jana Sangh] has been routed in Jammu,' she told Mir Qasim: 'Is this not a major victory for secular forces? . . . Far from harming the cause of secular and democratic forces in J&K, our strategy has strengthened it.'[49]

The subsequent attempts at unseating Farooq Abdullah have been documented in rich detail by the then governor of Jammu and Kashmir— and the prime minister's cousin—B.K. Nehru.[50] The dismissal had to await the exit of Nehru and the appointment of Jagmohan as governor. Nehru's retrospective verdict on this sordid episode is worth recalling. The Kashmiris, he wrote, 'were convinced now at the second dethronement of their elected ruler that India would never permit them to rule themselves . . . it was the last straw that broke the camel's back and to which the *intifada* . . . can be traced'.[51]

Indeed, New Delhi had won a pyrrhic victory. Since the demise of Jawaharlal Nehru, successive central governments, mostly under Indira Gandhi, sought to continue the erosion of the state's autonomy that had begun under him while attempting to resuscitate popular legitimacy in the state. As Nehru had realized, Sheikh Abdullah held the key to any potential solution. But Abdullah held fast to his demand for giving expression to popular will and restoring the state's autonomy. The war of 1971 at once altered the geopolitical balance in the subcontinent and decimated Abdullah's negotiating position. Thereafter, he could only return to power by placing his imprimatur on the destruction of the state's autonomy and at the sufferance of the Congress party. In hindsight, Abdullah's choice deepened popular alienation in the Valley, especially among the Muslim youth. Indira Gandhi's subsequent attempts to retain control in the state, culminating in the arbitrary dismissal of Farooq Abdullah, created widespread disaffection—a necessary condition for the onset of an armed conflict. Kashmir had traversed the tortuous route from autonomy to insurgency. This journey was hardly preordained, but it may hold a mirror to the illusions of our own times.

PART IV

ON RAMACHANDRA GUHA

15

RAM GUHA: A RADICAL PROGRESSIVE

MADHAV GADGIL

THE YEAR WAS 1981. I was at the Forest Research Institute (FRI) in Dehradun at the invitation of my entomologist friend, Dr Sen Sharma, to give a talk on elephant social behaviour. At the end of the talk, my friend introduced me to the then twenty-three-year-old Ram, saying that Ram's father, a chemist, was his colleague at FRI, and that Ram was interested in talking to me. I found Ram full of enthusiasm, and greatly enjoyed chatting with him over the next hour and a half. Ram had been brought up in Dehradun and had studied in the Doon School, following which he had obtained a bachelor's degree from St Stephen's College and a master's from the Delhi School of Economics. These were all highly prestigious educational institutions where many of the rich and famous, including Rajiv Gandhi, Karan Singh, Jyotiraditya Scindia and Mani Shankar Iyer, had studied. But Ram had no false airs. He explained that he was a nature lover, fond of the Himalayas. He was fascinated by birds from a young age, and at the age of twelve had written an article on the birds of Dehradun's New Forest in the *Newsletter for Birdwatchers*. He now wished to switch to sociology from economics and had just begun his doctoral research on the Chipko movement at the Indian Institute of Management in Kolkata.

CHIPKO

The British started plundering the natural resources of the Himalayas. The pace only increased after independence. The cost of this exploitation was being imposed on the local people, who were suffering in many different ways, with huge landslides and floods that washed away entire villages. An important cause of this damage was the felling of trees. Trees were being supplied to newer and newer enterprises at throwaway prices. One such enterprise manufactured badminton rackets.

The Chipko movement had begun in 1973 as a result of people's struggle to halt the felling of trees against their wishes. It had attracted a great deal of public attention with extensive news coverage. This movement had a long history. People had been registering their protests in many different ways over decades. A great deal of documentation was available on such protests. After the Second World War, students of history had given up focusing exclusively on those in power and had begun to record history centred around common people. Studies were appearing on how people at the bottom of society struggled to fulfil their aspirations. Ram was interested in working on the Chipko movement employing this new paradigm.

I was a biologist primarily interested in ecological issues. Since 1971, I was engaged in field studies on hilly regions in forested tracts. I was exploring how the paper mills were mercilessly exploiting forest resources, how centuries-old sacred groves were being cut down to feed the plywood mills. I, too, was very much fascinated by the Chipko movement. Indeed, I was planning to proceed from Dehradun to Bemru village in Garhwal to participate in a ten-day eco-development project of Dasholi Gram Swaraj Sangh, a leading organization involved in the Chipko movement. Ram and I discussed his research methodology. Like all other students of history, he was going to focus on historical documents. I suggested that the written documents often give an incomplete, perhaps distorted, view of reality. So, by all means, Ram should study the documents, but Chipko was a living, ongoing movement, and Ram must complement his archival research with fieldwork involving people on the ground. Ram is a very friendly soul and he easily gets along with all sorts of people. He readily accepted my suggestion and launched on his path-breaking work on Chipko.

KOLKATA

It was clear from that first chat in Dehradun that Ram was a young man of remarkable intelligence, brimming with curiosity. His love of nature, his concerns about people, his egalitarian beliefs, his faith in democratic processes, all of this was in tune with my own inclinations. So, when the professor he was working with at the Indian Institute of Management asked me to serve on his thesis committee, I readily agreed. At that time, my good friend Kailash Malhotra, a brilliant student of the anthropologist Irawati Karve, was a professor in the anthropometry and human genetics unit of the Indian Statistical Institute in Kolkata. We were collaborating on a number of studies in the field of human ecology. From time to time I used to visit Kolkata to work with Kailash and continued my interactions with Ram.

Ram was a person with a very broad range of interests, spanning natural history, literature, music, sports, society, polity, economy and history. He was also a talented cricket player and had played alongside Kirti Azad and Arun Lal on the St Stephen's College cricket team. With his wide-ranging interests and extensive reading, he was doing brilliantly in the then newly fashionable quiz contests. Ram was the runner-up in the popular all-India quiz contest hosted by Siddharth Basu. Among the rival contestants was one of the founders of Infosys, Nandan Nilekani, at that time a student in IIT Bombay. Naturally, they had struck up a friendship. Ram is well acquainted with many such personalities, but is as courteous to common people as to the rich and famous.

AN ACCOMPLISHED WRITER

Ram had by then launched into a career in writing. Beginning in 1982, he began contributing to the left-leaning magazine, *Frontier*, always writing without fear or favour. He even criticized J. Krishnamurti, revered by many and declared to be an avatar of Krishna by Annie Besant. He had also started writing on cricket, a game he loved and understood well, bringing his sociological perspective to bear on the history of the game. I too enjoyed writing and was very much interested in history and in sports, having once been a Maharashtra state junior high-jump record holder. Naturally, I thoroughly enjoyed Ram's writing.

Ram's PhD thesis on the Chipko movement—set in the framework of how disempowered people explored new avenues of struggle to protect their interests—combined careful examination of historical documents and live interactions with people in the field. I read the thesis with great care, thoroughly enjoying the experience. In 1980, the forestry establishment had attempted to float a new forest policy that would have further consolidated power in what is the biggest landlord in India (the forest department), leading to a vigorous public debate. In a significant contribution to this debate, Ram published a paper in 1983 on forestry in British and post-British India in the *Economic and Political Weekly*, demonstrating his mastery of writing that was at once scholarly yet readable.

Then he published *The Unquiet Woods*, a path-breaking study of Indian environmental history based on his PhD thesis on the Chipko movement. I had at that time been working for well over a decade on management of natural resources in India and exploring how these experiences fitted in the broader framework of history, sociology and ecology. I had been toying with the idea of summarizing all of this in the form of a book but had made little headway. Ram obviously had a deep understanding of the issues involved and much information that complemented what I had gathered as a part of my own studies. Even more importantly he was an accomplished writer. So, I proposed to Ram that we collaborate on a book on the ecological history of India. He liked the idea, and happily accepted a position as an assistant professor of management studies at the Indian Institute of Science (IISc) in Bengaluru.

Ram had a long family association with the IISc His father, a chemist, had obtained his master's and doctoral degrees at the IISc. K. Venkataraman, who was married to Ram's aunt, was a well-known chemist and had served for many years as the first Indian director of the National Chemical Laboratory. He was very fond of Ram and declared that Ram should be his last PhD student. But Ram did not find the science laboratory to his liking. So, Venkataraman told Ram that he should do a thesis with his daughter, Ram's cousin Dharma Kumar, a leading economic historian. But economics too did not agree with Ram and he turned to sociology.

Ram certainly wrote a first-rate PhD thesis in the scholarly tradition of the universities. But he was not cut out for the routine of an academic career. He had very wide interests and was a talented writer. His special skill lay in exploring new fields and writing learned yet readable articles and books. Beginning with his monograph on the Chipko movement, he has written a series of books that have become popular, but are packed with novel information and insights. As of today, he has written fourteen books and edited eight. His *India after Gandhi* has established itself as the leading study of India's post-Independence history. Only three of his books have been co-authored, and I have the privilege of being one of those co-authors. Our book, *This Fissured Land*, an ecological history of India, written over a quarter of a century ago is still being regularly reprinted and is being used as a textbook in many universities.

Ram served on the faculty of the IISc for two years and then moved first to Delhi University and then to the Nehru Memorial Museum and Library. Following this stint, he has devoted himself to independent writing and visiting assignments in different universities for the last two decades. He lives in Bangalore; his wife Sujata is a book designer and a partner in the design firm, Ray and Keshavan. Ram, writing from home, devoted a great deal of his time to looking after their two children, Keshav and Iravati, when they were young and Sujata was busy with her own work.

Sports Historian

Ram has written a most enjoyable and entertaining book on the history of cricket, *A Corner of a Foreign Field*, shedding new light on the subject in his own inimitable fashion. When the sport was striking roots in India and accomplished Indian cricketers were beginning to emerge, the two most notable names were the batsman Ranjitsinhji, born the prince of Nawanagar, and the bowler Palwankar Baloo, born to a poor, Dalit family. Palwankar Baloo developed into an outstanding spinner while working as a labourer on the grounds of the European Gymkhana in Pune on a salary of Rs 3 a month. He was then employed by the English captain of the European Gymkhana team to give him batting practice, paying him 8 annas every time Baloo managed to dismiss him. As his reputation grew, Baloo was invited to play for the Hindu Gymkhana team. While Hindu Gymkhana was winning matches thanks to Baloo's bowling skills, his teammates would not allow him to eat his meals or drink his tea alongside them. Justice M.G. Ranade criticized them severely for such behaviour, and Lokamanya Tilak felicitated him in the teeth of protests by traditional Pune society. As knowledgeable a cricketer as Vijay Merchant has remarked that Indian cricket gained respect due to Ranji's batting and Baloo's bowling. While we continue to remember Ranji through many events such as the Ranji trophy matches, Baloo has been totally forgotten.

Ram is utterly free of any prejudices relating to caste, creed, colour or wealth. He has particular sympathy for the have-nots. Naturally, Ram has celebrated Baloo's accomplishments in his book. Ram, a truly committed scholar, put in a remarkable amount of effort to collect the relevant information, and to understand the society and the way it functioned in Baloo's time. He arranged to get all the news relating to Baloo that was published in Lokamanya Tilak's Marathi newspaper, *Kesari*, translated in English. He then followed up on Baloo's family history and contacted some of his kin in the Thane-Dombivli areas of Greater Mumbai. Mama Varerkar, a contemporary of Baloo's and a progressive writer and thinker, has written a Marathi play inspired by Baloo's life titled *On the Doorstep of the Prison*. The name of the play reflects Varerkar's conviction that the higher-caste society has imprisoned itself to its own serious detriment through its prejudices. Ram managed to lay hands on a copy and turned up one day in my house with a request to carefully read the play, explain it to him from beginning to end, and tell him what the play suggested about the society of that time.

BIOGRAPHER

Verrier Elwin was a British anthropologist, as aware as Ram is today of the inequities of Indian society. He was married to a Gond lady, was greatly respected by Jawaharlal Nehru and played an important role in the formulation of state policies towards tribals in the early years of Indian independence. Ram wrote a biography, *Savaging the Civilized*, bringing out many new facets of Elwin's life. This biography became so well known that close friends of two Bharat Ratnas, Atal Bihari Vajpayee and C.N.R. Rao, requested Ram to write their biographies. This would have been a golden opportunity to come close to these two famous and influential personalities. But Ram was not at all tempted and politely declined to oblige them.

So, going beyond Bharat Ratnas, Ram embarked on a biography of the father of the nation, Mahatma Gandhi. An enormous amount has already been written on the Mahatma, yet Ram came up with a lot of new information and insights. He visited the school where Mahatma Gandhi had studied and many places where he had stayed in South Africa. The two-volume study is a major contribution to our understanding of India's freedom movement.

JOURNALIST

Apart from his books, Ram is a very popular newspaper columnist. His English articles regularly appear in leading newspapers such as *The Hindu, Hindustan Times* and *Telegraph*. These are translated and regularly published in many Indian languages. In today's iniquitous society, the gulf between the educated, better-off middle classes and the increasingly impoverished masses of India is rapidly widening. As a result, much of the material reaching the middle classes entirely fails to bring out the stark reality of the distortions in the course of development in India. Ram's writing is a notable exception.

For a long time now, Goa has been afflicted by the tyranny of the rich. Three of my good friends have been victims of this state of affairs. Bismark Dias has died under very suspicious circumstances, Hanumant Parab escaped by the skin of his teeth from a murderous attack, and Ravindra Velip was taken into custody on flimsy excuses and while lodged in the jail was attacked by hired goondas. When I informed Ram of these tragic occurrences, he came to Goa on his own and exposed this reality through an article in the *Hindustan Times*. The article concludes with this statement: 'Although most Indian and foreign tourists may not know or care, something is very rotten in the state of Goa. The citizens of Goa know and care, since they see and experience it all the time.'

I am a very good friend of Ram's, so I wanted somebody who had never personally met Ram to spend some time with him and tell me of his impressions. Luckily, my good friend Subodh Kulkarni, a devoted social worker, had the opportunity to spend two days in April 2016 accompanying Ram on his visits to the families of Bismark Dias and to the village of Ravindra Velip. He has jotted down the following impressions at my request:

> Wherever we went, whether to Father Bismark's house or Ravindra's Caurem village, he was very alive to the situation, carefully absorbing all relevant information. He wasted no time in talking about irrelevant matters, did not use his mobile phone at all or indulge in photography or sit down to make long notes in a notebook. To me this was most unusual behaviour. While very much alive to the present, he always places situations in its historical context. He is totally committed to carefully listening and understanding

while talking to people. He avoids making any remarks about any individual, institution or political grouping, but tries to understand the root causes of what has been going on and the driving forces behind these happenings.

He successfully brought out late Father Bismark's personality by gently getting all his relatives to talk about him. Bismark's house was, of course, engulfed in grief following his untimely death; nevertheless, we could come to understand Bismark's childhood and youth, his embracing the profession of a Christian priest, his love of music and of environment and all the struggles he was involved in as we talked to his mother, sister and brothers. Ram's transparent honesty persuaded these people to talk to him freely from their hearts. He talked with a great deal of sympathy to Ravindra and his colleagues, and sincerely expressed his respect and admiration for their struggles. This has certainly given a great moral boost to the people of Caurem in their grave difficulties. What was most impressive throughout was his complete honesty, simplicity and genuine humanity.

Moral courage

Ram has come to be widely admired and respected since a fairly young age entirely on the strength of his own achievements. Lakhs of readers read his newspaper columns. They learn a great deal from his completely unbiased, factually accurate and forthright exposition of what is happening all around us today. Ram is a well-known public speaker and attracts huge audiences wherever he may be speaking in India. His scholarly but highly readable books are in great demand. The *New York Times* felicitated him as the best writer of non-fiction in India. Leading universities like Yale confer on him their honorary degrees. The president of India decorated him with the Padma Bhushan.

I am fortunate enough to know many people of considerable achievements including Padma Vibhushans, Bharat Ratnas and Nobel laureates. But Ram stands out among them all. He is as simple and sincere today as he was when he met me as a twenty-three-year-old student. Ever since that time, he has been marching ahead, looking for no favours, and fearing nobody. That is why he continues to contribute to nation-building through his meaningful and impactful writings.

16

THE UNQUIET RAM

RUKUN ADVANI

IT MAY BE best for me not to begin my recollections of Ram along the standard template which recommends the phrase 'The first time I met . . .' The reason is that our first meeting was inconsequential. Apparently, we met on a college badminton court forty-five years ago, in about July 1974. Since Ram did not go on from this badminton court to become the father of Deepika Padukone, this first encounter's location, at least, was not an augury of the direction of Ram's future fame.

I have no idea what Ram was doing near a badminton court in the mid-1970s because his interests lay in a corner of a different field, the cricket pitch. His agenda even then was anti-Hindutva, though it took a peculiar shape because it had become mixed up with his interest in cricket. His aim in those days was to disprove the Hindu idea of reincarnation by circumventing his own afterlife through becoming either Bishan Singh Bedi or Erapalli Prasanna in this life. Failing either of those two options, he seemed to have resigned himself to a third, which was to become Gundappa Vishwanath.

Since I was far from passionate about cricket, for the remainder of our college years Ram and I lived proximate lives without ever coming close. I knew roughly who he was, and I also knew precisely what 'type' he was— he was what was called in those days a 'sports type'. This knowledge was a subconscious certainty somewhere inside me that if there was a fellow in our college who was never going to amount to anything intellectually, his name was Ram Guha. He would develop his muscles, grow into a hunk, even perhaps wear a turban, and the climax of his aspiration would—to put it with the studied inaccuracy of those mystified by cricket enthusiasts—be to draw Viv Richards out of the crease and bowl him round his legs. To my mind in those days Ram Guha was someone who could be safely written off and forgotten about.

I was not alone in thinking this way. The college we went to was full of bright people who were all mostly determined to join the IAS, and they too seemed to think Ram didn't stand much chance of becoming a bureaucrat. In an ironic way, and for the wrong reasons, they were right. We all thought Ram would never make it into the bureaucracy because he seemed keener on the square drive than the intellectual drive, less interested in his present IAS prospects than the future prospects of E.A.S. Prasanna. But the real reason, which perhaps no one saw, was that Ram was too restless, too passionate, too wayward, and too interested in too many things—such as playing bridge, participating in quizzes, and casually pursuing as many women as possible—to fit into the Procrustean mould that shapes most bureaucrats.

So I forgot Ram quite comprehensively for many years until in the mid-1980s we ran into each other quite by chance at the wedding of a friend we had in common. I was by this time an editor at the Oxford University Press (OUP) and Ram seemed keen to woo me with his passion for the PhD in sociology he'd been working on at the Calcutta IIM. I expressed interest in hearing what he'd been up to and invited him to drop in at the OUP. Some days later, Ram arrived in my office to discuss the book he had in mind. What he did not know was that I had only invited him out of sheer curiosity—curiosity over why this man who I recalled as the failed reincarnation of Bishan Bedi had been so animated about some Garhwali village where, apparently, the women had taken to embracing tree trunks. Had his failure to make it to the Indian Test team as a spin bowler bowled him clean out of his own mind?

You can imagine my surprise at our meeting, during which a man I'd by now mentally certified as a lunatic at a loose end started telling me about how the Subaltern Studies series had helped him understand narratives of dissent that were forged at a distance from nationalism. He spoke also of E.P. Thompson and someone called Sartono Kartodirdjo, a name so alien and impossible to pronounce that it could only have been of some exalted foreign academic. The realization slowly dawned on me that the man in my office had turned himself into a scholar. It seemed a bad case of spin taking another turn: the Ram I'd seen worship at the altar of Bishan Singh Bedi and Gundappa Vishwanath was now worshipping at the altar of Chandi Prasad Bhatt and Sunderlal Bahuguna. It was a transformation nearly inconceivable, most unanticipated, and quite absolute. I did not foresee then that this was only the first of several radical changes of direction in Ram's intellectual life.

Nor was *The Unquiet Woods*, Ram's first book, which was published by the OUP in 1989, something that either I or anyone else at the time could have seen for what it was—the starting point of the unusually variegated career of a writer and intellectual. My recollection of it thirty years on is still sharp—because of the exceptional clarity and accessibility of the prose in which it was written. Having edited the early volumes of Subaltern Studies and Ranajit Guha's *Elementary Aspects of Peasant Insurgency*, I was just about getting used to the somewhat arcane terms in this kind of Indian history-writing about protest and dissent, the only greatly readable exception to the general trend being the prose of David Hardiman who, like Ram, seemed interested in an audience not confined within cloisters. The prose of these two seemed to me modelled on a template traceable back to E.P. Thompson, in those days perhaps *the* important historian in the intellectual genealogy of every liberal and left historian. For my humdrum editorial purposes when facing the script of Ram's first book, this was a wonderful lineage because it emphasized a vital interpenetration of complexity of thought and clarity of expression, which basically meant that I as editor had to do very little work as far as straightening out prose went.

In fact, in Ram's writing ever since I have found very little that needs straightening out because he instinctively stays clear of obscurity. In his first monograph, though matters were frequently complex and complicated, the prose was never gratuitously 'complicating' issues—an activity academics had begun taking a fancy to around then. His arguments and analyses were never the sort that could only be unravelled and properly understood by an intellectual elite already thoroughly immersed in the literature. Ram was writing from the start for seriously interested and ordinarily intelligent readers, unswayed by the value fashionable academics put on fatuous obscurity. This partly accounts for the considerable success even of his first book, despite it being on a specialized subject.

Since I edited at about this same time the historian Shahid Amin's first book—which was about peasants who harvested sugar cane, whereas Ram's was about peasants who opposed the harvesting of trees—I remember thinking of the similarities and contrasts between the two. The similarities are clear: both *Sugarcane and Sugar* and *The Unquiet Woods* are important monographs in their areas (though Ram's work seems more pioneering because forest history had not been done whereas the agricultural economy had); both authors know their fields from the inside, in the anthropological sense, even while writing histories of peasant life (in this sense Amin is in fact better grounded). But the central contrast, from the editorial perspective, is clearer: getting into the world of Shahid Amin's peasants entails an intellectual struggle for the non-specialist and the non-academic reader, whereas getting into the world of Ram Guha's protesting peasants is, for the same kind of reader, not difficult at all. The obvious conclusion for me as an editor, then, was that Ram Guha was likely to be the historian-as-writer, while Shahid Amin was always going to be an inspiration only to other historians. This is not to belittle academic writing wholesale, because of course much academic writing can only be in a language which by consensus is best suited to convey information of an esoteric nature to specialists and the learned, and which might be seriously diluted if too much effort were put into making it accessible to a general readership. But in the Indian context, I realized through Ram that academic prose is rather commonplace—in both senses of the word—whereas it is rare to find a genuinely archive-besotted scholar who can write attractive prose for a non-scholarly audience.

In this sense, Ram was pioneering in a second way: he had not only moved from sports to peasants, he had also honed a style of writing about them for which most other Indian scholars had little capacity and less inclination. Later it also became clear to me as an editor that the first-rate scholarly minds with a literary bent who write accessible prose and whose books sometimes sell in decent numbers—people such as Sunil Khilnani, Mukul Kesavan, Nayanjot Lahiri, Sanjay Subrahmanyam, Harjot Singh Oberoi, Nandini Sundar and Srinath Raghavan—are looked on with suspicion by some of their colleagues because the hegemonic axiom of the academic world is that scholars must complicate what seems simple. Ram, on the other hand, was trying out the Thompsonian alternative in a novel way in the context of Indian history. His writing was based on the assumption that the academic can complicate what seems simple even while simplifying what seems complicated. This underlying theory is, I think, central to understanding the nature of Ram's prose, which took Indian scholarly writing out of its long confinement within academia. From my limited editorial perspective, I see Ram as having implicitly encouraged academics such as Harjot Oberoi and Nayanjot Lahiri and many more such who, in the wake of the example set by *The Unquiet Woods*—and without doubt of the example of other similar books that they have later read—wrote wonderfully readable monographs.

For any editor who wants to make books that sell in large numbers, which is what every editor wants, chancing upon a writer among the anthropologists is to hit upon 'a gem of purest ray serene'. I'm not sure how clearly it is seen outside editorial offices that when Ram wrote *The Unquiet Woods* he was pioneering not just Indian environmental history but also a somewhat new way of writing an Indian monograph. Because as an editor I tend to think of books as belonging to particular stylistic genres, I see that before the arrival of Ram's first book, the great Indian monographs were Sumit Sarkar's *Swadeshi Movement* and Irfan Habib's *Agrarian System*, both solid tomes in an altogether different style. True, historians of an older generation such as Ashin Dasgupta, S. Gopal, Tapan Raychaudhuri and Ranajit Guha were prose writers whose work showed their immersion not just in Marx and Gramsci but also Tagore and Shakespeare. But such people remained inspiring essentially within academic portals and their work, excluding Gopal's excellent biography of his father, stayed strictly within the boundaries of the ivory tower. Though it is possible to trace in Ram's work the inspiring example of S. Gopal as biographer of both Jawaharlal Nehru and S. Radhakrishnan, it would still have to be said that, unlike Ram, no one in the earlier generation of Indian historians—not even S. Gopal—caused such a considerable and influential outward expansion of historical prose. This is evident merely by listing the many genres within which Ram's historical knowledge took root: the popular biography, the large synthesizing text, the short historical memoir, the punchy feuilleton, sports history, political polemic, and the memorable newspaper op-ed.

His independent-mindedness gradually became more and more evident from the fact that he was never afraid of venturing into what were considered the by-lanes of history not worth exploring. He explored them, and in doing so showed new directions. In a sense, only after Ram's *Elwin* and *Gandhi*, for example, could you have Lahiri's *Ashoka*, as well as the many biographies now that are based on sound scholarship but not written only for the scholarly. In this sense, as the forefather of a style of writing, Ram indirectly enabled several Indian scholars to make something like a decent supplementary income from their learning.

Other things followed from my early apprehension of Ram's writing abilities, and by other things I mean other books by Ram. Once an editor knows that the historian he has on his hands is a writer for possibly large audiences and not a scholar who will write largely for historians, it becomes mainly a matter of making encouraging noises every time the writer says he wants to write on Topic X or Topic Y. This was the policy I followed with Ram. Some time after *The Unquiet Woods*, he said he had quite a lot of journalistic stuff on Indian cricket and cricketers. Sure enough, I soon got the script of his first cricket history, *Wickets in the East*, another book I recall as not requiring editorial inputs. He subtitled it 'An Anecdotal History'. It may seem facetious, but it may not be stretching a point to say that there was also something new about this kind of titling. Historians in India did not write sports history; nor, if they intended being serious, did they write proper histories that they then advertised as 'anecdotal'. Ram may not have realized it at the time, but in retrospect it looks to me like he was cocking his first snook at academic prose. I think the day will come when some student in an English department will, deploying Lacan and Saussure, examine *Wickets in the East* as an author's subconscious Freudian attempt to parody the prose of scholars, even perhaps to say out loud that though he hadn't got his doctorate from Oxbridge or Harvard, he'd show them he could write casual scholarly history of a kind they hadn't conceived of in India.

It is often asserted that so-and-so Budding Writer was 'discovered' by so-and-so Great Editor, and a fair number of these great editors have made their careers by listing the budding writers they apparently discovered. As I see it, the plain truth is that I discovered no budding writer in Ram Guha; it was as if he hit the perfect square drive and I, standing at fine leg, took the catch; or—to put it without wishing to offend every cricketer—we happened to find each other and hit it off. And at the time we did, he was pretty full-budded already and his resemblance to a flower that would soon be in full bloom was not in doubt. My own experience is that budding writers arrive at editorial offices, and the editor sitting in the editorial offices where they arrive is in luck if they later happen to become famous and hand them books that sell in large numbers. Ram Guha was from the word go rather like an unstoppable force, a volcano spilling over with more ideas for books that he wanted to write than his brain was able to contain. In addition to spilling the beans on all these future books of his, he also had the pleasant habit of trying out on me all the possible titles that these books might one day have. Sometimes he would call on the phone and the entire call could become a discussion over half an hour of the absolutely appropriate title of a book that he intended writing five years after our conversation. The man was bursting with ideas for unwritten books that were springing unbidden out of him. For me, as his editor, there was something quite soothing about his frenzy over matters so far off, because there was no immediate script to worry about and convert into a book. It is naturally much easier for editors to cluck in sympathy over scripts in the realm of dreams. The advantage is also that the author hears editorial clucking as a sign that his collected works have been accepted. In Ram's case, my clucking improved into cooing and billing, indicating that I was willing to sign on, there and then, his collected works.

A related point is that if sheer chance had not made sure I happened to be the editor sitting in that OUP office, he would have met some other editor at the OUP and been published with as much success. No eighteenth-century publisher could have stopped publishing Mozart's frenetic outpouring, and no twentieth-century editor could have done anything other than publish the catch of fine books that Ram Guha was throwing at him. In this sense, my feeling is that the exceptional writer isn't discovered by an editor, he merely throws himself into the arms of an editor who then becomes an octopus and embraces the writer for good, making sure never to let go.

This is not the same thing as saying that Ram's books would have been identical under any editorial hand. Of course, every editor brings their particular skills and distinctive perspective to every book they edit, and it is generally true that like a valued hairdresser, a valued editor can for long stretches be thought irreplaceable by the generously grateful author. In that sense, I think Ram and I got on like a house on fire and he felt he could flick everything I threw at him with the finesse of Vishwanath executing a square cut. So he stuck with me, for which I was in return grateful, because the OUP was finding it easier to sell his books than most of its other academic titles.

Ours was what is called in academic terminology a symbiotic relationship. In publishing this is a bonding of mutual benefit between author and editor. This symbiotic relationship that Ram and I established with *The Unquiet Woods* continued for perhaps twenty-five or more years. It included the time over which he changed from an environmental historian to a cricket writer to a sociologist to a biographer to an anthologist to a writer of the advanced synthesizing text called *This Fissured Land* to an essayist. The nice thing for me was that while Ram was intellectually diversifying and reincarnating himself in all these ways, he remained at an emotional level consistently affectionate and sentimental, always taking the lead in a friendship which we both cherished and sustained through regular letters and emails. If I were to start detailing the many ways in which he helped me—mainly on account of his enthusiastic commitment to the editor who had published his first book—I would end up with a very large memoir. But, in brief, Ram became a kind of propagandist for the OUP and for me, so that a number of writers and books I later published and made money out of were directed to me by his propaganda campaigns in our favour. After Anuradha Roy and I started Permanent Black, we often recalled how Ram was among our closest supporters and went far out of his way to ensure that we were never short of books to publish, those by him as well as by writers who listened to his advice.

It seems ironic to me, therefore, that rather than editors attributing their success to writers, it is writers who more often attribute so much of their success to their first editor. Sometimes this can be for good reason, especially in the area of fiction writing, where the number of writers is very large and the number of high-class editors and presses quite small. Fiction writers are repeatedly turned down, and when in the end a press accepts them they are over the moon. But this situation has no connection with how my relationship with Ram began, nor with his first book which, because of his sentimental generosity, is now in print with Permanent Black.

There are two reasons why Ram's attribution of some of his writerly success to me is overgenerous. The first is that it would have been obvious to every history editor that Ram's first book was an unusually competent monograph that, on account of its original theme and unusually cogent style, would embellish any serious academic history list. The second reason is that when it came to scholarly publishing, in the mid-1980s the OUP had no serious competitor. Ravi Dayal had made the press's stature virtually unassailable, so, even if Ram had wanted to publish elsewhere, there was no real elsewhere. All academics in those days, from Amartya

Sen to M.N. Srinivas to Ranajit Guha, headed for the OUP, and I think Ram came into my life because he had no choice in the matter.

More important were the vibes between Ram and me. Some off-spinners are known to strike up a good rapport with a particular wicketkeeper, and this stumps larger numbers. It also works as a metaphor for success in the making of books. The author and editor have to hit it off and feel relaxed in their exchanges, saying what they like with no fear of the occasional political incorrectness being misunderstood or forwarded. This was so with Ram. It made the creative process of making his books pleasurable and easy. If I asked him to clarify or modify or explain or expand or delete, he was receptive. If I had an extraneous literary idea which I suggested might be squeezed into something he had written to make it look brighter, he was mostly pleased and made the insertion. If he asked me to read several versions of a script that he was writing and then revising and re-revising, I was happy to.

I have published more books by Ram, and over a longer stretch of time, than I have with anyone else. In my longish professional life as an editor and publisher, my relationship with him has been the most important I have had with an author. So, although I hope he writes many more books, and with equal or greater success, I also secretly hope he does not write so many that he grows even fonder of some of his future editors than he has been of me.

17

THE MANY RAMS OF
RAMACHANDRA GUHA

DAVID GILMOUR

MY FIRST IMPRESSION of Ram Guha was that he was like an intellectual of about sixty or seventy years ago. With his rough tweed jacket and baggy trousers, his tousled hair, his round-lensed spectacles and his rather shambling gait, he looked like a figure of the 1930s; underneath his jacket he wore a patterned jersey that might have been knitted for George Orwell. Furthermore, he talked in the way that bhadralok scholars used to talk, rapidly and excitedly on a very wide range of subjects.

Yet, I soon realized, he was not really garrulous—an adjective much used by British rulers to denigrate Bengali intellectuals—he was simply more interested and better informed than almost anyone else. About twenty years ago we went to Trent Bridge to watch a cricket match, I in my stripy blazer, he in his tweed jacket and Orwell's jersey. We travelled to the ground with Sunil Khilnani and my son in a motor car, a rather ropey old vehicle that Sunil had recently bought from a friend. It was a day–night match, an one-day international (ODI) between Australia and Pakistan, and as we returned to the car park shortly before midnight, Sunil suggested that, as he had only recently passed his driving test and had never driven in the dark, it might be better if I drove home. Reluctantly, I agreed, and, while I navigated the outskirts of Nottingham and set off on the long dreary journey down the M1 to

266

London, Ram in the back seat kept up an inquisition that lasted two hours. Had I read the current issue of the *New York Review*? Did I agree with so and so's piece in the latest *Times Literary Supplement*? What did I think of a denunciatory article in the *London Review of Books*? He is sometimes a difficult chap to keep up with.

Over the last twenty years I have known Ram in various guises, but there are earlier incarnations that I could not know. I never knew Ram the anthropologist, Ram the trainee sociologist or Ram the nearly-Marxist, the Calcutta student who gave away his cricket books in order to find room on his shelves for a Marxist library that included the ninety volumes of Lenin's collected works. Nor, more regrettably, have I seen much of Ram the ecologist, although we have similar views on the environment—we have been on expeditions into the Nilgiris, and we have enjoyed good country walks in Britain, in the hills of lowland Scotland and southern England.

The first Rams I was acquainted with were Ram the fledgling biographer, then struggling through several drafts of his biography of Verrier Elwin, and Ram the historian of Indian cricket, a subject he found easier to write about and which resulted in what I consider his most enjoyable book, *A Corner of a Foreign Field*. Yet, whatever difficulties he had with Elwin—with an Indian editor (helpful though he happened to be), with Western publishers (unhelpful though they were) and with his own problems in making the transition from anthropology to biography—*Savaging the Civilized* is a wonderful book. Ram was able to empathize with his subject in a variety of different ways—especially with Elwin's Gandhism, his anthropological work and his concern for India's tribal peoples, even if he did not—and does not—share his subject's taste for marrying tribal women. Not the least of the book's charm is the way that it is amiably sprinkled with cricketing metaphors, with how Elwin might be 'stumped' or forced 'onto the back foot', and how some Indian minister would go 'out to bat' on his behalf.

The next Rams I knew were the Rams that everyone knows, Ram the biographer of Gandhi and Ram the chronicler of modern India. These are great books, which I read in draft form, but I do not think there is much point in my talking about them to an audience which knows so much more about these subjects than I do. Instead, I would like to say something about Ram the essayist and political journalist because his articles reveal more about his mind and his character than anything else he writes.

An English journalist once said of my father, Ian Gilmour, a left-wing Tory who was a minister in Ted Heath's government and briefly (until he criticized her) in Margaret Thatcher's, that he was a man of 'liberal views, illiberally held'. Much the same could be said of Ram, who liked—and was liked by—my father, and who once described himself as a moderate who sometimes expressed his views in 'an extreme fashion'. I think that one of the best decisions he ever made was to refuse a professorship in Delhi, which would have made him part of the 'academy'. I am someone who rejected academic life because I wanted to write about different subjects and different countries, but Ram had more serious reasons. He wanted to be independent, not to be part of any 'school', not to have to defer to colleagues or to the prevailing fads of a particular department. He is not an intellectual of the seminar or the cafe table but a scholar of the archives and his own desk. He rejected the academic fervour of Delhi for what, in intellectual terms, is the backwater of Bangalore.

Ram's independence has allowed him to attack, at some personal risk, targets in all areas of the particular spectrum. He will assail with equal vehemence both the enthusiasts of Hindutva and the communists of West Bengal. Yet he will also criticize those parties and their representatives that might be closer to him in ideological terms but have failed to perform their duties, whether because they are corrupt, stupid or merely incompetent. If I were Rahul Gandhi and I had read Ram's articles, I would long ago have disappeared from public life.

One of the aspects of Ram's essays that I most appreciate is the personal experience, his memories of the people and places he has encountered in the course of his career. Authors acquire human proportions, they give their readers a sense of intimacy when they write about their 'haunts', in this case when Ram describes his love of the now defunct Premier Book Shop in Bangalore and of a cafe nearby known, depending on whether one is a native of the city, as Parade's or Koshy's, and when he writes of his memories of some venerable Mumbai institutions such as the Oxford University Press or about the journal, the *Economic and Political Weekly*, and its remarkable editor, Krishna Raj. Ram's essays also recount stories of his travels, often by rail. Most of us travel nowadays to see places and sample their cuisine, the classic priorities of the modern tourist. But these are not Ram's priorities, certainly not in Britain. Naturally, he travels to deliver lectures and to work in the archives, but he also travels to see people, frequently people he has never met before, and to go long distances to do so, especially if they are very old men such as Nirad Chaudhuri in Oxford or E. P. Thompson in Worcestershire. Ram could never have been one of those young historians who make their name by setting out to destroy the reputations of the previous generation. Of course, older scholars may often be wrong and out of touch, but Ram is aware of how much one can learn from them just by listening and prompting them with the right questions. They have been through so much, they can tell one so much. I am someone who found it easier to become friends with my parents' friends than with my children's, but I could seldom make friends with my grandparents' friends, as Ram did, for example, with that great ICS officer, C. S. Venkatachar.

I will end on that most personal note, that of friendship. Ram is someone who takes friends seriously. Many of our generation seem to regard friendship as a rather fluid phenomenon, something that prospers with the help of proximity and occasion and which tends to fade when faced by distance or unavailability. Ram will have none of this. Friendship is friendship, whatever distant continents the friends might live in. And for him friendship is not just about people enjoying each other's hospitality, me going to Coonor to be pampered by him and his beautiful wife Sujata or him coming to Oxfordshire to be looked after by my equally lovely Sarah. It is a duty, a sort of moral commitment, and one that has to be regularly serviced. Talking recently about an old friendship of his that seemed to have lapsed, he said sadly that at our age—and I must confess here that I am five years his senior—it is so difficult to make new friendships that one must do everything possible to preserve existing ones. If he feels that friends are being remiss about keeping in touch, he sends them—or at least he sends me—rather peremptory emails titled 'What's up?' followed by the sentence 'I haven't heard from you for a long time', which immediately makes one feel guilty, although I have to say in my defence that any dereliction in this context has been two-sided.

Many of us drift into friendships, after rather liking someone at a dinner or a cocktail party; it is often a casual, take-it-or-leave-it affair, something that doesn't really matter whether it works out or not. Ram is different, in this respect as in so many others. If he wants someone as a friend, he will travel hundreds of miles to ensure that the friendship is kept flourishing. I will never forget how twenty years ago he came to do some research in Edinburgh, where I then lived, and, following an introduction from a mutual friend, turned up at my doorstep in tweed jacket, baggy trousers and Orwell's jersey. He was at his wittiest and most irrepressible, perhaps even 'garrulous'. Afterwards, he summed up the encounter in a sentence that may not have been his most stylish but which perfectly described the episode, 'I felt that we hit it off first ball.'

18

'WHAT DO THEY KNOW OF HISTORY WHO ONLY HISTORY KNOW?'

SURESH MENON

IT MIGHT HAVE been England's first cricket tour, but it was aborted even as the players prepared to cross the Channel. 'A pitch had been prepared in the Champs Elysees,' wrote Frank Keating. But at Dover, the captain announced, 'Bad news, chaps, the game's off'. It was 1789, the French Revolution got in the way.[1]

On the day the Bastille was stormed, the Earl of Winchilsea was clean-bowled by William Bullen in the Hampshire-Kent match at Hambledon. Many saw a moral in this. The English historian G.M. Trevelyan spelt it out thus: 'If the French nobility had been capable of playing cricket with their peasants, their chateaux would never have been burnt'.[2]

Trevelyan wrote that almost a century and a half after the event. It was convenient to believe that cricket had abolished class, with peasants and nobles playing the game together. As the writer Robert Winder said, cricket inspires happy delusions.[3]

Still, the point is not so much about the importance of cricket as its perceived importance. It had a role in society. Yet, Trevelyan himself did not think so while writing a social history of England in the nineteenth century. As C.L.R. James says in *Beyond a Boundary*: 'A famous Liberal historian [Trevelyan] can write the social history of England in the 19th century, and two famous Socialists [Raymond Postgate and G.D.H. Cole,

271

The Common People] can write what they declared to be the history of the common people of England, and between them never once mention the man who was the best-known Englishman of his time. I can no longer accept the system of values which could not find in these books a place for W.G. Grace'.

Have historians short-changed cricket? There are many histories of cricket. At the turn of the century, Derek Birley wrote *A Social History of English Cricket*, the story of how the sport was 'snatched from rustic obscurity by gentlemanly gamblers and became the latest metropolitan fashion'.

This came some four decades after James asked: 'What do they know of cricket who only cricket know?' To understand the game, you had to understand, or at least acknowledge, its historical, cultural and social contexts.

A People's History of Sports in the United States by Dave Zirin and similar books speak of the influence of politics on sport—and might come as a revelation to those who believe that sport and politics do not mix (or even ought not to mix).

Each of these books is a classic, but all of them emphasize the impact of history and culture and economics and politics and personalities on sport. Yes, it helps us understand sport better, to contextualize it, to read into it deeper meanings and discover more profound connotations. In *Bad Sports*, Zirin writes about how in America, 'For a generation now, baseball has been a highly leveraged real estate urban development plan where people happen to play a game'. In India, we can think of the IPL (Indian Premier League) as a highly leveraged television serial ideal for selling products where people happen to play a version of a popular game.

Yes, sports do count. But we are loath to concede that the traffic might also move in the opposite direction. It is easy to understand that sport affects economics or that it plays a significant role in the cultural development of a community. But history? No, that would be pushing it too far, we conclude, and move on to other things.

Three examples from sport, however, will help us understand sport's impact on history better.

In 1947, Jackie Robinson became the first African American to play major league baseball in America. The impact was rapid and far-reaching. It opened the doors for the ethnic minorities to enter the world of Whites-only sport, but more importantly, hastened the end of segregation. As

Michael Mandelbaum, director of the American Foreign Policy programme at the Johns Hopkins University, put it, 'Robinson is an important figure in American history because of the particular, and particularly oppressed, status of African-Americans in the life of the nation and because baseball was the first visible institution in American civil life in which they were able to participate on equal terms with whites'.[4]

A couple of decades later, the Cape Coloured cricketer Basil D'Oliveira had an important role to play in the dismantling of apartheid in South Africa. Denied opportunities in his own country, D'Oliveira looked towards England. With help from the commentator John Arlott, he arrived there in 1960 to play league cricket. Six years later, he was playing for England. In 1968, he was chosen for the tour of South Africa. It didn't happen so easily, though.

First, there were attempts to bribe him to withdraw from the tour even before the team was picked. A businessman in South Africa (with the knowledge of Prime Minister John Vorster) offered him a lucrative 'coaching' assignment. In England, the Marylebone Cricket Club (MCC) secretary Billy Griffith tried to persuade him to withdraw in the larger interest (i.e. his own). Meetings went on in two countries which initially seemed to have the same plan: keep D'Oliveira out.

The English selectors, despite his knock of 158 in the final Ashes Test at The Oval—the last before the tour—hemmed and hawed, and finally named him a standby for the tour, leading to a public outcry. Many felt that England ought not to be told whom to pick or drop by another country. D'Oliveira's non-inclusion was seen as an act of cowardice.

Then the medium-pacer Tom Cartwright pulled out because of an injury, and now D'Oliveira was in the team. The following day, South Africa barred the team from visiting. South Africa's sporting ban began soon after—it was twenty-two years before the country, now led by Nelson Mandela, was allowed to re-enter international sporting competition. What came to be known as the 'D'Oliveira Affair', was according to Mandela, a 'decisive phase in his movement's eventual triumph'.

Historian Ramachandra Guha understands that sport affects not only the world around it but also the world that lies in the future.

The third example is of Palwankar Baloo, a left-arm spinner of 'low-caste' origin who led the Hindus and claimed over 100 wickets on the first all-India tour of England in 1911.

Guha's *A Corner of a Foreign Field* introduces us to Baloo, whom he calls the first great Indian cricketer. Baloo could not dine at the same table as his teammates at the Hindu Gymkhana when he started out. He had to drink his tea in a terracotta cup that was then shattered so others wouldn't have to drink from it. Yet, his exploits on the field helped erase some of the prejudices against him and those like him, off the field. When he was dropped from the team, there was a public outcry.

On his return from the successful tour of England in 1911, a function was organized by the Depressed Classes of Bombay to felicitate Baloo. B.R. Ambedkar gave the welcome speech. Ambedkar would become the greatest of all 'lower-caste' politicians and reformers, and this was his first public appearance. Although later Baloo and Ambedkar fought on different sides in an election, the cricketer was the politician's hero. In *A Corner of a Foreign Field* Guha calls Baloo a 'pioneer in the emancipation of Untouchables'.

In his book on cricket and race,[5] Jack Williams asserts that race was at the heart of cricket throughout the twentieth century. In India, it wasn't race so much as caste (and class, since the two moved in the same circles) that mattered.

Baloo played his last first-class match in 1920, and Palwankar's brothers—Shivram, Vithal and Ganpat—also played for the Hindus, with Vithal breaking another barrier by captaining the team. If this were a work of fiction, this might be the place to tie it all up by asserting that since then, the caste system has been wiped out in India, that the successors of Baloo, like those who came after Robinson and D'Oliveira, enjoyed the fruits of his work and are liberated.

Sadly, reality lacks the roundedness of fiction. But while admitting this, the efforts of those such as Baloo and Ambedkar, and the importance of those early steps, cannot be underplayed. *A Corner of a Foreign Field* narrates the story with compassion. It could have been a classic of post-caste India, but it is still a post-colonial text and exciting revisionist history. The story was generally ignored by historians because of its origins in cricket, and by cricket writers because it seemed an obscure chapter in history. It took an exceptional writer to reach out between the two stools where the story seemed to have fallen, and bring it to our attention. Here finally was a historian who also wrote with understanding on cricket.

The large canvas helped Guha paint a history of India as told through cricket, rather than a history of cricket full of matches and runs and wickets. It asked—and answered—the question: How did this most British of games become so thoroughly domesticated in the subcontinent?

The sociologist Ashis Nandy had provided a glib, attractive one-line answer: 'Cricket is an Indian game accidentally invented by the British'. He began his book *The Tao of Cricket* with this premise, but didn't follow through.

For the social historian, says Guha, mass sport is a sphere of activity that expresses, in concentrated form, the values, prejudices, divisions and unifying symbols of a society. Yet, historians generally ignore it.

It has become a habit to connect the way a country plays its sport—soccer in Brazil, cricket in India—to its national character. When the Indian Ranjitsinhji was charming all of England with his batting at the turn of the twentieth century, he was so fresh, so daring, so original that a contemporary said he 'never played a Christian stroke in his life'.

Neville Cardus, never one to hold himself back when describing a favourite player, wrote, 'The light that shone on our cricket fields when Ranji batted was a light out of his own land, a dusky, inscrutable light. His was the cricket of black magic indeed. A sudden sinuous turn of the wrist and lo! The ball had vanished—where? The bowler knowing he had aimed on the middle stump saw as in a vision the form of Ranji all fluttering curves. The bat made its beautiful pass, a wizard's wand. From the middle stump the ball was spirited away to the leg side boundary'.[6]

It was easy for Ranji to inspire poetry. Talent apart, he was a prince, and therefore an exotic Eastern gentleman.

Baloo was at the opposite end of the exotic scale. He was an 'invisible man', to use the novelist Ralph Ellison's evocative phrase. Princes were noticed. 'Untouchables' were not.

Sport has been viewed through various glasses. Marxists have their interpretations, Dalits too (some point to the number of educated Brahmins who filled the teams and ask if that is a commentary on the poor availability of education and infrastructure for the disadvantaged). But history hadn't been looked at through the glasses of sport.

'I do not support the placing of sports history in a ghetto of its own', writes Guha. 'The attempt should be to use ignored or previously marginal spheres, such as sport or gender or environment to illuminate the historical centre itself'.

Historian and cricket lover Guha's favourites in the respective fields are both named Thomson. One with a P, as in the social historian E.P.

Thompson, and the other without a P as in A.A. Thomson. E.P. Thompson has written about meeting Jawaharlal Nehru as a boy and being asked about his batting technique; A.A. Thomson has no such crossover story. Both were outstanding writers, but neither could have written *A Corner of a Foreign Field*. That needed a combination of the Thomsons, and an Indian who asked the question: What do they know of history who only history know?

ABOUT THE CONTRIBUTORS

Rukun Advani edited Ramachandra Guha's first book, *The Unquiet Woods*; subsequently he edited *This Fissured Land, Wickets in the East, Savaging the Civilised, An Anthropologist among the Marxists, Environmentalism: A Global History, How Much Should a Person Consume?* and *The Last Liberal.* He has edited books by other authors as well.

Aditya Balasubramanian is a lecturer in economic history at Australian National University. His book on ideas of free economy and the emergence of opposition politics is forthcoming from Princeton University Press.

Amita Baviskar is a sociologist who studies the cultural politics of environment and development. She teaches at Ashoka University. She is the author of *In the Belly of the River: Tribal Conflicts over Development in the Narmada Valley* and *Uncivil City: Ecology, Equity and the Commons in Delhi.*

Madhav Gadgil is an ecologist, the founder of the Centre for Ecological Sciences, Indian Institute of Science, and a staunch believer in democratic decentralization. He headed the Western Ghats Ecology Expert Panel, 2010. He is one of Ramachandra Guha's early mentors and collaborators.

David Gilmour is a historian and biographer whose works include *The Ruling Caste* (a history of the Indian Civil Service), *The British in India* (a social history) and biographies of Lord Curzon and Rudyard Kipling.

Venu Madhav Govindu is a biographer of the Gandhian economic philosopher and constructive worker, J.C. Kumarappa. He is currently working on a thematic history of Gandhi's life and work in the 1930s. He is an associate professor at the department of electrical engineering, Indian Institute of Science, Bengaluru.

Shashank Kela is a writer and scholar. He is the author of a historical monograph, *A Rogue and Peasant Slave: Adivasi Resistance 1800–2000*, a novel, *The Other Man*, and numerous essays and articles.

Madhav Khosla is an associate professor of political science at Ashoka University, the Ambedkar Visiting Associate Professor of Law at Columbia University and a junior fellow at the Harvard Society of Fellows. His books include *India's Founding Moment* and the *Oxford Handbook of the Indian Constitution*.

Prashant Kidambi is an associate professor of history at the University of Leicester. He is the author of *Cricket Country: The Untold History of the First All India Team* and the lead editor of *Bombay Before Mumbai: Essays in Honour of Jim Masselos*.

Joan Martinez-Alier's research interests are ecological economics, political ecology, agrarian studies, environmental justice and the environmentalism of the poor and the indigenous. He is co-director of the EJAtlas (www.ejatlas.org), a global database mapping environmental justice movements, based at the Institute of Environmental Science and Technology, Autonomous University of Barcelona (ICTA-UAB).

Suresh Menon is contributing editor, *The Hindu* and founder-editor of *Wisden India Almanack*. He has been writing on cricket for nearly four decades. His books include *Sachin Unplugged, Pataudi: Nawab of Cricket*, and *Bishan: Portrait of a Cricketer*.

Akshaya Mukul is an independent researcher and a journalist. He is the author of *Gita Press and the Making of Hindu India* (2015). He is writing the first English biography of noted Hindi writer Sachchidananda Hirananda Vatsyayan Agyeya.

Meera Anna Oommen is associate director of Dakshin Foundation, Bangalore, and has interests in environmental history, human-animal relationships, local knowledge systems, qualitative networks and bounded rationality.

Dinyar Patel is an assistant professor of history at S.P. Jain Institute of Management and Research in Mumbai. He is the author of *Naoroji: Pioneer of Indian Nationalism* and has co-edited two volumes: *Dadabhai Naoroji: Selected Private Papers* (with S.R. Mehrotra) and *From Ghalib's Dilli to Lutyens' New Delhi: A Documentary Record* (with Mushirul Hasan).

Jahnavi Phalkey is a film-maker and historian of science and technology. She is the founding director of Science Gallery Bengaluru, and Sir Asutosh Mukherjee Visiting Professor at the National Institute of Advanced Studies. Jahnavi is the author of *Atomic State: Big Science in Twentieth Century India,* and the producer-director of the documentary film *Cyclotron.*

Srinath Raghavan is professor of international relations and history at Ashoka University. He is the author of several books, including *The Most Dangerous Place: A History of the United States in South Asia.*

Brototi Roy, a PhD candidate, is based at the Institute of Environmental Science and Technology, Autonomous University of Barcelona (ICTA-UAB) researching on environmental justice movements in India using the lenses of political ecology and ecological economics.

Arupjyoti Saikia is professor of history at the department of humanities and social sciences, Indian Institute of Technology, Guwahati. His publications include *A Forests and Ecological History of Assam, Century of Protests: Peasant Politics in Assam since 1900*, and *The Unquiet River: A Biography of the Brahmaputra.*

Kartik Shanker is an evolutionary ecologist at the Centre for Ecological Sciences, Indian Institute of Science. He is a founder trustee of Dakshin Foundation, Bangalore and editor, *Current Conservation*. He is also the author of *From Soup to Superstar: The Story of Sea Turtle Conservation Along the Indian Coast*, a history of sea turtle conservation in India.

Nandini Sundar is professor of sociology at the Delhi School of Economics, Delhi University. *The Burning Forest: India's War against Maoists* is her most recent book.

A.R. Venkatachalapathy, historian and Tamil writer, is a professor at the Madras Institute of Development Studies, Chennai. Awarded the V.K.R.V. Rao Prize (history, 2007) and Vilakku Virudhu (lifetime contribution to Tamil literature, 2018), Chalapathy's publications in English include *Tamil Characters: Personalities, Politics, Culture*; *Who Owns That Song?: The Battle for Subramania Bharati's Copyright*; *The Province of the Book: Scholars, Scribes, and Scribblers in Colonial Tamil Nadu* and *In Those Days There Was No Coffee: Writings in Cultural History*.

ACKNOWLEDGEMENTS

THIS VOLUME IS based on a workshop organized to celebrate Ramachandra Guha's scholarship in April 2018, the year he turned sixty. In our experience, it has never been easier to organize an event, and for this, our primary thanks must go to Ramachandra Guha himself for creating such a network of friends and admirers. Every single person we asked to contribute—whether as paper presenter, chair or discussant, or in terms of financial support—responded with enthusiasm and instant agreement.

The workshop was divided into four panels, each reflecting one aspect of Guha's work: environmental history and politics, sports, contemporary political history, biography and the nation. Each session was chaired and discussed by wonderful scholars who spoke knowledgeably about Guha's work and contextualized it within a larger sphere of scholarship: Niraja Gopal Jayal, Nayanjot Lahiri, Mukul Kesavan, Rudrangshu Mukherjee, Mahesh Rangarajan and Ghazala Shahabuddin. We are grateful to Mukul Sharma, Madhav Gadgil and Shekhar Pathak for their extended conversation on environmental politics in India, and to Pradeep Magazine, Sharda Ugra and Rahul Bhattacharya for a fascinating discussion on the social history of sports. These conversations and the papers by Vinay Sitapati and Harish Damodaran have not been reproduced here. We are grateful to all the contributors to this volume, whether in terms of research articles or reflections on Guha.

The workshop was generously funded by Ashoka University, with support from Oxford University Press and Penguin Random House. We are especially grateful to Ashish Dhawan, Venkat Eswara, Pratap

Bhanu Mehta, Rudrangshu Mukherjee and Malabika Sarkar at Ashoka University. Pratap Mehta and Rudrangshu Mukherjee not only saw this through but also spoke at the workshop. Manish Sabharwal, Guha's long-term friend in Bengaluru, offered to fill any gap in funding through a personal contribution, so we could go ahead knowing we had backup, which was a huge comfort. IIC was as usual very easy to work with, and we are especially grateful to Sutapa Abbas for all her help. Rekha Natarajan, Naveen Chaudhury and Madhur Malhotra of OUP, Meru Gokhale, Hemali Sodhi and Tarini Uppal of Penguin Random House—all took an active, personal interest in making it possible.

Vinay Sitapati, Madhav Khosla, Akshaya Mukul and the fantastically able Arpit Gaind ensured that all the organization went smoothly, for which we are truly grateful. Vinay Sitapati deserves special thanks for his leading role in organizing the conference. Sumit Guha, K. Sivaramakrishnan and Mekhala Krishnamurthy provided valuable suggestions at the inception.

We are delighted to have this volume published by Penguin Random House. As Ramachandra Guha's long-standing publisher they were our first and natural choice. We are grateful to Meru Gokhale for enthusiastically accepting the project and to Tarini Uppal, Paloma Dutta and Aparna Kumar for taking it forward.

NOTES

Introduction

1. Interview with John Kenneth Galbraith, *Outlook*, 20 August 2001.
2. Some other Indian public intellectuals like Arundhati Roy or Romila Thapar are not on Twitter, and we are not counting Twitter in Indian languages.
3. S. Sagarika, D. Mishra and J. Pal, 'Influencers in Indian Political Journalism', University of Michigan, 2020. Accessed at http:/joyojeet.people.si.umich.edu/influencers-in-indian-political-journalism/
4. Ramachandra Guha, *Patriots and Partisans* (New Delhi: Penguin Books, 2013).
5. Adam Sisman, *A.J.P. Taylor: A Biography* (London: Mandarin 1995, p. 87.
6. Ramachandra Guha, 'The Arun Shourie of the Left', *The Hindu*, 26 November 2000; N. Ram's interview with Arundhati Roy, 'Scimitars in the Sun', *Frontline*, 6 January 2001.
7. Ramachandra Guha, 'Liberals, Sadly', *Indian Express*, 24 March 2018.
8. 'Hindutva Hate Mail', Guha, *Patriots and Partisans*, pp. 59–73.
9. 'Here's Why the ABVP thinks Ram Guha is Anti-National', The Wire, 2 November 2018.
10. Ramachandra Guha in conversation with John Harriss, 'Reflections', *Development and Change*, 46:4 (2015), pp. 875–92.

11. Max Weber, 'Science as a Vocation', H.H. Gerth and C. Wright Mills (eds), *From Max Weber: Essays in Sociology*, (London: Routledge, 1948), p. 137.

12. Guha and Harriss, 'Reflections', p. 89.

13. Guha's awards include the Leopold-Hidy Award of the American Society for Environmental History, the Daily Telegraph/Cricket Society Prize, the Malcolm Adiseshiah Award for Excellence in Social Science Research, the Ramnath Goenka Award for Excellence in Journalism, the R.K. Narayan Prize, the Sahitya Akademi Award and the Fukuoka Asian Culture Prize. He has been awarded the Padma Bhushan by the Government of India and an Honorary Doctorate by Yale University. In 2019, he was recognized as Honorary Foreign Member of the American Historical Association. His books have been at the top of bestseller lists several times, and in May 2008, Foreign Policy included him in the top 100 public intellectuals of the world.

14. David Arnold and Stuart Blackburn, *Telling Lives in India: Biography, Autobiography and Life History* (New Delhi: Permanent Black, 2004).

15. Ramachandra Guha, 'Gandhi's Formative Years', *Financial Times*, 20 September 2013.

Part I: Environment and Equity

Chapter 1: Empire's Nature in the Garo Hills: A Microhistory of India's Environmental Movements

1. The kheddah department was responsible for the entire administration of elephants in the custody of the Indian government; Rudyard Kipling, *The Jungle Book* (New York: The Century Company, 1920), p. 217.

2. For a fine examination of the British imperial forestry programme in Meghalaya, see B.G. Karlsson, *Unruly Hills: A Political Ecology of India's Northeast* (New York: Berghahn Books, 2011).

3. This phrase has been drawn from Amy R. W. Meyers and Margaret Beck Pritchard, *Empire's Nature: Mark Catesby's New World Vision* (Chapel Hill: University of North Carolina Press, 1998).

4. Jamini Mohan Ghosh, 'The Afghan Fortress in Mymensingh: The Story of Bokainagar', *Bengal Past and Present*, (1924), pp. 56–58; F.A. Sachse, *Bengal District Gazetteers: Mymensingh* (Calcutta, 1917);

W. Van Schendel, '"Madmen" of Mymensingh: Peasant Resistance and the Colonial Process in Eastern India, 1824 to 1833', *Indian Economic and Social History Review*, 22:2 (1985), pp. 139–73; Gautam Bhadra, 'Paglai Dhum: Mymensingh er Krishak Vidroha', in idem, *Iman O Nishan* (Calcutta: Subarnarekha, 1994).

5.   *An Account of the Burman Empire and the Kingdom of Assam*, Compiled from the works and manuscript documents of the following most eminent authors and public functionaries viz. Hamilton, Symes, Canning Cox Leyden, F. Buchanan, Morgan, Towers, Elmore, Wade, Turner, Sisson, Elliot &c. & c, (Calcutta, 1839), p. 132.

6.   Parimal Chandra Kar, *British Annexation of Garohills*, (Calcutta: Nababharat Publishers, 1970); M. Momin (ed.) *Readings in History and Culture of the Garos: Essays in Honour of Milton S. Sangma* (Delhi: Regency Publications, 2003); Milton S. Sangma, *History and Culture of the Garos* (New Delhi: Books Today, 1981); Alexander Mackenzie, *History of the Relations of the Government with the Hill Tribes of the North-East Frontier of Bengal* (Calcutta: Home Department Press, 1884), p. 255.

7.   William Carey, *A Garo Jungle Book or the Mission to the Garos of Assam* (Philadelphia: The Judson Press, 1919), p. 2.

8.   Ratneswar Mahanta, '*Garo Britanta*', N. Saikia (ed.) *Assam Bandhu (1885–86)*, (Guwahati: Assam Publication Board, 1984), pp. 33–36, 169–72, 528–30; J.N. Bhuyan (ed.) *Ratneswar Mahanta Rachanwali* [Collected Works of Ratneswar Mahanta] (Guwahati: Assam Publication Board, 1977), pp. 201–10.

9.   Lord Lindsay, *Lives of the Lindsays* (London: John Murray, 1849), p. 176.

10. D. Sutherland, *The Regulations of the Bengal Code in Force in September 1862 with a List of Titles and an Index* (Calcutta: Savielle and Cranenburgh, 1862), pp. 1019–023.

11. Mackenzie, *History*, 255.

12. Letter from A. Davidson, principal assistant to governor general, to Captain F. Jenkins, agent to the governor general North East Frontier, 15 September 1834, in ibid., p. 109.

13. Letter from F. Jenkins, agent to the governor general to C. Macsween, chief secretary, Government of Bengal, 'Organising Expedition Against Garos to Collect Fines and Tributes Imposed on Them, Judicial (Criminal)', 10 November 1834, Consultation No. 56, in

Simonti Sen (ed.), *North East (1830–1873): Select Documents*, Part 1 (Kolkata: Directorate of State Archives, 2018), p. 107.

14. Ibid.
15. *The Imperial Gazetteer of India*, Vol. 12 (Oxford: Clarendon Press, 1908), p. 174.
16. Letter from A. Mackenzie, officiating secretary to Government of Bengal, judicial department to the secretary to Government of India, Home Department (Calcutta, July 1872), No. 4415 in Sen, (ed.) *North East*, p. 113.
17. Baboo Ram Nath Chuckerbutty, *English, Bengali, and Garrow Vocabulary* (Calcutta: Bengal Secretariat Press, 1867).
18. 'The Empress versus Burah and Book Singh', *The Indian Law Reports: Calcutta Series*, Vol. 3 (Calcutta: Thacker, Spink & Co., 1878), p. 84.
19. Mackenzie, *History*, p. 216.
20. Robert Montgomery Martin, *The History Antiquities, Topography, and Statistics of Eastern India: Puraniya, Ronggopoor and Assam*, Vol. 3 (London: W.M.H. Allen and Co., 1838), p. 684.
21. For details on the rebellion of the Pagal Panthis, see, Van Schendel, '"Madmen" of Mymensingh', pp. 139–73; Bhadra, 'Paglai Dhum', pp. 20–164.
22. Maheswar Neog, (ed.) *Guru Charit Katha* (Guwahati: LBS, 1999).
23. George Watt, *The Wild and Cultivated Cotton Plants of the World* (New York, Bombay, Calcutta: Longmans, Green and Co., 1907), p. 10; Joseph G. Medlicott, *Cotton Hand-Book, for Bengal* (Calcutta: Bengal Printing Company, 1862), pp. 102–03.
24. Watt, *The Wild*, p. 110; Carey, *A Garo Jungle Book*, p. 19.
25. *Report on the Administration of Bengal (1872–73)* (Calcutta: Bengal Secretariat Press, 1873), p. 61.
26. Watt, *The Wild*, p. 110.
27. Ibid.
28. Carey, *A Garo Jungle Book*, p. 19.
29. Mackenzie, *History*, p. 216.
30. *An Account*, p. 135.
31. Ibid., p. 136.
32. Jayanta Bhushan Bhattacharjee, 'The Garos under the Zemindars, 1765 to 1816', *Proceedings of the Indian History Congress*, 3 (1969), pp. 334–35; *An Account*, p. 134.

33. Mackenzie, *History*, p. 255.
34. S. Kumar, 'State "Simplification": Garo Protest in Late 19th and Early 20th Century Assam', *Economic and Political Weekly*, 40:27 (2-8 July 2005), p. 2944; W. J. Williamson, *General Administration Report of the Garo Hills District for the year 1875–76* (Shimla: Government Central Branch Press, 1876), p. 2.
35. *An Account*, p. 131.
36. *Report on the Administration of Bengal (1872–73)*, p. 61.
37. 'The Treaty of Commerce between Assam and the East India Company in 1793', C.U. Aitchison, *A Collection of Treaties, Engagements and Sanads*. Vol. II. Treaty No. XXXV (Calcutta, 1909), pp. 134–37.
38. *Deposition of Nilkanta Mukherjee*, p. 691.
39. Ibid.
40. *Progress Report of Forest Administration in the Province of Assam 1876–77*, 2; *Progress Report of Forest Administration in the Province of Assam 1875–76*, p. 3
41. 'Timber Trade in Assam', *Indian Forester*, 4 (1879), p. 47.
42. For practices of shifting cultivation in the Garo Hills, see, Bela Malik, 'The "Problem" of Shifting Cultivation in the Garo Hills of North-East India, 1860–1970', *Conservation and Society*, 1:2 (2003), pp. 287–315.
43. Letter from deputy commissioner, Garo Hills, 11 September 1882, No. 749 quoted in Government of India, 'Report on the Investigations into the Alleged Grievances of the Garos in the Goalpara and Garo Hills Districts, Eastern Bengal and Assam', Para. 3. *Proceedings of the Government of India*, Department of Revenue and Agriculture, Branch Land Revenue, A, Nos. 28–29, File no. 507 of 1907 (April 1908) National Archives of India (NAI), p. 593.
44. Ibid., para. 2, p. 593.
45. Ibid., para. 6, p. 594.
46. The Garos could cut trees for jhum but 'they cannot sell any trees, reserved or unreserved, to outsiders', 'Deposition of Nilkanta Mukherjee' in GOI, *Report on the Investigations*, p. 691.
47. Ibid.
48. Ibid.
49. S. Eardley-Wilmot, *Notes of Tour in Darrang, Kamrup, Garo Hills and Goalpara Forest Divisions of Assam in 1906*, (Calcutta: Office of the Superintendent of Government Printing), p. 6.

50. Eardley-Wilmot, *Notes*, p. 7.
51. Quoted in S. Eardley-Wilmot, *Forest Life and Sport in India* (London: Edward Arnold, 1910), p. 7.
52. *Progress Report of Forest Administration in the Province of Assam, 1875–76*, p. 3
53. Ibid., p. 3
54. Government of India, *The Sylhet Jhum Regulation, 1891*, Proceedings of the Government of India, Legislative Department. File no. 85-98. May 1891, NAI.
55. Wilmot, *Forest Life*, p. 8.
56. R. Morrieson, 'Report on the Causes of the Late Disturbances in Pergunnahs Sherepore and Allapsing' (12 November 1825), quoted in Van Schendel, '"Madmen" of Mymensingh', p. 142.
57. GOI, *Report on the Investigations*, p. 599.
58. Mihir N. Sangma, *Unpublished Documents on Garo Affairs* (New Delhi: Scholar Publishing House, 1993), p. 135.
59. Court order of A. Playfair, deputy commissioner Garo Hills to Banuram Nokma (20 February 1905) in Sangma, *Unpublished Documents*, p. 136.
60. GOI, *Report on the Investigations*, p. 602.
61. Stephen Fuchs, *Rebellious Prophets: A Study of Messianic Movements in Indian Religions*. (New York: Asia Publishing House, 1965), p. 115; From J.C. Arbuthnott, commissioner Surma Valley and Hill Districts to the chief secretary to Government of Eastern Bengal and Assam (11 and 30 May 1907), GOI, *Report on the Investigations*, Appendix, 1, part 1, no. 164 (hereafter Arbuthnott, *Report*), p. 7; T.K. Sangma, *Political Movement of Sonaram R Sangma and its impact upon the Garo Society,* unpublished doctoral thesis (Gauhati University, 2002), chapter 3.
62. Arbuthnott, *Report*, 7.
63. Arbuthnott, *Report*, 8.
64. 'Statement of Sonaram Sangma', GOI, *Report on the Investigations*, p. 620.
65. Ibid.
66. 'Deposition of Sonaram Sangma', GOI, *Report on the Investigations*, p. 621.
67. 'Deposition of Sonaram Sangma', GOI, *Report on the Investigations*, p. 619.

68. Sangma, *Unpublished Documents*, p. 30.
69. 'Deposition of Sonaram R. Sangma', GOI, *Report on the Investigations*, p. 621.
70. GOI, *Report on the Investigations*, 628. For lawyer Jacob's role in Birsa Munda case, see K. Suresh Singh, *The Dust-storm And the Hanging Mist: a study of Birsa Munda and his movement in Chhotanagpur, 1874–1901*, (Calcutta: Firma K. L. M, 1966).
71. Ibid., p. 128.
72. Kumar, 'State "Simplification"', pp. 2941–2947.
73. 'In the Matter of Reserved Forests in Garo Hills', Memorandum from Sonaram Sangma and others to Earl Minto, viceroy of India (Calcutta: 9 February 1906) in Sangma, *Unpublished Documents*, p. 125.
74. Arbuthnott, *Report*, p. 593.
75. 'Deposition of Sonaram Sangma', GOI, *Report on the Investigations*, p. 623.
76. Ibid.
77. 'Note on Forest Reservation', GOI, *Report on the Investigations*, p. 595.
78. Santo Barman, *Zamindari System in Assam during British rule: A Case Study of Goalpara District* (Guwahati: Spectrum Publications, 1994).
79. GoI, *Report on the Investigations*, pp. 700 and 702.
80. *The India List and India Office List for 1905* (London: Harrison and Sons., 1905), p. 428.
81. 'Note on Forest Reservation', GOI, *Report on the Investigations*, p. 594.
82. Ibid.
83. 'Deposition of Malbay Sirdar of Songsak', GOI, *Report on the Investigation*, p. 676.
84. 'Deposition of Bancha Garo', GOI, *Report on the Investigation*, p. 672.
85. 'Deposition of Eneng Nokma', GOI, *Report on the Investigations*, p. 676.
86. 'Deposition of Malbay Sirdar of Songsak', GOI, *Report on the Investigation*, p. 676.
87. 'Arasing Nokma's Ryots Were Fined Rs. 50', GOI, *Report on the Investigations*, p. 659.

88. 'Deposition of Nacheng Nokma of Dobu', GOI, *Report on the Investigations*, p. 661.

89. 'Deposition of Jangsa Nokma', GOI, *Report on the Investigations*, p. 675.

90. 'Deposition of Singiram Nokma', GOI, *Report on the Investigations*, p. 660.

91. 'Deposition of Arasing Nokma', GOI, *Report on the Investigations*, p. 659.

92. 'Note on Forest Reservation', GOI, *Report on the Investigations*, p. 596.

93. 'Deposition of Rijan Nokma of Naphak', GOI, *Report on the Investigations*, p. 675.

94. 'Deposition of Singiram Nokma', GOI, *Report on the Investigations*, p. 660.

95. 'Deposition of Bangran Nokma of Cheran', GOI, *Report on the Investigations*, p. 693.

96. These statements of Sonaram are taken from 'Deposition of Sonaram Sangma', GOI, *Report on the Investigations*, pp. 623–25.

97. A. Playfair, Deputy Commissioner, Garo Hills, Proceeding against Sonaram Sangma, Garo of Roamari Salpara village in the district of Goalpara under section 110 Cr.P.C (14 February 1905), Sangma, *Unpublished Documents*, p. 201.

98. Deposition of Jito Garo, proceeding against Sonaram Sangma, Garo of Roamari Salpara village in the district of Goalpara under section 110 Cr.P.C (14 February 1905), Ibid., p. 203.

99. 'Deposition of Nacheng Nokma', GOI, *Report on the Investigations*, p. 661.

100. 'Deposition of Thonang Garo of Gabul', GOI, *Report on the Investigations*, p. 672.

101. Deposition of Janggat Garo, proceeding against Sonaram Sangma, Garo of Roamari Salpara village in the district of Goalpara under section 110 Cr.P.C (14 February 1905), Sangma, *Unpublished Documents*, p. 202.

102. 'Deposition of Motjing Nokma of Rongapgiri near Rongrenggiri', GOI, *Report on the Investigation*, p. 662.

103. 'Deposition of Banjang Nokma of Sinal', GOI, *Report on the Investigations*, p. 675.

104. 'Deposition of Malbay Sirdar', GOI, *Report on the Investigations*, p. 676.

105. 'Note on Forest Reservation', GOI, *Report on the Investigations*, p. 594.
106. Arbuthnott, *Report*, part 1, no. 164.
107. 'Note on Forest Reservation', GOI, *Report on the Investigation*, p. 594.
108. 'Note on Forest Reservation', GOI, *Report on the Investigations*, p. 594.
109. 'Note on Forest Reservation', GOI, *Report on the Investigations*, p. 593.
110. 'We were afraid to annoy the forest people by complaining', 'Deposition of Jangsa Nokma', GOI, *Report on the Investigations*, p. 675.
111. 'Note on Forest Reservation', GOI, *Report on the Investigations*, p. 595.
112. Ibid., p. 5.
113. Ibid., p. 595.
114. Ibid., p. 596.
115. Ibid., p. 601.
116. 'Note on Impressment of Labour', GOI, *Report on the Investigations*, p. 602.
117. 'Notes Recorded by the Financial Secretary to Government and Conservator of Forests on the Questions Regarding Forest Reservation in the Garo Hills', Ibid., Appendix III, p. 771.
118. Ibid.
119. Letter from H. Lemesurier, officiating chief secretary to the government of Eastern Bengal and Assam to the secretary, GOI, Department of Revenue and Agriculture (26 November 1907), GOI, *Report on the Investigations*, pp. 559–567.
120. Letter from R.W. Carlyle, secretary to GOI, Department of Revenue and Agriculture to chief secretary, Government of Eastern Bengal and Assam (20 March 1908), no. 29 no. 358-507-2, Ibid., pp. 773–75.
121. A.C. Sinha, *Beyond the Trees, Tigers and Tribes: Historical Sociology of the Himalayan Forests* (Delhi: Har-Anand, 1993), p. 122.
122. A.J. Kurien, S. Lele, H. Nagendra, 'Farms or Forests? Understanding and Mapping Shifting Cultivation Using the Case Study of West Garo Hills, India', *Land*, 8:9 (2019), p. 8 and p. 133.

Chapter 2: The Heart of the Matter: Studying Institutional Structures in Historical Perspective

1. For a criticism of the judgment, see Armin Rosencranz and Sharachchandra Lele, 'Supreme Court and India's Forests', *Economic and Political Weekly*, 43:5 (2–8 February 2008), pp. 11–14.

2. Ramachandra Guha, *The Unquiet Woods: Ecological Change and Peasant Resistance in the Himalaya* (Delhi: Oxford University Press, 1989); Madhav Gadgil and Ramachandra Guha, *This Fissured Land: An Ecological History of India* (Delhi: Oxford University Press, 1992).

3. Richard H. Grove, *Green Imperialism: Colonial Expansion, Tropical Island Edens and the Origins of Environmentalism, 1600–1860* (Cambridge: Cambridge University Press, 1995).

4. Sumit Guha, 'Claims on the Commons: Political Power and Natural Resources in Precolonial India', *India's Environmental History*, Vol. I, (eds) Mahesh Rangarajan and K. Sivaramakrishnan (Ranikhet: Permanent Black, 2012).

5. Kathleen D. Morrison, 'Conceiving Ecology and Stopping the Clock: Narratives of Balance, Loss, and Degradation', *Shifting Ground: People, Animals, and Mobility in India's Environmental History*, (eds) Mahesh Rangarajan and K. Sivaramakrishnan (Delhi: Oxford University Press, 2014).

6. Tarsh Thekaekara, et al., 'Notes from the Other Side of a Forest Fire', *Economic and Political Weekly*, 52:25–26 (24 June 2017).

7. Jaydev Mandal and T.R. Shankar Raman, 'Shifting Agriculture Supports More Tropical Forest Birds than Oil Palm or Teak Plantations in Mizoram, Northeast India', *The Condor*, 118 (2016), pp. 345–359.

8. Ramachandra Guha, 'Forestry in British and Post-British India', *Economic and Political Weekly*, 18:44 (29 October 1983), pp. 1882–1896.

9. See Nandini Sundar, Roger Jeffery and Neil Thin, *Branching Out: Joint Forest Management in India* (Delhi: Oxford University Press, 2001).

10. Sharachchandra Lele and Ajit Menon, 'Introduction', *Democratising Forest Governance in India*, (eds) Idem (Delhi: Oxford University Press, 2014), pp. 2–3.

11. Ghazala Shahabuddin, *Conservation at the Crossroads: Science, Society, and the Future of India's Wildlife* (Ranikhet: Permanent Black, 2010).

12. Mahesh Rangarajan, M.D. Madhusudan and Ghazala Shahabuddin, 'Introduction', *Nature without Borders*, (eds) Idem (Delhi: Orient Blackswan, 2014).

13. Shahabuddin, *Conservation at the Crossroads*, chapter 3; Meghna Krishnadas, Umesh Srinivasan, Nandini Velho and Sachin Sridhara,

'Turning the Page in Forest Governance: Science and Bureaucracy', *Economic and Political Weekly*, 46:50 (10 December 2011), pp. 10–13; Pradip Krishen, 'Introduction', Peter Wohlleben, *The Hidden Life of Trees* (New Delhi: Allen Lane, 2016), pp. xvii–xviii.

14. Kanchi Kohli and Manju Menon, 'The Making of Forest Re(Publics)', *Democratising Forest Governance*.

15. Karuna Dietrich Wielenga, 'The Emergence of the Informal Sector: Labour Legislation and Politics in South India, 1940-1960', *Modern Asian Studies*, 54:4 (2020), pp. 1113–1148.

16. Sharachchandra Lele, 'What is Wrong with Joint Forest Management?', *Democratising Forest Governance*, p. 53.

17. Oliver Springate-Baginski, Madhu Sarin and M. Gopinath Reddy, 'Resisting Rights: Forest Bureaucracy and the Tenure Transition in India', *Small-scale Forestry*, 12 (2013), pp. 107–124.

18. Ibid; Kohli and Menon, 'The Making of Forest Re(Publics)', *Democratising Forest Governance*, pp. 287– 290.

19. The major monographs include Mahesh Rangarajan, *Fencing the Forest: Conservation and Ecological Change in India's Central Provinces 1860–1914* (Delhi: Oxford University Press, 1996); K. Sivaramakrishnan, *Modern Forests: Statemaking and Environmental Change in Colonial Eastern India* (Delhi: Oxford University Press, 1999); and S. Ravi Rajan, *Modernising Nature: Forestry and Imperial Eco-development 1800–1950* (Oxford: Oxford University Press, 2006).

20. Sushil Kumar and Shashi Kant, 'Bureaucracy and New Management Paradigms: Modelling Foresters' Perceptions regarding Community-based Forest Management in India', *Forest Policy and Economics*, 7 (2005), pp. 651–669.

21. Forrest Fleischman, 'Understanding India's Forest Bureaucracy: A Review', *Regional Environmental Change*, 16 (Supplement 1) (2016), S153–S165.

22. The category of protection forests was established in 1894.

23. *Indian Forester*, 2:1 (July 1876), pp. 57–63.

24. *Indian Forester*, 7:4 (April 1882), pp. 363–369.

25. K. Sivaramakrishnan, 'The Politics of Fire and Forest Regeneration in Colonial Bengal', *Environment and History*, 2:2 (1996), pp. 145–194.

26. The arguments in the subsequent section are derived from a larger research project on south Indian forests, where I hope to examine them in more detail.

27. For a history of *Lantana camara* in India, see Ramesh Kannan, Charlie M. Shackleton and R. Uma Shaanker, 'Reconstructing the History of Introduction and Spread of the Invasive Species, *Lantana*, at Three Spatial Scales in India', *Biological Invasions*, 15 (2013), pp. 1287-1302. For its potential role in forest fires, see Bharat Sundaram, et al., 'Ecology and Impacts of the Invasive Species, *Lantana camara*, in a Social-Ecological System in South India: Perspectives from Local Knowledge', *Human Ecology*, 40:6 (2012), pp. 931–942.

28. Indian Forest Records (New Series), Silviculture, Vol. I, No. I: *A Preliminary Survey of the Forest Types of India* by H.G. Champion (Delhi: Manager of Publications, 1935, reprinted 1961), p. iii.

29. Darwin's whole career is emblematic of this tradition.

30. Dan H. Nicolson, C.R. Suresh and K.S. Manilal, *An Interpretation of Van Rheede's Hortus Malabaricus* (Koeltz: Koenigstein, 1988), p. 17.

31. For a representative career, see H.J. Noltie, *Robert Wight and the Botanical Drawings of Rungiah and Govindoo* (Edinburgh: Royal Botanic Garden Edinburgh, 2007).

32. Indian Forest Records, Vol. II, Part II: *The Silviculture of Hardwickia binata* by D.O. Witt (Calcutta: 1910).

33. Vasant K. Saberwal, 'Science and the Desiccationist Discourse of the 20th Century', *Environment and History*, 4:3 (1998), pp. 309–343; Vasant K. Saberwal, 'Bureaucratic Agendas and Conservation Policy in Himachal Pradesh, 1865–1994', *Indian Economic and Social History Review*, 34:4 (1997), pp. 465–498.

34. Saberwal, 'Bureaucratic Agendas', pp. 493–494.

35. K. Sivaramakrishnan, 'Landlords, Regional Development and National Forestry Projects: Midnapore, 1930s–1960s', *A New Moral Economy For India's Forests?* (eds) Roger Jeffry and Nandini Sundar (Delhi: Sage, 1999), pp. 87–89. For teak plantations in Jharkhand, see Guha, 'Forestry in British and Post-British India'.

36. N.C. Saxena and Madhu Sarin, 'The Western Ghats Forestry and Environmental Project in Karnataka: A Preliminary Assessment', *A New Moral Economy*, p. 186.

37. Peter Wohlleben, whose popular account, *The Hidden Life of Trees*, became an unexpected bestseller, worked as a forester in Germany.

38. M.K. Ranjitsinh, *A Life with Wildlife* (New Delhi: HarperCollins, 2017); Mahesh Rangarajan, 'Striving for a Balance: Nature, Power, Science and India's Indira Gandhi, 1917–1984', *Conservation and Society*, 7:4 (2009), pp. 299–312.

39. Shahabuddin, *Conservation at Crossroads*, pp. 87–88.

40. Sundar et al., *Branching Out*.

41. N.H. Ravindranath, Madhav Gadgil and Jeff Campbell, 'Ecological Stabilization and Community Needs: Managing India's Forest by Objective', *Village Voices, Forest Choices: Joint Forest Management in India* (eds) Mark Poffenberger and Betsy McGean (Delhi: Oxford University Press, 1996), p. 303.

42. Sundar et al., *Branching Out*; Shahabuddin, *Conservation at Crossroads*, chapter 6.

43. Bhaskar Vira, 'Implementing Joint Forest Management in the Field', *A New Moral Economy*, p. 267.

44. For Bengal, see Sivaramakrishnan, 'Landlords, Regional Development and National Forestry Projects'; for Tamil Nadu, see Siddhartha Krishnan, 'Of Land, Legislation and Litigation: Forest Leases, Agrarian Reform, Legal Ambiguity and Landscape Anomaly in the Nilgiris, 1969–2007', *Conservation and Society*, 7:4 (2009), pp. 283–298.

45. Sundar, et al. (2001), pp. 71–72.

46. Kohli and Menon, *Democratising Forest Governance*, pp. 287–290.

47. Asmita Kabra's 'Conservation Induced Displacement: A Comparative Study of Two Indian Protected Areas', *Conservation and Society*, 7:4 (2009), pp. 249–267, compares contrasting rehabilitation outcomes in Karnataka and Madhya Pradesh.

48. In 1990–91, 62 per cent of forests in Arunachal Pradesh were designated as unclassified state forests under community ownership. Amitava Mitra, 'Environment and Sustainable Development in the Hilly Regions of North-east India: A Study in Arunachal Pradesh', *International Journal of Social Economics*, 25: 2/3/4 (1998), p. 198.

49. Raghu Chundawat, *The Rise and Fall of the Emerald Tigers: Ten Years of Research in Panna National Park* (Delhi: Speaking Tiger, 2018).

50. Shahabuddin, *Conservation at Crossroads*, chapter 5; Shashank Kela, *A Rogue and Peasant Slave: Adivasi Resistance 1800–2000* (Delhi, Navanyana, 2012), pp. 364–365.

51. Stephanie Mansourian, 'Understanding the Relation between Governance and Forest Landscape Restoration', *Conservation and Society*, 14:3 (2016), pp. 267–278; Mark Poffenberger et al., 'Communities Sustaining India's Forests in the Twenty-first Century' in *Village Voices, Forest Choices*.

52. The website of the EPA contains a short history and a number of documents from its early years.

Chapter 3: The Authoritarian Biologist Reloaded and Deep Ecology Redux: Conservation Imperialism and the Control of Knowledge, Money and Space

1. Ramachandra Guha, 'Radical American Environmentalism and Wilderness Preservation: A Third World critique', *Environmental Ethics*, 11 (1989), pp. 71–83; Ramachandra Guha, 'The Authoritarian Biologist and the Arrogance of Anti-humanism: Wildlife Conservation in the Third World', *Ecologist*, 27:1 (1997), pp. 14–20.

2. John MacKenzie, *The Empire of Nature: Hunting, Conservation and British Imperialism* (Manchester: Manchester University Press, 1988); Richard Grove, *Green Imperialism: Colonial Expansion, Tropical Island Edens and the Origins of Environmentalism, 1600–1860* (Cambridge: Cambridge University Press, 1995); David Arnold and Ramachandra Guha (eds), *Nature, Culture, Imperialism: Essays on the Environmental History of South Asia* (Delhi: Oxford University Press, 1995).

3. William Cronon, 'The Trouble with Wilderness; or, Getting Back to the Wrong Nature', *Uncommon Ground: Rethinking the Human Place in Nature*, (ed.) William Cronon (New York: W. W. Norton & Co., 1995), pp. 69–90.

4. Michael D. Spence, *Dispossessing the Wilderness: Indian Removal and the Making of the National Parks* (Oxford: Oxford University Press, 1990); M. Kat Anderson, *Tending the Wild: Native American Knowledge and the Manipulation of California's Natural Resources* (Berkeley and Los Angeles: University of California Press, 2013).

5. William Cronon, *Changes in the Land: Indians, Colonists, and the Ecology of New England* (US: Hill & Wang, 1983); Alfred Crosby, *Ecological Imperialism: The Biological Expansion of Europe, 900–1900* (Cambridge: Cambridge University Press, 2004).

6. Mark D. Spence, *Dispossessing the Wilderness: Indian Removal and the Making of the National Parks* (New York: Oxford University Press, 1999), p. 4.

7. Guha, 'A Third World Critique'.

8. Guha, 'The Authoritarian Biologist'.

9. Dan Brockington, *Fortress Conservation: The Preservation of the Mkomazi Game Reserve, Tanzania* (US: Indiana University Press,

2002); Dan Brockington, 'Community Conservation, Inequality and Injustice: Myths of Power in Protected Area Management', *Conservation and Society*, 2 (2004), pp. 411–32.

10. Mac Chapin, 'A Challenge to Conservationists', *World Watch*, 17:6 (2004), pp. 17–31.

11. Mark Dowie, 'Conservation Refugees: When Protecting Nature Means Kicking People Out', *Orion*, (November–December 2005), pp. 16–27; Mark Dowie, *Conservation Refugees: The Hundred-Year Conflict between Global Conservation and Native Peoples* (Boston: The MIT Press, 2011).

12. Jon-Paul Rodriguez et al., 'Globalisation of Conservation: A View from the South', *Science*, 317 (2007), pp. 755–56.

13. James Igoe and Dan Brockington, 'Neoliberal Conservation: A Brief Introduction', *Conservation and Society*, 5 (2007), pp. 432–49; Bram Büscher et al., 'Towards a Synthesized Critique of Neoliberal Biodiversity Conservation', *Capitalism, Nature, Socialism*, 23 (2012), pp. 4–30.

14. Paul Robbins, *Political Ecology: A Critical Introduction* (Blackwell Publishing, 2004).

15. Piers Blaikie, *The Political Ecology of Soil Erosion in Developing Countries* (UK: Routledge, 1985); Piers Blaikie and Harold Brookfield, *Land Degradation and Society* (Routledge, 1987); Raymond Bryant, 'Beyond the Impasse: The Power of Political Ecology in Third World Environmental Research', *Area*, 29 (1997), pp. 5–19; Raymond Bryant, 'Power, Knowledge and Political Ecology in the Third World: A Review', *Progress in Physical Geography*, 22 (1998), pp. 79–94.

16. Rosaleen Duffy, 'War by Conservation', *Geoforum*, 69 (2016), pp. 238–248.

17. See also Roderick Neumann, 'Moral and Discursive Geographies in the War for Biodiversity in Africa', *Political Geography*, 23 (2004), pp. 813–837; Nancy L. Peluso and Peter Vandergeest, 'Political Ecologies of War and Forests: Counterinsurgencies and the Making of National Natures', *Annals of the Association of American Geographers*, 101 (2011), pp. 587–608; Bram Buscher and Robert Fletcher, 'Under Pressure: Conceptualising Political Ecologies of Green Wars', *Conservation and Society*, 16 (2018), pp. 105–13.

18. Nicholas D. Smith, 'Plato on Knowledge as a Power', *Journal of the History of Philosophy*, 38 (2000), pp. 145–68.

19. Imam Ali (599–661 CE), as recorded in the tenth-century book *Nahj Al-Balagha*.

20. Rachel Carson, *Silent Spring* (US: Houghton Mifflin Company, 1962).

21. Michael E. Soul., 'What is conservation biology?', *BioScience*, 35 (1985), pp. 737–34; Daniel Janzen, 'The Future of Tropical Ecology', *Annual Review of Ecology, Evolution and Systematics*, 17 (1986), pp. 305–24.

22. Michael E. Soule, *Conservation Biology: The Science of Scarcity and Diversity* (Sunderland: Sinauer Associates Inc., 1986); Richard B. Primack, *A Primer of Conservation Biology* (Sunderland: Sinauer Associates Inc., 1995).

23. Robert H. MacArthur and Edward O. Wilson, *The Theory of Island Biogeography* (Princeton: Princeton University Press, 1967).

24. Jared Diamond, 'The Island Dilemma: Lessons of Modern Biogeographic Studies for the Design of Natural Reserves', *Biological Conservation*, 7 (1975), pp. 129–146.

25. Daniel S. Simberloff and Lawrence G. Abele, 'Island Biogeography Theory and Conservation Practice', *Science*, 191 (1976), pp. 285–286; Daniel S. Simberloff and Lawrence G. Abele, 'Refuge Design and Island Biogeographic Theory—Effects of Fragmentation', *American Naturalist*, 120 (1982), pp. 41–56.

26. P. Barber et al., 'Advancing Biodiversity Research in Developing Countries: The Need for a New Paradigm', *Bulletin of Marine Sciences*, 90 (2014), pp. 187–210.

27. Alphonsa Jojan et al., 'Critiquing Narrow Critiques of Convention on Biological Diversity', *Economic and Political Weekly*, 53:44 (3 November 2018), pp. 16–18; Dyna Rochmyaningsih, 'Indonesia Gets Tough on Foreign Scientists', *Science*, 365 (2019); pp. 304–305.

28. Reidpath and Allotey, 'The Problem of "Trickle Down Science"', *BMJ Global Health*, 4 (2019), pp. 1–3.

29. Divakaran Prathapan et al., 'When the Cure Kills—CBD Limits Biodiversity Research', *Science*, 360 (2018); pp. 1405–1406. For a critique, see, Alphonsa Jojan et al., 'Critiquing Narrow Critiques'.

30. Daniel D. Reidpath and Pascale Allotey, *BMJ Global Health* (2019).

31. Peter Kareiva and Michelle Marvier, 'What is Conservation Science?', *BioScience*, 62 (2012), pp. 962–969.

32. Michael E. Soul., 'The "New Conservation"', *Conservation Biology*, 27 (2013), pp. 895–897.

33. Philip Cafaro and Richard B. Primack, 'Species Extinction Is a Great Moral Wrong: Sharing the Earth with Other Species Is an Important Human Responsibility', *Biological Conservation*, 170 (2014), pp. 1–2.

34. For the debate, see https://www.elsevier.com/connect/speciesextinction-is-a-great-moral-wrong

35. See https://www.editage.com/insights/norway-joins-the-ranks-ofgermany-and-sweden-cancels-subscription-with-elsevier

36. William M. Adams, *Against Extinction: The Story of Conservation* (UK: Earthscan, 2004); Brockington, *Fortress Conservation*; Chapin, 'A Challenge to Conservationists'; Dowie, 'Conservation Refugees'; Grove, *Green Imperialism*; Roderick Neumann, *Imposing Wilderness: Struggles over Livelihood and Nature Preservation in Africa* (US: University of California Press, 1998).

37. Edward O. Wilson, *Half-Earth: Our Planet's Fight for Life* (London: Liveright Publications, 2016).

38. George Wuerthner, Eileen Crist and Tom Butler, (eds), *Protecting the Wild: Parks and Wilderness, the Foundation for Conservation* (London: Island Press, 2015).

39. Bram Buscher et al., 'Half Earth or Whole Earth: Radical Ideas for Conservation and their Implications', *Oryx*, 44 (2017), pp. 482–484.

40. Michael Rosenzweig, *Win-Win Ecology: How the Earth's Species Can Survive in the Midst of Human Enterprise* (Oxford: Oxford University Press, 2003).

41. Ibid.

42. Robin Chazdon et al., 'Beyond Reserves: A Research Agenda for Conserving Biodiversity in Human-modified Tropical Landscapes', *Biotropica*, 41 (2009), pp. 142–153.

43. Philip Cafaro et al., 'If We Want a Whole Earth, Nature Needs Half: A Response to Büscher et al.', *Oryx*, 51 (2017), p. 400.

44. Robert T. Lackey, 'Science, Scientists and Policy Advocacy', *Conservation Biology*, 21 (2007), pp. 1–17; Kai M.A. Chan, 'Value and Advocacy in Conservation Biology: Crisis Discipline or Discipline in Crisis?', *Conservation Biology*, 22 (2008), pp. 1–3.

45. Arian D. Wallach et al., 'Summoning Compassion to Address the Challenges of Conservation' *Conservation Biology*, 32 (2018), pp. 1255–1265.

46. Adrien Treves, Francisco J. Santiago-Avila and William S. Lynn, 'Just Preservation', *Biological Conservation* 229 (2019), pp. 134–141.

47. William Kymlicka and Sue Donaldson, *Zoopolis: A Political Theory of Animal Rights* (Oxford: Oxford University Press, 2011); Martha C. Nussbaum, *Creating Capabilities* (Cambridge: Harvard University Press, 2011); Martha C. Nussbaum, 'Working with and for Animals: Getting the Theoretical Framework Right', *Journal of Human Development and Capabilities*, 19 (2018), pp. 2–18.

48. Meera A. Oommen et al., 'The Fatal Flaws of Compassionate Conservation', *Conservation Biology*, 33 (2019), pp. 784–787.

49. Ibid.

50. Amy Dickman. et al., 'Trophy Hunting Bans Seriously Imperil Biodiversity', *Science*, 365 (2019), p. 874.

51. Amy Dickman et al., 'The Moral Basis for Conservation: How Is It Affected by Culture?' *Frontiers in Ecology and the Environment*, 13 (2015), pp. 325–331.

52. Ibid., p. 329 and 330.

53. Wallach et al., 'Summoning Compassion'.

54. Guha, 'A Third World critique'.

55. See Peter Bille Larsen and Dan Brockington, (eds), *The Anthropology of Conservation NGOs: Rethinking the Boundaries* (Switzerland: Palgrave Macmillan, 2018).

56. Christine MacDonald, *Green, Inc.: An Environmental Insider Reveals How a Good Cause Has Gone Bad* (Connecticut: The Lyons Press, 2008).

57. Nnimmo Bassey, 'IUCN Attempts to Greenwash Shell with Flawed Report on Oil Disaster in Ogoniland', *IC* (September 2013).

58. Matthew Bishop and Michael Green, *Philanthrocapitalism: How the Rich Can Save the World* (New York: Bloomsbury Press, 2008), p. 59.

59. For a critique, see Michael Edwards, *Just another Emperor? The Myths and Realities of Philanthrocapitalism* (UK: The Young Foundation, 2008).

60. Richard H. Thaler and Cass R. Sunstein, *Nudge: Improving Decisions about Health, Wealth and Happiness* (US: Penguin, 2009).

61. John Mbaria and Mordecai Ogada, *The Big Conservation Lie* (Auburn: Lens & Pens Publishing, 2017).
62. Ibid. p. 44.
63. Mark Dowie, *Orion* (2005); Dan Brockington and James Igoe, 'Eviction for Conservation: A Global Overview', *Conservation and Society*, 4 (2006), pp. 424–470.
64. Tom Warren and Katie J.M. Baker, 'WWF Funds Guards Who Have Tortured and Killed People', Buzzfeed News (2019).
65. John Mbaria and Mordecai Ogada, *The Big Conservation Lie* (2017).
66. Ibid.
67. Edward O. Wilson, *Half-Earth: Our Planet's Fight for Life* (2016).
68. Helen Kopnina et al. 'The "Future of Conservation" Debate: Defending Ecocentrism and the Nature Needs Half Movement', *Biological Conservation*, 217 (2012), pp. 140–148.
69. Sammy Zahran et al., 'Stress and Telomere Shortening among Central Indian Conservation Refugees', *Proceedings of the National Academy of Sciences*, 112 (2015), pp. 928–936.
70. Guha, 'A Third World Critique'; see also Karl S. Zimmerer and Kenneth R. Young, (eds), *Nature's Geography: New Lessons for Conservation in Developing Countries* (Madison University of Wisconsin Press, 1998).
71. Kartik Shanker, Meera Anna Oommen and Nitin Rai, 'Changing Natures: A Democratic and Dynamic Approach to Biodiversity Conservation', *India Futures*, (eds) Ashish Kothari and K.J. Joy (India: Authorsupfront Publishing Services Private Limited, 2017).
72. Mahesh Rangarajan, 'Environmental Histories of South Asia: A Review Essay', *Environment and History*, 2 (1996), pp. 129–143.
73. Milind Wani and Ashish Kothari, 'Protected Areas and Human Rights in India: The Impact of the Official Conservation Model on Local Communities', *Policy Matters*, 15 (2007), pp. 100–114.
74. Michael Lewis, 'Cattle and Conservation at Bharatpur: A Case Study in Science and Advocacy', *Conservation and Society* 1 (2003), pp. 1–21.
75. Ramachandra Guha, *How Much Should a Person Consume?: Environmentalism in India and the United States* (Berkeley: University of California Press, 2006).
76. Ibid.
77. Mukul Sharma, 'Passages from Nature to Nationalism: Sunderlal Bahuguna and Tehri Dam Opposition in Garhwal', *Economic and*

Political Weekly, 44:8 (21 February 2009), pp. 35–42; Mukul Sharma, *Green and Saffron: Hindu Nationalism and Indian Environmental Politics* (Hyderabad: Orient Blackswan, 2011).

78. Kartik Shanker and M. Muralidharan, 'For Conservation to Work, We Need to Rescure Crocodiles from Animal Rights, The Wire, 11 November 2018.

79. Grove, *Green Imperialism*; Guha, 'The Authoritarian Biologist'.

80. David Western, 'Populations, Resources and Environment in the Twenty-first Century', *Conservation for the Twenty-First Century*, (eds) David Western and Mary Pearl (Oxford: Oxford University Press, 1989).

81. Arun Agrawal, 'Dismantling the Divide between Indigenous and Scientific Knowledge', *Development and Change*, 26 (1995), pp. 413–439.

82. Kartik Shanker and Meera Anna Oommen, 'Engaging Communities in Resource Monitoring: The Political Ecology of Science as the Language of Power', *Radical Ecological Democracy* (October 2018).

83. Elinor Ostrom, *Governing the Commons: The Evolution of Institutions for Collective Action* (Cambridge, UK: Cambridge University Press, 1990).

84. Bryan G. Norton, 'The Cultural Approach to Conservation Biology', *Conservation for the Twenty-First Century*, (eds) David Western and Mary Pearl (Oxford: Oxford University Press, 1989); Bryan G. Norton, 'Biodiversity and Environmental Values: In Search of a Universal Earth Ethic', *Biodiversity and Conservation*, 9 (2000), pp. 1024–44.

85. Millennium Ecosystem Assessment, *Ecosystems and Human Well-Being: Synthesis* (Washington DC: Island Press, 2005) p. 155.

Chapter 4: Nation's Body, River's Pulse: Narratives of Anti-dam Politics in India

1.   Mahesh Rangarajan, 'The Politics of Ecology: The Debate on Wildlife and People in India, 1970–95', *Economic and Political Weekly*, 31:35-36-37 (14 September 1996), pp. 2391–2409. Also see Jairam Ramesh, *Indira Gandhi: A Life in Nature* (New Delhi: Simon & Schuster, 2017).

2. Amita Baviskar, *In the Belly of the River: Tribal Conflicts over Development in the Narmada Valley* (Delhi: Oxford University Press, 1995).
3. Ramachandra Guha, 'Ideological Trends in Indian Environmentalism', *Economic and Political Weekly*, 23:49 (3 December 1988), p. 2581.
4. Chitra Padmanabhan, 'Recovering Budhni Mejhan from the Silted Landscape of Modern India', *The Hindu*, 2 June 2012.
5. Daniel Klingensmith, *'One Valley and a Thousand': Dams, Nationalism and Development* (New Delhi: Oxford University Press, 2007).
6. 'When the Big Dams Came Up', *The Hindu*, 20 March 2015.
7. Speech delivered on 8 July 1954 at the opening of the Nangal Canal, *Jawaharlal Nehru's Speeches Vol. 3 (1953–1957)*, (Delhi: Publications Division, Government of India, 1970).
8. Adivasi, which literally means 'original inhabitants', is the term used by and for communities designated as Scheduled Tribes by the Indian government. While the present-day circumstances of different adivasi groups vary, most trace their identity to forest-based cultures and have been deeply affected by land alienation. By most indicators of human development such as infant mortality, life expectancy, income, food security and education, adivasis fare the worst in the Indian population. For a comprehensive review of the literature on historical and contemporary adivasi issues, see Nandini Sundar (ed.), *The Scheduled Tribes and Their India: Politics, Identities, Policies, and Work* (New Delhi: Oxford University Press, 2016).
9. Satish Deshpande, *Contemporary India: A Sociological View* (New Delhi: Penguin India, 2003).
10. Ravi Hemadri, Harsh Mander and V. Nagaraj, *Dams, Displacement, Policy and Law in India*, Working Paper, (Cape Town: World Commission on Dams, 1999).
11. Virginius Xaxa, 'Protective Discrimination: Why Scheduled Tribes Lag Behind Scheduled Castes', *Economic and Political Weekly*, 36:29 (21 July 2001), pp. 2765–2772.
12. Padmanabhan, 'Recovering Budhni Mejhan'.
13. Among some adivasi communities, especially those that have adopted some Hindu customs, a wedding ceremony involves the bride and groom placing floral garlands around each other's necks. Garlanding is also a common way of welcoming honoured guests, so

it is puzzling that the Santhal elders should have interpreted Budhni Mejhan's actions quite so strictly.

14. Shekhar Singh, Kulan Amin and Ashish Kothari, 'Evaluating Major Irrigation Projects in India', *Big Dams, Displaced People: Rivers of Sorrow, Rivers of Change*, (ed.) Enakshi G. Thukral (New Delhi: Sage, 1992).

15. An early exception in the colonial period was the 1920s agitation against the Tata power company's dam on the Mulshi river near Pune in Maharashtra. For an account of this movement, see Rajendra Vora, *The World's First Anti-Dam Movement: The Mulshi Satyagraha, 1920-1924* (Delhi: Permanent Black, 2009). Also, between 1975–78, thousands of affected adivasis protested against land acquisition for the Chandil dam on the Subarnarekha river in present-day Jharkhand and succeeded in securing better compensation. The struggle against dams on the Koel and Karo tributaries of the Brahmani river in Jharkhand started around the same time, continuing into the millennium when the projects were cancelled due to such sustained opposition.

16. Ramachandra Guha, *The Unquiet Woods: Ecological Change and Peasant Resistance in the Himalaya* (Delhi: Oxford University Press, 1989).

17. Centre for Science and Environment, *The State of India's Environment: The Second Citizens' Report* (New Delhi: Centre for Science and Environment, 1984).

18. Ramachandra Guha and Joan Martinez-Alier, *Varieties of Environmentalism: Essays North and South* (New Delhi: Routledge,1997).

19. Amita Baviskar, 'Red in Tooth and Claw? Searching for Class in Struggles over Nature', *Social Movements in India: Poverty, Power, and Politics*, (ed.) Raka Ray and Mary F. Katzenstein (Lanham, MD: Rowman and Littlefield, 2005), pp. 161–78.

20. Rajni Kothari, *State against Democracy: In Search of Humane Governance* (Delhi: Ajanta Publishers, 1988).

21. Guha, 'Ideological Trends'.

22. Prakash Karat, 'Justification for Imperialist-Financed Activities', *Economic and Political Weekly*, 20:18 (4 May 1985), p. 812.

23. Anuj Bhuwania, *Courting the People: Public Interest Litigation in Post-Emergency India* (New Delhi: Cambridge University Press, 2017).

24. Kalpavriksh and Hindu College Nature Club, *Narmada Valley Project: Development or Destruction?* (Delhi: Kalpavriksh, 1984).

25. A few individual dams had already attracted adverse attention: the dam on the Tawa had resulted in extensive waterlogging in its command area; the one near Bargi had miscalculated the submergence area such that many resettled villagers were flooded out again and forced to move.

26. Amita Baviskar 1995, op. cit.

27. Vijay Paranjpye, *High Dams on the Narmada: A Holistic Analysis of the River Valley Projects* (New Delhi: Indian National Trust for Culture and Heritage, 1990).

28. Suhas Paranjape and K.J. Joy, *Sustainable Technology: Making Sardar Sarovar Project Viable* (Ahmedabad: Centre for Environment Education, 1995).

29. It is not possible to encapsulate here the entire trajectory of the Narmada Bachao Andolan or all the dimensions of its ideology and practice. Fuller accounts can be found in Baviskar, *In the Belly of the River*; Ranjit Dwivedi, *Conflict and Collective Action: The Sardar Sarovar Project in India* (New Delhi: Routledge, 2006); and Alf Gunwald Nilsen, *Dispossession and Resistance in India: The River and the Rage* (New Delhi: Routledge, 2010).

30. Bharat is the Hindi work for the country and is used politically to refer to its rural, vernacular part.

31. Oliver Mendelsohn and Upendra Baxi (eds), *The Rights of Subordinated Peoples* (Delhi: Oxford University Press, 1994). 'The Greater Common Good' was also the title of a powerful essay by acclaimed author Arundhati Roy that helped revive public interest in the Narmada Andolan when it had received a setback in the Supreme Court. See Arundhati Roy, 'The Greater Common Good', *Outlook*, 24 May 1999.

32. For details and discussion of such strategies, see chapter 9 in Baviskar, *In the Belly of the River*.

33. Ramachandra Guha, *Savaging the Civilized: Verrier Elwin, His Tribals, and India* (New Delhi: Oxford University Press, 1999).

34. Sanjeev Khagram, *Dams and Development: Transnational Struggles for Water and Power* (Ithaca, NY: Cornell University Press, 2004).

35. For a discussion of the politics of claiming indigenous status for adivasis, see Amita Baviskar, 'The Politics of Being "Indigenous"', *Indigeneity in India*, (eds) Bengt G. Karlsson and Tanka Subba (London: Kegan Paul, 2006), pp. 33–50.

36. Michael Levien, *Dispossession without Development: Land Grabs in Neoliberal India* (New York: Oxford University Press, 2018). Also see Kenneth Bo Nielsen and Patrik Oskarsson (eds), *Industrialising Rural India: Land, Policy and Resistance* (New Delhi: Routledge, 2016).

37. David Harvey, *The New Imperialism* (New York: Oxford University Press, 2003). Also see, Saturnino Borras Jr, Ruth Hall, Ian Scoones, Ben White and Wendy Wolford, 'Towards a Better Understanding of Global Land Grabbing: An Editorial Introduction', *Journal of Peasant Studies*, 38:2 (2011), pp. 209–216.

38. Felix Padel and Samarendra Das, *Out of this Earth: East India Adivasis and the Aluminium Cartel* (New Delhi: Orient Blackswan, 2010).

39. See Kenneth Bo Nielsen, *Land Dispossession and Everyday Politics in Rural Eastern India* (London: Anthem Press, 2018); and Sarasij Majumder, *People's Car: Industrial India and the Riddles of Populism* (New York: Fordham University Press, 2018).

40. Preeti Sampat, 'Special Economic Zones in India: Reconfiguring Displacement in a Neoliberal Order?' *City and Society*, 22:2 (2010), pp. 166–182.

41. Pollution from industries and rapidly growing cities is also a major threat to river water quality but will not be discussed here. On this subject, see Kelly D. Alley, *On the Banks of the Ganga: When Wastewater Meets a Sacred River* (Ann Arbor, MI: University of Michigan Press, 2002); Amita Baviskar, 'What the Eye Does Not See: River Yamuna in the Imagination of Delhi', *Economic and Political Weekly*, 46:50 (10 December 2011), pp. 45–53; Victor Mallet, *River of Life, River of Death: The Ganges and India's Future* (New Delhi: Oxford University Press, 2016). Nor will I discuss the recent project to make the Ganga river navigable, a project with far-reaching ecological implications. For analyses, see studies and articles by Manthan Kendra at https://www.manthanindia.org/work-theme/inland-waterways/articles-waterways/.

42. Amita Baviskar, 'The Damned Brahmaputra', *India Today*, 7 September 2009.

43. A farmers' organization in Assam state, Krishak Mukti Sangram Samiti, has been opposing these dams but has made little headway since they are to be constructed in another state (Arunachal Pradesh).

44. Emmanuel Theophilus, *Mahakali: Ghost River*, Unpublished manuscript (2018).

45. See Joanna Van Gruisen, 'Ken-Betwa Link: Creating, Not Solving, Water Woes', *Current Conservation*, 11:1 (2017), pp. 4–10

46. Raksha Kumar, 'Where is the Data to Support the Government's Rationale for Linking the Ken and Betwa Rivers?' Scroll, 26 March 2017.

47. A rare departure from this silence seems to be a student organization from the Idu Mishmi Scheduled Tribe in the Dibang river valley, who number only 12,000, that has voiced concerns about the implications of tens of thousands of migrant construction workers coming to live in the area for decades, drastically changing its cultural politics. See Neeraj Vagholikar and P.J. Das, *Damming Northeast India: Juggernaut of Hydropower Projects Threatens Socialand Environmental Security of Region* (Pune: Kalpavriksh, Aaranyak and ActionAid India, 2010), p. 7.

48. Charles Tilly, *Popular Contention in Great Britain, 1758–1834* (New York: Routledge, 2005).

49. Guha and Martinez-Alier, *Varieties of Environmentalism*, p. 13.

50. The most contentious of these claims relates to the fifteenth-century Babri Masjid in Faizabad, north India, which was demolished on 6 December 1992, by a mob of Hindu nationalists on the grounds that it stood on the birthplace of Ram, a Hindu deity. The leadup to the demolition whipped up anti-Muslim sentiments and the riots that followed resulted in large-scale violence across the country, including the deaths of more than 2000 people, mainly Muslim. After protracted litigation, the Supreme Court awarded the disputed site to Hindu plaintiffs in November 2019, months after the Hindu supremacist Bharatiya Janata Party had been returned to power with a massive parliamentary majority.

51. Mary Douglas, *Purity and Danger: An Analysis of Concepts of Pollution and Taboo* (London: Routledge, 1966).

52. Angana P. Chatterji, *Violent Gods: Hindu Nationalism in India's Present, Narratives from Orissa* (Hyderabad: Three Essays Collective, 2009). Also see Amita Baviskar, 'Adivasi Encounters with Hindu Nationalism in MP', *Economic and Political Weekly*, 40:48 (26

November 2005), pp. 5105–13; and Nandini Sundar, 'Teaching to Hate', *Economic and Political Weekly*, 39:16 (17 April 2004), pp. 1605–1612.

53.   Padel and Das, *Out of this Earth*.

54.   In the case of contemporary anti-dam campaigns, culturalist claims were also successfully invoked by Buddhist communities in Sikkim state to stop a project on the Teesta river. See Vibha Arora, '"They are All Set to Dam(n) Our Future": Contested Development through Hydel Power in Democratic Sikkim', *Sociological Bulletin*, 58:1 (2002).

55.   See their website: https://sandrp.in/.

56.   Ishan Kukreti, 'Supreme Court stays Uttarakhand High Court's Order Declaring Ganga and Yamuna "Living Entities"', *Down to Earth*, 7 July 2017.

57.   Ramachandra Guha, 'The Authoritarian Biologist and the Arrogance of Anti-humanism: Wildlife Conservation in the Third World', *Ecologist*, 27:1 (1997), pp. 14–20.

Chapter 5: Weaving Our Way through Environmental Justice Movements in India

1.   Ramachandra Guha, 'The Past and Present of Indian Environmentalism', *The Hindu*, 27 March 2013.

2.   Ramachandra Guha and Madhav Gadgil, *This Fissured Land* (Delhi: Oxford University Press, 1992); Ramachandra Guha and Madhav Gadgil, *Ecology and Equity* (New Delhi: Penguin, 1995); Ramachandra Guha and Joan Martinez-Alier, *Varieties of Environmentalism: Essays North and South* (Abingdon: Earthscan, 1997).

3.   Leah Temper et al., 'The Global Environmental Justice Atlas (EJAtlas): Ecological Distribution Conflicts as Forces for Sustainability', *Sustainability Science*, 13:3 (2018), pp. 573–84.

4.   Leah Temper et al., 'Mapping the Frontiers and Front Lines of Global Environmental Justice: The EJAtlas', *Journal of Political Ecology*, 22:1 (2015), pp. 255–278.

5.   For India, until 2019, the EJAtlas has drawn mainly on efforts by Swapan Kumar Patra (at Jawaharlal Nehru University between 2012 and 2015), Federico Demaria, Daniela Del Bene, Radhika Mulay, Eleonora Fanari and us.

6. Arnim Scheidel et al., 'Ecological Distribution Conflicts as Forces for Sustainability: An Overview and Conceptual Framework', *Sustainability Science*, 13:3 (2018), pp. 585–98.

7. Willi Haas et al., 'How Circular is the Global Economy?: An Assessment of Material Flows, Waste Production, and Recycling in the European Union and the World in 2005', *Journal of Industrial Ecology*, 19:5 (2015), pp. 765–77.

8. Joan Martinez-Alier et al., 'Is There a Global Environmental Justice Movement?', *Journal of Peasant Studies*, 43:3 (2016), pp. 731–755.

9. Joan Martinez-Alier, *The Environmentalism of the Poor: A Study of Ecological Conflicts and Valuation* (New Delhi: Oxford University Press, 2005).

10. Brototi Roy, 'Ecological Distribution Conflicts in India: A Bird's Eye View', *Ecologia Politica*, 55 (2018).

11. EJAtlas, 'Kaziranga Conflict: Rhinos and Poachers', 2017.

12. Sanjay Barbora, 'Riding the Rhino: Conservation, Conflicts, and Militarisation of Kaziranga National Park in Assam', *Antipode*, 49:5 (2017), pp. 1145–1163.

13. 'Protest Meet Against Proposed Eco-Sensitive Zone', *Assam Tribune*, 9 July 2019.

14. 'Rally at Bagori Tomorrow against SC Directive', *Assam Tribune*, 9 May 2019.

15. Eleonora Fanari, 'Relocation from Protected Areas as a Violent Process in the Recent History of Biodiversity Conservation in India', Ecology, *Economy and Society—The INSEE Journal*, 2:1 (2019), pp. 43 –76.

16. EJAtlas, 'Land and Livelihood Conflicts in Bhitarkanika Wildlife Sanctuary and Mangrove Forest, Odisha', 2018.

17. 'Odisha Villagers Residents Stage Protest against Illegal Prawn Farms', *New Indian Express*, 25 June 2019.

18. Ramachandra Guha, *The Unquiet Woods: Ecological Change and Peasant Resistance in the Himalaya* (New Delhi: Oxford University Press, 1999).

19. EJAtlas, 'Appiko Movement. Western Ghats', 2014.

20. Manisha Rao, 'In the Margins: Environment, Resources and Livelihoods in the Appiko Chaluvali', *Journal of Social and Economic Development*, 14:2 (2012), pp. 155–181.

21. 2017 marked the thirtieth anniversary of the Save Western Ghats March, which was started in 1987–88 to conserve the 1600-odd km long Western Ghats spanning six states, and home to a diverse flora and fauna as well as to many human communities and cultures. More information at http://www.savethewesternghats.org/

22. EJAtlas, 'Brewery Project Destroying Jhinkargadi Forest in Balarampur Village, Odisha', 2018.

23. EJAtlas, 'Fishworkers Struggle in Kerala', 2018.

24. Nalini Nayak, 'The Kerala Fishworkers' Struggle', *A Space within the Struggle*, (ed.) Ilina Sen (New Delhi: Kali for Women, 1990), pp.141–59.

25. John Kurien, *Towards a New Agenda for Sustainable Small-Scale Fisheries Development* (Trivandrum: South Indian Federation of Fishermen Societies, 1996).

26. Mathew Aerthavil, *Fishworkers Movement in Kerala (1977–1994)* (New Delhi: India Social Institute, 2000).

27. Ibid.

28. EJAtlas, 'Sterlite Copper Smelter Unit, Tamil Nadu, India', 2018.

29. The Centre for Science and Environment (CSE) published a book called *Slow Murder* on the deadly story of vehicular pollution in India in November 1996. The CSE applied the term also to the struggle against endosulfan in cashew plantations in Kerala.

30. EJAtlas, 'Unilever Refused Responsibility for Kodaikanal Mercury Poisoning', 2018.

31. The song came out in 2015, written and performed by Chennai-born rapper Sofia Ashraf titled *Kodaikanal Won't* and a second one came out in 2018 titled *Kodaikanal Still Won't* performed by Amrit Rao, Sofia Ashraf and T.M. Krishna.

32. Sarah Hiddleston, 'Poisoned Ground', *Frontline*, 2:19 (24 September 2010).

33. EJAtlas, 'Ennore Coal Power Plant and Fisherfolk Protest, North Chennai, India', 2017.

34. The song can be heard and viewed in this link: https://video.scroll.in/826772/watch-tm-krishna-sings-to-arouse-people-intopreventing-chennais-environmental-degradation.

35. EJAtlas, 'Kashipur Anti-bauxite Mining Movement', 2017.

36. EJAtlas, 'Kudankulam Nuclear Power Plant', 2016.

37. 'Anti-Kudankulam protests turn violent, one killed in police firing', *Times of India*, 10 September 2012.

38. EJAtlas, 'Kudankulam Nuclear Power Plant', 2016.

39. Starting from the Narmada Bachao Andolan, India has witnessed many cases of dam conflicts. There is a featured map dedicated to environmental justice movements in Himachal Pradesh, most of which are about dams: https://ejatlas.org/featured/himachal_pradesh.

40. EJAtlas, 'Nyamjang Chhu Dam and Hydropower Expansion in Tawang, Arunachal Pradesh', 2016.

41. Sangeeta Barooah Pisharoty, 'Police Firing, Hydel Projects Cast Long Shadow over Arunachal's Sensitive Tawang Region', The Wire, 3 May 2016.

42. Arpita Bisht and Julien-François Gerber, 'Ecological Distribution Conflicts (EDCs) over Mineral Extraction in India: An Overview', *The Extractive Industries and Society*, 4:3 (2017), pp. 548–63.

43. Sofia Avila, 'Environmental Justice and the Expanding Geography of Wind Power Conflicts', *Sustainability Science*, 13:3 (2018), pp. 599–616.

44. Brototi Roy and Joan Martinez-Alier, 'Environmental Justice Movements in India: An Analysis of the Multiple Manifestations of Violence', Ecology, *Economy and Society—The INSEE Journal*, 2:1(2019), pp. 77–92.

Part II: The Makers of Indian Democracy

Chapter 6: Travels within the Self: M. Lakshmi and Her Letters from London

1. Tanika Sarkar, 'A Book of Her Own. A Life of Her Own: Autobiography of a Nineteenth-Century Woman', *From Myths to Markets: Essays on Gender*, (eds) Kumkum Sangari and Uma Chakravarti (New Delhi & Shimla: Manohar and Indian Institute for Advanced Study, 1999), p. 85.

2. Malavika Karlekar, *Voices from Within: Early Personal Narratives of Bengali Women* (Delhi: Oxford University Press, 1991), p. 11.

3. Binodini Dasi, *My Story and My Life as an Actress*, Rimli Bhattacharya (ed.) (New Delhi: Kali for Women, 1998).

4. Antoinette Burton, *Dwelling in the Archive: Women Writing House, Home, and History in Late Colonial India* (Delhi: Oxford University Press, 2003), p. 4.

5. It was Tamil convention to affix the honorific 'Ammal' to the names of respectable women. Though all of her writings were published under the name Lakshmi Ammal I refer to her throughout this essay as Lakshmi.

6. Interestingly, Lakshmi wrote the entry on her father in the Tamil encyclopedia, *Kalaikkalanjiyam* (Chennai: Tamil Valarchi Kazhagam, 1961), p. 218.

7. R.S. Subbalakshmi (1886–1969) aka Sister Subbalakshmi. A child widow, she is said to be the first Hindu woman to graduate in the Madras Presidency. In 1912, she founded the Sarada Ladies Union to bring together like-minded middle-class women interested in social issues. She also founded Sarada Illam, a home that provided rehabilitation and education for widows. The first principal of the Lady Willingdon College that provided teacher training, she was an active member of the All-India Women's Conference and the Women's Indian Association.

8. Lady Andal (1894–1969). Widowed early in life, Andal had the benefit of a good education. Against great odds, she married Justice M. Venkatasubba Rao, and in 1928 founded the Madras Seva Sedan, an institution to support destitute children and women, with her own resources.

9. Mary Clubwala Jadhav (1909–1975). A Parsi philanthropist based in Chennai, she organized relief for injured soldiers in World War II and was the founder of the Madras School of Social Work.

10. P. Sri. (ed.), *Munnila* (Chennai: Dinamani, 1944). In the October 1924 issue of *Panchamirtam* she published an abridged translation of a lecture by one Prof. Soddy from his *The Future of Economics and Scientific Thought*.

11. 'Tamil Vacanam' [Tamil Prose] published under the pseudonym 'Sri' was published in the inaugural issue of the celebrated Tamil monthly, *Kalaimagal*, 1:1 (January 1932). (It is from Kalki's review of this issue that we know the author's identity.); 'Tamilum Aangilamum' [Tamil and English], *Kumari Malar*, 5:11 (December 1948); 'Nigalchi Chithiram' [Portrait of an Event], *Chintanai*, September 1948. It is interesting to note that all these pieces are structured as a conversation between a few women rather than as essays with a single authorial voice.

12. Personal communication from Girija Madhavan, the daughter of Mukta Venkatesh, Madhaviah's youngest daughter. I am also grateful to Dr P.N. Aruna, granddaughter of Madhaviah's nephew P.N. Appuswami for sharing information.

13. For a biography in English, see Sita Anantha Raman, *A. Madhaviah* (New Delhi: Oxford University Press, 2005). Su. Venkatraman, *A. Madhaviah* (New Delhi: Sahitya Akademi, 1999), published in the Makers of Indian Literature series, provides an overview of his life and work. On his novels, see P.G. Sundararajan (Chitti) and S. Sivapathasundaram, *Tamil Novel: Noorandu Varalarum Valarchiyum* (Chennai: Christian Literature Society, 1977), esp. pp. 29–43.

14. Sudhir Chandra, *The Oppressive Present: Literature and Social Consciousness in Colonial India* (Delhi: Oxford University Press, 1992), p. 18.

15. Arvind Krishna Mehrotra (ed.), *An Illustrated History of Indian Literature in English* (New Delhi: Permanent Black, 2006), pp. 96–7; K.R. Srinivasa Iyengar, *Indian Writing in English* (New Delhi: Sterling, 1962, 2006), p. 325.

16. I met 'Mukta-amma' in 2002 in Mysore. She was a hundred years old then, but healthy and busy painting watercolours. We had lunch together: while she ate everything served on the table, I had to avoid some dishes due to medical advice!

17. I fondly remember Dr Meenakshi Tyagarajan, Madhaviah's granddaughter. Her house was right next to my office, the Madras Institute of Development Studies, Chennai. Living independently, she was a person of considerable achievement in her own right with a PhD in economics from the US in the 1950s, and a career in the research wing of the Reserve Bank of India. A voracious reader, towards the end of her life, she translated into English the first Tamil novel, Mayuram S. Vedanayakam Pillai's *The Life and Times of Pratapa Mudaliar* (New Delhi: Katha, 2005) and her own grandfather's novel, *Padmavati* (New Delhi: Katha, 2005). She also wrote a short book in Tamil on the early Tamil novelists.

18. This was written possibly in 1893, but published only in the 1970s, and therefore unavailable as a model to his contemporaries.

19. Sundararajan and Sivapathasundaram, *Tamil Novel*, p. 43.

20. In a curious case of appropriation, Vakulabharanam Rajagopal has traced a Telugu version of this novel: published in 1916 from Kakinada, the book itself does not carry the name of the translator/ editor but, according to Rajagopal, the British Library's catalogue identifies him as R. Kaustubham. Titled *Minakshi: Oka Brahmana Balika Sonta Caritra* (identical to the Tamil title), it is a faithful translation 'with some differences in details'. Rajagopal, 'Man with a Woman's Voice: Reading Minaksi's Fictional Autobiography', *Itihas*, 28 (January-December 2002).

21. Anantha Raman, *A. Madhaviah*, p. 46. The relevant footnote cites an article by P.N. Appuswamy and an interview with her granddaughter T. Meenakshi (Dr Meenakshi Tyagarajan). According to Rajagopal, the editor of the Telugu version notes the same detail of its serialization in the *Social Reform Advocate* and its translation by 'an educated woman relative'. I have not been able to trace this translation. A new translation of this novel, by Vasantha Surya, is appended to Anantha Raman, *A. Madhaviah*, pp. 121–88.

22. A.R. Venkatachalapathy, 'Excising the Self: Writing Autobiography in Colonial Tamilnadu', *In Those Days There Was No Coffee: Writings in Cultural History* (New Delhi: Yoda Press, 2006).

23. Subramania Bharati, *Kanavu* (Puducherry: Published by author, 1910).

24. Mattison Mines, *Public Faces, Private Voices: Community and Individuality in South India* (Berkeley: University of California Press, 1994), p. 4.

25. Jeeviya Charithira Churukkam was probably published in the later 1930s. For a recent critical edition see Stalin Rajangam (ed.), Rettamalai R. Srinivasan, *Jeeviya Charithira Churukkam* (Nagercoil: Kalachuvadu Pathippagam, 2017).

26. Tanika Sarkar, 'A Book of Her Own', p. 97.

Chapter 7: The Singing Satyagrahi: Khurshedben Naoroji and the Challenge of Indian Biography

1. Ramachandra Guha, 'A Bare Cupboard', *Times Literary Supplement*, 30 August 2002, p. 12.

2. Her legal name appears to have been Khurshedbanoo, and, aside from Khurshed, the shortened form of her name was occasionally

rendered as Khorshed. For the sake of consistency, and in order to distinguish her from other members of the Naoroji family, I have referred to her as Khurshedben throughout this article.

3. Khurshedben's three elder sisters—Perin, Gosi and Nurgis—married three brothers of the Captain family, a wealthy Bombay Parsi family. Some sources erroneously refer to Khurshedben as Khurshed Captain, but Khurshedben never married and hence kept her maiden name.

4. Parinaz Gandhi, 'In the Tradition of Dadabhai Naoroji', *Parsiana*, March 1993, p. 69.

5. Rustom P. Masani, *Dadabhai Naoroji: The Grand Old Man of India* (London: G. Allen & Unwin, Ltd, 1939), pp. 338 and 346; Behramji Malabari to Dadabhai Naoroji, 14 October 1893, National Archives of India (hereafter referred to as NAI), Dadabhai Naoroji Papers, M-32 (360).

6. Khurshedben Naoroji (hereafter referred to as KN) to Dadabhai Naoroji, in Virbai Naoroji to Dadabhai Naoroji, 14 April 1906, NAI, Dadabhai Naoroji Papers, uncatalogued item.

7. Email correspondence with Roger Jeffery, director, Edinburgh India Institute, University of Edinburgh, 8 November 2014.

8. Bhikhaiji Rustomji Cama to Dadabhai Naoroji, 22 November 1906, NAI, Dadabhai Naoroji Papers, C-13 (7); Nawaz Mody, 'Perin Captain: From Dadabhai to Mahatma Gandhi', *Women in India's Freedom Struggle* (Mumbai: Allied Publishers, 2000), pp. 206–7; 'History Sheet of Madame Bhikhaiji Rustom K.R. Cama', August 1913, NAI, Home Department—Political, Part B, p. 61.

9. A number of Khurshedben's letters are currently missing from Jawaharlal Nehru's papers at the Nehru Memorial Museum and Library, *Jawaharlal Nehru Correspondence, 1903–47: A Catalogue* (New Delhi: Vikas Publishing House, 1988), p. 368; *Collected Works of Mahatma Gandhi* (Delhi: Publications Division, Ministry of Information and Broadcasting, 1958–1994) (hereafter referred to as *CWMG*), Vol. 35, 292.

10. 'History Sheet of Madame Bhikhaiji Rustom K.R. Cama'; 'Bombay Chamber Orchestra: Third Popular Matinee', *Times of India*, 1 August 1925, p. 14.

11. 'From My Musical Sketch-Book', *Times of India*, 31 December 1950, p. 3; Artemis Leontis, 'An American in Paris, a Parsi in Athens', *A Singular Antiquity: Archaeology and Hellenic Identity in Twentieth-*

Century Greece, ed. Dimitris Damaskos and Dimitris Plantzos (Athens: Mouseio Benaki, 2008), p. 359.

12. Eva Palmer Sikelianos, *Upward Panic: The Autobiography of Eva Palmer-Sikelianos*, (ed.) John P. Anton (Chur, Switzerland: Harwood Academic Publishers, 1993), p. 97.

13. Ibid., pp. 97 and 98; Leontis, 'An American in Paris, a Parsi in Athens', p. 363.

14. Sikelianos, *Upward Panic*, pp. 98–99; Leontis, 'An American in Paris, a Parsi in Athens', p. 366.

15. Sikelianos, *Upward Panic*, p. 98; Leontis, 'An American in Paris, a Parsi in Athens', p. 368; KN to Eva Palmer Sikelianos, 20 December 1924, Benaki Museum Historical Archives, Eva Sikelianou Papers.

16. KN to Sikelianos, 3 April 1925 and 'Sunday' 1925, Benaki Museum Historical Archives, Eva Sikelianou Papers.

17. 'Bombay Chamber Orchestra: A Successful Concert', *Times of India*, 21 January 1928; *CWMG*, Vol. 37, p. 351; *CWMG*, Vol. 38, p. 346; KN to Pyarelal Nayyar, 2 July 1931, Nehru Memorial Museum and Library (hereafter referred to as NMML), M.K. Gandhi (Pyarelal) Papers (hereafter referred to as MKG[P]P), XVth instalment, S.N. 29.

18. KN to Mohandas K. Gandhi (hereafter referred to as MKG), 22 April 1930 and 1 May 1930, NMML, MKG(P)P, XVth instalment, S.N. 29; *CWMG*, Vol. 43, p. 349.

19. Numerous works mention but offer no sufficient citation for Khurshedben's supposed protest to Gandhi about excluding women from the Salt March. Aparna Basu, 'The Role of Women in the Indian Struggle for Freedom', *Indian Women: From Purdah to Modernity* (Delhi: Vikas Publishing House, 1976), 23; *CWMG*, Vol. 43, pp. 169–70, p. 239; 'Procession in Honour of Bhagat Singh', *Bombay Chronicle*, 26 September 1931, p. 7.

20. *CWMG*, Vol. 50, p. 266; *CWMG*, Vol. 55, pp. 197–98.

21. *CWMG*, Vol. 55, p. 197; KN to Devadas Gandhi, n.d., NMML, Devadas Gandhi Papers.

22. KN to Devadas Gandhi, n.d., NMML, Devadas Gandhi Papers.

23. *CWMG*, Vol. 52, p. 269; KN to Sikelianos, 24 January 1936, Benaki Museum Historical Archives, Eva Sikelianou Papers; KN to MKG, 3 June 1935, NMML, MKG(P)P, XVth installment, S.N. 29; MKG to KN, 5 June 1935, NMML, MKG(P)P, XVth installment, S.N. 29; *CWMG*, Vol. 59, p. 73 and p. 76.

24. *CWMG*, Vol. 66, p. 209, p. 210.

25. MKG to KN, 21 October 1940, NMML, Fateh Chand Papers, uncatalogued item.

26. KN to MKG, 11 April 1940 and 26 September 1941, NMML, MKG(P)P, XVth instalment, S.N. 29.

27. KN to MKG, 19 May 1940, 27 September 1940 and 17 November 1940, NMML, MKG(P)P, XVth instalment, S.N. 29.

28. KN to MKG, 17 November 1940, NMML, MKG(P)P, XVth instalment, S.N. 29.

29. KN to MKG, 2 December 1940, NMML, MKG(P)P, XVth instalment, S.N. 29; KN, speech, n.d., NMML, Fateh Chand Papers, uncatalogued item; KN to MKG, 2 December 1940 and 30 September 1941, NMML, MKG(P)P, XVth instalment, S.N. 29.

30. KN to MKG, 17 November 1940, NMML, MKG(P)P, XVth instalment, S.N. 29.

31. KN to MKG, 19 May 1940, 21 October 1940 and 13 May 1940, NMML, MKG(P)P, XVth instalment, S.N. 29.

32. KN to MKG, 5 May 1940, 17 November 1940 and 13 May 1940, NMML, MKG(P)P, XVth instalment, S.N. 29.

33. Mohammad Jan to MKG, 7 December 1940, NMML, MKG(P)P, XVth instalment, S.N. 29; KN to MKG, 17 November 1940, NMML, MKG(P)P, XVth installment, S.N. 29; D.G.H. de la Fargue to KN, 8 May 1940, NMML, MKG(P)P, XVth instalment, S.N. 29.

34. KN to MKG, 2 December 1940 and 3 December 1940, NMML, MKG(P)P, XVth instalment, S.N. 29.

35. *CWMG*, Vol. 74, pp. 208-9, p. 210.

36. 'Security Prisoners—Kurshedben [sic] Naoroji. Retransfer of— from Bhagalpur Jail to Yeravda Central Prison. Cancellation of Restrictions Imposed on Her', 1944, Maharashtra State Archives, Home Department—Special Branch, file no. 20.

37. KN to MKG, 24 October 1941, 2 October 1940, 17 November 1940 and 30 September 1941, NMML, MKG(P)P, XVth instalment, S.N. 29.

38. KN to MKG, n.d., 31 March 1941 and 30 September 1941, NMML, MKG(P)P, XVth instalment, S.N. 29.

39. KN to MKG, 31 March 1941, 5 May 1940 and 30 September 1941, NMML, MKG(P)P, XVth instalment, S.N. 29.

40. KN to MKG, 13 May 1940 and 11 June 1940, NMML, MKG(P)P, XVth instalment, S.N. 29.

41. Ibid.

42. Mohammad Jan to MKG, 7 December 1940, NMML, MKG(P)P, XVth instalment, S.N. 29.

43. KN to S.K. Patil, 9 October 1944, NMML, Bombay Pradesh Congress Committee Papers, file no. 80; *CWMG*, Vol. 81, p. 365; 'Proposed Indian Medical Mission for Viet-Nam,' *Bombay Chronicle*, 16 January 1947, p. 5; *CWMG*, Vol. 81, p. 399; *CWMG*, Vol. 90, p. 468.

44. KN to Brijkrishanji, 8 January 1948, NMML, Fateh Chand Papers, uncatalogued item.

45. Sarosh A.D. Naoroji, who died on 21 June 1980, was the last surviving sibling. Sita Anantha Raman, *Women in India: A Social and Cultural History*, Vol. 2 (Santa Barbara: Praeger, 2009), p. 165.

46. 'Bombay Concert', *Times of India*, 24 January 1951, p. 5.

47. 'Tit-Willow', *Time*, 25 September 1944, p. 40.

Chapter 8: 'Grocer, Tailor, Champion Wrestler': The Transnational Career of Buttan Singh, c. 1900–1912

1. *Age* (Melbourne), 17 October 1904, p. 6; *Advertiser* (Melbourne), 25 May 1904, p. 6.

2. *Age* (Melbourne), 7 November 1904, p. 9.

3. Ibid.

4. *Age* (Melbourne), 8 November 1904, p. 6.

5. *Sydney Sportsman*, 23 November 1904, p. 8.

6. Simon Wilde, *Ranji: The Strange Genius of Ranjitsinhji* (London: Aurum, 1999); Satadru Sen, *Migrant Races: Empire, Identity and K.S. Ranjitsinhji* (Manchester University Press: Manchester, 2004).

7. On Jamsetji Marker, see Prashant Kidambi, *Cricket Country: The Untold History of the First All India Team* (Penguin Random House India: Delhi, 2019), pp. 225–32.

8. S. Mazumdar, *Strong Men over the Years: A Chronicle of Athletes* (Lucknow, 1942), pp. 64–74; Joseph S. Alter, 'Gama the World Champion: Wrestling and Physical Culture in Colonial India', *Iron Game History*, 4:2 (October 1995), pp. 3-9.

9. On Baloo's career and times, see Ramachandra Guha, *A Corner of a Foreign Field: The Indian History of a British Sport* (London: Picador, 2002) and Kidambi, *Cricket Country*.

10. Clare Anderson, 'Introduction to Marginal Centers: Writing Life Histories in the Indian Ocean World', *Journal of Social History*, 45:2 (Winter 2011), pp. 335–44; Samia Khatun, *Australianama: The South Asian Odyssey in Australia* (Hurst: London, 2018).

11. On 'imperial globalization', see T.N. Harper, 'Empire, Diaspora and the Languages of Globalism, 1850–1914', *Globalization and World History*, (ed.) A.G. Hopkins (Pimlico: London, 2002), pp. 141–66.

12. Sunil Amrith, *Migration and Diaspora in Modern Asia* (Cambridge: Cambridge University Press, 2011), pp. 25–56.

13. Ibid.

14. Neeladri Bhattacharya, *The Great Agrarian Conquest: The Colonial Reshaping of a Rural World* (SUNY: Buffalo, 2019), pp. 385–441; Tom Kessinger, *Vilayatpur 1848–1968: Social and Economic Change in a North Indian Village* (Berkeley: University of California Press, 1974), pp. 90–92.

15. Ian Simpson, 'Decent Fellows, Making an Honest Living in India: Indian Hawkers in White Australia', *History Australia*, 13:3 (2016), pp. 321–34.

16. Thomas R. Metcalf, *Imperial Connections: India in the Indian Ocean Arena, 1860–1920* (Berkeley and Los Angeles: University of California Press, 2007), pp. 102–35; Isabella Jackson, 'The Raj on Nanjing Road: Sikh Policemen in Treaty-Port Shanghai', *Modern Asian Studies*, 46:6 (November 2012), pp. 1672–1704.

17. Simpson, 'Decent Fellows', pp. 323–24.

18. Kessinger, *Vilayatpur*, p. 92.

19. Stuart Macintyre, *A Concise History of Australia* (Cambridge: Cambridge University Press, 2004), pp. 121–55.

20. Anthony T. Yarwood, 'The Dictation Test—Historical Survey', *The Australian Quarterly*, 30:2 (June 1958), pp. 19–29; A.C. Palfreeman, 'Non-White Immigration to Australia', *Pacific Affairs*, 47:3 (Autumn 1974), pp. 344–57.

21. Yarwood, 'Dictation Test', p. 25.

22. Kama Maclean, 'Examinations, Access and Iniquity within the Empire: Britain, Australia and India, 1890–1910', *Postcolonial Studies*, 18:2 (2015), pp. 115–32.

23. Margaret Allen, '"Innocents abroad" and "Prohibited Immigrants": Australians in India and Indians in Australia 1890–1910', *Connected Worlds: History in Transnational Perspective*, (eds) Ann Curthoys and Marilyn Lake (Canberra: ANU Press, 2005), pp. 111–24.

24. Nahid A. Kabir, 'The Economic Plight of the Afghans in Australia, 1860–2000', *Islamic Studies*, 44:2 (2005), pp. 229–50.

25. Simpson, 'Decent Fellows', pp. 325–28.

26. Maclean, 'Examinations', pp. 118–19

27. *Bulletin* (Sydney), 30 July 1903, p. 26.

28. Ibid.

29. *Bulletin* (Sydney), 3 August 1905, p. 15.

30. See, for instance, *Manchester Courier*, 23 September 1905, p. 10.

31. *Sportsman* (Melbourne),12 June 1900, p. 3.

32. Edward Hitchcock and R.F. Nelligan, *Wrestling: Catch-As-Catch-Can Style* (New York: 1912).

33. *Bulletin* (Sydney), 23 June 1900, p. 24.

34. *Argus* (Melbourne), 11 June 1900, p. 7.

35. *Wagga Wagga Express* (New South Wales), 16 June 1900, p. 3.

36. *Bulletin* (Sydney), 23 June 1900, p. 24.

37. Ibid.

38. Ibid.

39. *Herald* (Melbourne), 30 April 1903, p. 4.

40. *Sportsman* (Melbourne), 8 January 1901, p. 8.

41. *Leader* (Melbourne), 2 May 1903, p. 19.

42. *Bulletin* (Sydney), 9 May 1900, p. 26.

43. *Leader* (Melbourne), 2 May 1903, p. 19; *Argus* (Melbourne), 1 May 1903, p. 6. One newspaper put the figure at close to 4000. *Sportsman* (Melbourne), 5 May 1903, p. 4.

44. *Leader* (Melbourne), 2 May 1903, p. 19.

45. *Argus* (Melbourne), 2 June 1903, p. 6.

46. The dates of the fights have been extracted from contemporary Australian newspapers.

47. *Western Mail* (Perth), 2 January 1904, p. 38.

48. See, for instance, *Referee* (Sydney), 8 March 1905, p. 7.

49. *Age* (Melbourne), 13 February 1905, p. 6.

50. *Age* (Melbourne), 20 November 1906, p. 8.

51. Buttan Singh, Certificate of Exemption from Dictation Test, Fremantle, 28 June 1909, K1145, 1909/124, National Archives of Australia, Canberra.

52. We know the date because the Board of Trade in the United Kingdom collected information about passengers on ships arriving in, and departing from, the country from non-European ports. Buttan's name appears in the passenger list of the *SS Pericles*, which docked in London on 6 August 1909; *Board of Trade: Commercial and Statistical Department: Inwards Passenger Lists*; Series BT26, the National Archives, Kew, UK. Accessed via Ancestry.co.uk: UK, Incoming Passenger Lists, 1878 1960 (online database).

53. *Sportsman* (London), 24 August 1909, p. 2.

54. See Kidambi, *Cricket Country*, pp. 113–120.

55. *Scottish Referee* (Glasgow), 17 September 1909, p. 1.

56. *Health and Strength*, 6:9 (26 February 1910), p. 213.

57. Conor Heffernan, 'What's Wrong with a Little Swinging? Indian Clubs as a Tool of Suppression and Rebellion in Post-Rebellion India', *International Journal of the History of Sport*, 34: 7–8 (2017), p. 568.

58. *Sporting Life* (London), 27 December 1909, p. 2.

59. *Health and Strength*, 6:6 (5 February 1910), pp. 126–33; *The Times*, 25 February 1910, p. 21; *The Times*, 21 June 1910, p. 19; *The Times*, 19 December 1910, p. 18; *The Times*, 20 December 1910, p. 17.

60. *Sporting Life* (London), 2 February 1910, p. 6.

61. *Sporting Life* (London), 4 February 1910, p. 6.

62. Ibid.

63. *Sporting Life* (London), 14 May 1910, p. 3.

64. *Health and Strength*, 7:4 (23 July 1910), p. 96.

65. Ibid.

66. Ibid.

67. *Health and Strength*, 6:20 (14 May 1910), p. 521.

68. *Sporting Life* (London) 1 July 1910, p. 6.

69. *Health and Strength*, 7:15 (8 October 1910), p. 360.

70. *Sporting Life* (London), 30 September 1910, p. 5.

71. *Lancashire Evening Post*, 6 September 1910, p. 4; *Daily Mail* (Hull), 6 September 1910, p. 8.

72. *Sporting Life* (London), 30 September 1910, p. 5.

73. Kidambi, *Cricket Country*, pp. 241–45.

74. *Board of Trade, Commercial and Statistical Department: Outwards Passenger Lists*; Series BT27, the National Archives, Kew, UK. Accessed via Ancestry.co.uk: UK, Outward Passengers List, 1890–1960 (online database).

75. *Standard Union* (Brooklyn, New York), 8 March 1912, p. 14.

76. Matthew Taylor, 'The Global Ring? Boxing, Mobility, and Transnational Networks in the Anglophone World, 1890–1914', *Journal of Global History*, 8:2 (July 2013), p. 231.

77. For parallels with the career of Ranjitsinhji in England, see Sen, *Migrant Races*.

Chapter 9: Agyeya: Hindi Literature's First Freethinker

1. Rajiv Saxena, *Naya Path*, Issue 1, Year II, November 1954, Cited in a letter to Agyeya, 20 November 1954.

2. Agyeya's lady friend from Beijing, 2 December 1953, Agyeya Papers.

3. Krishna Dutt Paliwal (ed.), *Agyeya Ke Abhibhasan* (Lectures of Agyeya), Vol. II, (Delhi: Sasta Sahitya Mandal, 2012), pp. 176–182.

4. Hirananda Sastri, 'Excavations at Kasia', *ASI Annual Report 1910–11* (India, Calcutta: Superintendent, Government Printing, 1914), p. 65.

5. F.E. Pargiter, 'The Kasia Copper Plate' in *ASI Annual Report 1910–11*, op cit., pp. 73–77.

6. Interview with Agyeya's niece Jyotsna Brar, July 2018.

7. Autobiographical note by Hirananda Sastri for DAV College Jubilee Book, August–September 1936. Agyeya Papers.

8. Ram Kamal Rai, *Shikhar Se Sagar Tak: Agyeya Ki Jiwan Yatra* (New Delhi: National Publishing House, 1997), pp. 24–25.

9. Raghuvir Sahay and Gopal Das, *Agyeya Apne Bare Main*, (New Delhi: Publications Division, 2012), p. 133–34.

10. Sachchidananda's Prison Diary, Agyeya Papers, 27 December 1930.

11. Ibid.

12. Joshua Kalapati and Ambrose Jeyasekaran T, *Life and Legacy of Madras Christian College 1837–1978* (Chennai: Zha Communications, 2010), pp. 52–70.

13. Prison Diary, Agyeya Papers, 1930.

14. Ibid.

15. Agyeya, 'Kirnon Ki Khoj Main' ('In Search of the Rays'), *Arre Yayavaar Rahega Yaad* (New Delhi: Rajkamal Prakashan 2015, first published in 1953), pp. 62–97.

16. Rai, *Shikhar Se Sagar Tak*, pp. 41–42. See also S.H. Vatsyayan, *Atmaparak* (reprint of *Likhi Kagad Kore* and *Atmanepad* in

one volume) (New Delhi: National Publishing House, 1983), pp. 177–78.

17. Ibid.

18. Rai, *Shikhar Se Sagar Tak*, p. 38

19. Prison Diary, Agyeya Papers, 1930.

20. Ibid.

21. Ibid.

22. Ibid.

23. Ibid.

24. Vatsyayan, 'Meri Pehli Kavita', *Atmaparak*, pp. 24–25.

25. Agyeya, 'Parche', *Karmvir* (Khandwa), 6 January 1940, Agyeya Papers.

26. Raghuvir Sahay and Gopal Das, *Agyeya Apne Bare Main*, Interview to All India Radio, (New Delhi: Publication Division, Information and Broadcasting Ministry, 2012), pp. 118–19.

27. Transcript of Agyeya's interview to Romesh Shonak of Duke University, (Delhi, July–August 1973), Agyeya Papers.

28. Fourth Instalment of Kailashpatti's Statement. Information obtained from Kailashpatti, the absconder in the Lahore Conspiracy case, who was arrested at Delhi by the local CID on the night of 28 October 1930, Agyeya Papers.

29. Girwar Singh's Statement and Fourth Instalment of Kailashpatti's Statement, Agyeya Papers.

30. Delhi Conspiracy Case. B (File No. 85) (Delhi: Chief Commissioner's Office, Home Department (Confidential, 1930), Delhi State Archives.

31. Rejection Letter from W.N.P Jenkin, Superintendent of Police, Political, CID Punjab, 26 July 1934, Agyeya Papers.

32. Jainendra Kumar to Agyeya, 30 October 1936, Agyeya Papers.

33. Transcript of Agyeya's interview to Romesh Shonak of Duke University, (Delhi, July–August 1973), Agyeya Papers.

34. M.N. Roy, *'Bharat ki Punarjagriti'* ('India's Reawakening'), *Sainik* (Agra: 2 and 16 March 1937).

35. Agyeya, *'Pad-Grahan'* ('Taking Office'), *Sainik* (Agra), 16 March 1937, p. 7.

36. Dr A. Latif, *'Hum Khadaghast Hi Haren'* ('We Should Lose with the Sword in Our Hand'), *Sainik* (Agra), 23 February 1937, pp. 5–6.

37. Rai, *Shikhar Se Sagar Tak*, p. 59.
38. Agyeya to Banarsi Das Chaturvedi, 27 January 1937, Agyeya Papers.
39. H. Bruno to Agyeya, 24 December 1933, Agyeya Papers.
40. C.F. Andrews to Agyeya, 26 January 1937, Agyeya Papers.
41. Agyeya to Banarsi Das Chaturvedi, 27 January 1937, Agyeya Papers.
42. Jawaharlal Nehru to Agyeya, 3 January 1937, Agyeya Papers.
43. S.H. Vatsyayana, 'Modern (Post-War) Hindi Poetry', *Visva-Bharati Quarterly* (Calcutta: August 1937) pp. 137–51.
44. Khagendra N. Sen, 'A National Language for India: The Claim of Bengali (A Literary Symposium at the Rabi Basar)', *Modern Review*, (May 1938), pp. 505–07.
45. Agyeya, 'Hindi aur Bangla' (Hindi and Bengali), *Sampadakiya Vichar* (Editorial Comment), (Calcutta: Vishal Bharat, June 1938), pp. 703–04.
46. Ramananda Chatterjee to Agyeya, 9 July 1938, Agyeya Papers.
47. Ibid.
48. Agyeya to Ramananda Chatterjee, Agyeya Papers.
49. Snehal Shingavi, 'Agyeya's Unfinished Revolution: Sexual and Social Freedom in *Shekhar: Ek Jivani*', *Journal of South Asian Studies*, 39:3 (2016), pp. 577–591.
50. Peter Gaeffke, *Hindi Literature in the Twentieth Century* (Delhi: Manohar, 2019, originally published in 1978), pp. 47–50.
51. Prabhakar Machwe, *Modernity and Contemporary Indian Literature* (New Delhi: Chetana Publications,1978), p. 98.
52. Nikhil Govind, *Between Love and Freedom: The Revolutionary in the Hindi Novel* (New Delhi: Routledge, 2014), pp.114–15.
53. Vatsaraj to Agyeya, 30 March 1941, Agyeya Papers.
54. Transcript of Agyeya's interview to Romesh Shonak of Duke University, (Delhi, July–August 1973), Agyeya Papers.
55. Ibid.
56. Kumari Sarla Chandel to Agyeya, 1954, Agyeya Papers.
57. Sahay and Das, *Agyeya Apne Bare Main*, p. 19.
58. Nemichandra Jain to Agyeya, 25 January 1941, Agyeya Papers.
59. Onkar Shankar Vidyarthi to Agyeya, Agyeya Papers.
60. Shivdan Singh Chauhan, 'Godan aur Shekhar', *Sahityanushilan* (Delhi: Atma Ram and Sons, 1955), pp. 229–31.
61. Ibid.

62. M. Bajpai, 'Shekhar: Ek Jiwani', *Modern Review*, (February 1943), pp. 143–144.

63. Nagendra, *Vichar Aur Anubhuti* (Second Edition) (New Delhi: Gautam Book Depot), pp. 143–45.

64. Agyeya married Santosh Kashyap on 1 July 1940 in Delhi. She came from a prominent Kashmiri family. They drifted apart soon, lived separately for long and were divorced in 1945. Santosh married her cousin Balraj Sahni and Agyeya, in the next few years, drew closer to Santosh's niece Kapila Malik. They got married in 1956.

65. Pamphlet of Anti-Fascist Conference, Agyeya Papers.

66. Netra Singh Rawat, 'Upanyas: Vedna, Vasna, Anushashan', *Agyeya Se Sakshatkar*, (ed.) Krishna Dutt Paliwal (New Delhi: Arya Prakashan Mandal, 2012), pp. 229–57.

67. Krishan Chander to Agyeya, Agyeya Papers.

68. Kripa Sen to Agyeya, 3 January 1943, Agyeya Papers.

69. S.H. Vatsyayana, '*Ansh-Dan*' in *Atmaparak*, pp. 299–308. The letter written in March 1943 is not part of Agyeya Papers but was used in Atmanepad. Name was taken out but clearly it was to a woman and addresses all questions that Kripa raised on 3 January 1943. Some personal matter was also taken out. There is another letter to a second person, a male, explaining why he joined army.

70. Vatsyayan, *Atmaparak*, pp. 185–86.

71. Lucy Rosenstein (ed.), *New Poetry in Hindi: Nayi Kavita: An Anthology* (London: Anthem Press, 2004), pp. 1–9.

72. Transcript of Agyeya's interview to Romesh Shonak of Duke University, (Delhi, July–August 1973), Agyeya Papers.

73. Ibid; Barbara Lotz, '*Rahon Ke Anvesi*: The Editor of the *Saptak*-Anthologies and His Poets', *Hindi Modernism: Rethinking Agyeya and His Times*, Vasudha Dalmia (ed.) (Berkeley: Centre for South Asia Studies, 2012), pp. 125–31.

74. Transcript of Agyeya's interview to Romesh Shonak of Duke University, (Delhi, July–August 1973), Agyeya Papers.

75. Sahay and Das, *Agyeya Apne Bare Main*, pp. 133–34.

76. Agyeya to M.N. Roy, 4 March 1949, M.N. Roy Papers, Nehru Memorial Museum & Library.

77. Document of the meeting of the Indian Congress for Cultural Freedom March 28 to 31 (Bombay: Kannada Press, August 1951).

78. Eric D. Pullin, '"Money Does Not Make Any Difference to the Opinions That We Hold": India, the CIA, and the Congress for Cultural Freedom, 1951–58', *Intelligence and National Security*, 26:2-3 (2011), pp. 377-98; Minutes of Proceedings of the Executive Committee of the Indian Committee for Cultural Freedom, International Association for Cultural Freedom Records, Box 173, Folder 8, University of Chicago Library Special Collections Research Center.

79. Giles Scott-Smith and Charlotte A. Lerg (eds.), *Campaigning Culture and the Global Cold War: The Journals of the Congress for Cultural Freedom* (London: Palgrave Macmillan, London, 2017), pp. 287–288.

80. Martin Russell to Agyeya, 3 August 1951, Agyeya Papers.

81. Jayaprakash Narayan, 'To the Detractors', *Everyman's*, 13 October 1973), p. 4.

82. Jayaprakash Narayan, 'Statement of Policy', *Everyman's*, 7 July 1973, p. 4.

83. 'Dissent and the Soviet Establishment: Freedom for All Men', *Everyman's*, 22 September 1973. p. 7.

84. Jayaprakash Narayan, 'The Day Jayaprakash Narayan Turns a Foreign Stooge, There Will Be No Patriot Left in This Country', *Everyman's*, 13 April 1974. p. 6.

85. Transcript of Agyeya's interview to Romesh Shonak of Duke University, (Delhi, July–August 1973), Agyeya Papers.

86. Walt Whitman, *Song of Myself* (London: Penguin, 1986), p. 84.

87. Transcript of Agyeya's interview to Romesh Shonak of Duke University, (Delhi, July–August 1973), Agyeya Papers.

88. Interview with Namvar Singh (Delhi, June 2016).

Chapter 10: Alone at Home, Among Friends Abroad? B.R. Shenoy from Austrian School Monetary Economist to Cold-War Public Intellectual

1. Guha, *India after Gandhi: The History of the World's Largest Democracy*,' (London: Picador, 2007), p. 223.

2. I.G. Patel, *Glimpses of Indian Economic Policy: An Insider's View*, (London: Oxford University Press, 2002), p. 41; Patel (1924–2005) was a prominent government economist who went on to become

Governor of the Reserve Bank of India and Director of the London
School of Economics.

3.   Shenoy to Friedman, 20 January 1959, Folder 10, Box 33, Milton
       Friedman Papers, Hoover Institution Archives [hereafter HIA],
       Stanford, California, US. Milton Friedman (1912–2006) was the
       most prominent advocate of free markets in the twentieth century
       and spent much of his career at the University of Chicago. By the
       1960s, he had taken over the MPS. He received the Nobel Prize in
       Economics in 1976. Lanny Ebenstein, *Milton Friedman: A Biography*
       (Basingstoke: Palgrave MacMillan, 2007).

4.   R.K. Amin, 'Editors' Note', *Theoretical Vision: B.R. Shenoy*, (eds) R.K.
       Amin and Parth Shah (New Delhi: Centre for Civil Society, 2004), p. i.

5.   Nicole Sackley, 'The road from serfdom: economic storytelling and
       narratives of India in the rise of neoliberalism', *History and Technology*
       31:4 (2015), pp. 397–419.

6.   Some of the standout works in this field are Srinath Raghavan, *1971:
       A Global History of the Creation of Bangladesh* (Cambridge, MA:
       Harvard University Press, 2013) and David Engerman, *The Price
       of Aid: The Economic Cold War in India* (Cambridge, MA: Harvard
       University Press, 2018). For a rare glimpse of the Cold War for
       hearts and minds, see Gyan Prakash, *Mumbai Fables* (New Delhi:
       HarperCollins, 2010), pp. 161–70.

7.   Although 'Nehruvian era' ideas were themselves internally
       heterogeneous; C.A. Bayly, 'The Ends of Liberalism and the Political
       Thought of Nehru's India', *Modern Intellectual History* 12:2 (2015),
       pp. 475-84.

8.   So far, this paragraph follows Mahesh Bhatt and Mukund Trivedi,
       'Bellicoth Raghunath Janardan Shenoy—A Biographical Sketch',
       *Liberalism in the Less Developed Countries: Essays in Memory of
       Professor Bellicoth Raghunath Shenoy*, (eds) idem (Ahmedabad:
       Gujarat University, 1982), pp. i-xvi (hereafter 'Biographical Sketch').

9.   Krishna Kumar, 'Quest for Self-Identity: Cultural Consciousness
       and Education in the Hindi Region, 1880-1950', *Economic and
       Political Weekly*, 25:23 (1990), pp. 1247–9 and 1251–5.

10.   Sumit Sarkar, *Modern India 1885–1947* (Basingstoke: Macmillan,
       1983), pp. 72–4 and 150–1.

11.   Agnar Sandmo, *Economics Evolving: A History of Economic Thought*
       (Princeton: Princeton University Press, 2011), pp. 166–90 and 181–2.

12. D.E. Moggridge, *British Monetary Policy: The Norman Conquest of $4.86* (Cambridge: Cambridge University Press, 1972); S.L.N. Simha (ed.), *History of the Reserve Bank of India*, Vol. I: 1935–51 (Bombay: RBI, 1970), pp. 26–28.

13. G. Balachandran, *John Bullion's Empire: Britain's Gold Problem and India Between the Wars* (Richmond: Curzon Press, 1996).

14. *Report of the Royal Commission of Indian Currency and Finance* (London: HMSO, 1926).

15. Benjamin Zachariah, *Developing India: An Intellectual and Social History, c. 1930-50* (New Delhi: Oxford Press, 2005).

16. Susan Howson, *Lionel Robbins* (Cambridge: Cambridge University Press, 2011), p. 168 and p. 1080; D.H. Robertson, 'Obituary: Philip Barrett Whale', *The Economic Journal*, 61:242 (June 1951), pp. 439–442.

17. *History of the Reserve Bank of India*, p. 36.

18. Letter Dated 23 June 1932, Academic Record, Shenoy Student File, London School of Economics and Political Science.

19. Hayek (1899–1992), associated with the defence of classical liberalism and postwar defence of market society, was awarded the Nobel Prize in 1974 for his work on the theory of money and economic fluctuations.

20. Bruce Caldwell, *Hayek's Challenge: An Intellectual Biography of F.A. von Hayek* (Chicago: University of Chicago Press, 2004), pp. 156–63.

21. Robert Skidelsky, *Keynes: The Economist as Saviour, 1920-37* (London: Macmillan, 1992), pp. 350–78.

22. Skidelsky, pp. 454–9.

23. Jeffry Frieden, *Global Capitalism: Its Fall and Rise in the Twentieth Century* (New York: Norton, 2006), 278–338.

24. B.R. Shenoy, 'An Equation for the Price-Level of New Investment Goods', *Quarterly Journal of Economics* 47:1 (1932), pp. 138–49.

25. B.R. Shenoy, 'The Interdependence of the Price-Levels', *The Quarterly Journal of Economics* 48:2 (1934), 362–368.

26. Bhatt and Trivedi, 'Biographical Sketch'.

27. Titles included *Ceylon Currency and Finance* (1941), *The Postwar Depression and the Way Out* (1944), *The Bombay Plan: A Review of its Chief Financial Provisions* (1944), and *The Sterling Assets of the Reserve Bank of India* (1946).

28. B.R. Shenoy, *Postwar Depression and the Way Out* (Allahabad: Kitabistan, 1944), p. 29

29. B.R. Shenoy, *The Sterling Assets of the Reserve Bank of India* (New Delhi: Indian Council of World Affairs, 1946).

30. B.R. Shenoy, *The Bombay Plan: A Review of its Chief Financial Provisions* (Bombay: Karnataka, 1944).

31. This paragraph follows 'Academic Record'.

32. This paragraph follows Francine Frankel, *India's Political Economy, 1947–2004* (New Delhi: Oxford University Press, 2005), pp. 128–31.

33. B.R. Shenoy, 'A Note of Dissent', *Papers Relating to the Formulation of the Second Five-Year Plan*, (ed.) C.D. Deshmukh (New Delhi: Planning Commission, 1955), pp. 19–34 and 19–20.

34. Some countries like the Soviet Union, Poland, Czechoslovakia, Hungary, and Bulgaria, had claimed to grow at 12–16 per cent in recent years; Shenoy, 'A Note of Dissent', p. 24.

35. P.T. Bauer, 'B.R. Shenoy: Stature and Impact', *Cato Journal* 18:1 (199), pp. 1–10; Shleifer, 'Peter Bauer and the Failure of Foreign Aid', *Cato Journal* 29:3 (2009), pp. 379–90.

36. P.T. Bauer, *United States Aid and Indian Economic Development* (Washington, DC: American Enterprise Association, 1959).

37. Engerman, *The Price of Aid*, pp. 89–115; George Rosen, *Western Economists and Eastern Societies: Agents of Social Change in South Asia, 1950–70* (New Delhi: Oxford University Press, 1985).

38. Milton Friedman, 'A Memorandum to the Government of India 1955', Box 226, Milton Friedman Papers, HIA.

39. Angus Burgin, *The Great Persuasion: Reinventing Markets Since the Great Depression* (Cambridge, MA: Harvard University Press, 2012), p. 8.

40. 'Sound recordings of the Mont Pelerin Society meeting at Oxford in 1959' Tape 20, Side 1, Box 61, Papers of the Mont Pelerin Society, HIA.

41. 'Free Market Economy for India', mimeo, Box 79, Folder 13, Friedrich Hayek Papers, HIA.

42. Shenoy to Hayek, 13 October 1959, Ibid.

43. Hayek to Shenoy, 20 October 1959, Ibid.

44. Shenoy to Hayek, 22 December 1965, Box 50, Folder 1, Ibid.

45. Friedman to Shenoy, 27 February 1961, Box 33, Folder 10, Friedman Papers, HIA.

46. Shenoy to Friedman, 22 October 1963; Edwards, *The Conservative Revolution: The Movement that Remade America* (New York: The Free Press, 1999), p. 140.

47. Friedman to Shenoy, 27 February 1961; Friedman to Shenoy, 16 December 1959, Box 33, Folder 10, Milton Friedman Papers, HIA.

48. On Friedman's reinvention, which involved hosting his own television show and writing popular books, see Burgin, 152–85.

49. Milton Friedman, 'Exchange Rate Policy', *Swarajya*, 30 March 1963; Milton Friedman, *India Needs a Free Market Exchange Rate* (Bombay: Forum of Free Enterprise, 1963).

50. B.R. Shenoy, 'The Right Road to Indian Progress', *Fortune*, April 1960.

51. Gregersen to Ropke,, 4 June 1962, Document 139, Ropke Papers, Institute for Political Economy, Cologne. I am indebted to Quinn Slobodian for this reference.

52. 'The Cold War in India,' *Eastern Economist*, 8 August 1952, p. 1.

53. This larger phenomenon is developed and expanded in my forthcoming book, *Partisans of the Free Economy* (Princeton University Press).

54. For 1959, the figure was 139, 625; *Press in India*—Part I (New Delhi: Ministry of Information and Broadcasting, 1960), p. 58.

55. See the articles in Amin and Shah (eds), *Economic Prophecies: B.R. Shenoy* (New Delhi: Centre for Civil Society, 2004).

56. Shenoy, 'East and West Berlin: A Study of Free vs Controlled Economy', *Swarajya*, 6 August 1960.

57. *Fortune*, April 1960,137.

58. Shenoy to Friedman, 19 November 1964, Box 33, Folder 10, Milton Friedman Papers, HIA.

59. Shenoy to Hayek, 4 January 1971, Box 50, Folder 1, Friedrich Hayek Papers, HIA.

60. Shenoy's connection is briefly mentioned in Howard Erdman's classic *The Swatantra Party and Indian Conservatism* (Cambridge: Cambridge University Press, 1967) but receives greater treatment in my forthcoming book.

61. Interview with S.V. Raju, Bombay, 1 July 2014.

62. 'Gujarat Swatantra Split: Rajya Sabha Poll', *The Times of India*, 22 March 1968.

63. Shenoy to Friedman, 19 November 1964; Shenoy to Ramkrishna Bajaj, 1 May 1967, Subject File 25, Bajaj Papers, Nehru Memorial Museum and Library, New Delhi.

64. Shenoy to Hayek 3 June 1970, Box 50, Folder 1, Hayek Papers; Shenoy to Hazlitt, 18 April 1973, Document 18851_3, Hazlitt Papers, Henry Hazlitt Digital Archives, Universidad Francisco Marroquin. Accessed at http://www.hazlitt.ufm.edu/

65. Hazlitt to Sudha Shenoy, 20 March 1978, Document 18866_3, Hazlitt Papers.

66. Amin and Shah (eds), *Theoretical Vision*.

67. See, for example, *Das, India Unbound: From Independence to Global Information Age* (New Delhi: Penguin Books, 2000).

68. Adam Tooze, *Crashed: How a Decade of Financial Crises Changed the World* (New York: Penguin Books, 2018); Amartya Sen and Jean Dreze, *India: An Uncertain Glory* (Princeton: Princeton University Press, 2013).

Part III: The Making of Indian Democracy

Chapter 11: The Road to Sevagram

1. Thomas Weber, *Gandhi as Disciple and Mentor* (New Delhi: Cambridge University Press, 2007), p. 114.

2. Ramachandra Guha, *Gandhi: The Years that Changed the World 1914–1918*, (New Delhi: Penguin Random House India, 2018), p. 510.

3. This essay draws from work in progress on a thematic history of Gandhi's life and work in the 1930s.

4. Irfan Habib, 'Civil Disobedience 1930–31', *Social Scientist*, 25:9/10 (September/October 1997), p. 59.

5. The literature on Gandhi's role in the Pact is extensive. A succinct synopsis of the debate is available in Sekhar Bandyopadhyay, *From Plassey to Partition and After: A History of Modern India* (New Delhi: Orient Blackswan, Second Edition, 2015), pp. 320–321.

6. Dietmar Rothermund, *India in the Great Depression: 1929–1939* (New Delhi: Manohar Publications, 1992), p. 102.

7. Letter from Willingdon to Samuel Hoare, 3 October 1932, MSS EUR E240/6, British Library.

8.   Telegram to Private Secretary to Viceroy, 1 January 1932, *Collected Works of Mahatma Gandhi*, Vol. 48 (New Delhi: Publications Division), p. 474.

9.   *Time Capsule 1932: A History of the Year Condensed from the Pages of the Time*, p. 125.

10. Typescript dated 14 February 1934, MSS EUR E240/9 Part II, British Library.

11. Letter from Willingdon to Samuel Hoare, 3 October 1932, MSS EUR E240/6, British Library.

12. At the end of this period, it was decided to discontinue the mass campaign but retain individual civil disobedience. Even this was eventually suspended in April 1934.

13. This was to eventually lead to the Government of India Act of 1935 and the associated Provincial Elections.

14. For Nehru's critique of this period of Congress politics, see chapter 'Dual Policy of British Government' in Jawaharlal Nehru, *Autobiography*, various editions. For a fascinating exchange between Nehru and Gandhi on their political and economic differences in this period, see their correspondence reprinted as an Appendix in D.G. Tendulkar, *Mahatma*, Vol. 3 (New Delhi: Publications Division, New Edition (revised), 1961), pp. 305–319.

15. Joint statement by V.J. Patel and Subhas Chandra Bose, Pattabhi Sitaramayya, *History of the Indian National Congress: Volume I (1885–1936)* (Bombay: Padma Publications Limited, 1935), p. 942.

16. Preface, *Collected Works of Mahatma Gandhi*, Vol. 43, p. vii.

17. Clearing the Issue, 5 January 1930, *Collected Works of Mahatma Gandhi*, Vol. 42, pp. 432–435.

18. J.C. Kumarappa (Director), *An Economic Survey of Matar Taluka* (Ahmedabad: Gujarat Vidyapith, 1931).

19. Sashi Sivramkrishna, *In Search of Stability: Economics of Money, History of the Rupee* (New Delhi: Manohar Publishers and Distributors, 2015), p. 402.

20. Dietmar Rothermund, *An Economic History of India: From Pre-Colonial Times to 1991* (New York: Routledge, 1993), p. 85.

21. Rothermund, *India in the Great Depression*, p. 32.

22. For a survey of India's role in Britain's gold-sterling nexus, see G. Balachandran, *John Bullion's Empire: Britain's Gold Problem and India Between the Wars* (Richmond: Curzon Press, 1996).

23. An article on 'Gold Export', typescript dated 1931, Speeches/Writings by Others, S. No. 19, M.K. Gandhi Papers (Pyarelal Collection), XVth instalment, Manuscripts Division, Nehru Memorial Museum and Library.

24. 'Mr Andrews Back from India: The Economic Crisis', *Manchester Guardian*, 7 December 1933.

25. Rothermund, *India in the Great Depression*, p. 74.

26. Baren Ray, 'Introduction', *Gandhi's Campaign Against Untouchability 1933–1934: An Account from the Raj's Secret Official Reports* (New Delhi: Gandhi Peace Foundation,1996), p. 16.

27. J.P. Haithcox, 'Left Wing Unity and the Indian Nationalist Movement: M.N. Roy and the Congress Socialist Party', *Modern Asian Studies*, 3:1 (1969), p. 19.

28. Acharya Narendra Deva, *Socialism and the National Revolution,* Yusuf Meherally (ed.) (Bombay: Padma Publications Limited, 1945), p. 11 (emphasis added).

29. Observations on M.R. Masani's Socialistic Programme, 29 May 1934, *Collected Works of Mahatma Gandhi*, Vol. 58, p. 36.

30. It is worth recalling here that till 1936 the Congress Socialist Party called for a new leadership of the Congress party.

31. Tendulkar, *Mahatma*, Vol. 3, p. 304.

32. Discussion with Students, 21 July 1934, *Collected Works of Mahatma Gandhi*, Vol. 58, p. 220.

33. Every Congress Committee a Satyagraha Committee, Collected Works of Mahatma Gandhi, Vol. 71, p. 368.

34. Ibid.

35. Statement to the Press, 17 September 1934, *Collected Works of Mahatma Gandhi*, Vol. 59, p. 8.

36. Speech at Gandhi Seva Sangh, On or before 30 November 1934, *Collected Works of Mahatma Gandhi*, Vol. 59, p. 408.

37. Why Only Khadi?, 14 January 1940, *Collected Works of Mahatma Gandhi*, Vol. 71, p. 103.

38. Letter to G.D. Birla, 5 July 1932, *Collected Works of Mahatma Gandhi*, Vol. 50, p. 154.

39. While running the AIVIA, Kumarappa emerged as a champion of agrarian India and a deeply insightful thinker on economic decentralization and environmentalism. For more on Kumarappa's life and work as well as the AIVIA, see Venu Madhav Govindu and

Deepak Malghan, *The Web of Freedom: J.C. Kumarappa and Gandhi's Struggle for Economic Justice* (New Delhi: Oxford University Press, 2016).

40. *AIVIA Annual Report*, 1939, p. 1.

41. Speech at Gandhi Seva Sangh, op. cit.

42. Jayaprakash Narayan, *Socialism versus the All-India Village Industries Association: A Pamphlet*, 1935, *Jayaprakash Narayan: Selected Works* Vol. 1, Bimal Prasad (ed.) (New Delhi: Manohar, 2000), p. 136. In 1936, JP also authored another pamphlet *Why Socialism?* that, inter alia, attacked Gandhi.

43. Letter from Willingdon to the Samuel Hoare, 11 November 1934, MSS Eur E 240/8, British Library.

44. 'Government's Village Uplift Work "Political Contraception"', *Modern Review*, Vol. 58, No. 2, August 1935.

45. Letter to Home Secretary, Government of Bombay, 26 July 1933, *Collected Works of Mahatma Gandhi*, Vol. 55, p. 303.

46. For more on Bajaj, see B.R. Nanda, *In Gandhi's Footsteps: The Life and Times of Jamnalal Bajaj* (New Delhi, Oxford University Press, 1990).

47. Statement to the Press, 17 September 1934, *Collected Works of Mahatma Gandhi*, Vol. 59, p. 3.

48. Mira Behn, *The Spirit's Pilgrimage* (London: Longmans, 1960), p.191.

49. Speech at Akhil Bharat Sahitya Parishad, 24 April 1936, *Collected Works of Mahatma Gandhi*, Vol. 62, p. 345.

50. Letter to Mirabehn, 20 July 1936, *Collected Works of Mahatma Gandhi*, Vol. 63, p. 161.

Chapter 12: Flights of Freedom: German Émigrés, Aeronautics and Self-Reliance in India

1. Pnina Abir-Am, 'From Multidisciplinary Collaboration to Transnational Objectivity: International Space as Constitutive of Molecular Biology, 1930–1970', E.T. Crawford, T. Shinn, S. Soerlin (eds), *Denationalizing Science: The Contexts of International Scientific Practice* (Dordrecht, Kluwer: Academic Publishers, 1993), pp. 153–186.

2. Sigrid Schmalzer, 'Self-reliant Science: The Impact of the Cold War on Science in Socialist China', Naomi Oreskes and John Krige (eds),

Science and Technology in the Global Cold War, MIT Press, 2014. In the Chinese case, Schmalzer argues, '. . . despite the actual importance of transnational influences, the power of this representation fostered a belief in a uniquely socialist Chinese approach to science. With roots in the pre-1949 revolutionary period, this idea crystallized in 1958 and interestingly became even more sharply articulated through the international exchanges of the 1970s, as foreign scientists eager to bring home exotic epistemologies participated in the promotion of Chinese uniqueness. In a few cases at least, such claims to uniqueness went beyond shaping the way people talked about science to change the actual character of scientific knowledge produced in Cold War China.' The effort and outcomes at self-sufficiency in India is yet to be studied in all its fullness.

3. Skin friction drag, a component of profile drag, is resistant force exerted on an object moving in a fluid.

4. Following his PhD, (1923, *Beiträge zur Aerodynamik des Doppeldeckers or Contributions to biplane aerodynamics*) Nolini Kanto Bose was reader, Aligarh Muslim University (1925–27); mathematical officer, Irrigation Research Institute, Lahore (1927–43); director, River Research Institute, Bengal (1943–56); adviser, Government of Bengal, ministry of irrigation; and professor, Indian Statistical Institute, Kolkata. Bose studied the problem of waterlogging in connection with the irrigation system of Punjab. He was involved in the Ganga Barrage Project and was responsible for setting up a model station at Belghoria for carrying out model studies at different project sites of the Damodar Valley Corporation. He co-authored (with A.N. Khosla) the book, *Design of Weirs and Permeable Foundation*, rated as a standard reference work on underground foundations.

5. See Peter A. Davidson, Yukio Kaneda, Keith Moffatt, Katepalli R. Sreenivasan, *A Voyage Through Turbulence*. Among his other students who would become relevant to the Indian story were: Theodor vonKarman (PhD, 1908, *Untersuchungen über Knickfestigkeit*); and Oskar Tietjens (PhD, 1923, *Beitraege zum Turbulenzproblem*).

6. Ghatage studied vortex formation using the facilities of the Kolaba observatory for his MSc thesis.

7. Roddam Narasimha, 'The German Connection in Indian Aeronautical Science and Technology', paper presented at the

conference: Philosophy and Science—Indo-German Dialogues and Dimensions, Heidelberg, 2013.

8. G.D. Khanolkar, *Walchand Hirachand: Man, His Times and Achievements* (Bombay, Ratanchand Hirachand, 2007 [1969]).

9. Jagadish N. Sinha, *Science, War and Imperialism: India in the Second World War* (Leiden: Brill, 2008), pp. 108–111; Rajat K. Ray, *Industrialisation in India: Growth and Conflict in the Private Corporate Sector*, 1914–47 (New Delhi: Oxford University Press, 1982 [1979]), pp. 255–256. Gita Piramal, *Business Legends* (Penguin, 2010) deals with the HAL story until 1942 until the imperial government bought over Hirachand's share of HAL.

10. Anthony R. Carrozza, *William D. Pawley: The Extraordinary Life of the Adventurer, Entrepreneur, and Diplomat who confounded the Flying Tigers* (Dulles, VA: Potomac Books, 2012).

11. Aparajith Ramnath, *International Networks and Aircraft Manufacture in Late-colonial India: Hindustan Aircraft Limited, 1940–47*; unpublished manuscript of paper presented at the SHOT Annual Meeting, October 2015.

12. Secretary to the Government of India to Under Secretary of State for India, London, No. 12122, 8 April 1940 in E&O No. 1879/ 40; Enclosure A.

13. Documents of Hindustan Aircraft Ltd., (No. 4) 'Agreement between Hindustan Aircraft and William Douglas Pawley', 1940, Karnataka State Archives Library.

14. V.M. Ghatage and G.V.R. Rao, 'Measurement of Turbulence and Pitch of the Airstream in the 5feet x 7feet Tunnel of Indian Institute of Science', *Journal of the Indian Institute of Science* 28 (1946), pp. 1–9.

15. See among others: Mike Gruntman, *Blazing the Trail: The Early History of Spacecraft and Rocketry* (Reston VA: AIAA, 2004); Wolfgang W.E. Samuel, *American Raiders: The Race to Capture the Luftwaffe's Secrets* (University Press of Mississippi, 2004); Steven T. Koerner, 'Technology Transfer from Germany to Canada after 1945:A Study in Failure?' *Comparative Technology Transfer and Society*, 2:1 (2004), pp. 99–124; Jones, Evan, 'The Employment of German Scientists in Australia after World War II'; The University of Sydney School of Economics and Political Science, Working Papers ECOP2002-1, October 2002; U. Goni, *The Real Odessa: How*

Perón Brought Nazi War Criminals to Argentina (London: Granta, 2002); Howard Margolian, *Unauthorized Entry: The Truth about Nazi War Criminals in Canada, 1946–1956* (Toronto: University of Toronto Press, 2000); John Farquharson 'Governed or Exploited? British Acquisition of German Technology, 1945–48', *Journal of Contemporary History*, 32:1 (1997), pp. 23–42; J. Camarasa, *Odessa al Sur: La Argentina como Refugio de Nazi's y Criminales de Guerra* (Buenos Aires: Planeta, 1995); Matthias Judt and Burkhard Ciesla, *Technology Transfer outside Germany after 1945* (Amsterdam: Harwood Academic Publishers, 1996); J. Camarasa, *Los Nazis en La Argentina* (Buenos Aires: Editorial Legasa, 1992); L. Hunt, *Secret Agenda: The United States Government, Nazi Scientists and Project Paperclip, 1944–1990* (New York: St Martin's Press, 1991); John Gimbel, 'US Policy and German Scientists: The Early Cold War', *Political Science Quarterly*, 1:3 (1986), pp. 433–451; Christopher Simpson, *Blowback: America's Recruitment of Nazi's and its Effects on the Cold War* (New York: Weidenfeld and Nicholson, 1988); T. Bower, *The Paperclip Conspiracy: The Hunt for the Nazi Scientists* (Boston: Little Brown, 1987); John Gimbel, 'US Policy and German Scientists: The Early Cold War', *Political Science Quarterly* 1, No.3 (1986), pp. 433–451; C. Lasby, *Project Paperclip: German Scientists and the Cold War* (New York: Athenaeum, 1971).

16. Carl Glatt cites British Darwin Panel allocations of Germans to Australia of forty-four, India twenty-four, 'Canada about six and Pakistan probably only two'. Whether they all actually arrived in those countries is unclear; Carl Glatt, 'Reparations and the Transfer of Scientific and Industrial Technology from Germany: A Case Study of the Roots of British Industrial Policy and of Aspects of British Occupation Policy in Germany between Post-World War II Reconstruction and the Korean War, 1943–1951', 2 Vols. PhD Diss. (Florence: European University Institute, 1994).

17. See Ernst Heinrich Hirschel, Horst Prem, Gero Madelung, *Aeronautical Research in Germany: From Lilienthal until Today*; and Michael Eckert, *The Dawn of Fluid Dynamics: A Discipline Between Science and Technology* (Weinheim: Wiley-VCH GmBH, 2005).

18. Farnborough is seen as the birthplace of British aviation, and the site of both the UK's first powered heavier-than-air flight, and whereits

first military aviation units were formed. The Royal Aircraft Establishment in Farnborough, Hampshire, had five wind tunnels, one of which was built in 1935 to study how wind affected objects. The Hawker Hurricane aircraft which became the main force for victory in the Battle of Britain was tested here. The research carried on in these tunnels was secret and Havemann's work there could be explored further; P.J. Cooper, *Farnborough: 100 Years of British Aviation* (Midlands Publishing: 2006).

19. Max Born, *My Life and My Views* (New York: Charles Scribner, 1968).

20. B.V. Subbarayappa, *In Pursuit of Excellence: A History of the Indian Institute of Science*, (Tata McGraw-Hill: 1992) (note 19), p. 162; See especially, Rachel Lee, 'Constructing a Shared Vision: Otto Konigsberger and Tata & Sons', *ABE Journal* (2012), p. 2.

21. The historian David Edgerton suggests that between 125 and 140 of the Marut were manufactured at HAL; *The Shock of the Old*, pp. 124. David Donald, *The Encyclopedia of World Aircraft* (London: Aerospace, 1997), suggests that 147 were built.

22. For Tank's aeronautical design and engineering work in Juan Perón's Argentina see, Jonathan D. Hagood, 'Why does Technology Transfer Fail? The Technology Transfer Projects from Perónist Argentina', *Comparative Technology Transfer and Society* 4, No. 1 (2006) pp. 73–98; Ruth Stanley, *Rüstungsmodernisierung durch Wissenschaftsmigration? Deutsche Rüstungsfachleute in Argentinien und Brasilien 1947–1963* (Frankfurt am Main: Vervuet, 1999).

23. Michael J. Neufeld, 'The Nazi Aerospace Exodus: Towards a Global, Transnational History', *History and Technology*, 28:1 (2012), pp. 49–67.

24. See W. Wagner, *The History of German Aviation: Kurt Tank, Focke-Wulf's Designer and Test Pilot* (Atglen, PA: Schiffer Military/ Aviation History, 1998); H. Conradis, *Design for Flight: The Kurt Tank Story* (London: MacDonald, 1960).

25. Neufeld, 'The Nazi Aerospace Exodus', p. 57.

26. Narasimha, 'The German Connection', p. 7.

27. Hindustan Aircraft Limited (HAL), *Diamonds in the Sky: Sixty Years of HAL, 1940–2001* (New Delhi: Society for Aerospace Studies, 2001).

28. In a recent interview, Sitaram Rao Valluri offered an explanation for Bristol Siddeley's inability to provide engines: 'The idea was that

HF 24 would use a reheat version of Bristol Siddeley's Orpheus 703. Bristol Siddeley, at that point of time, was offering this version both to India and the NATO countries. But NATO unexpectedly dropped their project. Bristol Siddeley then offered to develop the reheat version for India at a cost of Rupees 5 crores. The offer was rejected. This was a serious blunder.' In *Avia, Journal of the Aeronautical Society of India* (April–August 2003) pp. 4–5. A reheat system for the Orpheus 703 engine was, in fact, built by the Gas Turbine Research Establishment—itself an outcome of the research and development from the manufacture of Marut—but the prototype crashed at take-off. After a few more efforts at integrating more powerful engines with the HF 24, HAL closed the door on this effort altogether.

29. Hagood, 'Why Does Technology Transfer Fail?', citing J. Singh, 'Defence: A Profile of Five Decades', *Independent India: The First Fifty Years*, (ed.) H. Karlekar (New York: Oxford University Press, 1998), pp. 92–115.

30. https://marutfans.wordpress.com/ (seen on 31 December 2019).

31. Among others, see Melvin Kranzberg, 'The Technical Elements in International Technology Transfer: Historical Perspectives', J.R. McIntyre and D.S. Papp (eds) *The Political Economy of International Technology Transfer* (Northampton MA: Edward Elgar, 1986).

32. Mitchell G. Ash and A. S.llner (eds), *Forced Migration and Scientific Change: Emigre German-Speaking Scientists and Scholars after 1933* (Cambridge, Cambridge University Press, 1996).

33. Neufeld, 'The Nazi Aerospace Exodus'.

34. Jeffry A. Engel, '"We Are Not Concerned Who the Buyer Is": Engine Sales and Cold War Security at the Dawn of the Jet Age,' *History and Technology*, 17:1 (2000), pp. 43–67; *Cold War at 30,000 Feet: The Anglo-American Fight for Aviation Supremacy* (Cambridge: Harvard University Press, 2007).

35. See especially Kris Manjapra, *Age of Entanglement: German and Indian Intellectuals across Empire* (Cambridge: Harvard University Press, 2014).

36. Other German engineers worked at different engineering schools or departments in the 1950's, for example, the earlier mentioned Hans A. Havemann (combustion engineering) at the Indian Institute of Science, W. Repenthin (aeronautical engineering) and R. Wallauscheck (instrument design) at the Madras Institute of

Technology; Robert Kraus and Hans Tishner at the Indian Institute of Technology Kharagpur. The legendary German female pilot, Hanna Reitsch, came to India in 1959 and established a gliding school. Between 1950–1980, Hindustan Machine Tools had eighteen German collaborating partners, sixteen from West Germany and two from East Germany. And finally, West Germany aided the establishment of the Indian Institute of Technology Madras.

Chapter 13: The Supreme Court and Democratic Consolidation

* This chapter draws extensively on Madhav Khosla, 'India's First Period: Constitutional Doctrine and Constitutional Stability', *From Parchment to Practice: Implementing New Constitutions* (Tom Ginsburg and Aziz Huq (eds), (New York: Cambridge University Press, 2020).

1. See Arend Lijphart, 'The Puzzle of Indian Democracy: A Consociational Interpretation', *American Political Science Review*, 90:2 (1996), pp. 258-68; Ashutosh Varshney, 'Why Democracy Survives', *Journal of Democracy*, 9:3 (1998), pp. 36-50; Devesh Kapur, 'Explaining Democratic Durability and Economic Performance', *Public Institutions in India*, (eds) Devesh Kapur and Pratap Bhanu Mehta (New Delhi: Oxford University Press, 2005), pp. 28-64; Ashutosh Varshney, *Battles Half Won: India's Improbable Democracy* (New Delhi: Penguin, 2013), pp. 11–15.

2. It should be further noted that the very topic of *India after Gandhi*— its attempt to deliver a contemporary history of India—was itself an argument about the means and ends of historical writing. See generally Ramachandra Guha, 'The Challenge of Contemporary History', *Economic and Political Weekly*, 43:26-27 (28 June 2008), p. 192.

3. See Sunil Khilnani, 'Nehru's Judgment', *Political Judgment: Essays for John Dunn*, (eds) Richard Bourke and Raymond Geuss (New York: Cambridge University Press, 2009) pp. 254–77; Madhav Khosla (ed.), Jawaharlal Nehru, *Letters for a Nation: From Jawaharlal Nehru to His Chief Ministers* (Gurugram: Penguin Allen Lane, 2014).

4. See Upendra Baxi, 'Taking Suffering Seriously: Social Action Litigation in the Supreme Court of India', *Third World Legal Studies*, 4 (1985), pp. 107-32; P.P. Craig and S.L. Deshpande,

'Rights, Autonomy and Process: Public Interest Litigation in India', *Oxford Journal of Legal Studies*, 9:3 (1989), pp. 356–73; Madhav Khosla, 'Making Social Rights Conditional: Lessons from India', *International Journal of Constitutional Law*, 8:4 (2010), pp. 739–65.

5. See Pratap Bhanu Mehta, 'The Rise of Judicial Sovereignty', *Journal of Democracy*, 18:2 (2007), pp. 70–83; Pratap Bhanu Mehta, 'The Indian Supreme Court and the Art of Democratic Positioning', *Unstable Constitutionalism: Law and Politics in South Asia*, (eds) Mark Tushnet and Madhav Khosla (New York: Cambridge University Press, 2015), pp. 233–60.

6. Granville Austin, *Working a Democratic Constitution: A History of the Indian Experience* (New Delhi: Oxford University Press, 1999), Chapters 1–6.

7. See Madhav Khosla, *India's Founding Moment: The Constitution of a Most Surprising Democracy* (Cambridge: Harvard University Press, 2020).

8. Rohit De, *A People's Constitution: The Everyday Life of Law in the Indian Republic* (Princeton: Princeton University Press, 2018).

9. Zachary Elkins, Tom Ginsburg and James Melton, *The Endurance of National Constitutions* (New York: Cambridge University Press, 2009).

10. Article 37, Constitution of India, 1950.

11. State of Madras v. Champakam Dorairajan, AIR 1951 SC 226.

12. See generally Charles Taylor, 'Interpretation and the Sciences of Man', *Review of Metaphysics*, 25:1 (1971), pp. 28–29.

13. State of Bombay v. F.N. Balsara, AIR 1951 SC 318.

14. F.N. Balsara, para 32.

15. Hanif Quareshi v. State of Bihar, AIR 1958 SC 731.

16. In Re the Kerala Education Bill, 1957, AIR 1958 SC 956.

17. See, for example, P.K. Tripathi, *Spotlights on Constitutional Interpretation* (Bombay: N.M. Tripathi, 1972), pp. 291–322.

18. Gautam Bhatia, 'Directive Principles of State Policy', *Oxford Handbook of the Indian Constitution*, (eds) Sujit Choudhry, Madhav Khosla and Pratap Bhanu Mehta (Oxford: Oxford University Press, 2016), pp. 644–61. Bhatia is quite right to note, as a doctrinal matter, that In Re the Kerala Education Bill is the case that signals a shift in the Supreme Court's approach.

19. On the relationship between the directive principles and fundamental rights, see, Craig and Deshpande, 'Rights, Autonomy and Process'; Khosla, 'Making Social Rights Conditional'; Bhatia, 'Directive Principles of State Policy'.

20. H.C.L. Merillat, *Land and the Constitution of India* (New York: Columbia University Press, 1970), pp. 52–78.

21. Namita Wahi, 'Property', *Oxford Handbook of the Indian Constitution*, (eds) Sujit Choudhry, Madhav Khosla and Pratap Bhanu Mehta (Oxford: Oxford University Press, 2016), pp. 943–63.

22. Austin, *Working a Democratic Constitution.*

23. Kameshwar Singh v. State of Bihar, 30 Indian Law Reports 454 (1951) (Patna High Court).

24. Kameshwar Singh, page 476.

25. Sankari Prasad v. Union of India, AIR 1951 SC 458. On the subsequent jurisprudence relating to amendments, see Madhav Khosla, 'Constitutional Amendment', *Oxford Handbook of the Indian Constitution*, (eds) Sujit Choudhry, Madhav Khosla and Pratap Bhanu Mehta (Oxford: Oxford University Press, 2016), pp. 232–50.

26. State of Bihar v. Kameshwar Singh, 1952 SCR 889 (Supreme Court [SC]), para 2.

27. Kameshwar Singh (SC), para 48.

28. See Surajpal Singh v. State of Uttar Pradesh, AIR 1952 SC 52; Visheshwar Rao v. State of Madhya Pradesh, 1952 SCR 1020.

29. Merillat, *Land and the Constitution of India*, pp. 140–149.

30. Austin, *Working a Democratic Constitution*, p. 80.

31. Surya Deva, 'Saving Clauses: The Ninth Schedules and Articles 31A-C', *Oxford Handbook of the Indian Constitution*, (eds) Sujit Choudhry, Madhav Khosla and Pratap Bhanu Mehta (Oxford: Oxford University Press, 2016), pp. 627–43.

Chapter 14: From Autonomy to Insurgency: Jammu and Kashmir in the Long 1970s

1. Ramachandra Guha, 'Opening a Window in Kashmir', *World Policy Journal* 21:3 (2004), pp. 79–94.

2. Ibid.

3. Srinath Raghavan, *War and Peace in Modern India: A Strategic History of the Nehru Years* (Ranikhet: Permanent Black, 2010), pp. 219–25.

4. 27 November 1963, *Lok Sabha Debates*, Vol. XII, Cols 1231–32.

5. Ramachandra Guha, *India after Gandhi: The History of the World's Largest Democracy* (London: Macmillan, 2007), p. 430.

6. J.J. Singh to Indira Gandhi, 11 June 1967, Subject File 87, Jayaprakash Narayan Papers (III Instalment), Nehru Memorial Museum and Library (NMML). Also see, Rakesh Ankit, 'Sheikh Mohammad Abdullah of Kashmir, 1965–1975: From Externment to Enthronement', *Studies in Indian Politics*, 6:1 (2018), pp. 88–102 (quote on p. 92).

7. Mir Qasim, *My Life and Times*, (Bombay: Allied Publishers, 1992), pp. 117–18.

8. Letter to Indira Gandhi enclosing note on 'Regional Autonomy in Jammu and Kashmir', 10 July 1967, *Kashmir and Beyond 1966–84: Selected Correspondence between Indira Gandhi and Karan Singh*, (ed.) Jawaid Alam (New Delhi: Viking, 2011), pp. 57–68.

9. Mir Qasim, *My Life and Times*, p. 119.

10. Haksar to Indira Gandhi, 14 September 1967, cited in Ankit, 'Sheikh Mohammad Abdullah of Kashmir', p. 94.

11. Haksar to Indira Gandhi, 9 June 1967, Subject File 113, P.N. Haksar Papers (III Instalment), NMML.

12. Ibid.

13. Abdullah to Kaul, 7 October 1967, Correspondence with Sheikh Abdullah, T.N. Kaul Papers, NMML.

14. Note on meeting with Abdullah, 11 October 1967, Subject File 13, T.N. Kaul Papers, NMML.

15. Abdullah's note on meetings on 10 and 12 October 1967, Correspondence with Sheikh Abdullah, T.N. Kaul Papers, NMML.

16. Note on meeting with Abdullah, 12 October 1967, Subject File 13, T.N. Kaul Papers, NMML.

17. Ibid.

18. Ibid.

19. Note on meeting with Abdullah, 7 November 1967, Subject File 13, T.N. Kaul Papers, NMML; Abdullah's note on this meeting, Correspondence with Sheikh Abdullah, Ibid.

20. Note on meeting with Abdullah, 7 January 1968, Subject File 13, T.N. Kaul Papers, NMML.

21. Radha Kumar, *Paradise at War: A Political History of Kashmir* (New Delhi: Aleph, 2018), p. 101.

22. Abdullah to Narayan, 6 March 1969, Subject File 93, Jayaprakash Narayan Papers (III Instalment), NMML.

23. Narayan to Abdullah, 20 March 1969, Ibid.

24. Abdullah to Narayan, 30 April 1969, Ibid.

25. Wajahat Habibullah, *My Kashmir: The Dying of Light* (New Delhi: Viking, 2001), p. 35.

26. Karan Singh to Indira Gandhi, 23 November 1970, *Kashmir and Beyond*, pp. 174–78.

27. Haksar to Indira Gandhi, 31 December 1970, cited in Jairam Ramesh, *Intertwined Lives: P.N. Haksar and Indira Gandhi* (New Delhi: Simon and Schuster, 2018), pp. 176–77.

28. Ankit, 'Sheikh Mohammad Abdullah of Kashmir', p. 96.

29. Narayan to Indira Gandhi, 26 March 1971, Subject File 93, Jayaprakash Narayan Papers (III Instalment), NMML.

30. Srinath Raghavan, *1971: A Global History of the Creation of Bangladesh* (Ranikhet: Permanent Black, 2013).

31. Mir Qasim, *My Life and Times*, p. 136.

32. R.K. Patil to Narayan, 10 April 1972, Subject File 93, Jayaprakash Narayan Papers (III Instalment), NMML.

33. Haksar to Indira Gandhi, 2 June 1972, Subject File 53, P.N. Haksar Papers (I and II Instalments), NMML.

34. Sarabhai to Haksar, 10 June 1972, Subject File 214, P.N. Haksar Papers (I and II Instalments), NMML.

35. Haksar to Indira Gandhi, 12 June 1972, Ibid.

36. Abdullah to Parthasarathi, 23 August 1974, *Article 370: A Constitutional History of Jammu and Kashmir*, (ed.) A.G. Noorani (New Delhi: Oxford University Press, 2011), p. 403.

37. Agreed Conclusions, 13 November 1974; Beg to Parthasarathi, 13 November 1974, *Article 370*, pp. 403–7

38. Indira Gandhi to Abdullah, 16 December 1974, Ibid., p. 408.

39. Abdullah to Indira Gandhi, 29 December 1974, Ibid., p. 411.

40. Mir Qasim, *My Life and Times*, pp. 141–42.

41. M.L. Fotedar, *The Chinar Leaves: A Political Memoir* (New Delhi: HarperCollins, 2015), pp. 101–2; Mir Qasim, *My Life and Times*, p. 143.

42. Indira Gandhi to Natwar Singh, 14 April 1975, K. Natwar Singh, *Treasured Epistles* (New Delhi: Rupa, 2018), p. 15.

43. Mir Qasim, *My Life and Times*, pp. 150–52.

44. Indira Gandhi to Mir Qasim, 2 July 1983, Subject File 78, B.K. Nehru Papers, NMML.

45. Entry of 18 May 1976, B.N. Tandon, *The PMO Diary-II: The Emergency* (Delhi: Konark Publishers, 2006), p. 335.

46. I.K. Gujral, *Matters of Discretion: An Autobiography* (New Delhi: Hay House, 2011), p. 83.

47. Karan Singh to Indira Gandhi, 14 July and 24 October 1980, *Kashmir and Beyond*, p. 293, p. 299.

48. Report on a Visit to Kashmir for Submission to Prime Minister, 5 July 1981, Subject File 12, T.N. Kaul Papers, NMML.

49. Indira Gandhi to Mir Qasim, 2 July 1983, Subject File 78, B.K. Nehru Papers, NMML.

50. B.K. Nehru, *Nice Guys Finish Second* (New Delhi: Penguin 1999), pp. 616–713.

51. Ibid., p. 716.

Part IV: On Ramachandra Guha

Chapter 18: 'What Do They Know of History Who Only History Know?'

1. Frank Keating, 'A Pre-Tour Wrangle with India Is Par for the Course', *Guardian*, 3 December = 2001.

2. G.M. Trevelyan, *English Social History: A Survey of Six Centuries* (London: Longmans Green & Co, 1946).

3. Robert Winder, *The Little Wonder: The Remarkable History of Wisden* (London: Wisden, 2013).

4. Michael Mandelbaum, *The Meaning of Sports: Why Americans Watch Baseball, Football, and Basketball and What They See When They Do* (New York: PublicAffairs, revised edition 2005).

5. Jack Williams, *Cricket and Race* (Oxford: Berg Publishers, 2001).

6. Neville Cardus, *The Summer Game* (Rupert Hart-Davis, revised edition 1948).

INDEX

Abdullah, Farooq, 244–45
Abdullah, Sheikh, 228–43, 245
    Indira accord, 241, 243–44
Adivasi, xiii, xvi–xvii
    culture, 64
    dams, development projects and
        displacement, 58–60, 63–64,
        66, 68, 82
    movements, 63–64, 66, 68, 74,
        82
    panchayats, 33–34
advertising on television, 272
Aeronautical Development
    Establishment, Bangalore, 209
aeronautics and self-reliance: India,
    200–213
Aeronautics India Limited (AIL), 211
Afghanistan, 113, 120
Agarwal, Anil, 85
Agarwal, Bharat Bhushan, 160, 161
agrarian, agriculture, 8, 63, 65, 177
    agrarianism and wilderness, 30,
        51
    disruptions, 52
    economy, 184, 189, 191,
        196–97, 260

    expansion, 22
    and industrial capitalism, 129
    landscape, 16, 18, 75
    no-rent campaigns, 186
    and pastoral societies, 37
    prices, 190
    self-sufficiency, 172
    swidden (jhum), 3, 8–10
    systems, 25, 38, 189
Agyeya, Sachchidananda Hirananda
    Vatsyayana, xviii, 146–164
    anti–fascism, 159–61
    collaborationist, 147, 161
    the editor, 153–55
    early education, 148–51ICCF
        incident, 161–63
    marriage with Santosh Kashyap,
        158, 159
    1960 and the Emergency,
        162–64
    political journey, 147–50,
        152–57, 163–64
    a revolutionary, 147, 151–53,
        159
    see also Hindustan Socialist
        Republican Army

works:
 Chinta, 151
 Dusra Saptak, 146
 Nadi Ke Dwip, 146
 Shekhar: Ek Jiwani I and *II*, 146,
  148, 156–158
Aiyar, Justice N. Chandrasekhara, 226
ALCAN, Canada, 81
Alhambra tournament, 139–41
All India Radio (AIR), 158, 241
All–India Village Industries
 Association (AIVIA), 194–99
alumina refinery, Rayagada, 81–82
Amanullah, King of Afghanistan, 113
'Amar Vallari', 148
Ambedkar, B.R., 158, 168, 188, 274
Amery, Leo, 202
Amin, Shahid, *Sugarcane and Sugar*,
 260
Ananthamurthy, U.R., xviii
Ananthanarayanan, Justice M, 94, 98
Andal, Lady, 93
Andrews, C.F., 113, 154, 191
Aney, M.S., 158
animal
 behaviour and ecology, 22, 40
 human relations, 56
 protection laws, 47
 rights, 46, 51, 52
anti–colonial struggle, 118
anti–dam campaigns and politics,
 55–70
Anti–Imperialist League of the United
 States, 154
Anti–Sterlite People's Committee, 78
Appiko Movement, 75, 86
Arbuthnott, John Campbell, 11–12,
 14–20
Argentina, 206–07, 209–10
Arlott, John, 273
Arnold, David, xvii

Arya Samaj movement, 148
Asadhya Veena, 164
Asalambikai, Pandita, 96
Ash, Mitchell, 210
Ashraf, Sofia, 80
Asom Jatiyatabadi Yuba Chatra
 Parishad, 74
Assam Bandhu, 4
Auden, W.H., 162
Aurangzeb, Muhi–ud–Din
 Muhammad, 105
Austin, Granville, *Working a
 Democratic Constitution: A History
 of the Indian Experience*, 216, 226
Australia
 Immigration Restriction Act
  (IRA), 131
 Indian and other Asiatic
  immigrants, xviii, 130–32,
  134–37, 138, 144
 National Sporting Club, Sydney,
  135, 139
 White Australia (colour
  discrimination), 126–27,
  130–32, 134–35, 137
 wrestling, 126–37, 139–41
authoritarianism, 43–45, 52
autobiography genre, 92
 in Bengali, 91
 Indian women's narrative, 91,
  96–97, 103–04
 in Tamil, 91, 96–97
 Western understanding of, 103
Azad, Abul Kalam, 122
Azad, Chandrasekhar, 152
Azad, Kirti, 251
Azadi Ke Bees Baras, 162

Bacon, Francis, 40
Bahuguna, Sunderlal, 52, 75, 259
Bajaj, Jamnalal, 197–99

Bajpai, Mohanlal, 158
Baksh, Ahmed, 141–43
Baksh, Gama (Gulam Mohammed), 128, 141–42
Baksh, Imam, 141–42
Bakunin, Mikhail Alexandrovich, 152
Baloo, Palwankar, 128, 253–54, 273–74, 275
Baloo, Vithal, 274
Baluchistan, 120, 131
Bamzai, K.N., 244
Banaras, 147, 152, 167–69
Banaras Hindu University (BHU), 152, 166–67
Banderdubi, Kaziranga, human inhabitants evicted, 74
Bangladesh, creation of, 209, 238
Bannu, 116, 118, 119, 123, 119, 124,
Bardoli satyagraha, 189–190, 194
Basar, Rabi, 155
Bastille, day of storming, 271
Basu, Siddharth, 251
Bauer, Peter, 173–175, 179
bauxite mining, Odisha., 68–70, 72. *See also* Niyamgiri hills
Beckett, W. O., 7
Beddome, Richard Henry, 27
Bedi, Bishan Singh, 257, 258–59
Beg, Mirza Afzal, 232, 237, 238–41
begaar, 3, 4, 10, 13, 18, 20
Benade, J.M., 150
Bengal, 32–33, 57, 91, 155, 187, 193
    British administration and Garos, 5, 7, 8–11
    Eastern Bengal, 14, 19
    forest management, 26
    Private Forests Act, 1948, 33
    timber market, 8
    Zamindars and Garos, conflict, 4, 5–8, 10
Bengal Infantry, 138

Benjamin, R.B., 141, 142, 143
Berry, Bob, 140–41
Besant, Annie, 251
Bhabananda, 6
Bhagat Singh, 148, 152
Bhakhra Nangal dam, 58
Bharati, Subramania, 96
Bharatiya Janata Party (BJP formerly Bharatiya Jana Sangh), xi, 176, 229, 231, 232, 236, 244–45
Bhatt, Chandi Prasad, 259
Bhitarkanika National Park, 74
Bhopal Gas Tragedy, 71
Bhutto, Zulfikar Ali, 238–39
Bihar, 57, 120
    Land Reforms Act, 1950, 224
Bijni estate, 7, 11
    Garos and the zamindars, dispute, 13
biodiversity conservation conflicts, 73–75
biomass and land conflict, 75–78
Birley, Derek, 272
Blackburn, Stuart, xvii
Blitz, 163
Bloch, Marc, xi
Board of Control for Cricket in India (BCCI), xiii
Bohr, Niels, 205
Bombay Chronicle, 113
Bombay Prohibition Act, 1949, 219–20
Bose, Nandalal, 161
Bose, Nolini Kanto, 201
Bose, Subhas Chandra, 123, 188
    Indian National Army, 123
Brahmaputra, 8, 11, 66
    dams, 67
Brandner, Ferdinand, 209, 212
British rule, British administration. *See* colonial rule in India

British Indian army, 130, 161
Brockington, Dan, 39
Browning, Robert, 151
Buchanan, Francis, 6
Bullen, William, 271
Burma, 112, 129
    Japanese occupied, 202, 203
Burnham, James, 162
Burton, Antoinette, 92
Buttan (Bhuttan) Singh, the wrestler,
    xviii, 126–145
    in Australia, 126–29, 130,
        132–37
    in London, 137–43
    United States, 143–44

California Institute of Technology
    (Caltech), 204
Cama, Bhikhaiji Rustomji, 108,
    109
Captain, Gosi Naoroji, 106, 108, 109,
    111
Captain, Nurgis, 106, 109, 120
Captain, Perin Naoroji, 106, 108–09,
    111, 112, 120
Cardus, Neville, 275
Carey, William, 4, 7
Caribbean, 139
    Indian indentured labour, 129
Carson, Rachel, 41
Cartwright, Tom, 273
caste, caste and politics, xvii, xix,
    21, 33–34, 51–52, 55, 58,
    62–64, 86, 92, 94, 97, 103, 128,
    149–50, 188–89, 192, 219, 254,
    273–74
    caste–based reservations, 219
    and resource use, xvii, 21–22
Central Empowered Committee, 21
Central Intelligence Agency (CIA),
    146–47

Centre for Science and Environment,
    xv, 85
Centre of Civil Society, New Delhi,
    179
Chagla, Justice M.C., 163
Champakam Dorairajan. See State
    of Madras v. Champakam
    Dorairajan
Champaran satyagraha, 189
Champion, H.G., 27–28, 29
Champs Elysees, Paris, France, 271
Chandel, Sarla, 156–57
Chapin, Mac, 39
Chaturvedi, Banarsi Das, 155
Chatterjee, Ramananda, 154–55
Chaudhuri, Nirad, 269
Chauhan, Shivdan Singh, 157
Chelmsford, Lord, 149
chemical industries, impact on coastal
    ecology, 81
Chernobyl nuclear disaster, 82
China, 84, 131, 201, 203
    Kuomintang, 172, 202
Chipko movement, xv, 61, 63, 71, 75,
    76, 86, 249–50, 251–52
Chundawat, Raghu, 34
Churchill, Winston, 185
Citizenship (Amendment) Act (CAA),
    ix–x
Civil Disobedience Movement,
    colonial reaction, 184–88
    Gandhi suspended, 188, 192–93,
        197
    Muslims' participation, 198
    political crisis, 184–89, 190
    women's role, 106, 112–13, 123
Cleghorn, Hugh, 27
climate change, 36, 56, 66, 67
Cold War, xviii, 163, 165–66,
    176–79, 209–10, 212–13. See
    also Shenoy, B.R.

Cole, G.D.H., 271
colonial rule in India, 1–21, 34, 35,
    38, 49, 107, 117–23, 129–30
    aircraft manufacturing in India,
        200–03, 207–11
    forest policies and rules, 21–22,
        24, 50
    forest management in the Madras
        Presidency, 25–27
    and freedom struggle, 184–91
    in the Garo Hills, 3–20
    natural resources' exploitation,
        250, 252
colour, caste, and class bias in sports,
    271–75
common resources management, 53
communalism, xi, 198
Communist Party of India (CPI),
    159
Communist Party of India (Marxist)
    (CPI-M), 32
community ecology, 41
'compassionate conservation', 46
Compton, Arthur H., 150
Congress, 12, 35, 149, 158, 161, 163,
    172
    Faizpur session, 1936, 153
    Gandhi and, 156, 183–89,
        192–97
    and the Kashmir issue, 229,
        231–33, 236–37, 241–45
    and Khurshedben Naoroji,
        105–25
    Lahore session, 1929, 151, 154
    and revolutionaries, 147
Congress for Cultural Freedom
    (CCF), 146–47, 161–63. See
    also Agyeya, Central Intelligence
    Agency (CIA)
    Indian CCF (ICCF), 161–62
Congress Seva Dal, 151

Congress Socialist Party, 188, 192,
    193
conservation,
    colonial legacy, 50
    conservation biology, 37–40,
        41–44, 61, 67, 72
    'convivial conservation', 74
    cultural values and, 53
    and ecosystem, conflicts, 73–75
    human-nature relationship,
        50–52
    imperialism and control of
        knowledge, money and
        space, 37–53
Conservation International (CI), 47
Constituent Assembly of India, 230
Constitution of India, 216–27,
    230–31, 239–40
    Amendment, 1951, 222–26
    Amendment, 1955, 223, 226
    Article 370, 229, 230–31, 234,
        239
constitutional reform, 187
constitutionalism, 218, 222, 226–27
Convention on Biological Diversity
    (CBD), 39
converts to Christianity, 8, 94–95
Corner of a Foreign Field, A, xii, xviii,
    253, 267, 274–76
corporate partnerships, 47, 48
corporations and NGOs, nexus, 48
corruption, 60, 85, 139, 162, 173,
    177, 193, 229, 236, 268
cotton, 5–8, 16, 18
cow slaughter, 221
cricket, 257–58
    and class divisions, 271–76
    race, 271–74
    Guha on, x, 267, 274–75
Crozier, Frank, 140
rivers, cultural politics around, 56–57

cultural rights, 64, 67–68
Cultural Survival, 64

D'Oliveira, Basil, 273, 274
dacoits, 107, 117–21
Dalai Lama, 6th, 85
Dalgoma disturbances, 11, 17
Damodar Valley Corporation, 59
dams, large, x, 31. *See also* Narmada
　　Bachao Andolan
　　anti-dam politics in India, 55–70,
　　　84
　　dams and development, 61–64
　　displaced persons, 58–59
　　social movements (against), xvi,
　　　56, 71, 84
Dandi March, 113, 184, 189, 197
Dasgupta, Ashin, 261
Dasholi Gram Swaraj Sangh, 250
Dayal, Ravi, 264
De, Rohit, *A People's Constitution: The*
　　Everyday Life of Law in the Indian
　　Republic, 217
Deccan, 22, 26–27
Defence Research and Development
　　Organisation (DRDO), 36
deforestation, xvi, 22, 30, 61, 67, 71
Delhi Conspiracy case, 152
Delphic Festival, 109, 111
democracy in India, x, xvi–xviii, 53
　　and Supreme Court, relationship,
　　　214–27
Depressed Classes of Bombay, 274
Desh Sevika Sangh, 112
Deurchur Chang, Kaziranga, human
　　inhabitants evicted, 74
Deve Gowda, H.D., 83
development economics, 169, 173
Dhanwantri, 152
Dhar, D.P., 231, 234, 238–41
Dhawan, Satish, 210

Dhingra, Madan Lal, 138
Dias, Bismark, 255–56
Dickman, Amy, 46
Dinnie, George, 137
displacement by development projects,
　　49–50, 58–63, 67–68, 74, 102
Dongaria Kondh adivasis, 68–69
Dowie, Mark, 39

Eardley–Wilmot, S., 10, 14
East India Company (EIC), xvi, 3, 4,
　　5–7, 8
ecological issues, ecology, x, xv,
　　22–23, 26, 55, 61, 64, 67, 70,
　　251–53
　　conservation imperialism, 37–54
　　distribution conflicts, 72, 76
　　distribution conflicts, 72, 76,
　　　80–81, 85–86
　　forests, ecological value, 29–31
　　sustainable development, 56
Ecology and Equity: The Use and
　　Abuse of Nature in Contemporary
　　India, by Madhav Gadgil and
　　Ramachandra Guha, xv
economic
　　crisis, 189–92
　　decentralization, 196
　　growth and development, ix, 58,
　　　65–66, 173–74, 179
　　issues, 166–73, 176
　　liberalization, 56, 65, 179
　　planning, 168, 171–73
　　policy, post-liberalization,
　　　178–79
ecosystems, 46, 60, 67, 70
　　fragility, 69
Egypt and India, alliance for
　　aeronautical self-reliance,
　　209–11
Ehrenfeld, David, 39

EJAtlas, international atlas
of environmental justice
movements, 72–73, 76, 82,
85–86
Ellison, Ralph, 275
Elwin, Verrier, x, xiii, xiv–xv, xvii, 64,
254, 261, 267
Emergency, 242–43
'enclosure movement', 76–77
Engel, Jeffrey, 210
Ennore port, 81
environmental
conservation. *See* conservation
education, 50
issues: history, x, xv, xvi, 22, 24,
30, 43, 61, 69, 85, 252, 261
movement, xvi, 1–20, 21, 37, 51,
61, 71–87
politics, xvi, 52, 56, 62
projects, funding, 48
sustainability, 72
Environmental Protection Agency
(EPA), 35–36
Ezekiel, Nissim, xiv–xv, 161

*F.N. Balsara. See State of Bombay v.
F.N. Balsara*
Fateh Chand, 117, 119, 124
fisherfolk, fishing, 38, 66
ban on fishing, 74
and forest rules, fines and
penalities, 15, 75
illegal prawn industry, 74
illegal shrimp farms, shrimp
mafia, 75
industrial and utilities conflicts,
78, 80
mechanized fishing and tradional
industry, 76–77
nuclear conflicts, 83, 87
struggle, 76–78, 87

villages, devastation by pollution,
80–81
Fleishmann, Forrest, 24
Flugzeugbau, Focke–Wulf, 206
food imports, 177
foreign aid, 172–74, 176
foreign exchange, 173, 177
forests and forestry, xv, 22, 23, 25, 35,
72, 75, 85 252
bureaucracy, forest departments,
role of, xvi, 8–16, 18, 20,
24–25, 27–29, 31, 33–34,
35–36, 73–74, 252
colonial management in Madras
Presidency, 25–27
imperial interests, xvi, 3–20
after independence, 29–32
1970s to 1990s, reform or statsis,
32–35
Forest Act, 1878, xv
Forest (Conservation) Act (FCA) of
1980, 23–24, 32, 33, 36
Forest Research Institute (FRI), 1906,
Dehradun, xii, 27, 28, 29, 31
Forest Rights Act (FRA). *See*
Scheduled Tribes and Other
Traditional Forest Dwellers
(Recognition of Forest Rights)
Act; *See also* Chipko movement;
Niyamgiri Bachao Andolan;
Silent Valley movement
Fortune, 176, 177
freedom movement. *See* nationalist
movement. *See also* Gandhi,
M.K.; Civil Disobedience
movement
French Revolution, 271
Friedman, Milton, 165–66, 173–77
Friends of the Earth, 64
Frontier, 251
Fukushima disaster, 2011, 83, 87

Fuller, Joseph Bampfylde, 14

Gadgil, D.R., 168
Gajendragadkar, P.B., 233
Galbraith, John Kenneth, ix
Gamu (wrestler), 141–42
Gandhi, Devadas, 113, 114
Gandhi, Indira, 61
    and the Kashmir issue, 229,
        232–34, 236–45
    totalitarian streak, 163
Gandhi, Maganlal, 198–99
Gandhi, Mohan Das Karamchand,
    xi, xvii, 62, 100, 137–38, 149,
    183–199, 254, 267
    Civil Disobedience movement,
        106, 112–13, 123, 183,
        184–88, 184–89, 190,
        suspended by, 188, 192–93,
        197
    against Communal Award, 188,
        192
    Irwin Pact, 184–86
    and Khurshedben Naoroji, 106,
        108, 109, 111, 114–116,
        120, 122
    resigned from the Congress, 184,
        192–97
    value system, 156
Gandhi, Rahul, 268
Gandhi, Rajiv, 59, 82, 249
Gandhi, Sanjay, 243
Garhwal Himalaya, 75
Garo Hills, Garos
    British empire's forestry, 3–4,
        8–11
    defiant, 4–5
    forests: as Reserved Forests (RF),
        9–10, 15–20
    turbulent, 3, 11–14
    zamindars, cotton, 5–8

Gas Turbine Research Establishment,
    Bangalore, 209
Gayan Uttejak Mandli, Bombay, 109
gender bias, conflicts, xix, 22, 86,
    106
general elections
    1971, 237
    1977, 243
    1980, 243
Germany, 27, 120–21, 134
    German émigrés, aeronautics
        and self-reliance in India,
        200–13
    historicist school, 167
Ghatage, Vishnu Madav, 201,
    202–04, 207–08, 212
Ghosal, Surendra Nath, 13
Ghosh, Anjan, xiv
Gilmour, Ian, 268
Girwar Singh, 152
global movement for environmental
    justice, 72, 86
Global North, 47, 49, 61
Global South, 39, 44, 50
globalization, 129, 144
Godavarman judgment (*T.N.*
    Godavarman Thirumulpad vs
    Union of India and others),
    21, 33
gold, 86, 133, 136, 169, 190–91
    abolishment of control measures,
        177
    convertibility, 167
    distress, 191
    shortage, 167
    smuggling, 177
Gopal, S., 261
Gorbachev, Mikhail, 82
Gorkha Students Union, 74
Gotch, Frank, 143
Govind Das, Seth, 161

Grace, W.G., 272
grasslands, 22
    destruction in Palni Hills, 26
Great Britain. *See* United Kingdom
Great Depression, 41, 168, 190–91,
    194
Greater Kaziranga Human Resource
    Development and Environment
    Protection Committee, 74
Green Revolution, 60
Greenpeace, 47, 79, 87
Gregersen, Magnus, 175–76
Grove, Richard H., xvi, 22, 25
Guha, Ramachandra
    awards and honours to
        Ramchandra Guha, 256
    biographer and writer, x,
        xvi–xviii, 251–53, 254,
        267
    birth, xii
    career, x, xii–xv
    contemporary history, xviii–xx
    cricketer, xii–xiii
    environment and equity, x, xiii,
        xv–xvi
    friendships, 269
    'Honorary Foreign Member'
        of American Historical
        Association, xii
    journalist, 255–56
    moral courage, 256
    'Opening a Window in Kashmir',
        228–29
    a radical progressive, 249–56
    sports historian, 253–54, 267,
        273–75
Guha, Ranajit, 261
    *Elementary Aspects of Peasant
        Insurgency*, 259
Guha, S.R., xiii
Gujral, Inder Kumar, 243

Gunga Brahmn (Ganga Brahmin),
    126, 134–37
Gupt, Maithilisharan, 157
Gyatso, Lama Lobsang, 85

Habarghat pergana, 18
Habib, Irfan, *Agrarian System*, 261
Hackenschmidt, George, 136–37, 143
Hagood, Jonathan D., 206–07
Haksar, P.N., 233–34, 236, 237–39
Hanif Qureshi v. State of Bihar, 221
Hardiman, David, 259
Hardin, Garrett, 77
Hari Singh, Maharaja of Kashmir, 230
Harijan Tour (a social reform
    campaign against untouchability),
    192
Harris, R.G., 204
Harriss, John, xiv
Havemann, Hans A., 205
Hayek, F.A. von, 168–70, 174
    Constitution of Liberty, 175
    Road to Serfdom, 175
Hazardous Wastes (Management,
    Handling and Transboundary
    Movement) Rules, 2008, 78
Hazare, Kisan Baburao (Anna), 52
Hazlitt, Henry, 176, 178
Heisenberg, Werner, 205
Himalayas, Himalayan, xii, 61,
    66–67, 75, 115, 249, 250
Hindalco of Birla Group, 81
Hindi Sahitya Sammelan of Uttar
    Pradesh (UP), 160
Hindu, Hindus, xi, 156, 167, 232,
    273–74
    in Australia, 130–32, 134–35
    Christians, communal tension, 68
    conservatism, 192
    Muslims, relations, xi, 58, 67–68,
        106, 114–21, 198, 234

nationalism, 56, 68–69, 167
idea of reincarnation, 257
revivalism, 167
upper-caste, 63–64, 167, 188
Hindu Gymkhana, 253, 274
Hindu Mahasabha, 155
Hinduism, 52, 95
Hindustan Aircraft Limited (HAL)
(HAL), xiii, 202–04, 206–08,
210–13
Hindustan Socialist Republic
Association (HSRA), 147,
151–52
Hindutva and the communists, xi,
268
Hirachand, Walchand, 200, 202–03
Hobbes, Thomas, 40
Hobsbawm, Eric, xii
Hong Kong, 130, 202
human–nature relationships, 44, 50,
52
human rights, 62–63, 69–70, 163
and social justice campaigns, 51,
54
organizations, 74
violations, 39–40, 49
hunting, 15, 22, 38, 46, 51
hunting preserves, 38, 50
hydel power as renewable energy, 66

Ildek, Garo Hills, 16
Imperial Forestry Service, 27–28
imperialism, 40, 52, 62, 146
In Re the Kerala Education Bill, 1957,
221
India after Gandhi (2007), ix, xviii, xx,
165, 214–15, 228, 252
Indian Air Force (IAF), 207, 208–09,
211
Indian CCF (ICCF), 161–62
Indian Forest Act, 1927, 50

Indian Institute of Management
(IIM), xiii, xv, 249, 251, 258
Indian Institute of Science (IISc),
Bengaluru, xiv, 31, 202–06,
252–53
Aeronautical Engineering,
Department of, 204, 206,
208, 209
Centre for Ecological Sciences, 31
Indian Institute of Technology,
Hyderabad, 80
Indian Institutes of Technology
(IITs), 210
IIT Hyderabad, 80
Indian Mutiny, 1857, 138
Indian Premier League (IPL), 272
Indian rivers as 'living human entities',
69–70
Indian Space Research Organisation
(ISRO), 36
Indian Wildlife (Protection) Act,
1972, 51
indigenous and marginalized
communities, 38, 51
indigenous and scientific knowledge,
democratization, 53
Indo–China, 109, 123
industrial brewery project, movement
against, 75–76
industrial development, 168
industrial pollution, 41, 71, 78–80
and lack of environmental
liability, 71. See also Bhopal
Gas Tragedy
Industrial Revolution, 38
industrial and utilities conflicts, 78–79
industrialization, 56, 172, 195, 196
state led in USSR, 58
industry, in pre-colonial India, 101
inland water resources pollution. See
pollution

Institute of Economic Growth, Delhi,
    xiv
Intellectual Property Rights (IPR), 43
Intelligence Bureau (IB), 239
International Rivers Network, 64
International Union for the
    Conservation of Nature (IUCN),
    41, 47
Irslinger, Henry, 139
island biogeography, 41
interests, 251, 266–70

Jacob, 12
Jadhav, Mary Clubwala, 93
Jagmohan, 245
Jagran, 147
Jain, Nemichandra, 157, 160
Jainendra Kumar,147, 152–53
Jallianwala Bagh massacre, 149
James, C.L.R., xiv, 271
Jammu and Kashmir, xi, 149
    acceded to the Indian Union,
        230
    assembly elections, 1967, 232
    assembly elections, 1977, 243
    from autonomy to insurgency in
        1970s, xx, 228–45
    Constituent Assembly, 230
    regional divide, 232
Janzen, Dan, 39
Jayaprakash Narayan (JP), 120, 161,
    163, 196, 234, 236–37, 238
Jayaraman, Nityanand, 80, 81
Jenkins, Francis, 5
jet fighter, 206–09, 212
Jharkhand, 57, 81
Jhinkargadi forest, 75–76
jhum cultivation, 3, 8–10
Jinnah, Muhammad Ali, 121, 125
Johnson, Jack, 141
Johnson, Lyndon, 177

Joint forest management (JFM), 1990,
    21, 24, 32–33
'just preservation', 46

Kabir, Humayun, 158
Kachari tribe, 19
Kader, Abdul, 134
Kakar, Sudhir, 97
Kalpavriksh, 62
Kameshwar Singh v. State of Bihar,
    224
Karan Singh, 232, 237, 242, 243
Kareiva, Peter, 43
Karlekar, Malavika, 91
Karman, Theodore von, 204
Kartodirdjo, Sartono, 258
Karve, Irawati, 251
Kashipur, Raygada, Odisha, 66, 81
    anti-bauxite movement, 82
Kashmir People's Convention,
    Srinagar, 1968, 236
Kashmir. *See* Jammu and Kashmir
Kaul, T.N., 234–36
Kaziranga National Park, Assam, 52,
    73–74
Keating, Frank, 271
Kenya, national parks, 49
Kerala Fishworkers' Struggle, 76
Kerala Sastra Sahitya Parishad (KSSP),
    61
Kerala Swathantra Matsya Thozhilali
    Federation (KSMTF), 77
Kesari, 254
Kesavan, Mukul, xx, 260
Keshavan, Sujata xii, xiv, 253, 269
Keynes, John Maynard, *Treatise on
    Money* 169–70
khadi movement, 109, 111, 189, 193
Khan, Abdul Ghaffar Khan (Frontier
    Gandhi), 106, 113, 115, 116,
    121, 124, 198,

Khan, Ayub, 237
Khan, Mirza Ali, 121
Khan, Sikandar Hyat, 158
Khare, N.B., 158
Khilnani, Sunil, 260, 266
Khudai Khidmatgars, 113, 114, 117,
    121, 122, 198
Kipling, Rudyard, 3
knowledge, 17, 72, 196, 210–11,
    257
    lack of, 59
    money and space, conservation
        imperialism and control,
        37–54
    as power, 40
    production, administrative
        structures, 27–29, 30, 34,
        35, 166
Kocherry, Thomas, 77
Kodaikanal, Tamil Nadu, mercury
    poisoning, 79–80
    Campaign to Cleanup, 80, 86
kolya satyagraha, 86
Königsberger, Otto, 205–06, 208,
    213
Koodankulam, Tamil Nadu (spl
    variation Kudankulam)
    Chennai Solidarity Group for
        Koodankulam Struggle, 83
    nuclear conflict, 82–83
Krishna Pillai, H.A.
    Palayamkottai Henry Albert
        Krishna Pillai Kristhavanana
        Kathai, 94
    Pilgrim's Progress (Tr.), 94
Krishna, T.M., 80
Krishnamurti, J., 251
Krishnan, M, 94
Kulkarni, Subodh, 255
Kumar, Dharma, xii, xviii, 252
Kumarappa, J.C.,194, 196, 198

Kunzru, H.L., 158
Kurien, John, 76

Lahiri, Nayanjot, 260–61
    Ashoka, 261
Lahore Resolution, 121, 192
Lakshmi Ammal, M, xviii, 91–104
    letters from London (Seemai
        Kaditham), 97–103
Lal, Arun, 251
Lalkaka, Kavasji, 138
land
    acquisition, 9–14, 49, 51, 58–59,
        66–69, 80, 222–25
        compensation for, 3, 13–15,
        18–20, 59, 62, 65–69,
        78, 222–25
    community ownership, 53
    grab, 5–8, 49, 66
    reforms, 218, 222–27
    revenue assessment,189–90
Land Acquisition Act, 1894, 59
land and water sources pollution. See
    pollution
Land Conflict Watch, 85
Latin Catholic Fisherman's Federation
    (LCFF). See Kerala Swathantra
    Matsya Thozhilali Federation
    (KSMTF)
Leakey, Richard, 49
legal recourse, legal procedure
    regarding
    forest dwelling communities,
        23–24, 33, 50
    Garo struggle, 4, 7, 10, 12–13,
        16, 18
    Hydel projects, 85
    land acquisition, land issues, 59,
        62, 66–67, 69
    Project-Affected Persons, 67
    revolutionaries, 152

See also Supreme Court and democratic consolidation, legislature and judiciary, demarcation of power, 224–27
Lele, Sharachchandra, 24
Leontis, Artemis, 110, 125
Leopold, Aldo, 38
Liepmann, Hans, 204
Line of Control (LoC), 229
linguistic reorganization of states, 233
Linnaean, system of classification, 28
Species Plantarum, 28
London School of Economics (LSE), xiv, 168–70, 175
Lone, Abdul Ghani, 242
Lutze, Lothar, 160

MacArthur, Robert H., 41
Machwe, Prabhakar, 160
Madhaviah, A, 92–96, 97–98
  Clarinda, 94, 95
  Muthumeenakshi: Oru Brahmana Pennin Swasarithai, 95–96
  Padmavathi Charithiram, 93
  Satyananda, 94
  Savitri Charithiram, 95
  Thillai Govindan, 94
Madhaviah, Meenakshi, 92
Madhok, Balraj, 232
Madhya Pradesh, 33–34
Madras forest department, administrative structure, 27, 29
Mahajan, Justice Mehr Chand, 225–26
Mahakali river, 66
Mahanta, Ratneswar, 4
Malaviya, Madan Mohan, 166–67
Malaya, 129, 130
Malhotra, Kailash, 251
Manchester mills, 7
Mandela, Nelson, 273

Mandelbaum, Michael, 273
Mao Zedong, 62
Maoists, xi
marginalized communities, 43, 44, 50, 52, 70
Marine Regulation Act, demand for, 77
Marker, Jamsetji, 128
Marut, an Indian fighter bomber aircraft, 208–09
Marvier, Michelle, 43
Marylebone Cricket Club (MCC), 273
Masani, Minoo, 161, 162, 177
Mbaria, John, 48
Mehta, Ashok, 161, 163 (check spl variation Asoka)
Mehta, Ushaben, 107
Mejhan, Budhni, 57–58, 59
Merchant, Vijay, 253
mercury poisoning, 79
Messerschmitt, Willi, 205, 209, 212
migration of Indians, 128–31, 200, 205, 210
Millennium Ecosystem Assessment Report, 53
Miller, William, 93
Minto, Lord, 13
Mirabehn (Madeleine Slade), 199
Modern Review,155, 158
Modi, Narendra, 229
monetary policy, 169–70, 189–90
monsoon trawling ban, 77
Mont Pelerin Society (MPS), 165–66, 173–176, 177–78
More, Vishwanath, 161
Morrison, Kathleen D., 22
Mughals and Garos, 4, 5, 6, 17
Muir, John 38
Mukherjea, Justice Bijan Kumar, 226
Mukherjee, Syama Prasad, 158

Mukherji, S. Air Marshal, 207
Mulgaonkar, S., 163
Muller, H.J., 162
Multiple Action Research Group
     (MARG), 62
Mumford, Lewis, xiv
Munshi, K.M., 161, 162
Muslim League, 121
Muslim unrest in Jammu and
     Kashmir, 244–45
Mymensingh, Bangladesh, 4, 6

Nagarjuna Sagar dam, 58
Nagas, 236
Nagendra, 158
Naidu, Sarojini, 106, 154
Nala Venba, 100
Namvar Singh, 164
Nandy, Ashish, The Tao of Cricket, 275
Naoroji, Ardeshir, 107, 108
Naoroji, Dadabhai, 105, 107–09, 124
Naoroji, Khurshedben A.D. and the
     challenge of Indian biography,
     xviii, 105–125
     birth and formative years, 107–8
     imprisonment, long years in jail,
          107, 113–14, 119–20, 123
     work with Khan Abdul Gaffar
          Khan, 106, 113–24
     Indian nationalist activity,
          106–07, 111–25
     singing, 109–11
Naoroji, Mherbanoo, 108
Naoroji, Virbai, 107–08, 111
Narain, Sunita, 85
Narasimha, Roddam, 207, 213
Narayan, Jayprakash, 234, 236–37, 238
Narendra Deva, Acharya, 193
Narmada Bachao Andolan, 62–65,
     67, 69, 71, 76. See also Sardar
     Sarovar dam

Supreme Court's judgements, 65
National Aeronautical Laboratory
     (now the National Aerospace
     Laboratory), Bangalore, 209
National Alliance of People's
     Movement, 85
National Aluminium Company
     Limited (NALCO), 82
National Centre for Biological
     Sciences, Bangalore, 31
National Commission on Agriculture,
     30
National Conference (NC), 231, 233,
     242–44
National Fishworkers Union, 83
National Forest Policy
     Resolution,1988, 21, 33
National Green Tribunal (NGT), 78,
     84, 85
National Register of Citizens (NRC),
     ix
nationalism, nationalist movement
     (Indian freedom movement),
     101, 107, 111, 166–67, 178–
     79184–91, 197–98, 258
natural resources, 21, 33, 59, 62, 75
     British plundered, 250
     management in India, 252
Naya Path, 146–47
Nayyar, Pyarelal, 112
Nazi aviation industry, 206, 210, 212
Needham, Joseph, xii
Nehru, B.K., 245
Nehru, Jawaharlal, xii, xix, 57, 108–9,
     124, 172, 194, 254, 261, 276
     Abdullah accord, 230–31
     and Agyeya, 154–55, 161–62
     hegemony, 166–67, 209, 215
     disagreement with Gandhi, 188
     and the Kashmir issue, 228,
          230–31, 236, 245

vision of development and self-
   reliance, 58–59, 65, 209
Nehru Memorial Museum and
   Library, xiv, xix, 106, 117, 253
Neill, Jack, 138, 140
neoliberalism, 65
Neufeld, Michael J., 207, 210
New India Foundation (NIF), xx
New York Times, 163, 256
Nilekani, Nandan, xx, 251
Nirala, Suryakant Tripathi, 154
Nixon, Richard, 35
Niyamgiri Bachao Andolan, 69, 72
Niyamgiri hills, 66, 68
non Governmental organizations
   (NGOs), 39–41, 51, 64, 69
   funding, 47–49
   international, 87
   multinational, 42, 47
Non–Cooperation movement, 109,
   166, 189
non–violence, 106, 113, 114, 117,
   120, 193, 198
Norsk Hydro, Norway, 81
North–Eastern Frontier of
   Rungpore, 4
North–West Frontier Province
   (NWFP), 131, 198
   Khurshedben Naoroji's work,
      106, 113–24
   Russian invasion, 198
nuclear conflicts, 82–84
Nyamjang Chhu dam, Tawang, 84

Oberoi, Harjot Singh, 260–61
ocean grabbing, 87
Odisha, 66, 72, 74, 81–82
Ogada, Mordecai, 48
Olympic stadium, Berlin, 205
Opening a Window in Kashmir,
   228–29

Ostrom, Elinor, 53

Padmanabhan, Chitra, 59
Pagal Panthis, 6, 10, 11
Pagel, Wilhelm, 134
Pakistan, 266
   India, relations, 124, 231,
      234–35
   war, 1965, 209, 236
   war 1971, 238, 245
   and Kashmir issue, 228, 229–31,
      234–35, 236–37
   Pakistan issue (pre-
      independence), 121
   Sheikh Abdulla's visit, 229–31
Palat, R.M., 158
Paliwal, Krishna Dutt, 152, 153–54
Palkhowa, Kaziranga, human
   inhabitants evicted, 74
Palni Hills, 26
Panchamirtam, 98
Panchayati Raj Extension to
   Scheduled Areas (PESA) Act,
   1996, 33
panchayats, 11, 12, 33
Pancheshwar dam, Assam, 66–67
Panchet dam, Jharkhand, 57–58,
   59–60
Panna National Park, 34, 67
Parab, Hanumant, 255
parachute science, 42–43
Paris, 99, 106, 110–11
Parthasarathi, G., 239–41
Partition of India, 58, 123–24, 149
Pashtuns, 113, 114, 116–17, 120–21
   Pashtun dacoits, 107
   Pashtunistan, 122
Patel, I.G., 165
Patel, Vallabhbhai, 190, 198
Patel, Vitthalbhai, 188
Patkar, Medha, 62–63

Patna, 147, 148
Patnaik, Naveen, 76
Patriot, 163
Pawley, William D., 202, 203, 204
peasant movements, xv, 153
People's Movement Against Nuclear
    Energy (PMANE), 83
Permanent Black, 264
Perón, Juan regime, 206–7
Perryman, Jack, 136
Pertapa, Kala, 143
'philanthrocapitalism', 48
philanthropic donors, 42, 48
Pilnyak, Boris, *The Naked Year*, 152
Pinchot, Gifford, 38
Planning Commission, 36
Plato, *Republic*, 40
Plebiscite Front, 232, 235–36,
    237–38, 242
political ecology, 40, 44, 52, 85
politics, influence on sports, 272
pollution, 35, 56, 81, 85
    government control programmes,
        36
    industrial, 41, 71, 78–80
    of inland water resources, 77
    mercury pollution, 79–80
    urban air, xv
Poona Pact, 188, 192
population biology, 41
Postgate, Raymond, 271
Praja Parishad, 231
Prakrutik Sampad Surakshya Parishad
    movement, 82
Pran Nath, 167
Prandtl, Ludwig, 201, 204–05
Prasanna, Erapalli, 257, 258
Pratik, 146, 160–61
prawn industry, 74
Prayogvad, literary movement 160
Premchand, 147, 157, 164

Godan, 157
Primack, Richard B., 43
Pristianity, 49–50
Progressive Writers' Association
    (PWA), 160–61
'Project–Affected Persons' (PAPs),
    59, 67
Public Interest Litigation (PIL), 65
    against removal of human
        habitation in and around
        Kaziranga, 74
Pul, Kalikho, 85
Punjab, 29, 113, 120, 123, 141, 187
    Arya Samaj movement, 148
    overseas Indian migration,
        129–31, 134
purna swaraj, 188

Qasim, Mir, 231, 233, 237, 239,
    241–42, 244
Quit India Movement, 115, 125

Rabhas, 8, 18
racial discrimination, 31, 129
Radhakrishnan, S.,161, 261
Radical American Environmentalism,
    39
Radical Democratic Party, 147, 158,
    159
Radical Humanists, 153
railways, 129
    expansion, and forest fires, 26
    largest customer of the forest
        department, 9–10
Raj, Krishna, xviii
Rajagopalachari, Chakravarti, 120,
    177
Rajam Iyer, B.R. *Kamalambal
    Charithiram*, 93
Rajasimla, Garo Hills, 16
Rajendra Prasad, 120, 161

Raju, S.V., 178
Ramasamy, E.V., 149
Ramnath, Aparajith, 202
Ranade, Justice M.G., 253
Ranjitsinhji, Kumar Shri ('Ranji') Jam
    Saheb of Nawanagar, 128, 253,
    275
Rao, C.N.R., 254
Rao, V.K.R.V., 168
Rashsundari Devi, *Amar Jiban*, 91
Rashtriya Stree Sabha, 109
RSS xi, xiii
Ray and Kesavan, 253
Raychaudhuri, Tapan, 261
Regulation X of 1822 (Bengal Land-
    Revenue Settlement Regulation), 4
*Report of the Indian Central Banking
    Enquiry Committee*, 168
Reserve Bank of India, 36
resource use and preservation, 21
Rheede, Hendrik van (comp.), *Hortus
    Malabaricus*, 28
rhinos, 48
    poaching, 73–74
Richards, Vivian, 258
Right to Fair Compensation
    and Transparency in Land
    Acquisition, Rehabilitation and
    Resettlement Act (LARR), 2013,
    66–67
river projects, new, 69
River Valley and Hydroelectric
    Projects, Expert Appraisal
    Committee on, 84
riverine ecosystem, 60, 67, 69–70
rivers
    Ganga and Yamuna 'Living
        Entities', Uttarakhand High
        Court's declaration, 2017, 69
    integrity, 69, 71
    interlinking, 67

as 'living human entities', 69–70
    related politics, 64
Robinson, Jackie, 272–73, 274
Rolland, Romain, 151, 153
Roller, Benjamin Franklin, 141, 143
Rosenzweig, Michael, 45
Rossetti, Christina Georgina, 150
Rougemont, Denis de, 162
Roy, Anuradha, 264
Roy, Arundhati, x–xi
Roy, M.N., 146,147, 153, 159, 161
rural development programmes, 197
rural India, economic conditions, 190,
    194
    Mahatma's agenda, 196–97
Russell, Martin, 162
Russia. *See* Soviet Union
Russian nihilists, 152

Sabarmati Ashram, 112, 197, 198
Saberwal, Vasant K., 29
Sadiq, G.M., 231–33, 237–38
Sainik,152–54
sal (Shorea robusta), 8–10, 15, 26,
    30, 76
Salt March, 112–13, 183
salt tax, 189
Salwa Judum, xvii
Samantara, Prafulla, 76
sand mafia, 86
Sandow, Eugen,126
Sangma, Sonaram, 4, 11–20
Sankhala, Kailash, 32
Santhals, 58–60
Sapru, Tej Bahadur, 158
Sarabhai, Mridula, 113, 234, 239
Saraswati Bai, C, 96
Sardar Sarovar dam, x, 62, 64–65
Sarkar, Jadunath, xii
Sarkar, Sumit, 185
Swadeshi Movement, 261

Sarkar, Tanika, 91, 97
Sashi Kant, 24
Sastri, Hirananda, 148
Sastri, Justice M. Patanjali, 225
Savaging the Civilized: Verrier Elwin,
    His Tribals and India, 254, 261,
    267
Savarkar, V.D., 108
Save Mon Region Federation
    (SMRF), 84
Save the Western Ghats, 75
Sayed, Abu, 161
Scheduled Tribes and Other
    Traditional Forest Dwellers
    (Recognition of Forest Rights)
    Act, 2006 (Forest Rights Act,
    FRA), 23–24, 33–34, 51, 53, 66,
    68, 73
Scheduled Tribes, displaced residents
    of forested hills, 59
School of Forestry and Environmental
    Studies, Yale, xiv
Scott, David, 5
Segaon. *See* Sevagram
seismic zone, 67
self–respect movement, 149
Sen, Amartya, 264
Sen, Kripa, 158, 159
Setalvad, M.C., 163
Sevagram (Segaon), xviii, 119, 122,
    123, 183–99,
Shah, A.B., 161
Shahabuddin, Ghazala, 23
Shakespeare, William, 93, 102, 261
Sharma, Ramvilas, 160
Shastri, Lal Bahadur, 231
Shell, 48
Shelley, Percy Bysshe, 150
Shenoy, B.R., xviii, 165–179
    Indian free-market economist,
        166–73

and Mont Pelerin
    Society,173–176
Sherpur, 4
Shimla Conference, 1972, 238
Shivaji Bhonsale, 105
shola forest, 26, 79
shrimp mafia, 75, 86
Sikelianos, Eva Palmer, 106, 109–12,
    115, 125
Sikhs, overseas migration, 129–30
Silent Valley (rainforest), 61
    movement, 72
Singh, J.J., 232
Singh, L.P., 234
Singiram Nokma, 15, 16
Sinha, K.K., 161
SLOSS (Single Large or Several Small)
    dilemma, 41–42
small–pox epidemic in Garo Hills, 11
Smithsonian Institution, 32
social justice, 51, 63
    and environmental welfare, 61,
        69–70
social media, 76
social movements
    against large dams in India,
        56–57
    and environmental politics, 62
Social Reform Advocate, 95
social reforms, India, 93–95, 192
social–ecological system, 44, 50
Söllner, Alfons, 210
Soulé, Michael, 41, 43
South Africa, 137, 189
    apartheid, 273
    Indian indentured labour, 129
    M.K. Gandhi in, 137–38, 254
    sporting banned, 273
South Asia Network of Dams, Rivers
    and People (SANDRP), 69
South Asia, 105

forest conservancy, 21, 22, 24, 85
South Asians
    in Australia, 131, 134
    in London, 138
Soviet Union, Russia, 84, 163, 170,
    172, 198, 205, 206, 208, 209,
    210–11, 212
'Space for Giants', 49
Spender, Stephen, 162
sports, role in cultural development of
    community, 272–73
Spratt, Philip, 161, 162
Srinivas, M.N., 265
Srinivasan, Rettaimalai, 97
Srivastava, Sir J.P., 158
State of Bombay v. F.N. Balsara,
    219–21
State of India's Environment report, 61
*State of Madras v. Champakam
    Dorairajan*, 219–21
Stepniak, Sergey, *The Career of a
    Nihilist*, 152
Sterlite copper smelting unit,
    Tuticorin, Tamil Nadu, 78–79
Subaltern Studies, 258
Subbalakshmi, R.S., 93, 96
Subbarao, C.V., xviii
Sundar, Nandini, 260
Sundar, Nadini, 260
Sundaram, Lanka, 161
Supreme Court of India, 21, 69, 73,
    74
    and democratic consolidation,
        214–27
Survival International, 68
Sushil Kumar, 24
Swatantra Party, 176, 178
Sylhet Jhum Regulation, 1891, 10

Tagore, Rabindranath, 150, 155, 261
    Gitanjali, 151

Tamil Nadu, 91, 92, 94, 243
    fisherfolks' struggle, 77
    industrial and utilities conflicts,
        78–79
    infrastructure and built
        environment conflicts,
        80–81
    Janmam Abolition Act, 1969, 33
    nuclear conflicts, 82–83
Tamil Nadu Energy Company
    Limited (TNECL), 81
Tamil Nadu Pollution Control Board,
    78, 80
Tandon, Purshottam Das, 160, 161
Tank, Kurt, 200, 205, 206, 211, 213
Tar Saptak, 146, 160
Tara Singh, Master, 158
Tarakunde,V.M., 163
Tawang, Arunachal Pradesh, 84–85
Taylor, A.J.P., x
teak (Tectona grandis), 26, 30
Tennessee Valley Authority, USA, 57
Thapar, Romila, xii
Thatcher, Margaret, 268
The Nature Conservancy (TNC), 41,
    47
Third World, 37, 40
    modernization, 30
*This Fissured Land: An Ecological
    History of India*, by Madhav
    Gadgil and Ramachandra Guha,
    xv, 12, 21–22, 55, 252–53, 264,
    277
Thokje, 12
Thompson, E.P., xi, xiv, 259, 269,
    275–76
Thomson, A.A., 276
Thoreau, Henry David 38
Tietjens, Oskar, 204–5, 208, 213
tigers, 34, 45, 48, 67, 74, 126
Tilak, Bal Gangadhar, 253–54

timber trade and extraction, 3, 8, 25–26, 27, 29–32, 35
Trevelyan, G.M., 271
tribal state, 120
tribes and tribals, 4–5, 8, 55, 59, 72
    rights, 51, 66, 76
    subjugation by the empire, 18
Turkman Gate, Delhi: killing of protestors, 1976, 243
Tyagi, Mahavir, 207

Unilever's thermometer plant, Kodaikanal, 79–80
United Arab Republic, 209
United Kingdom, 120, 168, 171, 190, 205
United Nations Conference on the Human Environment (1972: Stockholm), 61
United States of America, 27, 144, 178, 273
    imperialism, 62, 146
    North America, 129, 133, 139, 143
    notion of pristine wilderness, 38–39
Unquiet Woods: Ecological Change and Peasant Resistance in the Himalaya, The, xv–xvi, 4, 21, 252, 259–62, 264
untouchability, 192, 198, 199
Upper Odai river, 78
Utkal Aluminium Industrial Limited (UAIL), 81–82
Uttarakhand
    forest panchayats, 34

Vaishampayan, Vishwanath, 152
Vajpayee, Atal Bihari, 254
Varerkar, Mama, On the Doorstep of the Prison, 254

Vedanayakam Pillai, S., Pratapa Mudaliar Charithiram, 93
Vedanta Limited, 68, 78
Vedanta-Sterlite, 79
Velip, Ravindra, 255–56
Vellalars, Murugankurichi Vellalars, 94
Venkata Raman, Chandrasekhara, 205
Venkatachar, C.S., 269
Venkataraman, K., 252
venture philanthropy, 48
Via Campesina movement, 78
Vidyarthi, Onkar Shankar, 157
Vishal Bharat, 154–55, 158
Vishwanath, Gundappa, 257, 259, 263
Viveka Chintamani, 95
Vogel, Jean Philip, 148
Vohra, Bhagwati Charan, 152
Vorster, John, 273

Wadia, J.B.H., 161
Wadiyar, Jayachamarajendra, 206
Walo Tangi, 119
Wanghanui river, 69
water management, 63
    conflicts, 84–85
Watt, George, 7
Waziri–inhabited regions, 116
Weber, Clarence, 126–27, 136–37
West Bengal, 30, 66, 268
Western
    conservation interventions, 41, 42, 44, 46
    cultural norms, 94
    cultural influences, 111–12
    material wealth, 99
Western, David, 53
Western Ghats, 26, 75
wetlands, 81
Wickets in the East, xii, 262
wild elephants, 4, 8, 16

wild nature, preservation of, 49
wild tribes, 4, 5
wilderness
    agrarianism and, 51
    political, 187, 241
    preservation movement, 39
Wildlife Conservation Society (WCS),
    47
wildlife conservation, xvi, 25, 32, 39,
    51–52, 61
Wildlife Institute of India (1982),
    Dehradun, 31
William, Carey, 4, 7
Williams, Jack, 274
Willingdon, Lord, 186–87,196–
    97,198
Wilson, E.O., 41, 44
Winder, Robert, 271
women
    English, 101–2
    Indian, 92, 102–3, 106, 108,
        111, 113, 191
World Forum of Fisher Peoples,
    Delhi, 78

World War I, 30, 98, 128, 129, 144,
    167, 190
World War II, 123, 146, 176, 194,
    206, 250
World Wide Fund for Nature
    (WWF), 41
Wirth Brothers Circus, Melbourne,
    Australia, 126–27, 135–37
Wyllie, William Hutt Curzon, 138

Yashpal, 152, 164
Yellowstone, 38
Yeltsin, Boris, 83
Yosemite, 38
Young Men's League, 236

zamindars, 8, 11, 14
    of Bengal, 4, 5, 10
    of Goalpara,4, 5, 7, 13, 14, 20
Zbyszko, Stanley, 141–43
Zirin, Dave
    Bad Sports, 272
    A People's History of Sports in the
        United States, 272